Learning Strategies
and Learning Styles

PERSPECTIVES ON INDIVIDUAL DIFFERENCES

CECIL R. REYNOLDS, *Texas A&M University, College Station*
ROBERT T. BROWN, *University of North Carolina, Wilmington*

DETERMINANTS OF SUBSTANCE ABUSE
Biological, Psychological, and Environmental Factors
Edited by Mark Galizio and Stephen A. Maisto

HANDBOOK OF MULTIVARIATE EXPERIMENTAL PSYCHOLOGY
Second Edition
Edited by John R. Nesselroade and Raymond B. Cattell

HISTORICAL FOUNDATIONS OF EDUCATIONAL
PSYCHOLOGY
Edited by John A. Glover and Royce R. Ronning

THE INDIVIDUAL SUBJECT AND SCIENTIFIC PSYCHOLOGY
Edited by Jaan Valsiner

LEARNING STRATEGIES AND LEARNING STYLES
Edited by Ronald R. Schmeck

METHODOLOGICAL AND STATISTICAL ADVANCES IN THE
STUDY OF INDIVIDUAL DIFFERENCES
Edited by Cecil R. Reynolds and Victor L. Willson

THE NEUROPSYCHOLOGY OF INDIVIDUAL DIFFERENCES
A Developmental Perspective
Edited by Lawrence C. Hartlage and Cathy F. Telzrow

PERSONALITY AND INDIVIDUAL DIFFERENCES
A Natural Science Approach
Hans J. Eysenck and Michael W. Eysenck

PERSONALITY DIMENSIONS AND AROUSAL
Edited by Jan Strelau and Hans J. Eysenck

PERSPECTIVES ON BIAS IN MENTAL TESTING
Edited by Cecil R. Reynolds and Robert T. Brown

THEORETICAL FOUNDATIONS OF BEHAVIOR THERAPY
Edited by Hans J. Eysenck and Irene Martin

A Continuation Order Plan is available for this series. A continuation order will bring delivery of each new volume immediately upon publication. Volumes are billed only upon actual shipment. For further information please contact the publisher.

Learning Strategies and Learning Styles

Edited by

RONALD R. SCHMECK
Southern Illinois University
Carbondale, Illinois

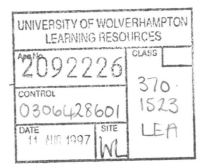
Plenum Press • *New York and London*

Library of Congress Cataloging in Publication Data

Learning strategies and learning styles / edited by Ronald R. Schmeck.
    p.   cm.—(Perspectives on individual differences)
Bibliography: p.
Includes index.
ISBN 0-306-42860-1
    1. Learning.2. Cognitive styles. I. Schmeck, Ronald R. II. Series.
LB1060.L4246   1988   88-12586
370.15′23—dc19   CIP

© 1988 Plenum Press, New York
A Division of Plenum Publishing Corporation
233 Spring Street, New York, N.Y. 10013

Printed in the United States of America

I dedicate this book to the following individuals in appreciation for their support during its preparation: N. Courtney, K. Harmon, S. Haynes, C. Labyk, P. McCarthy, C. Meade, C. Meek, A. Vaux, and my son Eric.

Contributors

John Biggs, Department of Education, University of Hong Kong, Hong Kong

J. P. Das, Developmental Disabilities Centre, University of Alberta, Edmonton, Alberta, Canada

Noel Entwistle, Department of Education, University of Edinburgh, Edinburgh, Scotland

John R. Kirby, Faculty of Education, Queen's University, Kingston, Ontario, Canada

Patricia McCarthy, Department of Educational Psychology, University of Minnesota, Minneapolis, Minnesota

Ference Marton, Department of Education, University of Goteborg, Molndal, Sweden

Gordon Pask, OOC Program, Faculty of Education, University of Amsterdam, Amsterdam, The Netherlands

Paul Ramsden, Centre for the Study of Higher Education, University of Melbourne, Parkville, Victoria, Australia

Z. L. Rockenstein, Department of Human Services, Western Carolina University, Cullowhee, North Carolina

Ronald Ray Schmeck, Department of Psychology, Southern Illinois University, Carbondale, Illinois

E. P. Torrance, University of Georgia, Athens, Georgia

Claire E. Weinstein, Department of Educational Psychology, University of Texas at Austin, Austin, Texas

Preface

A style is any pattern we see in a person's way of accomplishing a particular type of task. The "task" of interest in the present context is education—learning and remembering in school and transferring what is learned to the world outside of school. Teachers are expressing some sort of awareness of style when they observe a particular action taken by a particular student and then say something like: "This doesn't surprise me! That's just *the way he is.*"

Observation of a single action cannot reveal a style. One's impression of a person's style is abstracted from multiple experiences of the person under similar circumstances. In education, if we understand the styles of individual students, we can often anticipate their perceptions and subsequent behaviors, anticipate their misunderstandings, take advantage of their strengths, and avoid (or correct) their weaknesses. These are some of the goals of the present text.

In the first chapter, I present an overview of the terminology and research methods used by various authors of the text. Although they differ a bit with regard to meanings ascribed to certain terms or with regard to conclusions drawn from certain types of data, there is nonetheless considerable agreement, especially when one realizes that they represent three different continents and five different nationalities. Furthermore, the data upon which their concepts are based were gathered from widely differing cultural populations, and some of the theories were originally formulated without awareness of related work being done by some of the other authors who now appear next to them in the present text. Yet, in spite of such differing origins and differing perspectives, the authors show remarkable agreement regarding how best to conceptualize the educational process and the individuality of students. There is also considerable agreement regarding the best ways to apply the resulting theories in practice in order to improve education.

The second chapter, prepared by Noel Entwistle, recognizes that at the core of any "style" must lie something very basic which permeates a person's perceptions and subsequent behavior enough to produce those consistencies to which we apply the label "style" or, in his words, "orientation." It is his view that a major component of this core is the student's *motive*. He identifies three broad classes of motives: (a) pure interest in learning (or more broadly, in self-actualization); (b) the need to demonstrate self-worth coupled with the assumption that one will fail (constantly striving to avoid being "the fool"); and (c) the need to demonstrate self-worth coupled with the assumption that one will succeed (constantly striving to accumulate symbols of merit—e.g., praise and high grades). One of these three motives tends consistently to lie behind each of the "approaches to learning" discussed by Ference Marton in Chapter 3. Chapter 6, dealing with self-concept, relates nicely to Entwistle's discussion of motives.

Marton's Chapter 3 presents an overview of innovative, *qualitative* research into learning carried out at the University of Goteburg. Using interview data in which students describe their experience of learning in school settings, Marton has formulated conceptions of the process that parallel formulations that I and my colleagues developed on the basis of large-scale survey research in the United States. We both found that one can place a student's approach to the task of learning on a continuum that extends from *surface* (or as I've called it, "shallow") processing of symbols to *deep* analysis of the meanings that underlie symbols (including, ultimately, formulation of personal conceptions of reality). This surface to deep continuum can be used to describe how students' define learning, how they approach the task of studying, how they approach education in general, and to their approach to specific tasks such as reading and writing. All of this is discussed in the chapters of the present text.

The fourth chapter, by Gordon Pask, reviews some classic research which equals Marton's work in terms of the impact that it has had on other researchers—for example, myself (Chapters 1, 6, and 12) and Entwistle (Chapter 2). Instead of using interviews and the "retelling of texts" as Marton had, Pask relied upon one-to-one tutorials and computer-assisted tutorial systems in which students reveal their trains of thought by requesting specific bits of information and then demonstrate that they understand by teaching the information back to the researcher. Pask consistently uncovered two basic cognitive *strategies*, which can be called *styles* when they are used consistently across varied situations. The two styles/strategies are holist learning (paying special attention to global features of experience) and serialist learning (preferring detailed sequential analysis of experience and enjoying especially the specification of procedural rules).

In Chapter 5, J. P. Das presents a review of his work. Within the context of education, Das has applied the concepts of sumultaneous–successive coding processes and planning processes originally identified by the Russian psychologist Luria. Luria studied brain-injured patients to uncover cognitive processes, and Das and his colleagues (cf. Kirby's Chapter 9) have used psychological testing procedures (including factor analysis) to identify and assess these same processes in students and to determine ways in which they might account for and suggest ways of improving the level of functioning (e.g., reading) of those students in the school setting.

Patricia McCarthy and I make an attempt in Chapter 6 to tie what is known of social development and self-concept development to performance in educational settings, including a suggested connection between the person's social experience and his or her cognitive style. We describe research indicating that the quality of a learning outcome (the coded educational experience) is heavily influenced by the personality of the student. Students do not all derive the same conceptions from the same experiences, and this can be explained, in part, by differences in self-esteem which subsequently affect both perception and cognition (i.e., learning style). Possible connections between social experience and cognitive style are discussed further in the final chapter.

The style and strategy concepts developed in the first half of the book are applied to practical educational problems in the last half. In addition to applying the concepts to some classic problems in the areas of reading, writing, and creativity, the latter half of the text confronts such issues as situational determiners of style (the nature of the school setting) and how to change style.

In Chapter 7, Paul Ramsden discusses aspects of the educational setting that most influence students' approaches to the material to be learned. The way in which a course of study is structured can profoundly influence the ways in which students process information presented to them, and the ways the information is processed determine the nature of the codes left behind in memory. One of the interesting aspects of Ramsden's chapter is that he basically agrees with the concepts developed earlier in the text but argues nicely that style is quite flexible and really not very "stylistic" at all, in the sense that it is *not* "fixed."

In Chapter 8, John Biggs uses the surface–deep continuum discussed above to analyze differences in ways students approach the task of writing an essay. His analysis of writing is derived from and illustrated by interviews with students regarding their perceptions of the task of writing, and this data is related to questionnaire data regarding learning styles and some actual essays written by those same students. Anyone interested in either teaching writing or in using writing as a means of encouraging thinking should find Biggs' chapter fascinating.

Likewise, John Kirby's Chapter 9 applies the style and strategy concepts developed earlier in the book to the task of reading. Kirby's chapter complements Biggs' chapter in that he addresses another one of the basic skills involved in education. Kirby's chapter also complements Das' Chapter 5 in that Kirby and Das come from the same theoretical perspective and use similar methods. In my own final chapter, I have applied Kirby's analysis of how reading comprehension develops in a broader analysis of the development of cognitive style in general. He feels that the highest level of reading comprehension requires the integration of two earlier modes of cognitive functioning—global and analytic. The integration of the two is a difficult operation, and some individuals remain fixated at the global or analytic level of development.

Chapter 10, by Torrance and Rockenstein, presents an excellent overview of Paul Torrance's extensive research on creativity and it's relation to preferred mode of information processing. Rather than concluding that creativity is restricted to more global (or "right-brained") modes of processing, Torrance argues that both modes (right- and left-brained, or "global and analytic," to use Kirby's terms) have a strength that is required for a creative act to be carried through to fruition. The right-brained mode is associated with an aspect of creativity that Torrance calls "creating-by-inventing," while left-brained thinking is related to "creating-by-improving." Both functions are required for true creativity, and Torrance refers to such functioning as "whole-brained" (Kirby uses the term "synthetic").

In Chapter 11, Claire Ellen Weinstein describes her extensive research into the most effective ways of teaching students to use various learning strategies. Since a style essentially involves a special preference for one of the strategies, teaching students to use new strategies can result in modifications to their styles. As I mentioned above, I have addressed the question of modifying styles in Chapter 12, and it is my firm belief that the procedures developed by Weinstein are an effective means of accomplishing modifications. Also, her classification of the various learning strategies is extremely useful.

In Chapter 12, I summarize the text and go somewhat beyond the information presented therein to try to suggest new areas for future research and new ways of improving education. Based upon Kirby's work, I suggest that development of cognitive style proceeds from predominantly *global* to *analytic* and eventually, in self-actualizing individuals, to an *integration* of the global and analytic modes. I agree with Ramsden that the situation greatly influences the approach a person takes to it, but I argue that there is still a stylistic element that is often very resistant to change. The only individual who is truly flexible is one who has integrated global and analytic functioning. Most individuals strive for integration, but few achieve it.

Following up on some of the ideas presented by McCarthy and me in Chapter 6, I suggest in Chapter 12 that the difficulty encountered during integration relates to one's early social development, in particular, to the experiences affecting the development of one's concept of self, including one's self-esteem. I note that teachers cannot, of course, reconstruct students' personalities, but they *can* try to build on personal strengths and avoid inadvertently preying upon personal weaknesses. In so doing, it may indeed be possible for a *series* of teachers (in effect, the whole school experience) to alter personalities (and styles) of students in ways that broadly benefit the society that the school system serves.

Ronald Ray Schmeck

Carbondale, Illinois

Contents

PART II.   APPLICATIONS OF THE CONCEPTS OF STRATEGY AND STYLE

E. P. Torrance and *Z. L. Rockenstein*

Claire E. Weinstein

*Learning Strategies
and Learning Styles*

PART I

The Concepts of Strategy and Style

CHAPTER 1

An Introduction to Strategies and Styles of Learning

RONALD RAY SCHMECK

It seems appropriate to begin a book entitled *Learning Strategies and Learning Styles* with definitions of the terms *style, strategy,* and most basically, *learning.* Clarification of the meanings of these and other terms and important distinctions drawn between them will prepare the way for the remainder of the text. Learning can be described from various perspectives. I discuss three: the experiential, the behavioral, and the neurological.

WHAT IS LEARNING?

From the experiential (or phenomenological) perspective, learning is defined by individuals engaged in learning. The learners (students) describe their experience of events involved in learning. Learning, described in this fashion, can be categorized in several different ways, that is, everyone's experience of learning is not the same. At the extremes, one learner might describe learning as the literal retention of knowledge often achieved through repetition and recitation, while another might describe it as an interpretative process aimed at understanding reality. The authors of the present text use the label *conceptions of learning* to describe variation in students' interpretations of their experiences of learning.

RONALD RAY SCHMECK • Department of Psychology, Southern Illinois University, Carbondale, Illinois 62901.

In the present volume, Marton (Chapter 3) and Entwistle (Chapter 2) provide excellent descriptions of learning viewed from the phenomenological perspective, as do Ramsden (Chapter 7) and Biggs (Chapter 8). Marton suggests that educators can improve learning by encouraging students and teachers to define it more broadly, for example, to include personal development or self-actualization as a legitimate part of the process. He also suggests helping students enrich their internal characterizations of reality, helping them to "see" that reality from more than one perspective. Biggs describes important connections between the ways in which students view learning (or studying) and the ways in which they approach the task of writing essays; Kirby (Chapter 9) suggests similar connections with the task of reading.

The second perspective one can take when studying learning is behavioral. From this perspective, learning is an observable change in a person's reaction to an equally observable stimulus situation. The change in reaction (i.e., in behavior) is traditionally said to be relatively permanent once it has been learned. In any educational setting, we expect students' reactions to test events (e.g., examinations, essays, recitations) to change as a result of educational experiences. Thus, all educators view learning from a behavioral perspective at one time or another. I am including the cognitive view of learning in this behavioral category, since cognitive psychologists treat cognitive behavior similar to the ways other behavioral scientists treat other behaviors. Weinstein (Chapter 11) presents an excellent program for giving students training in the behavioral skills needed to improve their performance on test events. Similarly, Biggs provides suggestions for improving writing, and Das (Chapter 5) and Kirby (Chapter 9) suggest ways in which reading may be improved.

Finally, from the neurological perspective learning is the process whereby the nervous system is transformed by its own activity. It is the "tracks" left behind by thoughts, that is, neural activity changes the neurons that are active, and that change is the structural basis of learning. The change occurs as a direct result of the neural activity itself, that is, as a direct result of processing information. Das and Kirby take this perspective, as do McCarthy and Schmeck (Chapter 6) and Torrance and Rockenstein (Chapter 10). All derive important educational implications from such a neurological perspective, a perspective which may seem at first glance to be far removed from education.

McCarthy and Schmeck argue that educators should consider development of the *whole person* (including the person's nervous system) as one of the legitimate purposes of education. They argue, as does Entwistle, that even facts can be stored and referenced more effectively by embedding them in the overall conceptual framework of the student rather than simply repeating them until they are memorized. All of the authors of this text would agree that teachers should consider ways of stimulating greater varieties of neural activity (e.g., thinking and problem solving) in the classroom—perhaps focusing less on literal repetition and recitation. Simple repetition is deceptively rewarding since something observable is accomplished, but what is accomplished might, in reality, contribute very little to the overall development of the individual. In this latter regard, all of the authors argue in one way or another for a definition of learning that includes *integration* of mental contents and functions to promote versatility and formation of individuality and personal identity.

STRATEGIES, TACTICS, SKILLS, AND PROCESSES

The term *strategy* was originally a military term that referred to procedures for implementing the plan of a large-scale military operation. The more specific steps in implementation of the plan were called *tactics*. More generally, the term *strategy* has come to refer to the implementation of a set of procedures (tactics) for accomplishing something. Thus, a *learning strategy* is a sequence of procedures for accomplishing learning, and the specific procedures within this sequence are called *learning tactics* (Snowman, in press).

I have argued (Schmeck, 1983, 1988) that my own research with self-report questionnaires reveals strategies through factor analysis of students' responses to the survey questions. Schmeck, Ribich, and Ramanaiah (1977) wrote questionnaire items, each of which asked the students about a learning tactic (e.g., using imagery to remember the definition of a word). Factor analysis of students' answers to these questions revealed clusters of tactics, that is, clusters of questions, which could be combined to form inventory scales. These clusters of learning tactics served as operational definitions of learning strategies (Schmeck, in press). Furthermore, when the instructions to the questionnaire were worded so as to ask students to answer the scales as they learn "in general rather than a particular course," then I argued that the scores could serve as measures of what I called *learning styles* at that time but would prefer to call *learning orientations* for purposes of the present text. The distinction between the terms *style* and *orientation* is clarified below.

Kirby (Chapter 9) includes an excellent discussion of the subtle but important distinctions between strategies and tactics plus the closely related "skills." *Skills* are capacities, or abilities, which can be expressed in behavior at any time because they have been honed, or developed, through practice. Skills are the "tools" we have available in our cognitive "tool kits."

Kirby notes that a skill can be employed in either of two ways:

intentionally, through conscious decision; or automatically, without conscious decision. Strategies and tactics are conscious and intentional. Thus, if a conscious decision was made to implement a skill, tactics and strategies were involved. Skills are things we *can* do; strategies and tactics involve the conscious *decisions* to implement those skills. Also strategies and tactics involve *plans* (see Das, Chapter 5); a skill involved in a tactical or strategic maneuver is integrated into a plan of some sort. One way of conceptualizing students' plans is in terms of their *motives*, and Entwistle (Chapter 2) provides an excellent description of the types of motives observed in students seeking a university degree. He also suggests that motives are one of the chief determiners of the approach that a student takes to studying, and since motives tend to be stable, they help the researcher account for cross-situational (style-like) consistency in approach.

With regard to conscious decisions to employ skills, the experiential (or phenomenological) view of learning emphasizes that learning can be improved if skills are used more intentionally and responsibly and less automatically. Biggs, Entwistle, Marton, and Ramsden all agree with this phenomenological point of view. McCarthy and Schmeck argue that schools should help students learn about themselves, encouraging self-awareness as a way of promoting cognitive development. Both practitioners (e.g., Carl Jung, see Campbell, 1971) and researchers (e.g., Biggs, 1986) agree that such awareness is a key to developing responsible individuality. Pask (Chapter 4) describes a program for encouraging cognitive development by helping students become more aware of their present cognitive styles.

When analyzing educational problems, the terms *skill* and *strategy* are often confused. We have to remember that failure to carry out an activity doesn't necessarily imply lack of skill. Such a failure may mean that an individual knows how to carry out the activity but doesn't want to carry it out. In such cases, rather than providing training in a skill, we have to convince individuals to incorporate the skill into their motives and plans. This requires that they admit they are capable of the activity (i.e., that they accept responsibijity for the skill), see the benefits of including it in future plans, and actually make the strategic decision to use the skill when those plans are applicable. Entwistle, Biggs, and McCarthy and Schmeck all suggest that the concept of "locus of control" is applicable, with the responsible, planful student believing that life's rewards are "internally" (not "externally") controlled.

Several years ago there was an influx of training programs designed to teach individuals to be assertive, that is, to diplomatically achieve their rights. The lack of assertiveness was most often treated as a skill deficit. Thus, in a particular training program, students might practice saying to a person in front of them in a theater, "Sir, will you please be quiet; I cannot hear the performers." It is often the case that the student already knows how to say "Sir, will you please," etc. The real problem is, because of dependence and fear of rejection, he or she doesn't really want to make that statement. This then is a higher-level tactical and strategic problem rather than a skill problem, and training programs often failed to recognize the distinction. When individuals are already capable of employing a skill, they don't need training, they need education concerned with plans, strategies, and responsibility. Kirby points out that sometimes the problem is indeed one of insufficient practice with a skill, and then training is in fact called for. In this regard, Weinstein (Chapter 11) provides an excellent description of a proven behavioral training program for developing learning skills.

Before turning to the labels *style, approach,* and *orientation,* we need to consider the term *process,* as used by Das and Kirby. A process occurs at the most specific, neurological level of analysis and is even more specific, or less molar, than a behavior. Styles, strategies, tactics, and skills are all, theoretically, composed of processes. The question is, what level of analysis does one prefer? At the most differentiated and analyzed level we have processes, and at less differentiated and more general levels we have strategies and styles.

Both Das and Kirby distinguish between coding and planning processes, with *coding* involving the more literal recording of experience and *planning* involving integration of codes. Das and Kirby also distinguish between simultaneous and successive coding processes, with *simultaneous* coding processes being more gestaltic or global and *successive* processes being more sequential or serial. Also, both Das and Kirby suggest that individuals may be more proficient in the more-analytic successive processes or the more-global simultaneous processes and that this can contribute to the style-like quality of their behavior.

There is yet another term more general than strategy. That term is *style,* and I turn now to its definition and then to an important distinction between style and approach.

COGNITIVE STYLES

Escalona and Heider (1959) state with regard to their extensive developmental study of behavior:

> As one notes behavioral alterations from infancy to—in the case of our study—later preschool ages, one knows that not a single behavior has remained the same, yet one is struck with the inherent continuity of behavioral *style* and of the child's *pattern of adaptation.* (p. 9; italics added)

If ever we observe that an individual has an inclination to use the same strategy in varied situations, we can suspect the presence of a *style* (see Schmeck, 1988). However, for purposes of clarity, Entwistle and Ramsden reserve the word *style* to refer to the stable, traitlike consistency in one's approach to attending, perceiving, and thinking traditionally labeled *cognitive style*. They prefer the label *orientation* when referring to consistency in one's approach to learning in school and university setting, because they feel that the student's orientation to studying in schools and universities results from a combination of motives and styles during his or her perception of the classroom situation. This is clarified in the next section.

The authors of the present text agree that the major dimension of cognitive style affecting learning features global–holistic attention, perception, and thinking at one end and focused–detailed attention, perception, and thinking at the other. Witkin and his colleagues (e.g., Witkin, Moore, Goodenough, & Cox, 1977) used the terms *field dependent* and *field independent*, or *global* and *articulated*, to refer to attentional and perceptual elements of such a style dimension. Others have referred to "impulsive" and "reflective" styles (e.g., Kogan, 1976) and "category breadth" (Wallach & Kogan, 1965). Kirby uses the terms *global* and *analytic*. Pask refers to "holist" and "serialist" (or comprehension and operation) styles. Torrance and Rockenstein use the terms *right-brained* and *left-brained*. Das suggests that individuals can have stylistic preferences for simultaneous or successive coding processes. Even Marton, who emphasizes situational influences, discusses "holistic" versus "atomistic" ways of structuring experience, and these are very similar to the global versus analytic styles discussed by Kirby.

Kirby suggests that individuals move developmentally from global forms of information processing to analytic modes of processing and finally, if development continues, global processing is combined with analytic to achieve a synthesis—which Pask calls a "versatile style" and Torrance and Rockenstein call "whole-brain functioning." In terms of the field dependent versus independent styles with which most of us are familiar, Kirby's model suggests that we all begin development as predominantly field dependent individuals and acquire field independent skills as development progresses. However, the highest level of development from Kirby's point of view would not be extreme field independence but an *integration* of dependent and independent skills in the single flexible style that takes advantage of the benefits of both modes of functioning. In a sense then the most sophisticated, most developed style is no style at all but a versatile reduction in rigid cross-situational, style-like consistency.

The "behavioral styles" of Escalona and Heider (1959) are abstractions not necessarily visible in any particular behavior but evident only from the abstract perspective obtained through repeated longitudinal or cross-situational observations of many behaviors from the same individuals. Schmeck (1988) notes that it is only from such a perspective that styles (or style-like orientations) can be observed. As noted above, Schmeck (e.g., 1983, 1988; see also Biggs and Entwistle, this volume) advocated factor analysis of responses to self-report questionnaire items to highlight clusters of tactics (and skills) that suggest the presence of a strategy which, if used persistently across situations, can be taken to indicate the presence of a style. Das and Kirby similarly used factor analytic techniques but analyzed responses to standardized ability, achievement, and information processing tests to reveal clusters of abilities (or skills) that define different information processing modes.

Another method of studying styles used by some of the authors of the present text (e.g., Biggs, Entwistle, Marton, and Pask) is the "externalization" of students' thoughts through some sort of interview, teach-back, or think-aloud protocol. Pask has used the technique that he calls *teachback,* in which a student has to learn the material and then teach it to the experimenter. Similarly, Marton speaks of having his subjects "retell the text." Entwistle and Marton have similarly made extensive use of interview techniques in their work, which they describe in their respective chapters. Biggs used interviews to study writing, and in his chapter he presents some excellent examples (excerpts) of students' descriptions of their approaches to the task of writing.

As noted above, Entwistle, Pask, and Ramsden carefully reserve the label "style" for discussing the traitlike consistency in cognition that has come to be known as *cognitive style.* Traditionally, either end of a cognitive style continuum is equally effective in accomplishing its purpose. For example, it is assumed to be equally effective to extract meaning from text if the student focuses on details then extracts generalities (Pask's serialist, or operation, learning style) or if he or she concentrates on generalities and adds details only as needed (Pask's holist, or comprehension, learning style). However, Kirby argues that we should perhaps discard this requirement that either end of a style dimension be equally effective. Kirby feels that it is often the case that one mode of functioning (one end of the stylistic dimension) is better than the other for a particular task, and in that sense, either end of the continuum (either mode of functioning) provides only a partial solution to problems that demand both modes of functioning combined in a synthesis.

APPROACHES AND ORIENTATIONS

Two types of influence affect behavior: characteristics of the *person* (including genetics, cognitive style, and prior experience) and characteristics of the specific *situation* in which the behavior occurs. Distinguishing between these two sources of influence is complicated for the following reasons. First, there is no way to peruse the genetics, styles, and experiences that make up a person (or a *personality*). We can see components of personality only indirectly by observing behavior within varied stimulus situations. We cannot make direct observations of situational influences either. We see the influence of the stimulus situation only in the effects on someone's behavior.

If we keep a situation constant and look across people, we see situational influences; and if we keep the person constant and look across situations, we see the influence of personal style. However, the two are normally (e.g., in our classrooms) operating simultaneously in a sort of "chemical reaction" that, in the end, may be unanalyzable. Even when studying cross-situational consistency that is style-like, we still have to do it by presenting the subject with a situation, and then we have all of the complex person-by-situation chemistry operating once again within our testing situation. In other words, even when we study person variables with questionnaires, or by externalizing students' thoughts in interviews and think-aloud protocols, we still have to do it by presenting the subject with another situation.

As I noted earlier, it is recognition of this complex reality that led Entwistle, Marton, and Ramsden to adopt the terms *approach* and *orientation* for referring to the strategies and tactics observed in students engaged in studying. It is important to recognize that the origins of the concept of "approach" are experiential, or phenomenological (see Marton, Chapter 3)—the concept stresses relationships between intention, process, and outcome within a specified context as described by an individual. Thus, the approach an individual takes to a task is the result of a relation between person and environment, neither of which is observable without the other. Ramsden borrows the term *learning in context* from Laurillard to express this relational character of learning. Metaphorically, the relation is like a "chemical reaction," in which styles, genetics, and prior experiences influence perception of current situational cues and moderate behavior elicited or controlled by the current situation. Biggs, Entwistle, and Marton agree that an approach is made up of an intention (or more generally a motive) and a strategy. Biggs states that the two are combined through metacognitive processes to yield an approach (cf. Carl Jung's discussion of the role of self-awareness in stimulating the "transcendental function" (in Campbell, 1971).

Biggs views approaches quite flexibly. From his perspective, an approach is a paradigm with a general structure which may change in specifics according to the task. The term *modus operandi* comes to mind in the sense in which it is supposedly used by police to refer to the stylistic elements present in a particular criminal's approach to a particular type of crime. In the extremes, students can show an approach to college (the "orientation to education" discussed by Entwistle) or an approach to a particular task, which Biggs exemplifies with writing and Kirby with reading.

A surface approach to reading obviously involves different behaviors than a surface approach to writing, but they might share a common motive (get it over with quickly with minimal pain) and a common strategy (focus on lower-level components rather than higher-level ones, e.g., words and sentences rather than main ideas and themes). The reader interested in how the student's perceptual categorization of a situation can account for style-like consistency in strategy usage should refer to Entwistle's discussion of "internal versus external horizons." Kirby expresses the issue with regard to reading by saying that it is a question of focusing on "how they go about reading or how they go about life."

Entwistle has studied students who fairly consistently favor one type of approach to study, giving their study behavior a style-like appearance. He uses the term *orientation* rather than style to refer to this style-like consistency, because he believes that consistency in approach is still predominantly the result of the student's perception of the situation, mediated by his or her motives. As I've noted, Entwistle reserves the label "style" for that which he believes is most traitlike, that is, *cognitive style.*

Orientations have been conceptualized in at least two ways (see Entwistle, Chapter 2). *Orientation to studying* is the factor which summarizes approaches, motives, and styles; it includes an element of study methods and attitudes. *Orientation to education* is broader and involves life goals and purposes, reasons for taking courses at the university. As I said above, Kirby notes that, at the broadest level of classification, we could study one's orientation to life (or life-style). I have more to say about this in the next section.

FOCUSING ON THE PERSON VERSUS THE SITUATION

Traditionally, behavioral scientists disagree regarding the relative influence of an environmental situation and stylistic traits of the person who is confronted by that situation. In the present text, Ramsden argues strongly that we must focus on the situation, not the person. He states that "stability of orientations does not imply fixity. Orientations to studying are changeable and responsive to the context of teaching, evaluation, and curriculum" (Chapter 7). However, even Ramsden notes that personal, style-like *stability* in approach to studying can coexist with situationally sensitive *variability* in approach. Thomas and Bain (1984) report evidence that suggests that although a student with a reproducing orientation may be encouraged to take a deep approach by altering the situation, that student's approach is still likely to be more "surface" than that of a student with a meaning orientation to studying.

From an experiential or phenomenological perspective, any argument regarding which source of influence is most important (person or situation) is useless because the argument is not resolvable. A person in context is not simply the sum of the person and the context. We can focus on the person, looking across situations, or we can focus on the *situation*, looking across people, but in reality the two will always exist in a relation.

When it is a question of how to improve education, Entwistle, Marton, and Ramsden all argue that although we may not be able to say that the situation is "more important," the best way to improve education is still to focus on the situation, structuring it differently so that students perceive it differently. However, Das, Kirby, McCarthy and Schmeck, and Weinstein argue that there is also something to be gained by focusing on the person, believing that it is possible to improve functioning regardless of the situation by developing the person's skills through training and through encouragement of cognitive and emotional development (e.g., through increased self-awareness).

Säljö (1975) tried to structure a learning situation so that students would strive to understand the information that he presented to them. Most of the students flexibly modified their approach to the task depending on how it was structured. However, some of the students failed to engage in activities that would lead to meaningful understanding even when the situation was clearly one that should have encouraged such activities. Säljö's (1975) approach to research was experiential or phenomenological, including an emphasis on the person's perceptions. Thus, Sälljö argued that the students who persistently committed the information to memory in its literal form had for some reason perceived the situation as one demanding descriptive summaries rather than understanding. Why is it that Säljö was not able to alter the perceptions of these particular students?

Perception involves an act of classification, for example, this is "a test," or "a recital," or "a debate." The person classifies the situation, then behaves in ways that he or she has learned to be appropriate in that type of situation. When a particular motive is very dominant, a single perceptual category may excessively influence perception. In such cases, the person's behavior will be more stylized. For example, suppose that for a particular student the most important judgment in any situation is the likelihood that evaluation is involved, specifically its potential to "make him look foolish" (see Entwistle's discussion of the fear-of-failure motive). When a situation is judged to involve evaluation, such a student has a set procedure (or strategy) for responding to it—making his behavior appear very stylized. In his experiment, Säljö (1975) found that the students who persisted in remembering the text literally, even though understanding was called for, may have judged the situation to be an evaluative one and responded with their usual procedure—for example, repeat the text as literally as possible in order to avoid criticism.

The point that phenomenologists emphasize is that it's the student's perception that starts the whole thing. If teachers can structure classroom situations so that students perceive them differently, they will approach them differently (see chapters by Entwistle, Marton, and Ramsden, this volume). That approach worked with most of the students in Säljö's experiment, but not all of them. McCarthy and Schmeck argue that we can also influence perception by encouraging the overall cognitive and emotional development of the person.

On the cognitive side, development leads to increasing differentiation of perceptual categories revealing the uniqueness of events. On the emotional side, development brings with it freedom from excessive dependence on the approval of others to maintain self-esteem, and thus it brings freedom to pursue self-interests with deep approaches. In either case, stylistic rigidity is reduced, and integration or synthesis of various cognitive functions occurs, permitting versatility in functioning.

According to McCarthy and Schmeck, the catalyst for all of this is self-awareness or reflection of the mind upon itself. Such reflection stimulates the integration of information and development of planning skills (see Das, Chapter 5) as well as metacognitive control processes (see Biggs, 1986, also Chapter 8, this volume) that free the individual from compulsive, knee-jerk responding and raise cognitive functioning to a more responsible, conscious, intentional level (see chapters by Biggs, Entwistle, and Marton, this volume).

Finally with regard to development, Kirby notes that understanding requires skills that some students will not have automatized so that they can access and use them easily. These students may have to resort to literal, surface learning tactics—for lack of a better solution—until the prerequisite skill is acquired. We noted above that Kirby feels development of cognitive style proceeds from a prevalence of global, undifferentiated skills toward more analytic, differentiated functioning and finally achieves an integration of the earlier creative, global functioning with the analytic skills to form a synthesis that Torrance and Rockenstein call "whole-brained functioning." It is this latter synthesis that is necessary for understanding or for a deep approach to learning. Those students who have not achieved the synthesis will not be able to employ a truly deep approach or arrive at a true understanding. Thus, the reader will find that the present text contains two suggestions for improving education: changing the school setting in order to alter students' perceptions and changing the students themselves in order to alter their mode of functioning. The two suggestions are, of course, not at all conflictual. What is needed is that the teacher consider both perspectives: focusing sometimes on the student as figure and the environment as ground and sometimes on the classroom environment as figure and the students as ground. Such shifts in perspective can reveal ways of helping individual students as well as changes in overall procedure that help the class as a whole.

APPROACHES TO RESEARCH AND APPROACHES TO IMPROVING EDUCATION

Two broad approaches to, or perspectives on, research are presented in this book. The experiential, phenomenological perspective relies upon qualitative descriptions and the gradual, evolving conceptualization of research problems. This qualitative approach uses what are sometimes called emergent research designs and is somewhat more nondirective and discovery oriented than its alternative. The conceptions of qualitative researchers tend to be a bit more holistic and less reductionistic than those of quantitative researchers. A qualitative researcher describes situations as they are perceived by the participants rather than in terms of theories developed by psychologists in laboratory settings. Qualitative researchers fear that the laboratory settings used by many quantitative researchers have doubtful ecological validity.

The quantitative approach to research is more prescriptive and driven *a priori* by theory—focusing on testing or trying out hypothesized answers and solutions. It emphasizes preconceived research designs, manipulation of suspected causes, very specific *a priori* prediction of effects, and control of situational variables. It tends to be more reductionistic and laboratory oriented.

Educational researchers are interested in practical problems and solutions, and the types of solutions they propose tend to reflect their basic approaches to research. Advocates of qualitative analysis tend to spend more time considering (or "living with") basic questions and problems in the expectation that potential answers and solutions will emerge gradually along with the conceptualizations of the problem itself. Their research focuses upon the participants' perceptions and conceptualizations of experienced situations. The solutions they propose for educational problems similarly tend to emphasize students' perceptions and interpretations of the educational setting. For example, if some students place excessive emphasis upon literal retention of details, they must perceive the educational context as one in which such behavior is appropriate. Thus, we need to observe and conceptualize the factors that contribute to that perception. In so doing, ways will emerge for altering the educational context so as to alter the students' perception of and approach to it. In fact, Marton and Ramsden illustrate that some potential solutions have already emerged from qualitative–descriptive research.

On the other side of the coin, advocates of the more quantitative and prescriptive approach to research emphasize development and pre-testing of interventions developed in highly controlled settings. These interventions often take the form of training programs designed to control and change the students themselves. Weinstein provides an illustration of a training program carefully designed and thoroughly pretested for the purpose of altering students' approaches to learning by altering the students themselves, that is, by altering their study skills. Das and Kirby also mention training programs designed to alter students' information processing skills and strategies—in effect, altering their cognitive styles.

ADAPTING TO THE LEARNING CONTEXT

Why do some students literally commit to memory whatever they are to learn, while others attend to construction and revision of personal characterizations of reality? We've been emphasizing that the learning context, like all situations, is perceived before it affects behavior, and perception involves matching current experiences with patterns of prior experiences—"What manner of situation is this and what does it mean to me?"

If students are instructed to prepare for an examination or write an essay in a particular course, one can predict their behavior by inquiring: "What does an examination (or an essay) in this course *mean* to you?" In this manner, it is possible to begin to understand the patterns, including personal issues and motives, that enter into the student's perception of the learning context. If we probe sufficiently, we may find that for some students a test or essay is a potentially demoralizing and destructive situation, while for others, it is an opportunity to grow. For still others, it is an opportunity to dominate, or demonstrate superiority in a competitive, comparative manner. And for the remainder, it is a step in the earning of a certification that will help in obtaining gainful employment after graduation. In any case, Ramsden emphasizes that students attempt to cope with demands of the educational situation, and their thought processes during studying can be predicted from knowledge of their perceptions of the situations that they are trying to adapt to. Similarly, Entwistle suggests that if we know what a particular educational task *means* to a student we can predict how he or she will approach that task.

Many of the students who are expecting to be demoralized or destroyed will do what all people do in such situations, that is, they will generally be avoidant, obedient, attract as little attention as possible, and give the potential destroyer (i.e., the teacher) precisely what he or she seems to want. Thus, the students may try to commit to memory, in literal form, as many as possible of the teacher's beliefs and words as revealed within the lectures and textbooks of the class. This will be done under the influence of anxiety, which narrows attention even further to very specific and literal features of the information being processed (Schmeck, 1983).

Another way of saying all this is to say that a person's perception of a situation places that person into a "frame of mind." This frame of mind includes a scenario, or script, that has assumptions, expectations, roles, and concerns. Pask refers to this frame of mind as a *persona*. It can account for cross-situational consistency in students' behavior, such as their orientations to studying and to education, and it can also account for their conception of the learning process itself. Situations which place the person into the same frame of mind will be dealt with similarly, even though those situations might not seem similar to someone observing the person's behavior.

Thus, the person's frame of mind (or persona) can account for style-like consistency in his or her behavior, and that frame of mind is the result of his or her perception of the situation. Teachers can structure a situation so as to encourage a competitive frame of mind or a personal growth or self-actualization frame of mind. McCarthy and Schmeck point out that if we key into competition, some students will anticipate victory and others defeat, and both will behave according to their expectations. Likewise, they say that if we key into self-actualization, students will self-reference information and reflect upon their own functioning, thereby stimulating their continued cognitive development.

Another way teachers may influence perception and thereby influence learning is by encouraging a change in the scenarios, or scripts, that are part of the frame of mind that accompanies a perception. The teacher can ask a student, "what do you think will happen if (for example) you fail this test?" Then, student and teacher might discuss the student's beliefs and emotional expectations. Changes in scenarios or scripts occur through gradual developmental–experiential processes, which teachers can promote by structuring the educational situation so that the personal growth motive is engaged more frequently than either the need to prove something, the need to be dependent on someone, or the need to be taken care of. This is what Carl Rogers (1969) wanted educators to do, but the educational system has not always been sensitive to Rogers' recommendations. Both Marton and Ramsden discuss this problem of dealing with school systems that are not sympathetic to teachers who de-emphasize memorization and competition in favor of developing new interpretations of reality and continued self-actualization.

The case studies that Biggs presents in Chapter 8 show the influence of both situation and person variables. Both of his individuals are quite sensitive to evaluation pressure, always considering the preferences and biases of the instructor who will evaluate their essays. However, even when two of his participants have the same evaluator (and thus confront the "same" situation), one writes what she thinks is wanted and the other tends to write what she wants to say (see the discussion of "Emma" and "Anne" in Chapter 8).

The point is that student strategies and styles of learning should be, in principle, predictable and changeable based upon the types of analyses introduced in this text. The remainder of the present text elaborates upon the themes presented in this first chapter by presenting the views of some of the most experienced researchers in the field of education. The final chapter of the text summarizes these views and combines them to yield a broad analysis of the etiology of styles, strategies, and approaches to learning. The final chapter also elaborates upon suggestions regarding how the learning potentials of students might be improved.

SUMMARY

Learning strategies are combinations of cognitive (thinking) skills implemented when a situation is perceived as one demanding learning. In general, when a strategy is favored with a certain bias that ignores subtle variation in the situation, it suggests either the presence of a *cognitive style* or the presence of motives and personal experiences that affect perception and give rise to a style-like *orientation*.

Styles and motives reside within the person and relate to genetics and prior experience. Situational influences reside within the context but, like styles, cannot be observed directly. We see only behavior within specific situations, behavior influenced by both personal and situational factors as they interact during the individual's perception of the situation. Since we cannot separate the sources of influence, our authors suggest the term *approach* as a label for that which we can see, that is, the behavior of a particular individual in a particular situation. An approach reflects a *relation* between person and situation, and our authors differ somewhat with regard to the relative emphasis they place upon the two components.

Perception involves an act of classification in which a situation is matched to a pattern or prototype that evolved from past experiences (e.g., "an evaluation situation," "a self-expression situation," "a competition situation," etc.). This act of classification leads to transfer of the strategies found appropriate in prior encounters with the prototypical situations. In some students, the prototype includes expectations of failure and humiliation calling for self-effacing, obedient strategies that lead to literal repetition of the statement of authorities (e.g., teachers, authors, parents). Such repetitive, literal strategies yield only a fragmentary understanding. In other students, the prototypical pattern to which the situation is matched includes expectations for exciting and creative self-expression calling for a calm synthesis or integration of all cognitive functions.

We see in the following chapters that the teacher often has control of important aspects of the situation and can thereby affect the student by changing situational characteristics that affect how students perceive and approach the classroom situation (e.g., the teacher can sometimes de-emphasize competition). Furthermore, we see that the teacher can do things that encourage overall development of the personal strengths of individual students—strengths which may ultimately help them adapt to any situation, including a bad one, such as a poorly taught class. This way of thinking about the styles and strategies of learning is illustrated in greater detail within the subsequent chapters of the text.

REFERENCES

Biggs, J. (1986). The role of metalearning in study processes. *British Journal of Educational Psychology.*

Campbell, J. (1971). *The portable Jung.* New York: Viking Press.

Escalona, S. K., & Heider, G. (1959). *Prediction and outcome.* New York: Basic Books.

Kogan, N. (1976). *Cognitive styles in infancy and early childhood.* Hillsdale, NJ: Lawrence Erlbaum.

Rogers, C. R. (1969). *Freedom to learn.* Columbus, OH: Merrill.

Säljö, R. (1975). *Qualitative differences in learning as a function of the learner's conception of the task.* Gothenburg: Acta Universitatis Gothoburgensis.

Schmeck, R. R. (1983). Learning styles of college students. IN R. F. Dillon & R. R. Schmeck (Eds.), *Individual differences in cognition: Volume I* (pp. 233–279). New York: Academic Press.

Schmeck, R. R. (1988). Individual differences and learning strategies. In C. Weinstein, P. Alexander, & E. Goetz (Eds.), *Learning and study strategies: Issues in assessment, instruction, and evaluation* (pp. 171–191). New York: Academic Press.

Schmeck, R. R., Ribich, F. D., & Ramanaiah, N. (1977). Development of a self-report inventory for assessing individual differences in learning processes. *Applied Psychological Measurement, 1,* 413–431.

Snowman, J. (1986). Learning tactics and strategies. In G. D. Phye & T. Andre (Eds.), *Cognitive instructional psychology: Components of classroom learning* (pp. 243–275). New York: Academic Press.

Thomas, P. R., & Bain, J. D. (1984). Contextual dependence of learning approaches: The effects of assessment. *Human Learning, 3,* 227–240.

Wallach, M. A., & Kogan, N. (1965). *Modes of thinking in young children.* New York: Holt, Rinehart & Winston.

Witkin, H. A., Moore, C. A., Goodenough, D. R., & Cox, P. W. (1977). Field-dependent and field-independent cognitive styles and their educational implications. *Review of Educational Research,* 1–64.

CHAPTER 2

Motivational Factors in Students' Approaches to Learning

NOEL ENTWISTLE

INTRODUCTION

This chapter describes the theoretical background to, and the development and use of, an Approaches-to-Studying Inventory. This inventory covers the two main components consistently found to be predictive of academic success—organized study methods and active learning processes (Weinstein & Underwood, 1985)—but it also includes a series of motivational components. It is, of course, commonplace to attribute levels of attainment to the degree of effort exerted which, in turn, is explained in terms of the motivational characteristics of the learner. But the research based on the use of this inventory goes further. It indicates clearly that there are distinctive forms of motivation which affect the outcome of learning both quantitatively and qualitatively. The differing forms of motivation are associated with contrasting learning processes and, so, with qualitatively different outcomes.

The research into student learning traditionally has adopted psychometric techniques derived from work on the measurement of attitudes. The scales developed in such studies, however, have often lacked any convincing theoretical rationale. The pools of items have

NOEL ENTWISTLE • Department of Education, University of Edinburgh, 10 Buccleuch Place, Edinburgh, Scotland EH8 9JT.

been produced mainly from an examination of "how to study" manuals, rooted in speculative extrapolations from mainstream psychology and personal experience (Gibbs, 1981). An alternative methodology involves systematic analysis of interviews dealing with the tasks undertaken in everyday studying (Marton, Hounsell, & Entwistle, 1984; and Chapter 3, this volume). These studies have produced a series of concepts and categories describing aspects of student learning which are firmly rooted in the students' own experiences. The interrelationships between these concepts are beginning to provide one basis for developing scales with a sound rationale. Another theoretical basis can be found in cognitive psychology in relation to models of learning and memory and concepts such as levels of processing (Craik & Lockhart, 1972). Schmeck (1983) describes research involving the use of scales of learning processes derived from cognitive psychology. This chapter concentrates on quantitative research on approaches to learning which has made use of the concepts identified in interviews with students, but it also presents some evidence about the interrelationships of scales based on the two types of theory. The first task, however, is to establish the meaning of the main concepts and categories operationalized in the inventory and subsequently used in a discussion of the relationships between the concepts derived from qualitative research.

CONCEPTS FROM QUALITATIVE RESEARCH ON STUDENT LEARNING

The concepts emerging from research on student learning can be seen as describing aspects of the students' experience in terms of contexts which range from the broadest (the overall educational setting within the institution) to the narrowest (the content of a specific task). The most fundamental thread which seems to run through all these concepts, and provides a degree of coherence, is the student's motives or intentions. They produce a distinction between learning for personal understanding or development and learning necessitated by fulfilling the requirements of others in completing academic tasks to defined standards. The terms *intrinsic* and *extrinsic* describe this main distinction.

The concept of greatest generality to emerge from the qualitative studies is *educational orientation*, which has to be distinguished from *study orientation*, a less general term which emerges from the quantitative research to be described later on. Educational orientation derives from the work of Taylor (1983; Gibbs, Morgan, & Taylor, 1984) and describes the set of values and attitudes relating to education which the person holds at a particular time. The four main categories are *vocational*, *academic, personal,* and *social.* The first three of these categories may each be divided into extrinsic and intrinsic subdivisions, as shown in Table 1. Mere "intrinsic" is used to indicate that satisfaction is derived from the course content itself, while "extrinsic" refers to institutionalized aspects of the course (e.g., qualifications).

The four educational orientations can also be seen as distinctive sets of motives or forms of motivation. Indeed the first three of these describe attributes which were independently included in the quantitative studies presented in the main body of this chapter.

A concept with somewhat less generality is *conception of learning,* which was identified by Säljö (1982; Marton & Säljö, 1984) and has recently been extended by Van Rossum (1984). In qualitative studies students were asked what they understood by the word *learning.* The replies indicated a fundamental division between those who saw learning as reproducing a body of knowledge presented by the teacher and those who defined learning in terms of constructing their own understanding from a combination of formal knowledge and personal experi-

Table 1. *Students' Orientations to Higher Education*

Orientation	Aim	Concerns
Vocational		
Extrinsic	Obtaining a qualification	Perceived worth of qualification
Intrinsic	Being well trained	Relevance to future career
Academic		
Extrinsic	Progression up the educational ladder	Academic progress and performance
Intrinsic	Pursuing subject for its own sake	Choosing stimulating courses or topics
Personal		
Extrinsic	Compensation for past failures	Reassuring comments and pass marks
Intrinsic	Broadening horizons	New insights and challenges
Social		
Extrinsic	Having a good time	Facilities for sport and social activities

ence. Within this simple dichotomy there are up to six distinguishable categories, shown in Table 2 (cf. Marton, Chapter 3, this volume).

A more specific concept, but one which has had the most influence on the qualitative research in this area, was introduced by Marton (1975; see also Chapter 3, this volume). As a result of research into how students tackled the task of reading an academic article, he introduced the concept of *approach to learning* to describe what he saw as a fundamental difference in the focus of attention of students reading texts. The two categories he introduced were "deep" and "surface." In a *deep approach* the student starts with the intention to extract personal meaning from the text, and this leads to an active process of learning in which the student challenges the ideas, evidence, and arguments presented by the author, tries to see interrelationships among the ideas presented, and seeks links with personal experience and the outside world. This, in turn, implies that the student is reconstructing knowledge within a personal framework, that is, adopting a "holistic" approach in coding information into memory, in the sense that the activity is intended to establish a network of meaningful connections between the new information and previously established concepts, ideas, and factual information.

In a *surface approach* the focus of attention in reading a text is on the text itself. The student is concerned with verbatim recall of either the whole text or the facts and ideas presented in it. There is little or no personal engagement in the act of learning: it is seen as an external imposition. While the text is recognized to have meaning, the task presented is not seen as carrying personal significance. Students are thus concerned more with task completion than with improving their knowl-

Table 2. *Categories Describing Conceptions of Learning*

Category	Definition
Acquisition of knowledge	A vague quantitative conception of learning as involving "knowing a lot"
Memorizing	Storage of information for subsequent reproduction
Utilization of knowledge	Dawning realization that learning may involve more than memorizing facts, recognition that knowledge and skills can be useful in the real world
Abstraction of meaning	Recognizes that learning involves insights into relationships within subject matter and between subject matter and reality
Interpretative understanding	Learning seen as a means of understanding the world around us by reinterpreting knowledge
Self-actualization	Learning as personal growth and development

Adapted from Van Rossum, 1984.

edge and skills. As a result of this mechanical process of rote memorization, students may well fail to distinguish between essential points and
incidental facts or between principles and examples. They are unlikely
to relate evidence and conclusions or examine the argument in a critical
way. The process of learning thus can be seen as *sequential* or *atomistic*
(Svensson, 1976, 1984) in that it fails to include the crucial stage of
reorganization and reinterpretation, and the outcome is a more or less
complete reproduction of the text, which is unlikely to contain the central core of the author's message.

The original formulation of the approach-to-learning concept had a
narrow focus, being related to a particular type of learning task. Even
within this narrow focus there is clear evidence that the approach
adopted by the student is variable over time and over situation. And in
this variability the effects of motivation on approach become clear. Fransson (1977) investigated the effects of differing levels of intrinsic and
extrinsic motivation on students' approaches to reading an academic
article. He found that students who had found the article interesting or
relevant were more likely than others to adopt a deep approach. In
contrast, students who had found the experiment stressful, indicating
extrinsic motivation out of anxiety, tended to adopt surface approaches.

In subsequent research into students' everyday studying, the effects on approach of interest, in terms of assessment demands, have
been demonstrated (Entwistle & Ramsden, 1983; Laurillard, 1984). Students also reported how the enthusiasm and empathy of the lecturer
affects their approaches to studying (Hodgson, 1984; Ramsden, 1984). In
all these ways, approach has been found to be variable, depending on
both the content and the context of learning. But other research, looking
at a broader range of students' activities (including essay writing and
preparing for examinations), has shown considerable consistency in approach (Entwistle & Ramsden, 1983; Svensson, 1977). Although few
students were wholly consistent, most of them could be classified as
adopting either a deep or a surface approach to a majority of tasks. This
cross-situational consistency, taken in conjunction with the quantitative
findings to be discussed in the next section, led to the introduction of a
new term, *orientation to studying*. This term was chosen instead of the
more commonly used "style" because of the more limited sense in
which style is used in the research now to be discussed.

Pask (1976; Chapter 4, this volume) carried out laboratory studies of
students carrying out meaningful learning. He used the term *learning
strategy* to describe the distinctive ways in which students tackled a
problem-solving task. In his experiment students were forced to extract
meaning; they could not settle for a surface approach. But some students still focused their attention narrowly on the facts or details and on

logical relationships or procedures—a *serialist* strategy. Others, right from the beginning, tried to see the learning in a broader setting and were much more interested in grasping general relationships between ideas. They also seemed to rely heavily in their learning on analogies, illustrations, and anecdotes in bringing the academic learning closer to their everyday experience. This was described by Pask as a *holist* strategy.

Pask accepted that a student's strategy would be dependent on the nature of the task set, as Laurillard (1984) has shown in problem solving in everyday studying. But Pask also argued that students had preferred strategies which they would use first. These preferred strategies were identified as *styles of learning* which depend on contrasting processes of learning. A serialist strategy relies on *operation learning* (step-by-step concentration on particulars), while the process used in a holist strategy is termed *comprehension learning* (building up an overview). Academic learning in higher education generally seems to demand both these learning processes—a *versatile* style of learning. Students who rely too much on one or other process show characteristic *pathologies of learning*. Exclusive reliance on serialist strategies means that important relationships between ideas will be missed and useful analogies will be ignored. Pask described this category as *improvidence*. Repeated adoption of holist strategies implies a main concern with building up an overview. This tendency, termed *globetrotting*, is often also associated with an overreadiness to reach conclusions without examining the supportive evidence.

MOTIVATION IN STUDYING

The earlier atheoretical approaches to investigating studying had identified study organization, attitudes to courses and to teachers, and motivation as dimensions of importance. Perhaps the best known of the early inventories was the Survey of Study Habits and Attitudes (Brown & Holtzman, 1966). It contained four subscales: work methods (effective study procedures); delay avoidance (promptness in completing work); teacher approval (favorable opinions about teachers); and educational acceptance (approval of educational objectives).

In Australia, Pond (1964) showed the importance of time management and work organization in distinguishing high-achieving students from those who were less successful. Items relating to these dimensions were incorporated in a scale of study methods developed in Britain by Entwistle and Wilson (1970), who also included in their inventory items indicating academic achievement motivation. Subsequent factor analyses suggested the existence of two groups of items in both the study methods and motivation scales. The factors reflected study organization, study attitudes, and two forms of motivation described as achievement motivation and fear of failure. The distinctive nature of these two forms of motivation was confirmed both in interviews (Entwistle, Thompson, & Wilson, 1974) and through the use of cluster analysis (Entwistle & Wilson, 1977). This statistical technique separated three groups of successful students: one apparently motivated by hope for success (Atkinson & Feather, 1966), one by academic interest, and the final group by fear of failure (Birney *et al.*, 1969). Already it was clear that there were two forms of intrinsic motivation here, one which derived from the reinforcement of high academic self-esteem and the other from interest in the subject matter itself (Entwistle *et al.*, 1974).

Research by Wankowski (1973) showed that unsuccessful students were likely to have entered university for extrinsic reasons such as parental pressure or to obtain a "job ticket" rather than for intrinsic interest in a particular discipline. Wankowski also showed that students who were progressing normally had clearer short- and long-term goals. A scale which incorporated items distinguishing intrinsic motivation out of interest from extrinsic (vocational) motivation was subsequently developed by Biggs (1976).

DEVELOPING THE APPROACHES TO STUDYING INVENTORY

A 5-year research program was initiated in 1976 to build on the findings of a previous study (Entwistle & Wilson, 1977). This program was designed to draw on both qualitative and quantitative methodologies (Entwistle & Ramsden, 1983). Findings from this program, and from more recent work, provide the evidence used both in this chapter and in Chapter 7. The findings reported here relate mainly to quantitative findings, but the subsequent interpretation draws on the qualitative research as well.

The first pilot study carried out in the research program was an attempt to carry out a quantitative analysis to confirm Marton's conclusion that approach to learning was related to the outcome of learning. The criteria used by Marton to describe differences in outcome and in contrasting approaches were used with a questionnaire variant of Marton's interview procedure (Entwistle, Hanley, & Ratcliffe, 1979). The two sets of criteria were included in a factor analysis. Three interpretable factors were described. One factor linked surface approach and outcome, but two factors described contrasting aspects of deep approach and outcome. The first indicated a concentration on relating ideas without examining evidence in detail, while the second suggested a greater reliance on factual details but without a clear overview. This splitting of deep approach indicated that few of the students were able to carry through all the component processes demanded by a fully deep approach which would have resulted in a deep level of understanding. The division in deep approach was reminiscent of Pask's distinction between the two learning processes—comprehension and operation learning.

The next step in the research program was to measure approach to learning in a way which would allow the use of larger samples and quantitative analyses. Interviews with students were used both to confirm and extend the definitions of Marton's concepts and categories and to build up a pool of items for the quantitative parts of the program. The intention was to operationalize both "approaches to studying" and "styles of learning" in terms of the defining characteristics described by Marton (1975) and Pask (1976) in an inventory which also assessed the dimensions of study methods and motivation previously identified. Besides the two categories of approach introduced by Marton, interviews with students suggested the need for a third—"strategic approach." This category indicated an approach equivalent to what Miller and Parlett (1974) had described as *cue seeking*. Some students try to manipulate the assessment procedures to their own advantage by a careful marrying of their efforts to the reward system as they perceive it.

The process of operationalization involved rewriting the defining features of the main concepts and categories which had emerged from the qualitative analyses. This rewriting was based on the comments actually made by students in the interviews. As a result, the items had recognizable authenticity to students subsequently filling in the inventory. The pool of items defining each category was subjected to conceptual analysis in an attempt to ensure that the full meaning of each concept was covered without unnecessary overlap between items. This procedure produced a pilot inventory which was then developed through empirical item analyses alternating with further conceptual analysis. The pilot inventory contained 120 items (subsequently reduced to 106) and was presented in a 5-response Likert format.

Factor analysis of this inventory produced three main factors, each with a distinct motivational component (Entwistle, Hanley, & Hounsell, 1979). The first two factors also contained both an approach and a style. Factor I linked Deep Approach and Comprehension Learning with Intrinsic Motivation. Factor II indicated connections between Surface Approach, Operation Learning, and both Fear of Failure and Extrinsic Motivation. It also contained a substantial loading on Strategic Approach in this initial analysis. Factor III brought together Organized Study Methods, Positive Attitudes, and Achievement Motivation.

Biggs (1979) had independently described a similar structure linking study strategies and motivation. His inventory contained similar items but had been developed from a quite different theoretical rationale. He initially labeled his three factors Internalizing, Utilizing, and Achieving, containing the cognitive and motivational components shown in Table 3. The similarity between these two sets of factors is all the more remarkable when it is realized that Biggs was describing students in terms of a different inventory and within a different educational system (Australia). He has subsequently relabeled the first two factors Deep and Surface, in recognition of their close similarity to Marton's concepts (Biggs, 1985).

Discussion of the analyses of the pilot inventory led to several minor changes in items, but also to changes in the subscales. In particular, the factor describing the deep approach was strengthened by including two additional subscales. It had become clear from the preliminary item analyses, from the early interviews, and from continuing work by Marton and his colleagues, that deep approach involved both the *intention* to reach personal understanding and the learning *processes* involved in achieving that intention. Thus Deep Approach was subsequently used to describe a deep intention, while Relating Ideas and Use of Evidence covered the two main processes involved in understanding academic material.

The final inventory used in the research program contained 64 items spread across 16 subscales having internal consistency reliabilities (Cronbach alpha) between .78 (Extrinsic Motivation) and .32 (Strategic Approach), with a median value of .50. The lower values were associated with scales which applied more to one subject area than others. Coefficients for the four main domains had a median value of .72. A list of the subscales within four domains, together with indicative items, is presented as Table 4.

Table 3. Cognitive and Motivational Components of Learning Processes

Factor	Cognitive	Motivational
Internalizing	Meaning assimilation	Intrinsic
Utilizing	Fact–rote strategy	Extrinsic
Achieving	Study skills and organization	Fear of failure Need for achievement

From Biggs, 1979.

Table 4. Subscales within Four Domains and Indicative Items in the Students' Approaches to Studying Inventory

Domain with Subscales	Indicative item
Meaning Orientation	
Deep Approach	I usually set out to understand thoroughly the meaning of what I am asked to read.
Relating Ideas	I try to relate ideas in one subject to those in others, whenever possible.
Use of Evidence	When I'm reading an article or research report I generally examine the evidence carefully to decide whether the conclusion is justified.
Intrinsic Motivation	I find academic topics so interesting, I should like to continue with them after I finish this course.
Reproducing Orientation	
Surface Approach	I find I have to concentrate on memorizing a good deal of what we have to learn.
Syllabus-Boundness	I like to be told precisely what to do in essays or other assignments.
Fear of Failure	The continual pressure of work assignments, deadlines, and competition often makes me tense and depressed.
Extrinsic Motivation	My main reason for being here is that it will help me to get a better job.
Achieving Orientation	
Strategic Approach	When I'm doing a piece of work, I try to bear in mind exactly what that particular lecturer seems to want.
Disorganized Study Methods	I find it difficult to organize any study time effectively.
Negative Attitudes	When I look back, I sometimes wonder why I ever decided to come here.
Achievement Motivation	It is important to me to do things better than my friends.
Learning Style	
Comprehension Learning	I like to play around with ideas of my own even if they don't get me very far.
Globetrotting	I seem to be a bit too ready to jump to conclusions without waiting for the evidence.
Operation Learning	I generally prefer to tackle each part of a topic or problem in order, working out one at a time.
Improvidence	Although I generally remember facts and details, I find it difficult to fit them together into an overall picture.

ORIENTATIONS TO STUDYING

The target population for a national survey (Entwistle & Ramsden, 1983) using this inventory was students in their penultimate year of an honors degree who were studying in departments of English, history, economics, psychology, physics, or engineering. Sixty-six departments in universities and polytechnics across Britain agreed to take part. A total of 2,208 students completed the inventories, with a response rate of over 73%. The sample included 491 arts students, 852 in the social sciences, and 865 taking either pure or applied sciences.

The 16 subscales, together with indices of academic performance at school and in higher education, were included in a principal factors technique of factor analysis using the SPSS program. Four factors had eigenvalues greater than one and accounted for 55% of the variance. These factors were rotated to oblique simple structure. The factor structure loadings are shown in Table 5.

Table 5. Factor Structure of the Approaches to Studying Inventory

Approaches to Studying Subscales	Factors[a]			
	I	II	III	IV
School Attainment	−02	−13	−07	−15
Attainment in Higher Ed.[b]	31	−26	19	−39
Meaning Orientation				
Deep Approach	70			
Relating Ideas	65			
Use of Evidence	54			
Intrinsic Motivation	72			−25
Reproducing Orientation				
Surface Approach		57	30	36
Syllabus-Boundness	−41	58		
Fear of Failure		50		34
Extrinsic Motivation	−25	38	53	
Achieving Orientation				
Strategic Approach	29		48	
Disorganized Study Methods	−25			50
Negative Attitudes	−39			52
Achievement Motivation			45	
Learning Style				
Comprehension Learning	55			30
Globetrotting				52
Operation Learning		62	44	
Improvidence		68	26	

[a]Decimal points and loadings less than .25 omitted.
[b]Self-rating.

The four factors emerging from these analyses have been termed *orientations to studying*. The term *orientation* was chosen to indicate both a consistency of approach and the existence, in three of the factors, of both approach and motivation. The first factor was described as Meaning Orientation. It had high loadings on Deep Approach and both associated processes (Relating Ideas and Use of Evidence). Again these were associated with both Comprehension Learning and Intrinsic Motivation. Other loadings indicated links with syllabus-freedom and positive attitudes.

The second factor was equally clearly defined and was identified as a Reproducing Orientation. Its highest loadings brought together Surface Approach, Operation Learning, and Improvidence—all indicating an atomistic way of tackling academic work and a narrow concern with completing assessment requirements. As before, the associated motivational subscales were Fear of Failure and Extrinsic Motivation. This factor also showed negative loadings on academic performance in higher education. Although, theoretically, operation learning is considered to be a necessary part of a versatile, deep approach to learning, here it is associated with surface learning. This relationship suggests that students who prefer serialistic strategies may, perhaps through lack of time, become trapped in a reproductive mode of operation.

The remaining two factors were less distinct. The fourth factor was described as a Nonacademic Orientation, indicating predominantly disorganized study methods and negative attitudes toward studying. This factor did not have any distinctive motivational correlates, although interviews suggested that students showing this orientation were more concerned with social or sporting activities than with academic work. The remaining factor was labeled Achieving Orientation, as its highest loadings were on Strategic Approach combined with Extrinsic and Achievement motivations.

The inventory has been used by other research workers (Morgan *et al.*, 1980; Watkins, 1982, 1983). Their results generally confirm the importance of Meaning and Reproducing orientations and the lesser stability of the remaining two orientations. In one analysis Watkins (1982) found the Surface Approach combined with the defining features of the Nonacademic Orientation, while there was a separate factor describing an instrumental form of motivation. In a subsequent study Watkins (1983) suggested that the Reproducing Orientation was no longer distinct, but in that analysis the usual eigenvalue criterion was not applied, and as a result the pattern of loadings was compressed into three factors.

Comparisons with the original analyses can only effectively be made where the same technique of factor analysis and the same criterion for extraction of factors have been followed. Fortunately a direct comparison can be made with a study carried out by Diaz (1984) on a sample of 534 Venezuelan university students. One of the striking features of this investigation was the great care that was exercised in ensuring that the translation into Spanish was not just linguistically accurate but that the individual items carried the same meaning and referred to equivalent situations. The cultural, social, and academic differences between Britain and Venezuela combine to place a severe strain on the factor structure of the inventory. Table 6 shows that it survived the test remarkably well.

Analysis of principal factors was carried out, and the application of the eigenvalue criterion again led to four factors being extracted. These accounted for 52% of the variance, with Factors I and II together contributing 37% of the variance. Factor I was clearly Reproducing Orientation, linking its four subscales with Operation Learning and Improvidence, but also with Negative Attitudes. Factor II described Meaning Orientation equally clearly, and here it is interesting to see Comprehension

Table 6. Factor Structure of the Spanish Version of the Approaches to Studying Inventory

Approaches to Studying Subscales	Factors[a]			
	I	II	III	IV
Meaning Orientation				
Deep Approach		56		
Relating Ideas		69		
Use of Evidence		63		
Intrinsic Motivation		58		
Reproducing Orientation				
Surface Approach	66		40	47
Syllabus-Boundness	39		28	35
Fear of Failure	59			
Extrinsic Motivation	41			51
Achieving Orientation				
Strategic Approach	32	30		38
Disorganized Study Methods			54	
Negative Attitudes	48		42	
Achievement Motivation				50
Learning Style				
Comprehension Learning		29	44	29
Globetrotting	37		45	
Operation Learning	46	28		52
Improvidence	62			45

[a]Decimal points and loadings less than .25 omitted.

Learning and Operation Learning in combination, as indicated by Pask's theory. Factor III describes Disorganized Study Methods associated with Surface Approach and rather casual holist strategies (Comprehension Learning and Globetrotting). Factor IV shows the opposite learning pathologies (Operation Learning and Improvidence) but associated with a strategic, competitive approach and Extrinsic (vocational) Motivation.

In this analysis, again the motivational components play an important part in defining three of the four study orientations in exactly the same way as in the English language version. Combining the evidence with that of Biggs provides a convincing argument for this way of describing student learning and studying. But how does this structure relate to the dimensions derived from cognitive psychology?

APPROACHES TO STUDYING, MOTIVATION, AND LEARNING PROCESSES

Schmeck (1983) has described the development of an Inventory of Learning Processes which was based on Craik and Lockhart's (1972) ideas of levels of processing within the memory. This inventory contains scales of Deep Processing, Elaborative Processing, Fact Retention, and Methodical Study. At a descriptive level there would thus seem to be a likelihood of considerable overlap between this inventory and the one described in the previous section. However, the very different theoretical bases on which the subscales rest warn against expecting close agreement. Schmeck (personal communication) was able to have the two inventories completed by a sample of 269 students in Southern Illinois University. The product-moment correlations obtained between the two sets of subscales are shown in Table 7.

There is, in fact, little overlap between deep approach, or any of the subscales of Meaning Orientation, and Deep Processing. It appears that Schmeck's scale describes the avoidance of both Surface Approach and Improvidence and is also associated with self-confidence in studying (low Fear of Failure). It is, however, possible to compare Elaborative Processing with Meaning Orientation. Fact Retention, surprisingly, shows little connection with operation learning, being more closely related to Strategic Approach and the avoidance of Globetrotting. The highest correlation, as might be expected, is found between Methodical Study and organized study methods.

A more recent study has compared shortened versions of the two inventories in a British context (Entwistle & Waterston, 1985). Using the previously reported item analyses, 30 items were chosen from each inventory so as to maximize both discrimination and coverage. The sub-

Table 7. Intercorrelations between Subscales of the Approaches to Studying and Learning Processes Inventories

Approaches to Studying Subscales	Learning Processes Subscales[a]			
	Deep Processing	Elaborative Processing	Fact Retention	Methodical Study
Meaning Orientation				
Deep Approach	14	36	05	38
Relating Ideas	10	39	−03	30
Use of Evidence	23	34	06	32
Intrinsic Motivation	13	33	05	43
Reproducing Orientation				
Surface Approach	−39	−23	−07	−07
Syllabus-Boundness	−22	−22	−07	−20
Fear of Failure	−41	−22	−18	00
Extrinsic Motivation	−26	−19	−08	−05
Achieving Orientation				
Strategic Approach	21	18	26	34
Disorganized Study Methods	−28	−18	−16	−49
Negative Attitudes	−19	−15	−16	−26
Achievement Motivation	04	06	12	24
Learning Style				
Comprehension Learning	12	26	00	00
Globetrotting	−34	00	−27	−06
Operation Learning	−13	02	−06	08
Improvidence	−40	−14	−12	12

[a]Decimal points omitted.

scale structure of the Approaches to Studying Inventory was simplified by omitting four scales and relating subscales directly to the four study orientations. To facilitate comparison with the qualitative research on educational orientations, the emphasis in the Extrinsic Motivation scale was shifted slightly to allow it to be relabeled Vocational Motivation, whije a scale of Social Motivation was introduced. There were thus conceptual equivalents of all four main educational orientations: vocational, academic/achievement, personal/intrinsic, and social.

A common format for response was chosen (5-point Likert) and completed inventories were obtained from 218 first-year students at Edinburgh University (117 scientists and 101 in the arts and social science faculties).

Correlations between the subscales showed a similar pattern to those in Table 7 but with the overlap between corresponding subscales strengthened. Thus the correlation between Surface Approach and Deep Processing was −.50, while Deep Approach correlated .64 with

Elaborative Processing. The scales of Methodical and Disorganized studying correlated $-.67$, while Fact Retention again showed links with Strategic Approach, but only weakly (.15).

Using principal components factor analysis, four factors with eigenvalues greater than one were extracted. These factors explained 55% of the variance. The factor structure matrix is presented as Table 8, and similar results for the separate faculties have been reported elsewhere (Entwistle & Waterston, 1985).

The factor structure shows a very clear pattern linking the two inventories in the ways already indicated from the pattern of simple correlations. The first factor brings together low scores on Deep Processing with Surface Approach and Fear of Failure. It is also associated with both Improvidence and Operation Learning and with Globetrotting among scientists. This concentration on learning facts by rote is, however, negatively related to Fact Retention among scientists.

Table 8. *Factor Structure Derived from Shortened Version of Schmeck's and Entwistle's Inventories*

Inventory Subscales	Factors[a]			
	I	II	III	IV
Schmeck's inventory				
Deep Processing	−73	33	−26	
Elaborative Processing		81		
Fact Retention				61
Methodical Study		37	−83	
Meaning Orientation				
Deep Approach		83		
Intrinsic Motivation	−28	79		
Reproducing Orientation				
Surface Approach	77			
Fear of Failure	76			
Achieving Orientation				
Strategic Approach	28	31		61
Achievement Motivation		36		45
Vocational Motivation				57
Nonacademic Orientation				
Disorganized Approach	31		82	
Negative Attitudes	36	−46	38	
Social Motivation			67	
Learning Style				
Globetrotting	52		31	
Improvidence	69			
Operation Learning	66			

[a]Decimal points and loadings below .25 omitted.

The second factor suggests a substantial overlap between Elaborative Processing, Deep Approach, and both Intrinsic Motivation and positive attitudes to studying. Thus the personalizing of learning, which seems to be the hallmark of elaborative processing (Schmeck, personal communication), is strongly associated with both the intention to understand and the personal orientation towards education indicated by intrinsic motivation.

The third factor is composed mainly of items describing Disorganized Study Methods, and these are strongly linked with Social Motivation—another educational orientation.

The final factor is less clearly defined. In the total sample it brings together Fact Retention and Strategic Approach with both the remaining motivational scales, Achievement (academic orientation) and Vocational. In the two faculty samples, however, this tight grouping is dispersed. Among scientists, for example, Achievement Motivation is no longer strongly represented on this factor, forming instead an additional factor with Intrinsic Motivation, showing a negative loading on Vocational Motivation but no clear links with the process variables. Fact Retention is defined by items which are self-ratings of performance (I do well in exams . . ., I am very good at learning . . ., I have no trouble in remembering . . .), and Schmeck (personal communication) now regards this scale as indicating "self-efficacy." This factor can thus be seen as describing a self-confident, competitive, and strategic approach to studying, which is also likely to lead to academic success.

APPROACHES TO STUDYING IN SECONDARY SCHOOL

All the early work on approaches to studying was based on samples of students in higher education. Although it seemed likely that such a powerful explanatory concept as approach to learning would apply at earlier ages there was no direct evidence. There was some suggestion that even in the early stages of primary education pupils differed in the extent to which they sought personal meaning from the tasks teachers required of them. For example, Francis (1982, 1984) talked to children who were beginning to learn to read and write. She found considerable differences between their conceptions of what reading involved:

> In my own research . . . I have come to realise that . . . lack of understanding, or misunderstanding, can affect both motivation and strategies. . . . Although I have found children who thought that learning to read would take a long time . . ., there were others who thought the ability would come at some future date as an immediate enlightenment. In that case, they felt, why worry now? Others saw no disadvantage to classmates who were not

making progress, nor adults who could not read, and so had little inclination to read themselves. On the other hand, others could see advantages and felt these to be motivating. . . . Some children seem to be unable to talk at all about any activity connected with reading, whilst others reveal their lack of understanding in their comments. . . . I have [even] found children who did not realise that when their teachers were reading stories to them there was any connection with the book except through the pictures, or even perhaps through some sort of ritual action. . . . [Such] variations amongst children show . . . them to be individuals starting school with understandings and intentions of their own. . . . [And] I found (that) . . . those who understood something of the written word as a language form learned steadily, sometimes very quickly indeed, and with little or no forgetting, whilst those who lacked such understanding and were motivated only by the expectation that this was what happened in school or by the desire to please, learned much more slowly and forgot quite frequently. (Francis, 1984, pp. 15–18)

Although what Francis seems to be describing are deep and surface approaches among 5-year-olds, the connections with the concept introduced by Marton are too indirect to be sure. However, Selmes (1985), working in Edinburgh, has been using Marton's own interview technique to explore what approaches to studying are expected by teachers and reported by pupils at the top end of secondary school. He found a striking difference between what teachers were expecting of pupils before and after the external examinations taken at age 16 and above (0 Grade or 0 Level).

In the 0- Grade/Level phase the tasks were described over-whelmingly as demanding of, or conducive to, a surface approach. . . . The move to studying Highers or A-Levels involves a dramatic change in formal curriculum demands. . . . Teachers described the tasks (as involving) . . . the pupil taking greater responsibility for . . . learning. Pupils were expected to think about contributory ideas and concepts; to concentrate on understanding them; to integrate them; and often to relate them to their own ideas. (pp. 98–99)

The pupils above age 16 described approaches to studying which could be classified as either deep or surface using criteria very similar to those of Marton. Pupils also explained what affected their decisions about how they would study; these are summarized in Table 9. The effects on studying of teaching methods and assessment procedures have already been noted in studies in higher education. However, in schools, time constraints seem to have a very direct effect on pupils' approaches to learning.

Where pupils perceived time as being restrictive, surface approaches resulted; without such limitations deep approaches developed in the time space. In the tightly structured timetable of the secondary school . . . time would probably be more at a premium than in the more open undergraduate timetable. (Selmes, 1985, p. 153)

Even in higher education though, Ramsden (1984; Chapter 7, this

Table 9. Summary of Pupils' Perceptions of Influences on Their Approach to Studying

Task content and context influences	Perception of influence associated with	
	Surface approach	Deep approach
Teaching methods	Formal or repetitive	Informal
Studying tasks	Closed	Open
Type of assessment	Factual, closed response	Interpretive, open
Level of dependence	High	Low
Time available	Insufficient, restricted	Ample or unrestricted

Adapted from Selmes, 1985, p. 181.

volume) has demonstrated that a perceived heavy workload is associated with a greater tendency to adopt surface approaches to studying. Selmes (1985) went on to investigate the extent to which pupils adopted consistent approaches across different tasks. He found that

> sixth-form pupils have also been shown to describe individual consistency in approach. . . . Many of the interviewees were found to be predisposed to one or other approach, though all mentioned aspects of both approaches. . . . As with students, individual consistency and intertask variability can be said to characterise many senior pupils' approach to learning. (p. 154).

This consistency again allowed the construction of an inventory to identify dimensions which describe studying. The main defining items used in the student inventory were revised in the light of the comments made by pupils to Selmes and included as part of a longer inventory (Entwistle & Kozeki, 1985). Nine of the subscales in the student inventory were considered to be applicable to schoolwork. The intention was to retain, as far as possible, the main features of the Meaning, Reproducing, and Strategic orientations. However, as pupils have little opportunity for strategic studying, at least in the sense of cue seeking, the strategic approach was defined, instead, as a highly organized way of tackling schoolwork with an eye to good attainment. The processes of subscales of Meaning Orientation were omitted, as were the learning-style pathologies. Instead of Negative Attitudes, a more positive set of items was included as a subscale of Conscientiousness. Extrinsic Motivation was renamed Instrumental Motivation, as the vocational component could not be measured so directly at this age.

The final inventory contained 10 scales, each containing six items. The internal consistency measured by the Cronback alpha coefficient ranged from .45 to .79, with a median value of .59. Test–retest reliability with an interval of 3 weeks ranged from .63 to .77, with a median value of .73. The inventory was given in four British schools to a sample of 614

pupils aged between 13 and 17 years, most of whom were being prepared for external examinations and so were of above-average ability.
An equivalent sample of 579 pupils from Hungarian schools also completed a translation of the inventory prepared as part of a more extensive
comparative study (Entwistle & Kozeki, 1985). Estimates of school attainment were also collected.

    School Attainment was found to correlate positively with Deep Ap-
proach and Intrinsic Motivation (particularly among British girls). Negative correlations with attainment were found for Surface Approach, Fear
of Failure, and Instrumental Motivation (particularly among girls).
There were rather weak relationships between attainment and the subscales defining Achieving Orientation. An analysis of mean scores
showed that Hungarian pupils had consistently higher scores on all
three dimensions within the Meaning Orientation, while British pupils
were equally high on Reproducing Orientation. This difference was attributed to the effects of the emphasis on facts in the external examinations in Britain (Entwistle & Kozeki, 1985). In Hungary there had been a
drive against rote learning in schools, but the low scores on Serialist
Style indicated that this change may have gone too far, as a fully deep
approach requires both holist and serialist processes. Scores on the motivational components showed that Hungarian pupils had higher levels of
Intrinsic Motivation, while British pupils were found to be more competitive (higher Hope for Success). The Hungarians were more organized in their approaches, while the British seemed to be driven by the
extrinsic forms of motivation (Fear of Failure and Instrumental Motivation).

    The analyses which indicated the relationships between motivation
and approaches to studying are of most relevance here. Principal axes
analyses were followed by oblique rotation with delta set at zero. For
both samples three factors had eigenvalues in excess of unity. Table 10
shows the very close agreement between the factor structures in the two
samples. Factor I had its highest loadings on Conscientiousness and
Strategic Approach, with substantial loadings on Deep Approach and
Intrinsic Motivation. In the British sample, there were also loadings on
Serialist Style and Hope for Success. This factor could be seen as merging the Meaning and Achieving orientations found in the student analyses were it not for the exchange of Serialist for Holist styles of learning.
Factor II covered all the subscales of Reproducing Orientation in both
samples. Factor III reversed the emphasis of Factor I with Meaning
Orientation having the highest loadings. The inclusion of Holist Style
here, but not in the first factor, is reminiscent of the two factors of deep
approach and process reported by Entwistle, Hanley, and Ratcliffe
(1979), described previously in the subsection "Developing the Ap-

Table 10. Factor Loadings of Schools' Approaches to Studying Inventory in British and Hungarian Schools

Subscales	British schools[a]			Hungarian schools[b]		
	I	II	III	I	II	III
Meaning Orientation						
Deep Approach	53		75	54		87
Holist Style			62			57
Intrinsic Motivation	53		61	53		62
Reproducing Orientation						
Surface Approach		71			81	
Serialist Style	47	46			55	
Fear of Failure		61			58	
Instrumental Motivation		45			62	
Achieving Orientation						
Strategic Approach	71		34	70		36
Hope for Success	35		32		30	
Conscientiousness	85		43	88		38

Note. Decimal points and loadings below .30 omitted.
[a]N = 614. Percentage of variance extracted = 60.2
[b]N = 579. Percentage of variance extracted = 63.7

proaches to Studying Inventory. The merging of the Meaning and Achieving orientations should not be taken as implying any change in the basic conceptual structure. It may be that younger students see achievement more in terms of developing personal understanding until the extrinsic rewards begin to take precedence. It should also be noted that both samples were of above-average ability and, in light of recent work by Biggs (1985), the ability level, or the balance of different abilities within the sample, may affect the factor structure.

The similarity between the three main orientations from the Approaches to Studying Inventory and the factors identified independently by Biggs has already been stressed. He has recently been investigating the factor structure of his inventory for differing subgroups (Biggs, 1985). Among secondary school pupils he found the expected three-factor structure only for pupils high in both memory and reasoning scores. Samples high in only one cognitive component produced understandable two-factor solutions. For pupils with higher memory scores, Achieving Orientation merged with Reproducing Orientation, indicating a reliance on rote learning for achievement. Similarly, pupils with higher reasoning scores relied on a deep approach for achievement. Among pupils low on both cognitive components, the factor structure disintegrated, perhaps indicating a limited ability to introspect about learning processes.

In another interesting analysis of subgroups, Biggs divided pupils into "internals" and "externals," in terms of locus of control. While the internal group produced a two-factor solution with Meaning Orientation merging with Achieving Orientation, the external group again failed to produce a factor structure. Presumably the failure to recognize the personal responsibility for success or failure similarly limits accurate introspections about learning processes.

MOTIVATION AND APPROACHES TO STUDYING IN QUANTITATIVE ANALYSES

Bringing together the findings from the various versions of the Approaches to Studying Inventory, the existence of the three main orientations to studying can be accepted with some confidence. Although there is some variation in the factor structure depending on the age and composition of the samples, the three main orientations can be distinguished from age 12 upwards, in various subject areas, in the United States, Australia, Hungary, and Venezuela, as well as in Britain.

Meaning Orientation and Reproducing Orientation both bring together distinctive forms of motivation and approaches to studying. The items making up these factors can be grouped in ways which help to flesh out the meaning of the statistical factors. Thus Meaning Orientation not only contains the element of intrinsic motivation which indicates an inclination to learn out of interest, as a form of personal development, it may also be seen to indicate how the intention to understand is empirically and logically linked to subsequent learning processes necessitated by that intention. Taking these items together with those from Schmeck's (1983) inventory, these learning processes are found to include selection of salient material, organization of that material, reasoning, questioning, relating, and personalizing (Entwistle & Waterston, 1985).

Reproducing Orientation has fewer components, perhaps because the requirements of rote learning have not been articulated as fully. However, it is clear that the perception of learning as something imposed by an external authority completely changes the nature of the learning carried out. The learning is seen narrowly in terms of the prescribed syllabus and the specific task requirements. What is to be learned is limited to the knowledge presented, and so the processes of learning become altogether more mechanical, concentrating on overlearning and verbatim recall. Although considerable effort may still be put into this type of learning, there is less chance of even the details being remembered for any length of time (Marton, 1975). Even facts have to be embedded within a semantic framework if they are to be readily recalled out of the immediate context in which they were initially learned.

Achieving Orientation is distinct from the other two orientations, as it does not describe learning processes directly. Also, the forms of motivation it contains are more mixed, perhaps explaining its tendency to split into two. The strategic approach, linked to competitive achievement motivation, describes the tactics used by students mainly concerned with reinforcing their academic self-concept through "repeated demonstrations of intellectual mastery" (Entwistle & Wilson, 1977, p. 123). However, the other component of what was initially the Achieving Orientation describes a combination of careful planning, systematic study methods, positive attitudes, and conscientiousness which can be allied with deep, surface, or strategic approaches, depending on the student's individual conceptions of learning and purposes in studying.

These three or four main dimensions emerge from the quantitative analyses of the Approaches to Studying Inventory, but the interpretation of the combinations of constituent items is difficult without drawing on qualitative analyses of the students' own perceptions of how their conceptions and purposes relate to their learning processes.

MOTIVATION AND APPROACHES TO LEARNING IN QUALITATIVE ANALYSES

Qualitative research into student learning has not only made use of an additional set of concepts specific to the learning situation in higher education, it has also described the relationships between concepts in another way. The careful examination of interview transcripts indicates the causality, as interpreted by the students, of the relationships between different aspects of their own experiences. The analyses produce a series of categories within each concept, and the researchers examine the internal logical relationships between these categories, and between associated concepts, in terms of the connections experienced and reported by the students themselves. The links between concepts emerging from these qualitative analyses are described as functional relationships, as they avoid the possibility of spurious statistical artifacts which bedevil the interpretation of statistical relationships. It is, however, difficult within qualitative analysis to judge the relative strengths of the various relationships.

The easiest way to think about the relationships which exist between the concepts derived from the qualitative research on student learning is again to consider the relative breadth of each concept. The broader concepts, and their subsidiary categories, will to some extent encapsulate the narrower concepts. This hierarchy in terms of breadth can also be seen as indicating a temporal organization—a probable sequence of events (Entwistle & Marton, 1984). Such a sequence may be seen also as suggesting a chain of causality, but within the qualitative research tradition human actions are not seen as the inevitable outcome of preceding events. Multiple possibilities are accepted as the necessary consequence of the operation of human will and freedom of choice (Taylor, 1983).

The nesting of concepts one within the other can be illustrated by the following example. Starting from the broadest concept, educational orientation, a student who is categorized as being predominantly extrinsic and vocational in outlook can be expected to have both a reproductive conception of learning and to show an orientation to studying which relies on reproducing. In turn, this orientation to studying is likely to be associated with either an instrumental form of motivation or fear of failure. Such a student may thus be expected to bring to a specific academic task an intention to satisfy the lecturer's perceived requirements in a minimal, unthinking way—a surface approach. The learning processes used within this approach are likely to be predominantly rote memorization and the application of routine procedures chosen without systematic consideration of the nature of the task at hand. The outcome of such an approach can be, at best, no more than an accurate reproduction of certain marginally relevant aspects of what has previously been learned. It is logically impossible for fully surface approach to produce an imaginative reconstruction of previously unrelated ideas or information. The lack of personal engagement is also likely to have an effect on retention. Once the rote-learned material has been reproduced as required, it is subsequently readily forgotten. Comments from students suggest that it is almost as if the slate has been wiped clean to make room for other knowledge and experience anticipated to be more personally meaningful or relevant.

A second example of the relationships between concepts of decreasing breadth takes the opposite extreme. A student who is found to have an educational orientation which is predominantly intrinsic and personal is likely to see learning as involving interpretative understanding. Such a conception of learning can be expected to be associated with meaning orientation and intrinsic motivation. In tackling an academic task the intention is likely to focus on understanding—a deep approach. And that approach should include the processes which Pask describes as comprehension and operation learning—developing an overview and backing up conclusions with appropriate evidence. This can also be described as a versatile learning style. The probable outcome of such learning would be clear evidence of a deep level of understanding, re-flecting a personal reinterpretation of the topics covered.

These two examples show the simplest and most clear-cut patterns of relationships between categories and concepts. They rely on an un-ambiguous categorization into single categories. In reality, people have mixed motives and somewhat variable or inconsistent approaches to academic tasks. Thus, predicting a student's future actions on the basis of such characterizations of past events cannot be seen as more than a tentative anticipation of probable outcomes.

The quantitative findings have suggested that many students who intended to understand, failed to carry through the full process neces-sary to achieve a deep level of understanding. Few first-year students seemed able to carry out both comprehension and operation learning. The students who sought meaning were able to concentrate either on factual detail or on a broad overview, but they did not seem to use both processes in effective alternation. The statistical findings perhaps re-flected the effects of the strict time constraints under which students operate. Deadlines interfere with students' underlying intentions. Thus a serialist strategy towards understanding will finish up as a surface approach if the later stages of integration are omitted. And a holist strategy may result in a vague, unconvincing account if insufficient time has been spent in mastering the details. Also, a deep approach depends crucially on prerequisite skills and knowledge. If these are lacking, the student cannot carry out an intention to understand and may have to fall back on rote learning as a temporary expedient.

INTEGRATING QUALITATIVE AND QUANTITATIVE FINDINGS

Combining the results of both qualitative and quantitative analyses of student learning, it is possible to show in more detail the likely rela-tionships between at least the less-general concepts. Figure 1 shows the present stage of our understanding of these interrelationships. Again it must be stressed that this is a much oversimplified pattern which is unlikely to be found in precisely this form in reality.

The research on student learning is just beginning to describe dif-ferences in students' approaches to learning which are attributable to the distinctively different academic disciplines in which they are spe-cializing, or to the contrasting learning environments they meet in dif-ferent academic departments. Ramsden (1984; Chapter 7, this volume) has shown how a deep approach will demand a different balance of learning processes in contrasting academic disciplines. In particular, sci-ence students have to rely on operation learning much more than arts

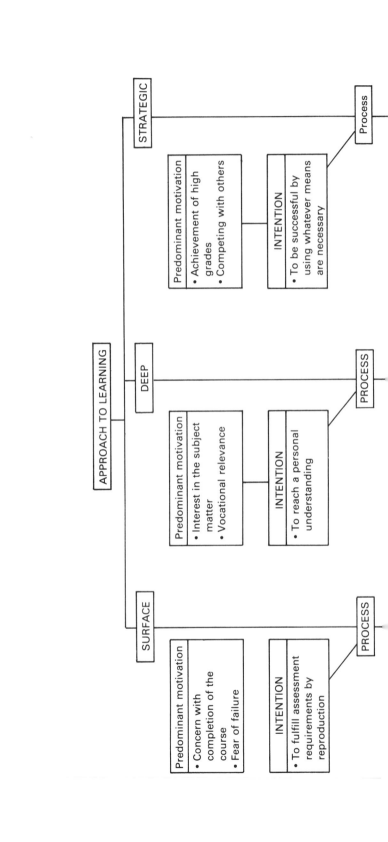

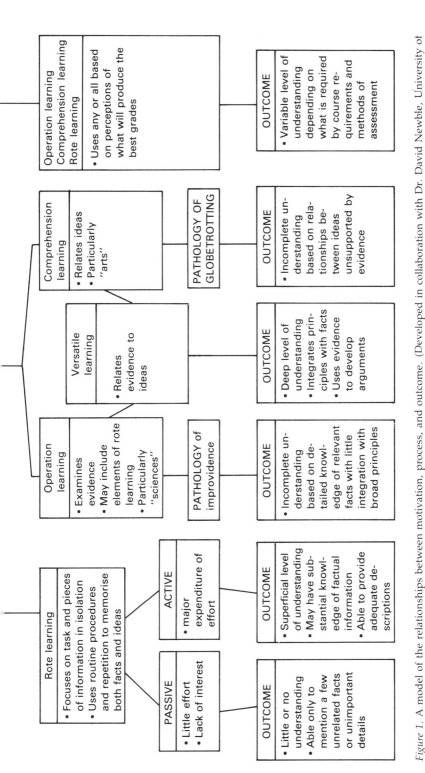

Figure 1. A model of the relationships between motivation, process, and outcome. (Developed in collaboration with Dr. David Newble, University ot Adelaide.)

students. Indeed, it is clear that rote learning of definitions, terms, or information is a necessary part of some disciplines and may play a prominent role in the early stages of learning a new topic. Thus the precise meaning of a deep approach will have to be reinterpreted within each subject area and even within each discipline, although the general intention of seeking understanding will remain the same.

The effects of departmental learning environments are also discussed by Ramsden (Chapter 7, this volume). He has identified a variety of ways in which students perceive their departments and has shown how these perceptions relate to approaches to learning. It seems that departments perceived as teaching effectively and enthusiastically, and as providing freedom for students to choose their own topics and modes of learning, facilitate a deep approach to learning (Hodgson, 1984). Departments which do not provide opportunities for choice and which impose a heavy workload are likely, unwittingly, to push students into surface approaches. While departments affect approaches to studying, they do not seem to affect either achievement motivation or study organization. Thus a complete model of student learning would have to include both the relatively consistent study habits and motivational patterns, as well as the interactions of departmental teaching methods and assessment procedures with students' approaches to studying (Entwistle, 1985).

The implications of these findings on the effects of academic context imply that departments influence the interest and relevance with which the material is perceived and also the level of apprehension about outcome (fear of failure). But they have less, if any, effect on achievement or vocational motivations. This research only describes, however, what is currently happening. It may be possible to help students change their current educational orientation by encouraging them to reconsider their priorities. If students are introduced to the results of the research on student learning, the consequences of their existing orientation in relation to academic progress may change their predominant motivation— with consequent changes in approach to studying. An attempt to embody this technique into a computer-based simulation of student learning is currently underway (Odor, Anderson, & Entwistle, 1988).

The research findings could also be made the basis of study skills courses which concentrated on helping the student to adopt learning strategies which take account of the differing demands of varying types of academic tasks (Biggs, 1985).

By ensuring that students become more aware of their own approaches, and of the implications of adopting them, it may thus be possible to improve the quality of learning outcomes. It will, however, be equally important for departments to provide learning environments which allow deep approaches to be pursued without unnecessary constraints.

REFERENCES

Atkinson, J. W., & Feather, N. T. (1966). *A theory of achievement motivation.* New York: Wiley.

Biggs, J. B. (1976). Dimensions of study behavior: Another look at a.t.i. *British Journal of Educational Psychology, 46,* 68–80.

Biggs, J. B. (1979). Individual differences in study processes and the quality of learning outcomes. *Higher Education, 8,* 381–394.

Biggs, J. B. (1985). The role of metalearning in study processes. *British Journal of Educational Psychology,* 185–212.

Birney, R. C., Burdick, H., & Teevan, R. C. (1969). *Fear of failure.* New York: Van Nostrand.

Brown, W. F. & Holtzman, W. H. (1966). *Manual of the survey of study habits.* New York: Psychological Corporation.

Craik, F. I. M., & Lockhart, R. S. (1972). Levels of processing: A framework for memory research. *Journal of Verbal Learning and Verbal Behavior, 11,* 671–684.

Diaz, D. (1984). *The identification of approaches to learning adopted by Venezuelan university students.* Unpublished M.Sc. thesis, University of Wales Institute of Science and Technology, Cardiff.

Entwistle, N. J. (1987). *A model of the teaching–learning process derived from research on student learning.* In J.T.E. Richardson, M. Eysenck, and D. Pipes (Eds.), Student learning research in education and cognitive psychology. London: Open University Press.

Entwistle, N. J., Hanley, M., & Hounsell, D. J. (1979). Identifying distinctive approaches to studying. *Higher Education, 8,* 365–380.

Entwistle, N. J., Hanley, M., & Ratcliffe, G. (1979). Approaches to learning and levels of understanding. *British Educational Research Journal, 5,* 99–114.

Entwistle, N. J., & Kozeki, B. (1985). Relationships between school motivation, approaches to studying, and attainment among British and Hungarian adolescents. *British Journal of Educational Psychology, 55,* 124–137

Entwistle, N. J., & Marton, F. (1984). Changing conceptions of learning and research. In F. Marton, D. J. Hounsell, & N. J. Entwistle (Eds.), *The experience of learning.* Edinburgh: Scottish Academic Press.

Entwistle, N. J., & Ramsden, P. (1983). *Understanding student learning.* London: Croom Helm.

Entwistle, N. J., & Waterston, S. (1985). *Approaches to studying and levels of processing: A comparison of inventories derived from contrasting theoretical bases.* Paper presented to the International Conference on Cognitive Processes in Student Learning, Lancaster University, England. Also, *British J. of Educational Psychology* (in press).

Entwistle, N. J., & Wilson, J. D. (1970). Personality, study methods and academic performance. *Universities Quarterly, 24,* 147–156.

Entwistle, N. J., & Wilson, J. D. (1977). *Degrees of excellence: The academic achievement game.* London: Hodder and Stoughton.

Entwistle, N.J., Odor, P., & Anderson, C. (1987). Anticipating the experience of higher education through computer simulation. *Higher Education, 16,* 337–355.

Entwistle, N. J., Thompson, J. B., & Wilson, J. D. (1974). Motivation and study habits. *Higher Education, 3,* 379–396.

Francis, H. (1982). *Learning to read.* London: Allen and Unwin.

Francis, H. (1984). *Minds of their own*. Inaugural lecture, University of London, Institute of Education.

Fransson, A. (1977). On qualitative differences in learning. IV—Effects of motivation and test anxiety on process and outcome. *British Journal of Educational Psychology, 47*, 244–257.

Gibbs, G. (1981). *Teaching students to learn*. Milton Keynes: Open University Press.

Gibbs, G., Morgan, A., & Taylor, E. (1984). The world of the learner. In F. Marton, D. J. Hounsell, & N. J. Entwistle (Eds.), *The experience of learning* (pp. 165–188). Edinburgh: Scottish Academic Press.

Hodgson, V. (1984). Learning from lectures. In F. Marton, D. J. Hounsell, & N. J. Entwistle (Eds.), *The experience of learning* (pp. 90–102). Edinburgh: Scottish Academic Press.

Laurillard, D. (1984). Learning from problem-solving. In F. Marton, D. J. Hounsell, & N. J. Entwistle (Eds.), *The experience of learning* (pp. 124–144). Edinburgh: Scottish Academic Press.

Marton, F. (1975). What does it take to learn? In N. J. Entwistle (Ed.), *Strategies for research and development in higher education*. (pp. 32–43). Amsterdam: Swets and Zeitlinger.

Marton, F., Hounsell, D. J., & Entwistle, N. J. (1984). (Eds.). *The experience of learning*. Edinburgh: Scottish Academic Press.

Marton, F., & Säljö, R. (1984). Approaches to learning. In F. Marton, D. J. Hounsell, & N. J. Entwistle (Eds.), *The experience of learning* (pp. 36–55). Edinburgh: Scottish Academic Press.

Miller, C. M., & Parlett, M. R. (1974). *Up to the mark: A study of the examination game*. London: SRHE.

Morgan, A., Biggs, G., & Taylor, E. (1980). *Students' approaches to studying the Social Science Foundation Courses: Preliminary studies* (Student Methods Group Report No. 4). Milton Keynes: The Open University, Institute of Educational Technology.

Odor, J. P. Anderson, C., & Entwistle, N. J., (1985). *The interactive simulation of student learning. Working Paper 1. The development of a systems representation of the simulation*. University of Edinburgh, Department of Education.

Pask, G. (1976). Styles and strategies of learning. *British Journal of Educational Psychology, 46*, 128–148.

Pond, L. (1964). A study of high achieving and low achieving freshmen. *Australian Journal of Higher Education, 2*, 73–78.

Ramsden, P. (1984). The context of learning. In F. Marton, D. J. Hounsell, & N. J. Entwistle (Eds.), *The experience of learning* (pp. 144–164). Edinburgh: Scottish Academic Press.

Säljö, R. (1982). *Learning and understanding: A study of differences in constructing meaning from a text*. Gothenburg: Acta Universitatis Gothoburgensis.

Schmeck, R. R. (1983). Learning styles of college students. In R. F. Dillon & R. R. Schmeck (Eds.), *Individual differences in cognition, Volume 1*. New York: Academic Press.

Selmes, I. P. (1985). *Approaches to learning at secondary school: Their identification and facilitation*. Unpublished PhD thesis, University of Edinburgh.

Svensson, L. (1976). *Study skill and learning*. Gothenburg: Acta Universitatis Gothoburgensis.

Svensson, L. (1984). Skill in learning. In Marton, F., Hounsell, D. J., and Entwistle, N. J. (Eds.) *The experience of learning*. (pp. 56–70). Edinburgh: Scottish Academic Press.

Taylor, E. (1983). Orientations to study: a longitudinal interview investigation of students on two human studies degree courses at Surrey University. Unpublished doctoral dissertation, University of Surrey, Guildford.

Van Rossum, E. J. (1984). Students' conceptions of learning and good teaching. Mimeographed article, University of Tilburg, Department of Educational Psychology, The Netherlands.

Wankowski, J. A. (1973). *Temperament, motivation and academic achievement* (2 volumes). University of Birmingham Educational Survey.

Watkins, D. (1982). Identifying the study process dimensions of Australian university students. *Australian Journal of Education*, 1982, 26, 76–85.

Watkins, D. (1983). Assessing tertiary study processes. *Human Learning*, 2, 29–37.

Weinstein, C. E., & Underwood, V.L. (1985). Learning strategies: the 'how' of learning. In J. W. Segal, (Eds.). *Thinking and learning skills* (Volume 1). Hillsdale, NJ: Lawrence Erlbaum.

CHAPTER 3

Describing and Improving Learning

FERENCE MARTON

Any description of differences between people in how they learn and any attempt to improve their ways of learning is contingent by logical necessity on what counts as learning. In both cases, what we mean by learning in terms of the description of outcome is frequently taken for granted. An alternative way of thinking about learning is to realize that what is learned (the outcome or the result) and how it is learned (the act or the process) are two inseparable aspects of learning. In the first part of this chapter, one sense of this relational nature of learning is illuminated. By means of some examples it is shown that the description of certain differences in how people learn corresponds to a given, in this case explicit, meaning of learning, reflected in the way in which differences in the outcome of learning are characterized. When it comes to the question of how learning is or should be described, the relational character of learning has, however, implications not only for the researcher but also for the educators who want to go about improving learning in real-life educational settings. In the second part of the chapter, another sense of the relational nature of learning is commented on. It is argued that as people's ways of learning represent relations between them and certain aspects of the world around them, any attempt to improve learning has to focus on the relationships as a whole and not on the individuals alone.

FERENCE MARTON • Department of Education, University of Goteborg, Box 1010, S 431 26 Molndal, Sweden.

is the one which is absolutely dominant within the educational system but far less frequent outside it. It is the kind of learning in which one is supposed to improve one's understanding of some phenomenon in the world around by means of taking part in a symbolic representation of that phenomenon, usually in the form of text.

DESCRIBING LEARNING

Researchers in psychology and education frequently make implicit and unwarranted assumptions. The implicit or taken-for-granted nature of these assumptions implies that it is mostly not realized that the assumptions are made.

An example of such an often unjustified tacit expectation is the belief that when college students are asked to read a fairly simple text in a learning experiment, they understand what the text is about and understand it more or less in the same way. In consequence, researchers mostly do not try to measure whether or not their subjects understand the text they are reading or to describe the *way* in which they understand it. When they look for some variation to be explained, they often assess what (or how much) the participants in the experiment remember of the text. If the outcome is described in this way, learning is operationally defined as the capability of recalling the text (or parts of it) in some form. If one, for instance, were to study the differential efficiency of strategies spontaneously used by people, or the effects of some instructions aimed at improving learning strategies, in relation to such a criterion, one would be able to judge, at best, to what extent one strategy or the other (spontaneous or induced) enhances the ease with which texts are recalled. However, it should be recognized that recall does not necessarily reflect understanding.

In the investigations of learning from texts or textbooks that have been carried out in our research group in Gothenburg, the above-mentioned assumption has never been made (whether or not all the subjects were university students). On the contrary, above all we wanted to find out what the subjects participating in the investigations thought the texts they had read were about. In accordance with this, after a subject has completed his or her reading in an individually run session, the first question we usually ask is, "Well, could you tell me what this text is about?" And, indeed, we have repeatedly found that the answers to this question differ dramatically even though the same text was read.

From time to time, we have been able to identify a limited number of qualitatively different ways in which the text as a whole has been understood. Once this variation is identified and characterized in terms of a set of categories of description (each category corresponding to a certain way of understanding), judges can classify the answers with a reasonable degree of reliability. A typical figure of the agreement between two independent judges classifying the answers, on the basis of a specification of the categories of description, would be above 70% for a set of four categories (see, e.g., Wenestam, 1980, pp. 65–66).

The texts we have used in our investigations have mostly been of a certain kind. In each text, there has been one (or several) principle(s) the author was trying to get across—he or she was introducing a certain way of viewing some phenomenon. The learning that is supposed to take place in such cases involves becoming capable of seeing something in a new way (the one argued for by the author). Whether or not, to what extent, or in which way learning, in this sense, has actually come about shows itself in the way in which the text is understood. The tacit assumption—which clearly may be wrong occasionally—is that the principle put forward in the text, that is, the way of seeing inherent in it, is new to all subjects in the experiment. To the extent that this assumption is unwarranted, we study *comprehension,* and not learning.

In these investigations, the description of the qualitative differences in how people understand the texts has thus been our starting point when trying to come up with an answer to the question, What makes a difference in learning? As was pointed out at the beginning of this chapter, any answer to such a question is dependent on what learning is tacitly taken to be. In the particular cases investigated, the *variation* in the understanding of texts has been our operational definition of "what is learned."

QUALITATIVE DIFFERENCES IN THE OUTCOME OF LEARNING

Wenestam's (1978) study offers a good example of qualitative differences in the outcome of learning from reading a text. The learning event was only one part of his investigation, the main aim of which was to find out how Swedish adults conceptualize the aims and functions of the welfare system. Fifteen subjects, six men and nine women, participated in individually run interview sessions; they were all students at a secondary school for adults and all 35 years old. The idea was that the reading of a text on the topic which the interview was supposed to cover could be used as a point of departure for a subsequent conversation. In this context, it is exactly this first part of the interview sessions which is of interest (and from which the findings in Wenestam's report are derived).

The text used in the experiment was a 1,350-word excerpt from a textbook on social studies for upper-level secondary school (roughly equivalent to junior college level). A more holistic view of the welfare system was argued for in the text, and the main thesis was that—paradoxically enough—many failures of the welfare system originate from its overly high level of ambition. With the aim of solving *all* problems, coercive measures are resorted to; this does more harm than good. It was claimed that it would be better if attempts were made to solve subproblems that are possible to solve, even if the more difficult problems remain.

This idea was illustrated by an example involving Erik Jansson, a married man with three children, who gets involved in fights and is well on the way to becoming an alcoholic. His wife suffers from a stomach ulcer from time to time and is often irritated with the children. The eldest child, a boy, plays truant and joins a gang that steals cars for fun.

In such a situation, it might be tempting to resort to coercive measures such as committing the father to an institution for alcoholics and the boy to a community home. But according to the author, such measures seldom lead to positive results. It would be better, he says, to try to improve the situation together with the clients instead of against their will, as in the case of commitment. This "remedial" approach would probably not lead to any immediate, radical results. But in the long run, improving the situation gradually is more humane, and the prospects of success are greater.

The subjects participating in the experiment were asked to read the text, and they were told that afterwards some questions would be asked about it. There were no time limits given for the reading. When a subject had finished reading, the experimenter asked, "Well, could you tell me what this text is about?"

Wenestam's study was chosen as an illustration because the qualitative differences in the understanding of the text seem very straightforward. Frequently, the description of the qualitative variation in terms of a set of categories of description is arrived at by means of thorough and extensive analysis (see, e.g., Marton & Säljö, 1984). In this particular case, however, the number of different ways of understanding the text is restricted to two, and the difference between these seems so distinctive that a simple listing of all the answers (or rather the beginning of them) to the above question would seem sufficient to make that difference obvious. The following is one group of answers from selected subjects (S), revealing one kind of understanding:

> S1   Yes, it's about how one should try to put right different things that are wrong here in society; that is, different people who have gone astray . . .
>
> S2   Yes, it's about certain problems just in society and it was illustrated by an example that was based on . . .

S3   Yes, it's about social welfare and help, of course; in particular, abuse of alcohol and juvenile crime. On the whole, it affects everything in the family, how they affect each other.

S5   Yes, it's about partly how social welfare is supposed to work and partly it's about an example here, this family and with this as the starting point, certain ideas are put forward about how things are and how they ought to be . . .

S8   Yes, it was about social welfare and a case involving a family was presented and that they wanted to have a more total approach in social welfare, that they shouldn't intervene because of one particular problem in the family; instead, there were usually several problems that formed the reason for everything.

S9   It's about the coordination of social measures in cases when the individual gets into trouble with the different authorities and that it's very difficult to help individual families needing help in so many places . . .

S10 It's about a family where the husband has a low-wage profession, he obviously has very many problems and they spread. . . . and then it says that one should have a different type of social welfare there which doesn't make such large demands on the individual. It would be freer.

S13 Yes, above all it's about social welfare and how to master it. Here, they take up an example of a family—do you want me to tell the whole story?

S15 Yes, it was about the care given us people by society, society's attempts to get people to function as normal individuals—that's how I see it. And some doubt has been expressed as to whether social welfare functions in the right way . . . and they give an example of a fairly normal family . . . and as I understand it, the question put is whether we can in some way change the form of social welfare . . . (Wenestam, 1978 pp. 7–8)

The other group of answers reveals another way of understanding the text:

S4   Yes, the text is about a family where the father is a low-wage worker . . .

S6   It's about a low-wage family, three children, where the father has an alcohol problem . . .

S7   Yes, there's a family with problems, the husband has alcohol problems and the wife is ill . . .

S11 If Erik Jansson and his tangled family life, you mean, or . . . ?

S12 Yes, there was a family here called Jansson . . .

S14 Yes, it's about a working-class family, Jansson is his name, Erik Jansson and his wife and three children. (Wenestam, 1978, pp. 8–9)

The expectation is thus that the difference between the two kinds of answers is straightforward enough. The subjects whose answers were brought together in the first group seem to think (and rightly so) that the text was about the social welfare system, while the subjects whose answers were put in the other group claim that the text was about Erik

Jansson and his family (without mentioning the welfare system in general terms).

The difference is rather striking. Judging from their answers, the subjects participating in the experiment had one of two distinctively different ideas of the content, although they read precisely the same text.

Now, the example of Erik Jansson and his family made up less than half of the text, its major part pursued a principal line of reasoning about the welfare system. Could the six subjects whose answers appear in the second group have entirely missed the fact that the welfare system was dealt with in the text? No, as their answers to the follow-up questions showed, they all noticed that the welfare system was a topic in the text. What they obviously did not see, however, was the superordinate character of what was said about the welfare system in relation to the example. In fact, these subjects did not see the example as an example.

In order to discover the principle–example structure of the text, one has to understand the principle (that social welfare often fails because of too high a level of ambition) and how it is illustrated by the example (the case of Erik Jansson and his family). And, indeed, with some possible exceptions, there was a close correspondence between the subjects' discovery of the principle–example structure and their understanding of the principle that is exemplified (as judged from their answers to other questions concerning the text). And it is exactly the meaning of the principle that links principle and example to one another. Without such an understanding the two could hardly be connected On the other hand, unless the two parts are seen in relation to each other, it is logically impossible to comprehend the principle intended by the author— given that we are using fairly advanced criteria for understanding. The two aspects—(a) relating or separating the two parts and (b) understanding the meaning of the principle that links the parts to each other— are dialectically interwined.

To sum up, as far as the variation in outcome is concerned, two different meanings of the text as a whole have been identified. According to one meaning, the text is about social welfare (illustrated by the case of Erik Jansson and his family). According to the other meaning, the text is about Erik Jansson and his family (*and* about social welfare— in some vague sense). The difference in meaning between the two kinds of understanding corresponds to the difference in the structure of those understandings. In the first case, one aspect (the Erik Jansson story) is *subordinate* to the other aspect (the principle). The principle is exemplified by the story, which is seen from the perspective of the principle. In the second case, there is the story of Erik Jansson and his family and there is the welfare system; the two things are, however, not explicitly related to each other.

The two related aspects of the qualitative differences in the outcome of learning thus concern (a) meaning, in the sense of the subjects' understanding of what the text refers to; and (b) structure, in the sense of the subjects' understanding of how the text is organized. We can thus speak of the *referential* and the *structural* aspects of outcome.

The dialectical relationship between these two aspects can be further illustrated by following Svensson (1984), who drew attention to some similarities between the Gestalt view of learning and thinking and our own way of characterizing differences in the understanding of texts read.

A Gestalt Experiment on the Role of Organization in Learning

Svensson (1984) reminds us of one of Katona's (1940) experiments, the results of which were published nearly five decades ago. Katona gave his subjects a series of figures to "learn". 581215192226. The task could be dealt with in different ways, but I relate here only the variation found within one of the conditions. Some of the subjects instructed to learn the series tried to memorize each numeral. Other subjects receiving the same instructions discovered a regularity in the series. They found that it could be structured in terms of numbers with the alternating differences of 3 and 4 between them.

$$5 \quad 8 \quad 12 \quad 15 \quad 19 \quad 22 \quad 26$$
$$3 \quad 4 \quad 3 \quad 4 \quad 3 \quad 4$$

Those who discovered this principle did not need any more time for rehearsing, and, needless to say, their long-term retention was much better than the retention of those who simply memorized the numerals. In order to remember the numerals by means of the principle, one has to know what the first numeral is. There is thus a kind of figure–ground relation between the first numeral and the others when the series is learned by means of the organizing principle. This figure–ground relation is absent when each numeral is memorized separately. So what does it take to arrive at the more efficient strategy? As long as one focuses on one numeral at a time, it is impossible to discover a principle which concerns the relation between the numerals. One has to view the numerals in relation to each other in order to see the regularity. When this is done the set of numerals changes meaning, it is viewed then as an ordered sequence. This change of meaning stems from a certain way of structuring what is given, but the structuring cannot be completed unless there has already been a change of meaning. The regularity (the sequence of numerals with the alternating difference of 3 and 4) can only be seen when the consecutive numerals are grouped together as 5, 8, 12,

15, and so forth, but the grouping cannot be made unless the idea of regularity is already present in some form.

Some of the conclusions that can be drawn from this experiment (as well as from Wenestam's study) are the following: First, the qualitatively different ways in which a certain material is understood correspond to qualitatively different ways in which the material is subjectively organized by the learner. Second, changes in meaning originate from acts of structuring, but acts of structuring presuppose changes in meaning—the two aspects of the learner's activity thus being intertwined in a dialectical interplay. Third, in order to establish a structure, that is, relations between components, these components have to be seen in relation to each other; they have to be seen as parts of the same whole.

THE CONSERVATION OF THE FIGURE–GROUND STRUCTURE

The example from Katona illustrated not only the relationship between the two corresponding aspects of outcome (the referential and the structural) but also the fact that aspects of the outcome of learning correspond to aspects of the act of learning. In the Wenestam (1978) study discussed earlier the difference between a hierarchical (vertical) and a sequential (horizontal) structure mirrors a corresponding difference between two alternative acts of structuring. From the point of view of the author, we may say that the intended (hierarchical, vertical) structure has been "tilted" or "horizontalized" in the sequential case. However, from the point of view of the subject, we cannot speak of horizontalization (of an existing hierarchical structure). He or she does not "tilt" or "horizontalize" anything, the text is apprehended in a sequential ("there was one thing and then then there was something else") manner to begin with. Under any circumstances, the differences between these two modes of understanding have been replicated several times (Marton & Säljö, 1978; Marton & Wenestam, 1978; Wenestam, 1980).

Säljö (1982, 1984) came across the same phenomenon in his penetrating study of an instance of learning through reading. In his description, the interrelatedness of the various aspects of learning became obvious, including the two-sides-of-a-coin nature of the relationship between act and outcome. Through this, his investigation also illuminates the analogy between the classical Gestalt experiment referred to in the previous section and learning of a more everyday kind.

Säljö used a textbook chapter about learning as his learning material, which, by the way, gives his study a somewhat convoluted character. In the introductory section, the principle of classical conditioning is explained. The text starts with an excerpt from a book written by a man telling about his experiences in one of the Greek military junta's torture chambers at the end of the 1960s. In the passage quoted—which is followed by an explanation given by the author of the chapter—the man describes how he, as a result of being tortured, has been conditioned to respond with convulsions at the mere sight of the pair of electrodes which have been used to torture him:

> "On the same day they applied the electrodes in a new way. Instead of placing them in the usual way, behind my ears, they rubbed them over my whole body—my arms, legs, everywhere. It felt like having a drill-bit in me, drilling in until you feel like you're going to fall apart. It was like being in the middle of a whirlwind, you feel like a piece of straw in a threshing machine. One of the leather straps broke and so they quit. I was very afraid. One of them listened to my heart. He said something to me, but I couldn't understand. Then they put me on a stretcher. I couldn't collect myself. I couldn't think about anything. Lethargy."
>
> "I don't remember if it was Karagounakis who came in afterwards. I only remember the stretcher and the leather bench, of course. New preparations. This time I had the feeling that everything was electrified. I got a shock as soon as I saw the electrodes, even before they had touched me with them. The man who held me was surprised. He only moved it in front of my eyes and I felt the current the whole time. He moved the electrode behind my head, where I couldn't see it; then I felt no electric current. Then he touched the back of my head slightly with the electrode and I jerked. The others came nearer to watch. They tried with the electrodes from different angles. It made no difference where they put it, as soon as it came into my field of vision I felt the current. That day they didn't ask any more questions. They laid me on the stretcher and took me back to my room."
>
> This example from a very unsettling event in one of the Greek military junta's torture chambers at the end of the 60's describes one form of learning in a dramatic way. Normally we do not feel shocks just from seeing electrodes or electric plugs of various kinds. However, the tortured prisoner in the example above had been exposed to experiences which caused him to react in a way quite unlike what he would have done had he never been tortured with electric current. We can say that this new reaction was learned. This form of learning is called *classical conditioning*. Contact with the charged electrode (unconditioned stimulus) . . . (Säljö, 1984, pp. 76–77)

As we can see, after the passage it first is pointed out that the extract is included in the text as an example of a form of learning called *classical conditioning*. The basic principle and the basic concepts are then explained and made explicit in relation to the example; the touch of the electrode is pointed out as the unconditioned stimulus, convulsion due to the touch as the unconditioned response, the sight of the electrode as the conditioned stimulus, and convulsion at the sight as the conditioned response.

By analyzing the way in which the subjects retold the text and answered specific questions about it, Säljö found two distinctively different ways of understanding the introductory part of the text. According to one, the first section was about classical conditioning, a form of learning which was illustrated by a torture scene:

Dave:

Well, this was a text about learning and it starts with a description of conditioning. At first there is an example from Greek torture. And this example is taken as a starting point to describe conditioning and all this about unconditioned stimulus, that's what it's called and conditioned . . . (original data provided by Roger Säljö)

According to the second way of understanding the same part of the text, it first dealt with a case of torture and *then* with classical conditioning:

Steve:

To start with there was a passage about torture in Greece. There was a Greek I guess, belonging to the resistance movement who is being tortured, and you get to know what feeling he has and . . . The first time he is being tortured he feels it physically, but then the next time he is brought in to be tortured, he just has to see those electrodes behind him, so that he cannot see them, he doesn't experience this pain and . . . But then they go on to talk about classical conditioning and instrumental conditioning. Classical conditioning that is when . . . (original data provided by Roger Säljö)

The main difference between these two ways of retelling the introductory part of the text seems to be that the hierarchical relation between the superordinate principle (classical conditioning) and subordinate example (torture scene) that we find in the text and in the first quote is absent in the second quote. There, "classical conditioning" and "torture scene" are simply two topics on the same level, one following the other. This means that the figure–ground relation in the text is not "conserved" by the learner. Conservation is of course only visible from the researcher's perspective when the structure of the text and the structure of the retelling (both as understood by the researcher) are compared. From the subject's point of view there is no figure–ground relation in the text as such which is preserved. The figure–ground relation is either constituted in the encounter between text and reading or not. In our example, classical conditioning is superordinate, hence figure, and the torture scene is a subordinate example, hence ground. When both are dealt with on the same level—"first this and then that"—there cannot be any figure–ground relation.

Why do some learners conserve the figure–ground relation in the text while others do not? The decisive factor seems to be *segmentation*. A figure–ground relation can only be established, discovered, or "conserved" to the extent that the two components, having the function of figure and ground, are seen in relation to each other. As was the case in the Gestalt experiment in the previous section, in order to discern a figure–ground structure, what is figure and what is ground must be viewed as parts of the same whole. If the text is segmented by the learner in such a way that the section on the explanation of the principle and the concepts of classical conditioning is cut off from the section on the torture scene, and both are read separately without being set in relation to each other, then it is impossible to consider one as being super- (or sub-) ordinate to the other. (It should be added that the term *figure–ground relation* is used here more or less in a metaphorical sense. Reading (or writing) the text in terms of a hierarchical structure means here that the subordinate part is seen from the point of view of the superordinate part. This is a very different meaning of "figure–ground relation" from the one suggested by the original Gestalt studies of perceptual phenomena, through which the term was established.)

As we have seen in both Wenestam's and Katona's experiments discussed earlier, there are differences in meaning corresponding to differences in structuring. This is the case here too. Differences in meaning are revealed by (or possibly stem from) differences in the context which formed the background against which the learners read the text. The first kind of structuring (in terms of whole–part relations) is linked with the interpretation of the first part of the text in terms of classical conditioning, as seen in the following dialogue between experimenter (E) and subject (S):

> *(Dave)*
>
> E: What are you thinking of when you say that you've experienced similar things yourself?
> S: Well, just think when you see a grape that sort of makes your mouth water and things like that. The smell of coffee and you start longing for a cup of coffee and so on.

The segmenting of the text in the form of isolating parts from each other (the second kind of structuring) is mostly linked with an interpretation of the excerpt at the beginning of the text in terms of political oppression (which is the most obvious idea if the excerpt is not put in relation to the subsequent part of the text):

> *(Steve)*
>
> E Do you remember the very first example in the text? I mean the example that the whole text started with?
> S: Yes, it was about torture.
> E: Could you recall it once again?
> S: (Recalls the example.)
> E: Why was it placed there, that example, would you say?
> S: Yes, well it was to show that you can scare people by torturing them, and

then that you can get people to really respect you if you want to be in a
position where you can deal with them easily, like the junta man wanted
to.
E: Yes, but what was this an example of . . . this here . . . ?
S: Well, political oppression, I think.

Clearly, associating the excerpt with political oppression is a very
reasonable thing to do. In fact, if we only consider the excerpt as such,
or, even more, if we consider it against the background of the book from
which it was originally taken, it is by far the best interpretation. As Säljö
points out, there is only one thing wrong with this way of understanding the text: it has been read without knowledge of the author's premise,
that is, without the realization of the communicative intent behind it.
The learner's attention has thus been focused on the text (or on its most
immediate referent) rather than on what it is about (according to its
communicative intent).

OUTCOMES OF LEARNING AND APPROACHES TO LEARNING

The picture emerging from the three examples is the following.
Qualitative differences in the outcome of learning have logically and
dialectically related structural and referential aspects. Structure refers to
how the outcome is arranged, and reference refers to *what* the outcome is
about. The variation that can be characterized in terms of these aspects is
similar in the three examples.

From the structural point of view in the examples taken from Säljö
and Wenestam the variation was between (a) a hierarchical structure,
within which one aspect is superordinate to the other in a figure–
ground relationship, and (b) a sequential structure, within which both
aspects are on the same level, without forming a figure–ground relationship. In the illustration taken from Katona, the main variation is
between a grouping pattern imposed on a series of numerals to be
learned and a plain sequential ordering of the numbers. In the first case,
a superordinate principle made the first number "figure" in the series
and the others "ground"; in the second case, the numbers were taken
one by one without any figure–ground structure.

There are corresponding referential aspects of the different outcomes in each case, that is, differences in perception of *what* the text was
about. From this referential point of view, the main difference in
Wenestam's and Säljö's studies is between understanding the principle
that holds the parts together and the understanding of the parts separately without any obvious relation to each other. In Katona's experiment, again the difference is between the discovery of the superordinate
principle versus the literal "understanding" of one number at a time.
Not only do the two aspects of the outcome of learning correspond

to each other, but they are also logically related to corresponding aspects of the *act* of learning. A structure arrived at always implies an act of structuring; a way of understanding something in the sense of a result always implies a way of understanding something in the sense of an act. Qualitative variation in learning as seen from the act perspective has been described by Svensson (1976) as differences in *approaches to learning*. Focusing on the structural or organizational aspect, he distinguishes between a *holistic* approach characterized by the learner's "direction toward understanding the text as a whole" and an *atomistic* approach characterized by the learner's "focusing on the sequence of text . . . [on] details and . . . [having] a lack of orientation towards the message as a whole" (p. 93). This description originates from an experiment (or rather a series of three experiments) on learning from texts.

All that was said about the act of learning in the cited examples (those from Wenestam's and Katona's studies) was derived from qualitative descriptions of performance, that is, outcome. (The line of reasoning was somewhat similar to this: Thinking about the text in terms of unrelated parts implies an act of segmentation, and thinking about the text in terms of a superordinate principle, linking the parts to each other, implies an act of understanding.) Svensson argued, however, that it is by no means self-evident how the outcome is to be described, and he based his characterization of both aspects of learning on two kinds of sources: performance data, that is, the subjects' answers to questions on the content of the text read, and experiential data, that is, the subjects' reports on their experience of the learning event.

Svensson thus used the *logical*, or internal, relationship between (the structural aspect of) approach and (the structural aspect of) outcome as a point of departure. The same line of reasoning has been followed in the present chapter and applies also to the relation between the referential aspect of approach and the referential aspect of outcome. This was not originally realized by Marton and Säljö (1976) when they presented their distinction between the deep and surface levels of processing, later called the "deep" versus "surface" approach (Marton & Säljö, 1984). They were focusing on the referential aspect. Specifically, they distinguish between the learner focusing on *what is signified* (the author's intention, that which the text is about) and on *the sign* (the text as such). In Wenestam's and Säljö's examples, the former means focusing on the overall thesis of the text, and the latter refers to focusing on the most obvious meaning of each part of the text. The distinction cannot be applied to Katona's example other than in a metaphorical sense—deep approach would then mean focusing on the principle that generates the grouping of figures, while surface approach would refer to focusing on the meaning (or rather the lack of meaning) of each figure in itself.

If we restrict the domain of applicability of the deep–surface distinction to learning from texts, and if we let it refer to what is actually taking place in the learning event, we can clearly see that this distinction refers to the referential aspect of the different approaches to learning just as the corresponding and logically related holistic–atomistic distinction refers to the structural aspect of those differences.

We could say that outcome represents the "what" aspect of learning and approach represents its "how" aspect. Furthermore—in accordance to what has been said here—it seems reasonable recursively to discern the "what" and "how" aspect again within both, in terms of their referential and structural aspects (see Figure 1). As the approach to learning has a holistic or atomistic aspect to it, so too does the outcome of learning have a hierarchical or sequential structural aspect. Our research has shown that the hierarchical outcome tends to coincide with the holistic approach, while the sequential outcome tends to coincide with the atomistic approach. The same parallelism exists with regard to the referential aspects depicted in Figure 1.

It may be tempting to look at the structure from a temporal point of view and consider approach and outcome as representing two temporally separate phases of learning: the ongoing process and—at its termination—the remaining result. Such a separation is, however, by no means justified. There is no meaning without the constitution of meaning, and, as was pointed out above, there is no structure without the act of structuring. The structure is simply a reflection (or measure) of the act of structuring. Moreover, the act of structuring consists of forming a structure all the time. A hierarchical structure mirrors an act of hierarchization, a sequential structure mirrors an act of sequentialization, and a changing structure mirrors at each moment the ongoing act of structuring. Not only the act but also that which is constituted thus has an extension in time.

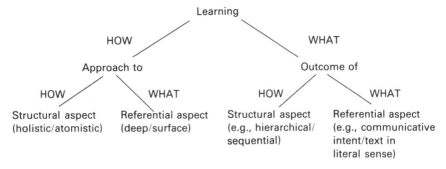

Figure 1. The logical structure of some categories used to describe learning from an experiential perspective.

Some Implications of the Model of Description

The first kind of possible implication of the model in Figure 1 is of a conceptual nature; in the present context we do not have to make a distinction between experience and conceptualization. We have here referred to the "what" and "how" aspects of learning on two consecutive levels. In the phenomenological tradition, the terms *noematic* and *noetic* refer to "that which is experienced" and "the act of experiencing," respectively (see, e.g., Ihde, 1977). There seems to be a structural similarity between this phenomenological distinction and our own way of distinguishing between the "what" and "how" aspects of learning. The aim of a phenomenological investigation is to study the immediate experience of various phenomena by "bracketing" our preconceived ideas, that is, by trying to describe those phenomena just as they appear to us and not as we conceptually expect them to be. In the investigations that have been referred to here, people's understanding of—or learning about—various topics have been the object of research. Both experience and conceptualization (which constitutes the kind of learning we have mostly been studying) are, however, of an intentional nature; experience is always the experience of *something*, and conceptualization is always the conceptualization of *something*. Both experience and conceptualization refer to relations between the individual and some aspect of the world around him or her. It should thus be possible, in spite of obvious differences from a psychological point of view, to apply the same model of description to the structure of human–world relations, regardless of whether they represent more or less pure experiences or more or less learned conceptualizations.

The second possible implication of the model in Figure 1 is of a methodological character: Just as the learner can take a holistic or atomistic view of what is learned, so too can the researcher take a holistic or atomistic view of the learner. The structural aspects of learning that have been dealt with here, and which are considered to be of decisive importance, are all of a macro character. They refer to ways of dealing with an entire text or with the main parts of it. These phenomena are simply not visible from the point of view of the details of the learner's performance only. Differences with regard to the overall structure of the understanding of the text (e.g., in terms of the distinctions between a hierarchical figure–ground structure and a sequential, horizontal structure) do not appear at all, for instance, in a propositional analysis of the subjects' recall of the text because the propositional analysis is used to investigate the correspondence between separate propositions in the text and separate propositions in the recall, and not to study the correspondence between the overall structure in the text and the overall structure in the recall. There seems to be a curious parallel between learners and researchers investigating those learners' way of learning. If the learners segment the text into parts which are focused on without relation to each other, that is, if they adopt what Svensson calls an atomistic approach, they will fail to discover the basic structure of the text. If researchers segment data on the learners' performance and experience into parts which are focused on without relation to each other, that is, if they adopt an atomistic approach in their research, they will fail to see whether or not the learner discovered the basic structure of the text.

IMPROVING LEARNING

We have thus arrived at a model of description in terms of which we can characterize qualitative differences in learning. There are two aspects of learning—approach and outcome—which, in turn, each have structural and referential aspects. All these aspects are logically related to each other, outcome to approach, referential to structural. But the one-to-one correspondence implied by the logical (internal) nature of the relationships holds only if the various aspects not only refer to the same phenomenon but also to the same data about that phenomenon. This is, however, most often not the case.

As was mentioned above, Svensson (1976) used a combination of performance and experiential data to characterize both approach and outcome. This has until now been a more or less unique procedure due to Svensson's unique epistemological stance. In investigations of the relationship between outcome and approach, performance data from either test or interview have commonly been used to describe outcome, and experiential data from either questionnaire or interview have been used to describe approach.

APPROACHES TO LEARNING IN THE INTERNAL AND THE EXTERNAL SENSE

Another issue that has yet to be clarified concerns the fact that experiential data on approach to learning may either concern the learners' experiences of what they are *doing* in the course of the learning event or what they are *trying* to do. This distinction seems fairly obvious. In the way it is used here, it seems to be related to a distinction of central importance within phenomenology, namely, that between internal and external horizon. In our interpretation, *external horizon* refers to the relations a phenomenon is seen to have to other aspects of a greater whole of which the phenomenon is a part. *Internal horizon* refers to the parts that a phenomenon itself is seen to have and to the relations seen between those parts. In accordance with this, while approach in the internal sense concerns how the content of the specific situation (i.e., the content of the text) is dealt with, approach in the external sense refers to how the broader situation is perceived (e.g., how will I be tested, why am I doing this, etc.).

Approaches to learning were dealt with in the internal sense in the first part of this chapter. Approaches to learning in the external sense also have two logically related referential and structural aspects. The referential aspect appears in the deep approach roughly as the learner "trying to understand" and in the surface approach as "trying to memorize." This difference corresponds to the difference with regard to the structural aspect: relating the reading of the text primarily to the reality the text describes, on the one hand, and relating the reading of the text primarily to the expected recall test, subsequent to reading, on the other. The following examples, taken from Marton (1974), may illuminate the distinctions made between approaches to learning in the internal versus external sense.

> *Deep approach (internal):*
>
> . . . or perhaps I stopped and thought about what they are actually saying. . . . If there was something I thought didn't agree and so on, then one stops and then if that really, that really follows from that, sort of, then it is really logical [and] one stops because of what they write and that sort of thing.
>
> *Surface approach (internal):*
>
> . . . haven't reflected on anything. I sort of read, when I read through it I read, I thought of the time, I sort of, I didn't read in order to think—I just read straight through it.
>
> *Deep approach (external):*
>
> I tried to look for . . . well, those main features . . .
>
> *Surface approach (external):*
>
> No, it was probably the worst, I was more tense and so on the first time, then I sort of sat and concentrated all the time. Now I had to sort of get as much as possible from this text so I'd be able to retell it later.

As was pointed out above, not only differences in outcome but also in approach (in the internal sense) can be characterized in terms of figure–ground relations. Both "the sign" and "what is signified" are present in the learner's consciousness in some way, both in connection with surface and deep approach; while in the surface approach "the sign" is figure and "what is signified" is ground, in the deep approach this relationship is reversed. This applies to the differences in approaches to learning in the external sense as well. While both the fact that reading is followed by some kind of test of retention and the fact that the text refers to some reality are present in some way in the learner's awareness, in connection with surface approach, "test" is figure, and with deep approach, "reality" (or referent) is figure.

In the first part of the chapter, where the internal horizon of learning was dealt with, reasoning was based on logical relationships between various aspects. In this second part, the step to a far less clear-cut realm has been taken. Several issues have been raised which we would expect to blur the correlation between approach and outcome. First, different data bases are as a rule used to describe the two aspects. Second, the distinction between the internal and the external sense of approach has not been made in previous publications. Third, the relation between approach, in the external sense, and outcome is always mediated by approach in the internal sense. While an external surface approach is likely to go with an internal surface approach, and external deep approach is necessary, but not sufficient, for an internal deep approach. (Differences in previous knowledge and understanding of the subject matter may be of decisive importance.) Fourth, the approach adopted may change during the learning event itself. An example (though extraordinary) can be found in Säljö's (1982) above-mentioned study. As was stated, the text he used was about learning. While the first part dealt with classical conditioning as a form of learning—the earlier examples given refer to that section—at the end of the text, some earlier studies on different approaches to learning were summarized. Some of the subjects in Säljö's study indeed realized the similarity between their own situation and what was described in the text.

> *(Dora)*
>
> E: Can you describe how you went about reading the article?
> S: Oh, well, first when I read it I sort of thought like this: right, now I'll try to remember as much as possible . . . and then I went on, and the more I read . . . when coming to the end of the article I could have burst out laughing because there they described the type of person I'd been myself at first, those who were trying to learn as much as possible . . . and then there were certain hints about . . . that you should try to find the meaning behind it all, so when I read it once again, I tried to make sense in quite a different way.

Against such a background, the relationship between approach and outcome reproduced in Table 1 is almost more clear-cut than one would have reason to expect it to be. van Rossum and Schenk (1984), from whose work the table is taken, have, by the way, used a general model for describing qualitative differences in outcome, focusing on structural aspects only—Biggs and Collis' (1982) SOLO (structure of observed learning outcomes) Taxonomy. This is an obvious difference from the more or less content-specific characterization of the variation in learning results that have evolved from data in the above examples from Wenestam (1978) and Säljö (1982) and, in fact, in most of the studies carried out

Table 1. Relation between Outcome of Learning and
Approaches to Learning

	Approaches to learning		
Outcome of learning	Surface	Deep	n
Multistructural	35	6	41
Relational	0	25	25
Extended abstract	0	3	3
	35	34	69

Note. After van Rossum & Schenk, 1984.

in our research group in Gothenburg. (For a discussion of this issue, see, for instance, Dahlgren, 1984.) The SOLO Taxonomy is discussed further in Chapter 8 (this volume) by Biggs.

Under any circumstances, investigations of the empirical relationship between approach and outcome have repeatedly revealed strong positive correlations, although not always as strong as in the case of van Rossum and Schenk's (1984) student (see, e.g., Marton & Säljö, 1976; Watkins, 1983; cf. Schmeck & Phillips, 1982).

CONCEPTIONS OF LEARNING

We have not yet dealt with the question of cross-situational consistency. It seems to be the case that at least within a rather narrow range of situations, such as those we found within academic studies, some people are more likely to adopt a deep and holistic approach to learning and come up with a better understanding than others (see, e.g., Svensson, 1976). How can we account for such an observation?

In an interview study, Säljö (1979) tried to find out in which way or ways people conceptualize learning. He found five distinctively different conceptions of learning. It was seen as

1. a quantitative increase in knowledge
2. memorizing
3. the acquisition of facts, methods, and the like, which can be retained and used when necessary
4. the abstraction of meaning
5. an interpretative process aimed at understanding reality

In their above-mentioned study, van Rossum and Schenk (1984) also investigated the relationship between the conceptions of learning in general held by the subjects and the approach they adopted (or intended to adopt) for a certain learning task. As can be seen in Table 2, there is a strong correlation between conceptions of and approaches to learning. Logically, one would expect that a deep conception of learning (characterized by categories 4 and 5 in Table 2) would be a necessary, but not sufficient, condition for a deep approach in the sense of the definition of the situation, just as earlier an external deep approach had been said to be a necessary but not sufficient condition for an internal deep approach ·in the sense of executing the task. It seems reasonable to assume that if someone holds a superficial conception of learning (one that can be characterized primarily in terms of categories 1 and 2 in Table 2), then he or she will adopt a surface approach in the external and the internal sense. A deep conceptualization, however, will not necessarily accompany a deep approach in the external sense. The qualities of the situation, may make the learner focus, for instance, on its demand characteristics. (The reader is here referred to Entwistle's Chapter 2, this volume, where the discussion of the "achieving" student suggests a sensitivity to demand characteristics in this manner).

The fact that a certain conception of learning can be a necessary but not sufficient condition is perhaps even more obvious in relation to outcome. As was pointed out in the summary of Wenestam's (1978) study, he had used a text in which it was argued that the welfare system might fail in many instances because of an overly high level of ambition. This thesis was illustrated by an example and supported by a fairly extensive line of reasoning. The author's intention was obviously to illuminate an aspect of the welfare system, probably new to the reader, and thereby somewhat alter the reader's conceptualization of it. The description of the learning outcomes reflected whether or not the subject participating in the experiment had become aware of the author's conceptualization of the welfare system.

Table 2. Relation between Conceptions of Learning and Approaches to Learning

	Approach to learning		
Conception of learning	Surface	Deep	n
1. Increase in knowledge	6	0	6
2. Memorization	19	4	23
3. Acquisition and utilization of facts	8	7	15
4. Abstraction of meaning	1	12	13
5. Understanding reality	1	12	13
	35	35	70

Note. After van Rossum & Schenk, 1984.

As Säljö (1982) points out, people with a surface, or what he in that particular context calls "flat," conception of learning (more or less corresponding to categories 1 and 2 in Table 2) do not include arriving at a new conceptualization in their definition of learning. Since they conceive of knowledge as "things to learn," they are looking for factual information to memorize in a learning experiment of the kind that has been described here. Parts of the text developing the conceptualization are dealt with by reducing them to pieces of information, about which Säljö says the following:

> Insofar as these messages are attended to by the subject, he or she appears to learn them as if they were "facts." Thus, they do appear in the recalls, but not as a result of an active search for what the writer intended to make known or of an attempt to reconstruct the chain of reasoning which is developed. Rather, they seem to appear as a result merely of remembering the actual statement made by the author. (p. 184)

Furthermore, Säljö tentatively states that

> if statements of this kind are not reduced to information they are understood as *points of view* and in consequence ignored as premises which would direct further reading. (p. 185)

Säljö makes these conclusions about learners with such an orientation:

> Since their implicit assumptions of learning and knowledge lead them to focus on "information," they can see no obvious way of dealing with much of what is said in the text, nor with the general line of reasoning developed. In fact, they act as if they lack what we might call a cognitive category corresponding to what we previously have described as a conception of a phenomenon. This of course does not mean that they do not have any preconceived ideas about the phenomenon dealt with prior to the reading of the particular text. What it does mean is that they do not see it as the purpose of the overall situation they are in to confront their preconceived assumptions with the ideas presented by the author. For them, changing one's conceptions of reality is not what has come to be associated with the specific task of learning in this kind of context. (p. 186)

LEARNING AS A CONCEPTUAL CHANGE

This last remark is especially interesting since it links studies of learning from texts on single occasions (usually lasting less than an hour) to studies of the effects of educational experiences (lasting a number of years) on students' conceptualization of the world around them. As Dahlgren's (1982) review shows, if we think of learning as a change between qualitatively different conceptions of phenomena or of aspects of reality, there is very little learning taking place in the educational system. Andersson and Kärrqvist (1981) conclude, for instance, that of the 16-year-old students in Sweden who have studied physics for several years, only 30% give the physical explanation of seeing in terms of light beams originating from a source being reflected off an object and hitting the retina. Most of the remaining 70% of the students give explanations in terms of a picture going from the object to the eyes, beams coming out of the eyes and hitting the object, or beams coming out of the eyes, hitting the object, and bouncing back to the eyes. If physics classes have not changed these conceptions, one has to wonder what such classes are accomplishing.

Dahlgren (1978) investigated the understanding of some basic economic concepts (such a price, inflation, and devaluation) in a group of university students, before and after one term of study in economics. The aim was to detect whether any conceptual changes were taking place in the students' understandings of economic aspects of the world around them. Dahlgren found qualitative differences in how the students thought about the phenomena in the questions (such as seeing the price of a commodity as a relation between supply and demand vs. considering it as an inherent quality of the commodity). The variation on the conceptual levels was there both before and after the course, but no trends toward improved understanding could be observed (although the group of students *sounded* more professional on the later occasion).

A third example can be taken from Johansson, Marton, and Svensson (1985). They report that quite a few students at a Swedish technological university seem to think in an Aristotelian rather than a Newtonian way in relation to some extremely simple problems, even after half a year of studies in mechanics at the postsecondary level. The following is one of the questions they were asked: A car is driven at a high constant speed straight forwards on a motorway; what forces act on the car? There were two distinctively different ways of answering this question. According to the first of these, and the one which is in line with Newtonian thinking, as the car moves with a constant speed, the forces acting in the direction of movement (the motive force of the engine) and the forces acting in the reverse direction (air resistence, friction) must be in balance. According to the second way of answering the question, which accords with Aristotle's view of motion, as the car moves, the forces in the direction of the movement have to exceed those acting in the opposite direction. Again, just as in the case of Dahlgren's (1978) above-mentioned study, there was a variation in the students' answers both before and after the course in mechanics, without any obvious trend toward a better understanding as a function of studying.

How is it possible that educational experiences so often fail to bring about conceptual changes in the most fundamental respects? The fact is that students may acquire huge bodies of knowledge (clusters of facts) without appropriating the conceptualizations on which those bodies of knowledge are based.

There is an important difference between the studies of learning from texts, referred to throughout this chapter, and studies of conceptual changes as educational effects. As we have seen, in the former case there is often an author whose intention is actually to bring about a change in the reader's conceptualization of the phenomenon dealt with in the text. Such an intention is, however, in most cases missing (at least explicitly) in educational settings. The conceptual foundations of the content of school subjects or disciplines are often taken for granted by teachers and by textbook writers. In terms of figure–ground relations, the conceptual foundations are the ground against which the rest of the content is thematized. In order to bring about the most important conceptual changes, figure and ground should be temporarily reversed, something which the students often do not manage to achieve on their own. Thus, they should be urged to focus periodically upon the conceptual foundations. Too many students go on thinking about the world as they have always done, in spite of the fact that they have acquired a large body of knowledge for describing the world and extensive sets of procedures for dealing with the world which are based on an entirely different conceptual perspective.

A RELATIONAL VIEW OF LEARNING

Approaches to learning (both internal and external) and conceptions of learning are of a relational character. They are not something that the individual *has,* and applies when necessary, but they represent what a learning event, a learning task, or a class of situations *is* for the learner. This may sound somewhat philosophical but has, nevertheless, the most down-to-earth implications.

If we were to think about approaches and conception as something located within the individual, as it were, it would make a lot of sense to try to change the individual or to try to change something *in* him or her, given that our aim is to improve learning. The alternative is to try to change the individual's experience, perception, or conception of *something.* This difference could be seen as a difference between a psychological and an educational perspective. Modern cognitive psychology has been very much concerned with describing what is taking place within the individual—within the "black box," as it were. This is, of course, by no means a logically necessary state of affairs, and the basic assumption has, in fact, been seriously questioned (see, e.g., Marton, 1984; Winograd, 1980).

Also, a relational perspective is easier to adopt in an educational context. The single individual is not or should not be the main object of interest in educational research. Rather, interest has to be focused on people in instructional settings, that is, on learners in a context. And reasonably, from a learning point of view, the content of learning should appear as the most important aspect of that context and hence be included in the description.

As things are now, however, thinking with regard to improvement in learning is dominated by a psychological perspective, as it is reflected in the way in which the most common concepts in the field, such as learning strategy, learning style, and metacognitive knowledge about learning are, as a rule, thought about. (The concept of "learning style" as it appears in the work of the British cybernetician Gordon Pask is an exception in this respect. See, e.g., Entwistle, 1978.)

It seems reasonable to pause at this point and briefly reflect upon the terminological apparatus was have arrived at. The distinctions made between approaches to learning in the internal sense, approaches to learning in the external sense, and conceptions of learning correspond to the distinctions between what one is actually doing in learning situations, what one is trying to do in learning situations, and what one thinks one is doing in learning situations. This trichotomy resembles the above-mentioned and more commonplace trichotomy between strategy, style, and metacognitive knowledge about learning.

No attempt is made here to clarify the exact nature of the relationship between the two sets of distinctions; it may suffice in this context to point only to the relational character of the concepts used in this chapter and within the research tradition from which they originate (see Marton, Hounsell, & Entwistle, 1984). As far as the alternative conceptual apparatus (resting mainly on the distinctions between strategy, style, and metacognitive knowledge) is concerned, outcome aspects of learning are usually not included in their characterization, although description of strategies, styles, and metacognition may very well be (externally) related to independent descriptions of the outcome of learning (see Schmeck & Phillips, 1982, for an exception).

Hierarchies of Relations. A further distinction, which cuts across the two traditions, is that between learning and studying. Svensson (1984) draws attention to the importance of distinguishing between learning skill and study skill. Svensson conceptualizes "learning skill" as a quality of the learner's performance of a learning task and "study skill" as the quality of the student's performance on a unit of studies. In the same way as we were able to identify qualitatively different ways in which a certain learning task can be carried out, corresponding to different skills, it is also possible to identify qualitatively different ways in which, for instance, the complex task of studying for a course is carried out. The complexity stems from the fact that, in addition to the way in which learning activities within the course are carried out, we also have to take into account things like the organization of those study activities, allocation of time used for studying, and more technical aspects of studying, such as note taking, preparation for exams, and so on. The most important point here is the idea that the concept of skill is related to "natural" units of activities, such as reading a text, taking a course, or carrying out studies. As a consequence of this, we can use the concepts of approach (both in the internal and the external sense) and conception in relation to studying, and we can speak of approaches to and conceptions of studying in a similar way as above, but in relation to larger complexes of activities. This line of reasoning should apply to the concepts of strategies, styles, and metacognitive knowledge as well.

An important point relates to the fact that notions like conception, approach (deep–surface or holistic–atomistic), horizon (internal or external), and skill are relative to the delimitations of the phenomenon made. Such a view of skill and of the distinction between a holistic and an atomistic approach has been very explicitly argued for by Svensson (1976). We can thus think of hierarchies of relations, where "wholes of the world" are delimited by the individual, differentiated in terms of their parts, and the parts again viewed as wholes in their own right and differentiated into parts anew and so on. *What is learned*, then, is skills, and they correspond to the qualities of relations between individual and task at differing levels of generalization.

At least two implications should follow from this. First, the fact that a relation may concern a very inclusive whole (e.g., "studies at university") would suggest a certain consistency of the quality of individual–task relations which are parts of that whole. This would relate to what some researchers call "style." Second, the use of simple dichotomies (compared with, e.g., the recursive applications of those dichotomies) gives a grossly oversimplified picture. We should also remember that qualitative differences in learning are not always dichotomous, and the dichotomies used for characterizing qualitative differences such as holistic–atomistic, deep–surface, hierarchical–sequential are not always applicable. Even when they are, they do not necessarily represent the most interesting differences (see, e.g., Svensson, 1984.)

The Origin of Relations. Approaches and conceptualizations should thus be considered as relations. As such, they would reasonably originate from earlier relations. An approach or a conception is far from being more typical of the approaching or conceptualizing individual than it is typical of the approached or conceptualized setting, task, or content. The five conceptions of learning found by Säljö (1979), for instance, obviously refer to schoollike learning situations. Giorgi (1985), who interviewed people about learning events in everyday contexts, arrived at far more different types of learning. Pramling (1983) also found a much wider variation of learning conceptions in her search for the roots of the idea of learning among preschool children. At the same time, she was able to show that as soon as we set up a schoollike situation, the difference between a deep and a surface approach (and the corresponding difference between holistic and atomistic approach) appears. She describes a situation where 5- to 6-year-old children were taught about various forms, such as a triangle, circle, square, and so on. Afterwards, the teacher asked them about what they had learned. Some children focused only on trying to come up with the right answers to the questions, while others connected what they had learned with the real world, beyond the immediate situation.

In a school environment, we are thus likely to find "school conceptions" of learning. Still, we find differences between individual cases as well. If we consider a single individual (and by doing so we "freeze" the interindividual variation), we will probably find a variation across situations. If we consider a single situation (and by doing so we "freeze" the intersituational variation), we will probably find a variation between individuals. We should thus preferably deal with a simultaneous variation in both dimensions and use relations as units.

The Improvement of Learning. There are at least three different ways in which learning can be improved from such a point of departure.

1. We should make up our minds about what kind of learning we value and then build an educational system that works toward that goal. If we think that students should go through conceptual changes bringing them in line with the fundamental ways of thinking underlying the discipline or the school subject they are studying, then we should operationalize our expectations (e.g., write examination questions) in accordance with that. Such learning surely means radical changes in the learners (or rather in the relation between them and the world around them). As it has been pointed out earlier:

> If we believe that the aim of education is qualitatively to change and improve the participants' way of apprehending their reality, we should judge and promote learning in accordance with this aim. Radical changes in thinking *due* to learning certainly presuppose radical changes in thinking *about* learning. (Marton, 1983, p. 302)

2. Defining the goals of education in this manner (e.g., in terms of examination questions requiring a deep understanding) may result in an

easy adaptation to those aims in a number of students. However, the shift in emphasis might be very difficult for other students. Thus, it is also important that we provide instructional means by which the students can obtain guidance to help them meet the expectations.

As was pointed out above, different understandings of the same phenomenon have both referential and structural aspects. We cannot directly make someone acquire a certain meaning, but we can possibly aid him or her to impose one structure on a phenomenon rather than another. One of the ways of doing so is to introduce a cognitive conflict which makes the learner reconsider his or her habitual way of delimiting the phenomenon in question. It is here we have to start. Let us reconsider the previous "car example."

Students at a Technological University answered the question, "A car is driven at high constant velocity straight forward on a motorway— what forces act on the car?" in two distinctively different ways. According to one, as the car is moving with a constant speed, the forces in the direction of the movement (from the engine) and those is the opposite direction (from air resistance and friction) have to be in balance. According to the second way of reasoning, as the car is moving, the forces in the direction of the movement must exceed those in the reverse direction. The car in question was thus apprehended as (a) moving at a constant velocity, due to the equilibrium of forces or (b) moving due to a motive inequilibrium of forces (Johansson, Marton & Svensson, 1985). The referential aspects of the two conceptions are "equilibrium" versus "motive inequilibrium." The structural aspects have to do with the way the phenomenon is delimited. In the first case, velocity is focused on, and constant velocity is compared (implicitly or explicitly) with acceleration or deceleration (negative acceleration). In the second case, movement is focused on, and it is compared (implicitly or explicitly) with rest. If we can get the students to consider the structure, to shift their focus, we may help them to discover the former meaning. In fact, a few students who answered the question according to conception (b) to begin with, changed their minds and came up with conception (a) when they, during the interview itself, shifted the focus of attention from movement to velocity.

The general, but as yet unexplored, idea is the following. The qualitatively different conceptions of various phenomena which we find, if we focus on learning as a change between qualitatively different conceptions of the same phenomenon, have both referential and structural aspects. This is in accordance with the model for describing the outcome of learning presented in the first part of this chapter. We can now use the structural aspect of a conception as a "lever," and by bringing about a change in how a phenomenon is delimited and focused on, we can also bring about a change in the meaning it has for the learner.

3. In addition to focusing the students' attention on a certain type of learning goal and aiding them by means of instructional measures to attain those goals, there is a third direction we can follow in order to improve learning. We can try to make the students aware of their own way of approaching a learning task and understanding its content, against the background of an awareness of the alternative ways of approaching the task and understanding the content. Realizing that there are different ways of thinking and different ways of going about a learning task can be a very efficient way, not only of enhancing one's understanding of the specific learning task, but also of transcending it, that is, of learning to learn in a very genuine sense of the word. Lybeck's (1981) work represents a highly content-oriented approach; he argues in favor of letting the student make their ways of thinking about the content explicit. He illustrates the efficiency of such an instructional strategy in the context of physics at secondary school level. While Lybeck primarily wants the students to reflect on each other's way of thinking about a concrete physical problem, Gibbs (1981) tries to make students reflect on each other's way of approaching various learning tasks. A recurring realization of these two somewhat differently focused intentions within the framework of ordinary course of activities would probably turn out to be a highly efficient alternative way of improving the student's learning. (The reader's attention is also directed to Weinstein's Chapter 11, this volume.)

It may be that none of these three ways of trying to improve learning is specific to a relational view of learning, but a combination of them probably is. The combination means that we are not dealing with the aims of learning *per se*, as they are operationalized in terms of examination questions, but we are dealing with these aims as they appear to the students. Neither are we dealing with the students' approaches as such, but rather in relation to the content of the learning task approached. And against the background of the combination of the three strategies, the instructional approach argued for should be interpreted as aiming at improving understanding, that is, at boosting the quality of the internal relation between learner and content.

The case for such a relational view of learning has been made in this chapter with reference to two interrelated theses. The intention of the first part was to argue that the description of learning arrived at by research is contingent on the conceptualization of learning embodied in the research community. The intention of the second part was to argue that the kind of learning that takes place in an educational setting is likewise contingent on the conceptualization of learning embodied in that setting.

Acknowledgments

The research reported here was financially supported by a grant from the Swedish Council for Research in the Humanities and Social" Sciences. Professor Lennart Svensson gave some most valuable comments on the first draft of this chapter and so did the editor of the present volume, professor Ronald Schmeck, on the second draft. I am greatly indebted to both. I am also indebted to professor Amadeo Giorgi of the Saybrook Institute, San Fransisco, for a most illuminating conversation concerning the temporal relationship between learning approach and outcome.

REFERENCES

Andersson, B., & Kärrqvist, C. (1981). Ljuset och dess egenskaper [The light and its qualities]. *EKNA-rapport nr 8, Institutionen för praktisk pedagogik, Göteborgs universitet.*
Biggs, J. B., & Collis, K. F. (1982). *Evaluating the quality of learning.* New York: Academic Press.
Dahlgren, L. O. (1982). Higher education—impact on students. *Department of Education, University of Göteborg,* 1982:02.
Dahlgren, L. O. (1984). Outcomes of learning. In F. Marton, D. Hounsell, & N. Entwistle (Eds.), *The experience of learning* (pp. 19–35). Edinburgh: Scottish Academic Press.
Entwistle, N. J. (1978). Knowledge structures and styles of learning: A summary of Pask's recent research. *British Journal of Educational Psychology, 48,* 255–265.
Gibbs, G. (1981). *Teaching students to learn: a student-centred approach.* Milton Keynes: Open University Press.
Giorgi, A. (1985). The phenomenological psychology of learning and the verbal learning tradition. In A. Giorgi (Ed.), *Phenomenology and the psychological research* (pp. 23–85). Pittsburgh: Duquesne University Press.
Ihde, D. (1977). *Experimental phenomenology.* New York: Putnam.
Johansson, B., Marton, F., & Svensson, L. (1985). An approach to describing learning as change between qualitatively different conceptions. In A. L. Pines & L. H. T. West (Eds.), *Cognitive structure and conceptual change* (pp. 233–257). New York: Academic Press.
Katona, G. (1940). *Organizing and memorizing.* New York: Columbia University Press.
Lybeck, L. (1981). Arkimedes i klassen [Archimedes in the class]. *En ämnespedagogisk berättelse.* Göteborg: Acta Universitatis Gothoburgensis.
Marton, F. (1974). Inlärning och studiefärdighet [Learning and study skill]. *Rapporter från Pedagogiska Institutionen, Göteborgs universitet,* nr 121.
Marton, F. (1983). Beyond individual differences. *Educational Psychology, 3,* 289–304.
Marton, F. (1984). Towards a psychology beyond the individual. In K. M. J. Lagerspetz & P. Niemi (Eds.), *Psychology in the 1980's* (pp. 45–72). Amsterdam: North-Holland.

Marton, F., Hounsell, D. J., & Entwistle, N. J. (Eds.). (1984). *The experience of learning.* Edinburgh: Scottish Academic Press.

Marton, F. & Säljö, R. (1976). On qualitative differences in learning: I. Outcome and process. *British Journal of Educational Psychology, 46,* 4–11.

Marton, F. & Säljö, R. (1978, July–August). *Level of difficulty viewed as a relationship between the reader and the text.* Paper presented at the 19th International Congress of Psychology, Munich, Germany.

Marton, F., & Säljö, R. (1984). Approaches to learning. In F. Marton, D. Hounsell, & N. Entwistle (Eds.), *The experience of learning* (pp. 36–55). Edinburgh: Scottish Academic Press.

Marton, F., & Wenestam, C-G. (1978). Qualitative differences in the understanding and retention of the main point in some texts based on the principle–example structure. In M. M. Gruneberg, P. E. Morris, & R. N. Sykes (Eds.), *Practical aspects of memory* (pp. 633–643). London: Academic Press.

Pramling, I. (1983). *The child's conception of learning.* Göteborg: Acta Universitatis Gothoburgensis.

Säljö, R. (1979). Learning in the learner's perspective. I. Some common-sense conceptions. *Reports from the Institute of Education, University of Göteborg,* nr 76.

Säljö, R. (1982). *Learning and understanding.* Göteborg: Acta Universitatis Gothoburgensis.

Säljö, R. (1984) Learning from reading. In F. Nartibm D. Hounsell & N. Entwistle (Eds.) *The experience of learning* (pp. 71–89). Edinburgh: Scottish Academic Press.

Schmeck, R. R., & Phillips, J. (1982). Levels of processing as a dimension of difference between individuals. *Human Learning, 1,* 95–103.

Svensson, L. (1976). *Study skill and learning.* Göteborg: Acta Universitatis Gothoburgensis.

Svensson, L. (1984). Skill in learning. In F. Marton, D. Hounsell, & N. Entwistle (Eds.) *The experience of learning* (pp. 56–70). Edinburgh: Scottish Academic Press.

van Rossum, E. J., & Schenk, S. M. (1984). The relationship between learning conception, study strategy and learning outcome. *British Journal of Educational Psychology, 54,* 73–83.

Watkins, D. (1983). Depth of processing and the quality of learning outcomes. *Instructional Science, 12,* 49–58.

Wenestam, C-G. (1978). Horisontalisering [Horizontalization]. Ett sätt att missuppfatta det man läser. *Rapporter från Pedagogiska Institutionen, Göteborgs universitet,* nr 157.

Wenestam, C-G. (1980). *Qualitative differences in retention.* Göteborg: Acta Universitatis Gothoburgensis.

Winograd, T. (1980). What does it mean to understand language. *Cognitive Science, 4,* 209–241.

CHAPTER 4

Learning Strategies, Teaching Strategies, and Conceptual or Learning Style

GORDON PASK

INTRODUCTION AND OVERVIEW

From the mid- to late 1960s, Brian Lewis, Bernard Scott, and I conjectured that learning strategies, teaching strategies, and even plans of action have characteristic types which can be differentiated (Lewis & Pask, 1964, 1965; Pask, 1961, 1970, 1972; Pask & Lewis, 1968; Pask & Scott, 1971, 1972, 1973). Individual difference psychologies have maintained a similar stance and with greater precision regarding the nature of strategies. An overview of the approach taken by my own group in the 1960s is described in the remainder of this section. Learning and teaching strategies can, under appropriate circumstances, be substantially exteriorized or externalized for observation. Protocols can serve this purpose, but we used maplike representations of what may be known or learned. These representations were open to continuous evolution as further topics and relations between them were added by learners.

Later, these representations were seen to be manipulable systematically and without the imposition of rules that insult freedom of thought or creativity (about mid-1970s). The maps and representations of topics (communicable, shared, or public concepts, rather than personal con-

GORDON PASK • OOC Program, Faculty of Education, University of Amsterdam, Grote Bickerstraat 72, Amsterdam, The Netherlands 1013 KS.

cepts) were called "entailment structures." Later still, Kallikourdis, Scott, and I discerned that entailment structures are special and restrictive cases of "entailment meshes," in which shared, public concept relations constitute expressions in a "protologic" (Lp) (Pask, 1975a, b; 1976 a, b, c; Pask & Scott, 1973; Pask, Kallikourdis, & Scott, 1975).

An *entailment structure* consists of topics and connections among topics which show how they may be derived or understood from other topics. The *entailment mesh* recognizes that the entailment of one topic from others is a momentary situation that occurs during action or explanation; in fact, the relationships between topics are *not* static and hierarchical. "Lp" refers to a *protologic* developed out of Conversation Theory which is a model of what underlies cognitive activity. It is not a model of logic or language itself but rather a "substrate" for them; hence the qualifier, "proto," meaning "underlying." Its rules involve the processes by which, for example, the normally heterarchical relationship between topics unfolds into hierarchies. Its details encompass conflict detection and resolution, analogy, generalization, and models of innovation and memory.

Conversation Theory is a summarization of our assumptions and rationale from this early period. Conversations are behaviors, but special kinds of behaviors with hard-valued observables in the form of concept sharings, detected as "understandings." Conversations are, we believe, the first basic data of psychological, social, or educational theory. We see later that people can even have conversations with themselves. Conversations which may lead to concept sharing need not be verbal. Often they are gestural, pictorial, or mediated through a computer interface.

Understanding, like many of the terms of Conversation Theory, has an everyday use that is evocative of its rigorous and almost technical meaning within Conversation Theory. An understanding involves not only the topics that are related and their relationship, but the ability to transfer and apply the relationship to new situations. An "agreement over an understanding" is a hard-valued event that can be detected in an experiment. It involves individuals, each of whom exteriorizes his or her understandings and confirms that the other's entailments reproduce his or her own, previously internal, concepts.

The entailment mesh constitutes a network or map of topics which have no hierarchy or direction. Paths on this map are a learning strategy or a teaching strategy. A learning strategy or a teaching strategy consists of paths on the map marked to indicate specific conceptual events like examining, trying to learn about, learning about a topic (shared concept), or understanding a topic in the related context of others from which it may be constructed, reconstructed, or recalled. Such paths may consist of simple trees, a hierarchical branching and looping, and they may or may not employ analogies as structures. They often involve the creation of analogies, and they may employ or create generalizations.

A *style* is a *disposition* to adopt one class of learning strategy or one class of teaching strategy in the conversation of a tutorial. In an art school, this is usually by demonstration. In a high school, it is usually by verbal communication or laboratory experience. The question remains, to whom does this stylistic disposition belong? Individual difference psychologists seem to take it for granted that the unitary, partly autonomous unit "owning" a disposition and opting for one or the other class of strategy is a person. Of course, this may be so, but a broader perspective is needed if we are to make sense of the facts. Conversation Theory offers one such broader perspective. In this theory, we specify an individual (a psychological individual, or P-Individual) as partly autonomous. The P-Individual is only *partly* autonomous because he or she is open to the information transfer of a concept-sharing conversation between persons or between mental organizations in one person (both, in our sense, P-Individuals).

"P-Individual" may appear clumsy, but the idea is essential because it allows one of the symmetries of Conversation Theory to exist. There can be many P-Individuals within one person (when I take different and possibly conflicting viewpoints) as well as a P-Individual that is made up of many persons, such as a school of thought or a religion.

The technical criteria of "organizational closure" and "informational openness," underlying this distinction, are hardly in the province of this paper. Likewise, there are very thorough technical criteria that underlie the theory's usage of the term *understanding*, already noted as a specific indicator of concept sharing. The interested reader will find a review in Pask (1983), which also gives reference to expositions in cybernetic, mathematical and logical terms. The basic ideas are, however, quite familiar in ordinary language. A P-Individual is a personna; an understanding is the ability of two or more P-Individuals to exchange "what," "how," and "why by that method" questions and to provide mutually satisfactory replies. Such a transaction, which embodies the slightly refined common meaning of understanding, is a concept-sharing act. Of course, the agreement over an understanding need not be and often is not complete; for example, your concept of "tortoise" or "knitting" may be quite different from mine. Hence, agreement must be taken to include agreement to disagree, with some knowledge of why and how we disagree. If there is some agreement and some concept sharing, then your personal concept of "tortoise" and my personal concept of "tortoise" are mutually enriched by whatever is shared in dialogue. Further, a shared or public concept of "tortoise," some of it yours and some of it mine, is created in the process and may be inscribed as a topic.

A topic, or shared concept, minimally consists of a description of how the concept is produced, that is, a means of recognizing or constructing or obtaining such a thing and a rationale for deriving it from other concepts. It is unlikely that such a statement would meet with much opposition if two or more P-Individuals in debate were necessarily individuals. However, Conversation Theory holds that P-Individuals are such that several may coexist in one brain (cf. Kelly, 1955, and Mildred Shaw's, 1980, insightful interpretation of Kelly's core-construct system).

At another extreme, particularly relevant in the context of educational or social institutions, there are P-Individuals that necessarily exist in several brains, for example, common norms or systems of rational belief. The hypothesis of Conversation Theory is that the dispositions to adopt certain learning strategies or teaching strategies, that is, styles, belong to P-Individuals of *any* type. This may imply that they are characteristics of people. More likely, as Laurillard once commented, they may characterize people in context, just as people have context bound, rather than absolute, personalities. (In the first and last chapters of this volume, Schmeck expressed a relativistic view, apparently consonant with this stance; cf. Ramsden, Chapter 7).

HYPOTHESES AND THE EARLY EXPERIMENTS

The hypotheses listed below are derived from Conversation Theory. So far, they have not been falsified, and the evidence obtained by other groups supports them. The present section of the paper concerns only one type of experiment, carried out in my own laboratory and in laboratory-monitored field studies. In both these and later experiments, I feel happier with detailed results. As many subjects as possible should be employed, but I am unconvinced by statistical amalgams of data, that this bias or preference is reflected in the studies.

The Existence of Learning Strategies

Early studies (e.g., Lewis & Pask, 1964) have shown that in perceptual motor learning under adaptively controlled conditions, learning strategies are in evidence. For example, in a coding task (Pask & Lewis, 1968) the differences are manifest in the detailed component-by-component records of response latency. In fact, it is possible to discriminate the *stringing* of sequential responses from *clumping*, in which the subjects act like a pianist playing a chord. Also, these tendencies are related in the domain of coding skills (Pask & Scott, 1971) to the strategy preferred and most effectively used in building up a complex response.

INTELLECTUAL LEARNING STRATEGIES

The first studies of intellectual learning took place in 1969 and are reported in Pask and Scott (1972) and summarized in Pask (1975a). In order to perform experiments of this kind, it is necessary to provide unfamiliar material to be learned. For this purpose, Dr. Scott produced taxonomies for two different types of "martian animal," the "clobbit" and the "gandelmuller." He provided graphic and written descriptions of each species: 40 cards in all, of which 10 showed typical subspecies; 15, contextual data about habits; 5, test types in the taxonomy; 7, physical characteristics; and 7 to indicate why names of parts or behaviors are used. Under free-learning conditions, the subjects could select cards as they wished and were required to give a tape recorded account of why any one was selected.

Upon analysis of data from about 26 subjects, it was possible to discriminate subjects who tested large, global predicates. In all cases the subjects satisfied a criterion of 10 or more on a standard 30-item taxonomy-based questionnaire administered when subjects thought themselves proficient. In addition, half of the selected subjects were required to teachback the information to a participant experimenter prior to completing the questionnaire. *Teachback* is an iterative process of explanation (of each species and its proper discrimination), correction, and further explanation. In comparative studies, teachback is replaced by similar-seeming but ineffective procedures.

The learning strategies are called *holist*, preferring global predicates and relations of topics, and *serialist*, preferring not to use such relations and learning step-by-step. These are paralleled by teaching strategies of each type. One qualification is required. The holist learner may be either irredundant, eschewing redundant data (often known as enrichment data), or redundant and apt to use such data. Generally, the redundant holist learns less rapidly, takes considerably longer, and has faster but less-accurate recall of any tutorial material. The irredundant holist is more selective about the material used in teaching. Schmeck (1983) refers to a redundant holist as an "elaborative processor."

MATCHED AND MISMATCHED LEARNING

It is easy to design and use a holist or serialist type of teaching program to guide a participant experimenter. This was done, with clobbits first and gandelmullers second, balanced against "gandelmullers" first and "clobbits" second. In each case, the instruction was iterative until complete mastery was secured. After that, subjects responded, several hours later, to test questions.

The matched consistently performed better than the mismatched. For example, the mismatched holists needed 4 to 7 iterative repetitions in contrast to 1 to 3 for matched serialists. Also, learners performing teachback are superior to learners with the ineffective control treatment regardless of whether they are serialists or holists. These results are, if anything, strengthened by later, detailed replications which also substantiate test-to-test reliability of the "clobbits" and the "gandelmuller" situations when their order is alternated (interscore correlations of .89).

In common with all such methods of exteriorizing concepts, any teachback process is likely to occupy 3 to 4 hours of effort, not counting the subsequent analysis of detailed data. Attempts to reduce the labor involved, by automatic control of administration and automatic recording, have been used with varying degrees of sophistication since the early 1970s. However, in order to be effective, the technique must be based upon a firm set of principles and, in the case of our group, those of conversation theory.

To summarize our findings at this early stage, the condition of understanding of a shared concept was obtainable by iterated teachback, and the resilience of an understood concept was affirmed by the superior retention of teachback learners. It was possible to specify learning strategies and teaching strategies as path markings (or classes of them) on a data representation, although, at the stage concerned, it was difficult to compare or refine them. Even so, the existence of distinct classes of strategy was sufficiently evidenced by the data in question. Strategic match or mismatch showed an influence upon learning—mismatch leading to difficulty in understanding and sometimes to complete misunderstanding of relevant topics. The converse result, that matching improves learning, was suggested, but it is less convincingly demonstrated because of an inherent ignorance of what the learner knows to begin with. These statements could, at this stage, only be demonstrated for the persons who participated, learners or teachers, but studies of the act of design suggested that the statements had greater generality (e.g., that designing can involve distinct P-Individuals in a single person).

A TYPICAL LARGER-SCALE SERIES OF EXPERIMENTS

A series of experiments, using partly automated methods, were carried out using 62 participants (who completed the series) from polytechnics of Kingston and Chiswick, United Kingdom. To indicate subject attrition in such detailed and lengthy experiments, the original sample contained 115 people, all selected by pretest in order to obtain rough equality of preferred strategy difference. These experiments were concerned with several issues: the means of determing learning strategy (i.e., the clobbit and the gandelmuller tests), the effect of securing understanding by teachback, stability over different subject matters (the operon cycle, the menstrual cycle, and an inductive inference task), and the influence of matched versus mismatched learning strategies.

Of the participants, 32 were exposed to the clobbit free-learning task to determine preferred learning strategy (holist or serialist). Then, the subjects engaged in a further session to perform the gandelmuller task in a matched or mismatched teaching program. Two-weeks later, they were taught the operon cycle in matched and mismatched conditions, and finally, they were given retention tests and teachback. Participants given ineffective control group teachback on clobbits received effective teachback on gandelmullers and on the operon cycle. Those given effective teachback on clobbits received ineffective teachback on gandelmullers and effective teachback on the operon cycle. All learning conditions were unrestricted. The remaining 30 students experienced similar sessions, but the free-learning task was the menstrual cycle, and the programmed tasks were the operon cycle and the inductive inference task. In both groups of participants, half of those receiving effective teachback had been selected and assigned as holists and half as serialist; half were presented with matched programs and half, mismatched.

The full experimental design and data for the development of the style indices appear in a series of reports (Pask, 1977, 1978, 1979). The most effective style assignment index consisted of the following set of measures: the frequency of naming, the intentions expressed by learners as to their goal for learning, and the details of the free-learning data when learners were directing their own paths (e.g., exploration of the subject matter), deliberate information search based on curiosity or uncertainty, search for one specific datum, search for several specific data, testing a single-predicate hypothesis, testing a large predicate or relational hypothesis. Some additional indices are obtained in sessions of free recall administered by the apparatus, notably when learners repeat certain topics and the extent to which the order of topics in free recall mirrors the order in which topics were covered during learning. As a further source of discriminative data, retrospective determinations of style were carried out after teachback and recall. Most determinations were influenced by whether or not the previous teachback was effective or ineffective (in the latter case, no explanations were obtained). Other tests (embedded figures, the "circles" test, the "analogies" test, and logical problem solving) were carried out, but yielded correlations that, although marginally significant, are modest.

Serial learners showed intention to search for specific data. Holist learners showed intention to test a large predicate or relational hypothesis. Holist learners selected a large number of data cards, while serialists selected a small number of data cards. Matched performance was better than mismatched performance. Matched task scores were better than mismatched task scores. Teachback performance was better than ineffective, control group teachback performance.

In addition, confidence was measured on the following dimensions: uncertainty about hypotheses, correct belief, uncertainty about the next topic to select, and belief in correctness of what to select next. These components are a multidimensional index of doubt. For holist learners uncertainty about the next topic to select and belief in correctness of what to select next were significantly higher than the others. For operation learners, correct belief was significantly higher than the other dimensions.

Perhaps the most puzzling, but also the most consistent, finding is the constancy of strategy type over all these tests as well as different-in-content learning situations. The enigma lies in the invariance of *personal* style, rather than P-Individual style. We should predict change in perspective with learning experiences for different learning contexts. In fact, these experiments started with a half-and-half split in each group, and there are in the 32-member group, 18 serialist and 14 holist learners. In the 30-member group, there are 17 serialist and 13 holist learners. Further, this constancy is manifest at all of the sampled intermediary phases. This was perplexing in that we approached the whole project with the assumption that context, or contextual demands, would far outweigh stylistic consistency as a determiner of choice of strategy, that is, we expected less consistency in an individual's choice of strategy. For more complete descriptions of these projects, the reader is referred to Pask (1977, 1978, 1979, 1983), and de Gelder (1981).

THE USE OF "CASTE" AND OF "INTUITION" AND THE NOTION OF STYLE

Just before 1973 a computer-regulated interface for exteriorizing conceptual events became operational as a laboratory exteriorizing tool. It is known as CASTE, or course assembly system and tutorial environment. Further, the "conceptual maps" of topics Pask (1975a,b) had been replaced by sophisticated, less-arbitrary forms of cartography. The representation employed was a form of entailment mesh.

As before, a *conceptual map* is an entailment structure, showing hierarchical connections (directed arrows) which indicate how the topics may be derived. The entailment mesh has relations rather than arrows, and it shows how particular entailments may arise for purposes of explanation or action. For example, I can explain (to use the very tired example from Conversation Theory) a circle using a compass and a plane ("By using the instrument of a compass, which works like such and such when used on a plane, a figure called a circle is made"). This shows how understanding a circle might entail the topics of compass and plane. However, (and this was the next step from entailment structure) it is equally valid to explain a compass from circle and plane ("A circle is made upon a plane by the manipulation of this instrument called a compass."). And again to explain a plane from circle and compass. Thus, the entailment mesh was developed, which does not contain any arrows and allows more of the everyday complexity, flexibility, and "chemistry" of understanding to be represented. An "understood topic" is one for which teachback has been obtained. Teachback involves not only saying what other topics that topic may be derived from, but also how those topics relate to reproduce the topic. It is not enough merely to parrot back a definition; the topic must be used in a novel way that shows the learner's ability to manipulate the topics and their entailments and produce a novel interaction.

CASTE was a laboratory installation that occupied two rooms. But a portable, less-powerful facility called INTUITION was developed that could be employed in schools and colleges, thus allowing for the representation of different types of learners in different institutional environments. Also, programs were designed for many subject matters, such as meiosis and mitosis, probability theory, physical chemistry, heat engines seen in the context of thermodynamics, the reign of Henry VIII, the Tsembaga ritual regulation cycle (an anthropological subject), diseases of the thyroid system, and many others.

These studies lasted for 6 years or more and covered an admixture of materials and types of learner, about 60 in the laboratory and some 95 completed (out of over 170 initiated) in colleges or schools. Typically, experiments with detailed, meticulous recordings lasted over spaced sessions between 7 and 12 hours each. These studies confirmed all of the original findings. For example, "understood" topics are resilient, people do adopt strategies of learning, a mismatch of learning and teaching strategies leads to no relevant learning, and matching leads to more effective learning than that achieved in an arbitrarily programmed situation.

As entailment meshes became recognized, it was possible to discriminate, with greater refinement, between types of learning strategy and their relation to inherent structures of subject matter, whether determined by an author's predilections, institutional constraints, or the subject matter itself. These distinctions, refined by using CASTE and INTUITION, are more clearly related to the content of this paper later when dealing with those strategies influencing dispositions called "styles."

Some distinctions, however, merit attention at this point. For example, among all holists, it is possible to recognize (a) those who depend upon the use of valid analogies or generalizations given within the material, that is, those having both contrast and similarity; and (b) those holists who depend upon the creation of valid analogies and generalizations between topics. This latter method incidentally seems to be one of the most productive ways of learning—by invention or discovery. These valid analogies are distinct from mere similitudes and overgeneralizations that do not contain contrasts and which are commonly found to be unproductive. The analogies that learners set down may be either valid or positively misleading. In the context of "hard to learn" subject matters, counterproductive holistic learning gives rise to casual *globetrotting*, a learning pathology.

Teachers, authors, or experts do much of the same (i.e., analogize productively or not). As a matter of fact, in the CASTE environment, the author–teacher–learning distinction becomes only one of dominant role. During the creation of the subject matter representation, clearly the author is dominant. Then, CASTE adopts the role of teacher whenever it presents material based on this underlying representation. However, the learner must teach the teacher what is not known, as well as certain aspects of his or her learning style. Also, the learner adopts the teacher's role in order to teach back the concepts to CASTE to confirm understanding, and finally, in its most full-blown form, CASTE allows the learner to become author.

Among serialistic learners, it is possible to distinguish at least the following two types. One is the operation, or local rule, learner who progresses logically, step-by-step, moving to a different context only when he or she has assimilated one portion thoroughly and often asking for tutorial guidance in which topics to tackle next. The other is the rote learner, who follows the prescribed and narrow path. Unless the subject matter is of trivial extent or the learner virtually has eidetic imagery, rote learners have little chance of success in making use of the knowledge they have acquired, although they may perform quite competently in multiple choice or other types of examinations where special memorization skill places them at an advantage.

From these descriptions it may appear that serial learners learn rules that holistic learners do not. If so, that misconception must be remedied. Successful serial and holistic learners both come to grips with rules, perhaps of their own making or perhaps inherent in the subject matter. The serial learner is inclined to focus upon local, small-predicate rules and the holstic learner upon global, large-predicate rules. The previously noted redundant holist tends to use dispersed and over-specified (i.e., enriched) rules, whereas the irredundant holist is happier with pure (i.e., minimally specified) rules. Finally, if this terse account still suggests that one type or another is at an advantage, then it is misleading. The evidence strongly suggests that successful learning does involve innovation or discovery but also the *integration* of both local and global rules. Both serial and holistic strategies are needed to achieve understanding.

TESTS OF CONCEPTUAL AND LEARNING STYLE

Soon after CASTE and INTUITION were in use, we became aware of the need for test learning situations yielding scores which could be used to predict which learning strategies were likely to be successful with certain individuals. A pair of tests were constructed. They have excellent covalidity and are based upon the same form of entailment mesh, relating topics (shared concepts) that have models as well as descriptions. They both require participants to learn a quantity of unfamiliar but thematic material. There are global as well as local rules, but prediction, in Bruner's (1975) sense of "going beyond the information given," is required of respondents, as well as the recall of whatever has been learned.

One test, the "Spy Ring History Test," is concerned with the development of an espionage network in which the agents have specific roles (local rules), and their activity, founded upon a logic of permission rather than implication, influences the form of network by global rules. Questions of both a predictive and a recall type are detailed, and it is possible to infer a great deal about how a student goes beyond the information predictively as well as how recall takes place.

The other test, matched and covalid, is concerned with the manufacture and distribution of heroin. The synthesis proposed in the heroin test is chemically possible but nowadays is uneconomic and always was rather hazardous. Both tests occupy about $3\frac{1}{2}$ hours and may be administered either manually or through a computer program. Further, provided that the form of the entailment mesh, with models included, is invariant, a user is able to manufacture versions which may be more suited to a given population. The originals are, henceforward, called the "Spies" and the "Smugglers" tests. Several alternative tests have been produced in other laboratories.

Since instruments of this kind are crude, relative to the scrutiny of

CASTE records or to the personal attention of one participant experimenter, it is only possible to detect general dispositions or styles of conceptualization and learning. However, these results have predictive value.

The scoring scheme of the latest version admits to considerable latitude. No particular scoring method is sacrosanct and there are numerous possibilities. Braten (1982), Laurillard (1980, 1981; Laurillard & Mirante, 1981), and Lindstrom (1983) have produced equally reliable and, in certain respects, more-informative scoring systems. All of the systems are reliable and yield useful correlation with aptitudes as well as specific skills and their performance.

Our own group uses the following indices:

1. A versatility index (V) based upon forecasting rather than given data, interpolative or predictive, and requiring the invention of more or less perspicuous analogy relations.
2. An index (X) chiefly of global pattern recall.
3. An index (Y) of global rule recall. The sum of Y and X is the score called *comprehension learning*, or C score.
4. An index (U) of local rule and operation recall. Rote learning of lists of messages, in contrast to the local rules that agents use, is discounted, so far as possible. Rule learning is known as an operation learning skill.
5. An index (R) of rote recall (chiefly of message lists). On the whole, with performance in mind, this index should be counted against the learner.
6. An index (S) of semantic recall.
7. A neutral (N) score, indicating that the material said to be studied has, in fact, been studied. This index has no discriminative stylistic value but, if it is below a reasonable level, the data may as well be discarded as guesswork.

In addition, learners are required to provide a written or pictorial account of what events they believe to have occurred during the period covered. This story given an adequate length and sufficient content, plays a quite crucial role in the analysis of results.

Cross correlation between the scores is passably high and reached the level for the V, U, and C scores of between .40 and .58 or .50 and .81 (depending upon the calculation of indices) for 74 learners. We used paired participants in teacher training colleges, youngsters at Queensgate school with mandatory "learning-to-learn" classes, and older persons at Henley grammar school/6th form and college/first-year university. Apart from the Queensgate group and one Henley group, there is a strong operation learning bias. The reverse difference appears for the groups first mentioned. The V score has the property of increasing if both C and U are high. But it was highest at Henley.

There are significant correlations between components of these stylistic tests and other psychometric instruments (analogies, progressive matrices, AH5, and others), but the correlations are smaller. There are large correlations between the V, C, and U indices (between .53 and .70) and learning success on CASTE for the Henley group and one group of teacher training students.

Academic performance is harder to assess. The U score relates most strongly to academic success in biology and physical chemistry, but there is also predominance of this operation learning style among all academically successful students, some being also versatile (V) and having sensible, but not often high, C scores. Others have found significant correlations with task performance, especially in various aspects of computer programming, and problem solving, in both laboratory and real-life situations.

STYLISTIC TESTS AND LEARNING TO LEARN

It is useful to add that these stylistic tests have been employed not only in various psychometric, style-discriminatory studies, but also in the context of specific "learning-to-learn" studies. Various researchers have maintained the existence of a general skill of learning to learn which is open to acquisition by most people. Learning to learn novel material is closely related to innovation and probably to the versatility index. It is possessed by some people who are able to approach and to appreciate novel contingencies or subject matters and to make their own way. They are able, on the one hand, to adopt roles and make decisions as individuals or as leaders in a group and, on the other hand, to organize and assimilate a body of subject matter with minimal direction from outside. The skills required (generally called learning-to-learn skills) may even be manifest in a design or invention context, where to some extent such skills are mandatory; in scholarship, where they are desirable; or in an action-oriented situation.

Among other methods of promoting these general learning-to-learn decision skills, we have the possibility of administering stylistic tests to a group and then giving them feedback regarding their scores. After this group has engaged in the same learning experience (say, of "Spies" or of "Smugglers"), the resulting scores are offered as indices of difference, explaining roughly how they are derived. The differences pinpoint the distinct strategies employed by the participants, and they encourage free discussion of the relative advantages of each approach. At the end, a cued recall review of the discussion is conducted by the leader. Similar situations have been engineered using CASTE in more interesting contexts (such as the Team Decision System, discussed later) and others have employed more socially oriented techniques.

The immediate results, although difficult to quantify, have yielded positive but far from dramatic results, the most salient beneficial effects being a marginal improvement. A far more useful and convincing result is that greater than 20% of participants, commonly mature people who have often to act in real-world group or individual projects, return after intervals of 6 months to 1 year and often at considerable inconvenience to ask advice upon their specific projects. They say that they have "got the idea" of the training sessions and, further, "have used their acquired skill." In the studies conducted by my own group, consultancy of this type is always promised. This is not a typical laboratory result, but a practical and heartening finding which deserves record since it suggests that researchers and professionals must perhaps expect an interval of 6 months to 1 year's duration before their labors bear fruit.

THE ENIGMA OF STRATEGY AND STYLE

In academic learning or innovative training, it looks as though people do adopt one or other type of strategy as a personal style. The prediction is that P-Individuals (persons, separate mental organizations in one person, or organizations identifiable as a group of people) should do so, but at the actual person level, our results seemed to be unduly positive. This finding, noted previously, remains enigmatic.

Our conjecture is that the person-oriented correlation can be largely ascribed to institutional constraints. These constraints, especially for preuniversity science students, are imposed by examination techniques and the necessary serialization of tuition, a point confirmed by the dominantly serial bias in style for this category of students. A less-prominent but holistic bias pertains to architecture and art students evaluated by jury methods or cumulative assessment. The institution, viewed as a P-Individual, determines that academic success shall depend upon a certain, and for the most part, serial orientation, and it is hard to recommend practical means of alleviating this state of affairs, especially since institutions provide a significant social as well as academic utility. The pity is that effective learning is not optimized by an enforced mismatch of style, and that point is borne out by noting that other-than-academic pursuits (be they astrology or pop music) have often been learned in a matched but scholastically atypical manner.

In order to demonstrate that fixity to persons does not always occur, rather fixity to P-Individuals (including whole institutions), it proved necessary to examine occupations in which changes of perspective are essential constituents and to reanalyze much of the standard data.

A series of experiments was carried out under classroom conditions over four sessions in a high school setting. The students were matched for their "streaming" in class, their assessed academic ability, and their age. Each session lasted a double period of about $2\frac{1}{4}$ hours. The design was balanced with respect to the stylistic tests Spies and Smugglers. Of the four sessions, one was devoted to the administration of a stylistic test. The next session was devoted to a test battery including Raven's Advanced Progressive Matrices and the Lancaster Learning Inventory. The next was devoted to the stylistic test not used in the first experiment, and the last to a test battery of the AH5 test, the analogies test, and the Inventory of Learning Processes.

So far as this study is concerned, there were 53 students completing Spies in the first session and 74 completing Smugglers in the first session. Correlations exist between stylistic tests and versatility, comprehension, and operation learning indices (as well as the neutral index). The correlations ranged from .47 to .70.

Between versatility and the normalized product of operation and comprehension learning there is a correlation of .84, indicating that both dispositions are needed in order to be versatile. The intercorrelations of comprehension learning and operation learning are about .55, and intercorrelations between these and problem-solving test scores (notably Raven's Progressive Matrices and the AH5) are fairly high, between .40 and .60. Correlations between the Spies and Smugglers test gave satisfactory values between .54 and .77. In fact, this consistency of the person's strategic preference across tests (and subject matters) is curiously high, as I noted above.

Due to the experiences of other researchers, the data obtained from this experiment were reanalyzed. The crucial matter was one open-ended question asking for an illustrated story of what the respondent believed to have caused the thematic changes that occur and how their predictions are made.

Only some of the students furnished intelligible accounts, susceptible to reanalysis. Some provided pictorial augmentation. Forty-four student respondents did so, and these results were examined using a pair of impartial judges. The judges opted for classification as "analytic" (outside the system) and "involved" (inside the system, i.e., as an agent or smuggler or inhabitant of the countries described in the thematic test material). Each of these 44 intelligible story responses were analyzed and classified with virtually no disagreement and assigned to the category of "analytic" or "involved." Of these, 25 people did change perspective from one test (context) to the next, and 19 people did not do so. Among the 25 people who changed perspective between tests (acted as different P-Individuals in the different tests), the intercorrelations between tests were between .04 and .50, and for those 19 who did not change, intercorrelations were between .65 and .90. Thus, some learners were more sensitive to context and more versatile in approach than were other learners. McCarthy and Schmeck (Chapter 6, this volume) and Schmeck (Chapter 12, this volume) maintain that this suggests a difference in personality development.

Design appears to be an occupation in which success depends upon frequent changes of perspective, but our first experiments, in the design of electronic circuits, gave disappointing results. The fact was that optimal design is, under these circumstances, substantially predetermined by the relevant stylistic stereotypes.

However, architectural design, examined in a fairly informed way at the Architectural Association School of Architecture in London, is a different matter altogether. In order to compromise between informality, open-endedness, and controlled rigor, experiments were carried out upon the design of an intruder alarm system (several designs being submitted due to variations in the brief). In this context, there is no significant correlation between the interpolated Spies and Smugglers stylistic tests, so that it seems people do not adopt the same style or act as the same P-Individuals throughout this design process.

In addition, further evidence comes from studies using a Team Decision System (TDS) in which stylistic test indices are admirable predictors of an ability to plan (a prerequisite of complex decision making) but not of *using* plans under conditions of overload. The TDS merits attention since it is able, used as a computer-regulated interface, to exteriorize strategies of action, tactics, and planning strategies where responsibility is delegated.

The method involves one or more "commanders," each in charge of at least two "ships," or any commander of necessity delegating tactic responsibility for at least two ships. The tactics ordained are subsequently executed (the "ship" is an independent microprocessor operating in a further independent, environmental processor, and a tactic is a context-dependent program). The method used is a measure of complex decision making.

In these studies, planning ability is predictable from stylistic tests. In fact, for a sample of 19 subjects who undertook two or three missions each lasting between 3 and 4 hours, the versatility correlation with planning was .95, the operation score .91, and the comprehension score .56. These figures, obtained by quantifying tactic construction, are highly significant. But there is no significant correlation between style and the effective use of tactics. Readers interested in planning should also consult Das (Chapter 5, this volume).

GENERAL CONCLUSIONS

It seems evident that distinctive learning strategies exist. These may be derived from unfoldments (pathways) of canonical, evolving representations (maps of topics and their relations) of what may be known or rationally believed, that is, an entailment mesh. Given this tangible form of both subject matter and individual strategy, it is possible to make detailed comparisons of strategies, whether they are of learning (how to learn about a shared concept) or action (how to reach a goal).

There are also certain distinct styles, or dispositions to adopt classes of strategy. The original conversation theory prediction was that styles would be characteristic of specific P-Individuals or partly autonomous mental organizations. Later it seemed that styles belonged to specific people and applied to learning situations involving a great variety of distinct entailment mesh.

More recent and detailed analyses of the initial data also support the original hypotheses, especially that one person may be the residence of several coexisting P-Individuals (points of view, perspectives, frames of mind) or to use Laurillard's phrase "people in context." I would also argue (along with Ramsden, Chapter 7, this volume) that the institutional constraints of an institution-sized "P-Individual" are to be held responsible for the initially apparent person-fixity of conceptual and learning style, which seemed both counterintuitive (a designer, for example, must change point of view) and inherently counterproductive. However, I am still perplexed by the extent to which some individuals persist in using the same strategy across contexts. Some students appear, of sheer necessity, to be institutionally consigned to a mismatched and ineffective form of intuition, examination, and the like, insofar as their style does not match the serialist style of academic or training institutions. Also, some persons seem more flexible, versatile, and context-sensitive than do other persons.

REFERENCES

Braten, S. (1982). Simulation and self-organization of mind. *Contemporary philosophy: A new survey, 2,* 189–218.

Bruner, J. S. (1975). Beyond the information given. In N. J. Entwistle & D. Hounsell (Eds.), *How students learn.* Lancaster, England: Institute for Research and Development in Post-Compulsory Education.

de Gelder, B. N. F. (1981). Cognitive transactions. In G. E. Laster (Ed.), *Applied systems and cybernetics.* New York: Pergamon Press.

Kelly, G. A. (1955). *The psychology of personal constructs* (Vols. I and II). New York: Norton.

Laurillard, D. M. (1980). *Interactive computer simulations in undergraduate teaching.* Paper presented at the 2nd International Microcomputers in Education Congress, London.

Laurillard, D. M. (1981). Interactive computer simulations in undergraduate teaching. *Proceedings of the Second International Microcomputers in Education Congress.* London: Harvester.

Laurillard, D. M., & Marante, G. J. (1981). *A view of computer-assisted learning in the light of conversation theory.* England: Milton Keynes.

Lewis, B. N., & Pask, G. (1965). The theory and practice of adaptive teaching systems. In R. Glasser (Ed.), *Teaching machines and programmed learning (Vol. II).* Washington, DC: National Education Association.

Lewis, B. N., & Pask, G. (1965). The theory and practice of adaptive teaching systems. In R. Glasser (Ed.), *Teaching machines and programmed learning (Vol. II).* Washington, DC: National Education Association.

Lindstrom, B. (1983). *Learning styles and learning strategies: Conversation theory—the work of Gordon Pask.* Sweden: University of Goteborg Press.

Pask, G. (1961). *An approach to cybernetics.* London: Hutchinson.

Pask, G. (1970). The meaning of cybernetics in the behavioral sciences. In J. Rose (Ed.), *Progress of Cybernetics, Vol. 1* (pp. 15–45). London: Gordon and Breach.

Pask, G. (1972). A fresh look at cognition and the individual. *International Journal of Man–Machine Studies, 4,* 211–216.

Pask, G. (1975a). *Conversation, cognition and learning: A cybernetic theory and methodology.* Amsterdam: Elsevier.

Pask, G. (1975b). *The cybernetics of human learning and performance.* London: Hutchinson.

Pask, G. (1976a). Conversation techniques in the study and practice of education. *British Journal of Educational Psychology, 46,* 12–25

Pask, G. (1976b). Styles and strategies of learning. *British Journal of Educational Psychology, 46,* 128–148

Pask, G. (1976c). *Conversation theory: Applications in education and epistemology.* Amsterdam: Elsevier.

Pask, G. (1977). *Learning styles, educational strategies and representations of knowledge: Methods and applications: Progress report 3.* London: Social Science Research Council.

Pask, G. (1978). *Learning styles, educational strategies and representations of knowledge: Methods and applications: Progress report 5.* London: Social Science Research Council.

Pask, G. (1979). *Learning styles, educational strategies and representations of knowledge: Methods and applications: Final report.* London: Social Science Research Council.

Pask, G. (1983). *Knowledge and innovation of decision makers: Final technical report.* London: U.S. Army Research Institute.

Pask, G., Kallikourdis, D., & Scott, B. C. E. (1975). The representation of knowables. *International Journal of Man–Machine Studies, 17,* 15–134.

Pask, G., & Lewis, B. N. (1968). The use of a null point method to study the acquisition of simple and complex transformational skills. *British Journal of Mathematics and Statistics, 21* 61–84.

Pask, G., & Scott, B. C. E. (1971). Learning and teaching strategies in a transformation skill. *British Journal of Mathematics and Statistics, 24,* 205–229.

Pask, G., & Scott, B. C. E. (1972). Learning strategies and individual competence. *International Journal of Man–Machine Studies, 4,* 217–253.

Pask, G., & Scott, B. C. E. (1973). CASTE: A system for exhibiting learning strategies and regulating uncertainty. *International Journal of Man–Machine Studies, 5,* 17–52.

Schmeck, R. R. (1983). Learning styles of college students. In R. Dillon & R. Schmeck (Eds.), *Individual Differences in Cognition.* New York: Academic Press.

Shaw, M. L. G. (1980). *Epistemological hierarchies in knowledge and expert systems.* Unpublished report. York University, Department of Computer Science, Toronto.

CHAPTER 5

Simultaneous–Successive Processing and Planning
Implications for School Learning

J. P. DAS

INTRODUCTION: PROCESSES, STYLES, AND STRATEGIES

This chapter reviews research which examined the relationship between two types of information coding processes (simultaneous vs. successive) and performance on measures of reading, recall, comprehension, inferencing, and arithmetic. In addition, wherever possible, relationships between planning and these latter measures are also discussed. In general, this presentation is based on the assumption that a process approach is vastly superior to one based upon styles and strategies.

There is an unstated responsibility for justifying this chapter in a book entitled *Learning Styles and Learning Strategies*. Where does "processing" stand in relation to styles and strategies? These terms have arbitrary connotations when used out of any context. *Abilities, processes, styles and strategies* are perhaps difficult to distinguish for a speaker of English and may signify much erudition when they can be differentially defined by psychologists. Fortunately, Biggs and Schmeck provide help. *Learning style* is a predisposition to adopt a particular learning strategy. A *strategy* is a pattern of information processing activities which is used to prepare for an anticipated test of memory (Schmeck, 1983). We may

J. P. DAS • Developmental Disabilities Centre, 6-123D Education North, University of Alberta, Edmonton, Alberta T6G 2G5 , Canada.

ignore the requirement that a memory test must guide learning strategy. Otherwise, we may not be able to use a learning style for acquiring knowledge without the necessity of passing a memory test. However, we do accept the rest of the definition.

How then does cognitive style relate to learning style, and what is cognitive style anyway? Schmeck cites Messick, who defines *cognitive style* as a general, habitual mode of processing information. Learning styles then are simply cognitive styles applied when individuals go about learning something (Schmeck, 1983). These various definitions may be difficult to remember because they are a little arbitrary. One more definition, however, has to be considered, which has to do with *cognitive strategy*. It entails operations and procedures that an individual may use to acquire, retain, and retrieve different kinds of knowledge and performance (defined by Rigney and cited in Biggs, 1984). Since acquisition, storage, and retrieval are included in information processing, cognitive style and cognitive strategy as defined respectively by Messick and Rigney may appear to the readers to be one and the same, except that style is latent and strategy is manifest.

Some readers may still remain unconvinced about the distinction between style and strategy. They may ask if strategies are always clearly manifested and if these definitions serve a practical purpose? In the background of scepticism already generated, should I introduce the definition of "processes"? Simultaneous and successive coding and planning (defined below) are cognitive processes; the processing takes place in the brain, whose nature it is to continuously process information. The brain is an active and dynamic processor engaged in seeking and selecting information and integrating it in a routine or novel manner. The structure of the brain, and its functions, ensure that we use or ignore some strategies, follow entrenched routines or original courses of actions.

But there is no place for a homunculus in the brain. How can we ascribe a "style" to a person or seek out the familiar strategies which characterize a person? The closest one could come to a homunculus without compromising one's status as a scientific thinker is to propose an "image", as conceptualized by Miller, Galanter, and Pribram (1960). An *image* is the accumulated and organized knowledge that an individual has about itself and its world. I think image and knowledge-base are conceptually very close. Image is the identity of the person, an aggregate of his or her memories, knowledge. and experience, and a base for cognitive style and strategies—for characteristic as well as atypical ways in which information is processed. I believe that beyond these, that is, the processing of information and the carrying out of actions, the person has no separate cognitive identity.

A psychologist or teacher may need to sort people into different classes or categories such as holistic versus serialistic, synthetic versus analytic, and subsequently infer the accuracy of such classification by inferring the strategies from samples of a person's behavior. This is not the concern of a *process* approach, which is *understanding* behavior. The object is to understand how the person goes about learning to spell or decode words or solve mathematics problems. What are the processes that contribute to good spelling, for instance? Do these involve both simultaneous and successive processes or predominantly successive ones at an early stage of school learning and both at a later stage? Then, would damage to the part of the brain mostly responsible for successive processing interfere with spelling acquisition if the child is in early school years?

Styles and strategies, it seems, can be compared to images and plans. Image reflects the sum total of a person's knowledge and experience, memory, and proclivities (as style does). *Plans* refers to the execution of a set or series of actions. Both images and plans are responsive to task demands, but at the same time they exist separately from those demands. Thus, they are trans-situational. They have an enduring if not a permanent stability similar to attitudes. Solution of a task may depend both on an adequate image of the problem as well as on the accurate execution of the planned activity. Sometimes, the problem is not well understood, and at other times, the steps for solution are not followed properly. Both affect performance adversely.

But can this be said of cognitive style and strategies? It seems not, if we accept the definition given earlier that strategy is style expressed in performance. If strategies are like plans, then they cannot be the mere manifestation of style (or image). Whereas one provides the source for the other, strategies must have a life of their own if we view them as plans. Thus cognitive strategies can go wrong even though the performer has the cognitive style that would facilitate task solution. By the same token, strategies may not reflect style accurately, hence the inferences about a specific style from the measurement of strategies cannot be highly reliable. The two do not correlate perfectly.

Those are my thoughts for the day on styles and strategies. Now turning to simultaneous–successive processes and planning, we face the problem of measuring them and using those measures for understanding the processes which are required in school-related tasks, such as reading and arithmetic. Processes are to be inferred; they are hardly observed. And in fact there is a fair amount of inferencing in ordinary observation. We arrange the conditions of a task so that in order to do the task, most individuals in a certain culture, educational level, and age will require the use of one process or the other. Not the exclusive use but, relatively speaking, a predominant utilization of either of the two coding processes or plans. We describe coding and planning in the next section. But let it be said here that having found such tasks, we assume that those who perform well on them must be proficient in the specific coding or planning process, and those who do not are not so proficient. Hence we came dangerously close to regarding processing proficiency as an ability. It is an ability, for that matter, anything is, when we compare the performance of an individual to a norm. However, our interest remains in the process, in knowing what cognitive processes were used in solving the problem. Once such process measures are found, that is, once we have determined to our satisfaction that the task provides an occasion for the predominant use of one of the coding or planning processes, then we resort to correlational analysis, or better, look in school performance for correlates of performance in our cognitive tasks. Reading and arithmetic have been considered for this purpose.

The logic is not perfect and may appear to be unacceptable at first. But it is the same logic which has been used to determine the psychological functions of different parts of the brain. The classic evidence for the localization of receptive and expressive language was correlational in nature; the correlates of brain dysfunction and behavioral changes provide much of the knowledge in neuropsychology. True, the statistical method of correlations is not popular in neuropsychology, and syndrome analysis instead of factor analysis is frequently used to determine brain–behavior relations (Das, Kirby, & Jarman, 1979; Luria, 1966). The evidence is correlational nonetheless.

There is one possible difference. Often the correlations obtained in neuropsychological investigations are supported by evidence from neuroanatomical and neurophysiological relations. The close connection between failure to use attentional resources, for instance, in a visual search task and injuries to both the prefrontal area and the limbic system is justified by the existence of numerous neural connections between the two parts of the brain. Do we have similar behavioral evidence, while correlationg school-related skills on the one hand and cognitive processes on the other?

The answer is yes, we better have, otherwise the correlations would have little relevance for understanding school learning. The evidence, of course, is psychological and psychoeducational rather than neurological in nature. For instance, simultaneous processing contributes significantly to the variance in comprehension among children who have a good vocabulary, but successive processing does not (McLeod, 1978), as is discussed later in some detail. By analyzing the processes involved in comprehension, in terms of grasping the pattern of ideas in the text and relating these ideas to each other (the essential core of simultaneous processing), one could expect such a positive correlation. What follows is the presentation of a series of studies on reading and arithmetic and their relation to simultaneous–successive coding and planning. In each study we have attempted to show that the relationship is anticipated from existing literature. But before these are presented, the concepts of coding and planning in the information-integration model are briefly discussed. In planning, the individual uses information that has been coded simultaneously or successively. As is clear in the following section, coding and planning are interdependent. The decision to use one kind of coding rather than the other is a planning function, as is also the utilization of coded information.

THE INFORMATION-INTEGRATION MODEL

Because of its process orientation, Luria's working-brain model provides an ideal neuropsychological framework for developing a model by which to describe cognitive processes. It is not surprising, then, that the model of information integration (Das, 1972, 1973a, 1980; Das, et al., 1975, 1979) has as its roots Luria's (1966, 1970, 1973, 1980) theory about the working brain. Whereas the Luria model is quite specific for describing neuropsychological functioning, the information-integration model is more appropriate for describing cognitive processing. As such, although the model described below is dependent on Luria's neuropsychological concepts, it goes beyond neuropsychology to include psychological principles of information processing. Some may even accept this model of cognitive processes without its neuropsychological metaphor.

BASIC PRINCIPLES

We described four basic components of information integration. They are (a) sensory input, (b) a sensory register, (c) a central processing unit, and (d) behavioral output (Das, 1973a, b; Das, et al., 1975, 1979). The first component of the information-integration model is sensory input. Sensory input may be presented to any of the sensory receptors. This input may be presented in a parallel, simultaneous manner or in a sequential, successive manner. For example, a chord played on a piano represents an auditory stimulus presented in a simultaneous manner. Watching a jet stream form in the sky represents a visual stimulus presented in a successive manner.

The information then reaches the sensory register which acts essentially as a buffer; it receives sensory information in the form initially coded by the sensory receptors and transmits the information to the central processing unit. This transition occurs in a serial fashion regardless of the mode and manner of stimulus presentation. Not all information received by the sensory register, however, is automatically transmitted to the central processor. A complex interaction between states of arousal and attention, coding of information, and planning—Luria's three functional units—determines what information is transmitted by the sensory register to the central processing unit.

The central processing unit comprises two major components: (a) simultaneous and successive processes, and (b) planning and decision-making processes. In simultaneous processing, separate units of information are synthesized into quasi-spatial, relational organization. Successive processes synthesize separate units of information into a temporally organized sequence. Planning includes a variety of processes associated with the generation of plans or strategies, selection and execution of plans, as well as decision making and judgment.

The type of processing that occurs in the central processing unit is not affected by either the mode or manner in which the sensory information was originally received by the sensory receptor. For example, a chord may be processed as a simultaneous set of notes, or it may be processed as a sequential series of segregated tones. Similarly, a jet stream may be processed sequentially in terms of a temporal series of events, or it may be processed simultaneously in terms of the relationship between the location of the stream and other points in the sky.

The actual type of information processing which is selected depends upon (a) the individual's preferred mode of processing (which is influenced by an individual's experience, sociocultural and genetic factors), (b) the task demands, and (c) the interaction between preferred mode and task demands. The first of these conditions may reflect a well-established habit. For example, a child who has memorized his or her addition facts using a number table may process a verbally presented addition problem simultaneously, examining a mnemonic number table and selecting the correct answer. A child who has learned addition facts through flashcard practice may, on the other hand, process the same addition problem sequentially, sorting through serially ordered memory traces for the correct problem and answer. Each child, when presented with the same addition problem printed on a worksheet containing a number line, may process the problem sequentially, using the number line to manually add the numbers.

The final component of the information-integration model is responsible for behavioral output. The output unit determines and organizes cognitive or motoric behavior as a function of task demands and planning processes. Output can be simultaneous or successive in nature and is independent of both input mode and manner of presentation and of manner of processing. For example. recalling a series of words according to semantic categories requires simultaneous processing at output, even though the words were presented successively and may have been processed successively. On the other hand, recalling the same list in correct serial order requires successive processing at output.

Research methods used with the information-integration model have been of two types, namely, confirmatory factor analysis to identify marker tests and experimental analysis of groups of individuals differing in terms of their processing skills. The early studies have mainly employed factor analytic techniques in order to verify the model and distinguish simultaneous, successive, and planning processes; more recent research has been concerned with detailing the interactions between different modes of processing and various cognitive behaviors relating to a variety of abilities, such as language, reading, writing, and arithmetic, which are discussed later.

The factor analytic method (see Das, 1973a;, Das *et al.*, 1975) was used initially to evaluate the information-integration model as distinct from, but complementary to, Luria's method of "syndrome analysis" (Luria & Artem'eva, 1970). Luria identified simultaneous and successive modes of processing on the basis of in-depth clinical assessment of a small number of individuals exhibiting behavioral symptoms characteristic of various brain lesions. Luria used tests that appear, theoretically, to have similar task demands. Similarities in performance across these tests were used to diagnose a deficient cognitive process or identify individual differences in processing.

In contrast, my students, colleagues, and I have identified simultaneous and successive modes of information processing and planning processes on the basis of factor analytic comparisons of the performance of a relatively large number of individuals drawn from a variety of populations, including normal and mentally retarded children and adults and various cultural and ethnic groups. Individual differences in performance across the tests were used, through factor analysis, to confirm the theoretically defined cognitive processes. Thus, whereas the clinical method uses individual differences to determine some deficit in cognitive processing, the factor analytic method uses individual differences to determine the reliable existence of some form of cognitive processing. The factor analytic studies of performance on various tests of simultaneous and successive processing across age, IQ, and different cultural groups have been reviewed in detail. The interested reader is referred to Das (1984a), for reviews of the factor analytic research pertaining to simultaneous–successive processes and to Das (1980, 1984b), for research on planning.

Knowledge-base was not explicitly mentioned in the original 1975

model. Perhaps this component does not have direct neuropsychological roots as do the coding and planning components of the model.
Although Luria's writings on the three functional divisions of the brain
(Luria, 1966, 1970) do not explicitly mention knowledge-base, nevertheless, in clinical practice neuropsychologists take this into consideration. A simple arithmetic problem of the "if two apples costs x cents"
variety may not be a good test of planning behavior for an adult who
cannot read, because of a possible deficiency in knowledge-base.

Knowledge-base is required for the operations performed by a
human as well as a computer. But the human knowledge-base is not
quite the same as in a computer, although the term as popularized by
Hunt (1980) is derived from the computer. The sum total of a person's
experiences, habits, and predispositions, conscious or unconscious,
must make up the knowledge-base. In this sense, knowledge-base
should resemble image as conceptualized by Miller, Galanter, and Pribram (1960, p. 17): the accumulated, organized knowledge that the orga-
nism has about itself and its world. As suggested earlier, image is analogous to the concept of cognitive style. All information processing may
thus be influenced by knowledge-base. Hence, I suggest that this "new"
component of the model should be located between reception of information and central processing.

FOCUS ON READING AND RECALL

Kirby and Das (1977) report the results of our first study in which
reading achievement and simultaneous–successive processing were related. The orientation of this study was very much in the tradition of
aptitude–treatment interaction approach. Since, at that time, it was
important to consider Jensen's two hierarchical levels of mental abilities
(Levels I and II), which were memory and reasoning, we contrasted the
explanation of reading measurement in terms of simultaneous–successive processing to an explanation based on Level I and Level II
abilities.

In the Kirby and Das research on reading, subjects were Grade 4
students. The simultaneous and successive tasks were pretty typical as
measures of the two kinds of coding processes: Raven's Coloured Progressive Matrices, Figure Copying, and Memory for Designs were the
marker tests for eliciting simultaneous processing, whereas Serial Recall
of Words, Visual Short-Term Memory, and Digit Span were the measures of successive processing.

Factor analysis of these tasks lead to two clear factors labeled as
simultaneous and successive. Factor scores were then derived for each

subject. Subjects were then divided into four contrasting groups by splitting the scores at the median. Those above were "high," those below were "low." The high-simultaneous, high-successive group had both scores above both medians, as did the high-simultaneous, low-successive group; low-simultaneous, high-successive and low-simultaneous, low-successive groups were formed. This standard procedure has been adopted in several studies following the Kirby and Das paper.

Reading vocabulary and reading comprehension scores were then analyzed for these four groups. The analysis of variance clearly showed that reading achievement, as measured by vocabulary as well as by comprehension, had significant main effects for each of the coding processes. Those subjects who were high on both modes of processing scored the highest on vocabulary and on comprehension, whereas those who were below median or low in both modes of processing scored the lowest. Those high in one coding process but low in the other had scores in between those two extreme groups. We concluded that the study not only revealed the importance of both modes of information processing for reading skills but also had implications for training. This study provided a direction for training, inasmuch as training in either form of processing, if successful, should increase the level of reading achievement.

The significance of the study for an aptitude–treatment interaction model was clear. We suggested that these modes of processing should prove suitable as aptitude variables. Since the two aptitudes, simultaneous and successive, are nonhierarchically related, that is, one is not superior to the other, educational programs which are designed to match aptitude to treatment should produce normal levels of achievement. If the two were hierarchical, like rote memory and reasoning, educational programming, which is based on memory, would result in a lower level of achievement.

Our concern for training, for compensatory programs, is thus closely linked with the objectives of our correlational studies. We have indeed constructed remedial tasks, which are rationally derived from the research on cognitive processes, and used them successfully to improve reading and, in some cases, arithmetic (see Das, Kirby, & Jarman, 1979).

FURTHER STUDIES ON CODING PROCESSES

The role of simultaneous and successive processing in reading and other linguistic functions, however, may vary between groups of subjects who are at different developmental levels. For instance, successive processing may be relatively more important for the mastery of initial decoding skills, although simultaneous processing is still needed. But for subjects who are at higher levels of fluent reading, simultaneous processing may be somewhat more relevant than successive processing (Cummins & Das, 1977). This becomes clear by considering the populations of mentally retarded and reading-disabled children. As shown in one of our experiments (Cummins & Das, 1977) on educatable mentally retarded children, simultaneous and successive factor scores, derived from the marker tests for these processes, were correlated with spelling, arithmetic, and oral reading subtests of the Wide Range Achievement Test. It was observed that successive-processing factor scores correlated significantly with oral reading and spelling subtests, while simultaneous processing was significantly related to arithmetic. The importance of successive-processing strategies for the development of decoding skills in the retarded children was recognized. We concluded that low levels of successive processing may be a limiting factor in the reading achievement of disabled readers.

Following Luria (1966), we acknowledge the importance of simultaneous processing for the discovery of conceptual relationships between objects and events, and obviously this process is expected to be involved at more advanced stages of reading. Do we have data to suggest this?

We reported another study (Cummins & Das, 1978) on normal Grade 3 students using the same median split procedure as described in the previous report. Subjects were divided into four groups on simultaneous and successive factor scores, and their decoding and comprehension scores were then compared. The analysis of variance showed significant main effects for simultaneous processing in both decoding and comprehension. The results were, so far, similar to those obtained for vocabulary and comprehension in the Kirby and Das (1977) study. However, the main effect for successive processing was not significant for any of the reading scores.

In order to investigate the suggested hypothesis that simultaneous processing is especially important at more-advanced stages of reading and successive, at least-proficient stages of reading, we examined the correlations between simultaneous and successive processes and comprehension scores for those subjects who were in the top and bottom half of each distribution. Despite the reduced variance in comprehension scores, simultaneous processing correlated significantly with comprehension in the top half, but not the bottom half, of the distribution. The decoding results were different. When the decoding distribution was similarly divided into top and bottom halves, the relationship between decoding and simultaneous processing was not found. From this, it can be concluded that simultaneous processing may be necessary for the development of a more-advanced level of comprehension skills.

The fact that in the present study, successive processing related less to reading performance than in the previous Kirby and Das (1977) study, may be due to the different criterion measures of reading which were employed by the school systems involved in the two studies. Alternatively, we can explain it in terms of IQ: the sample used by Cummins and Das (1978) had a higher mean IQ than the sample in the Kirby and Das study.

In summary, what emerges from the study reviewed by Cummins and Das (1978) is that among children who are likely to experience difficulty in reading, competence in successive processing is critical for reading achievement. However, among normal readers, at more-advanced levels of reading skills, simultaneous processing is equally, if not more, important in the reading process.

READING AND PLANNING FACTOR

The relationships between the cognitive processing variables and reading were further analysed, with particular emphasis on individual and group differences in planning, in a study by Das, Snart and Mulcahy (1982). In this research, three planning tasks were included along with simultaneous and successive tasks. The children were from Grades 4 and 5. From each of these grades, 30 normal readers and 15 reading-disabled children were tested. Grade 6 reading-disabled children were reading at the level of Grade 4 normal children, and the Grade 4 disabled readers were at Grade 2 reading level. Thus, there are four groups of children: Grades 4 and 6 normal readers and Grade 6 retarded readers, who are reading at Grade 4 level, and Grade 4 retarded readers, who are reading at Grade 2 level. All the children were given the marker tasks for simultaneous and successive processing as well as the planning tasks. Since the planning tasks have not been described before, I provide a brief account of them here.

The tasks were Trail Making, Visual Search, and Planned Composition. Trail Making is part of the Halstead–Reitan Battery, which has been used as a neurological screening test mostly for detecting frontal lobe dysfunctions. In the study, numbers were arranged from 1 to 16 or 1 to 25, scattered over a page. The subject's task was to draw a continuous straight line joining consecutive numbers, such as 1 to 2 to 3, and so forth. In a variation of the test, which was not used here, the numbers and letters of the alphabet are mixed together so that the subject is asked to join 1 to A to 2 to B to 3 to C, and so on.

The Visual Search task, like Trail Making, has been used as a test of frontal lobe dysfunction. In our studies, which used Visual Search, we had provided overhead transparencies which were viewed through a special apparatus. Each transparency had a field of figures, numbers, or letters, and the subjects were requested to find an instance of a target item which might be a number, figure, or letter. Two time scores were recorded. The first was the search time, which was the time taken by the subject to locate the target; the second was the execution, or movement, time, which was the reaction time to hit the target once it had been located.

Planned Composition has also been used as one of the marker tasks of planning. In this task the subject is asked to write a story after seeing a picture card. We have consistently used card number 2 of the Thematic Apperception Test (TAT). The subject's story is scored by averaging the rating of at least two teachers at the subject's school grade level. The criteria for rating include organization, expression, and individuality. The raters give a score between 1 and 7 to indicate their evaluation of the story, ranging from good to poor in each of the criteria.

Syllogistic Reasoning was the other planning task. We have used it previously as a measure of planning and have shown that it loads on the same factor as Trail Making, Visual Search, and Planned Composition (Das & Heemsbergen, 1983). The critical score in syllogistic Reasoning is not accuracy but the total time to solve a set of syllogisms which require the same strategy. For example, the syllogisms could be in the following form: John is taller than Bob, Bob is taller than Dick; conclusion, John is taller than Dick, true or false. A set of eight of these are given and the total time taken to solve them is recorded. In the next set the format of the syllogisms is changed: Dan is shorter than Jim, Mark is taller than Jim; conclusion, Dan is shorter than Mark, true or false. The idea here is to see if the subjects catch on to the strategy after they have gone through the first few syllogisms in the set. The sooner the subjects pick up on a strategy to solve the syllogisms in the set, the shorter the time to solve them.

Reading scores were obtained for both good and poor readers. Therefore, it was interesting to investigate the pssibility of qualitative and quantitative differences between groups which varied on reading competence, for instance, between the poor readers in Grade 6, who were equated in reading level to good readers in Grade 4.

The results of the Das and Snart (1982) study are very clear. All of the tasks—the two coding tasks and four planning tasks—could discriminate between the normal readers in Grades 4 and 6; the older children were superior to the younger ones. The normal readers, taken together, were also superior to the reading-disabled children, who were of the same chronological age as the normal readers. We tried to argue that since the tests contained both verbal and nonverbal tasks, as well as those which had a memory component and those which did not, the usual ability differences (verbal vs. nonverbal, memory vs. nonmemory) would not account for the results. In summary then, the analysis of the results demonstrated that the reading-disabled groups were poorer in planning tasks as well as in coding tasks.

The next question we asked of the data was as follows: Do the reading disabled differ from normal readers because of some unknown qualitative difference that may exist between the two groups, or is the ability difference in reading coexistent with individual differences in the coding and planning tasks? In other words, among the normal readers, do we find that ability differences in reading correlate with the subjects' scores in the various coding and planning tasks? Fortunately, we had obtained from school records decoding and comprehension scores for the normal readers. Decoding showed a significant correlation with Serial Recall, which was a marker test for successive processing, as well as with Planned Composition, a marker test for planning.

The Grade 6 results showed significant correlations of decoding with both Serial Recall and Figure Copying (a simultaneous-processing marker) as well as Planned Composition. Comprehension, on the other hand, did not correlate with Serial Recall in either of the two grades. Instead, in both Grades 4 and 6, significant correlations were obtained between comprehension, on the one hand, and Figure Copying as well as Planned Composition, on the other.

Thus, the results of the Das and Snart (1982) research in relation to decoding and comprehension support the conclusions from previous research by Cummins and Das (1977, 1978) in as much as we showed that (a) decoding at the lower grade may require successive processing, and (b) comprehension in any grade would require simultaneous processing. However, if the results can be replicated, we have to entertain the possibility that decoding, even at a higher grade, may also need simultaneous processing (because of the correlation obtained between Figure Copying and decoding in Grade 6). The relations among planning, decoding, and comprehension cannot be clearly interpreted because the only planning task that showed a significant correlation with either measure of reading ability was Planned Composition. Obviously, some common skills are shared between reading abilities and composition. The relationship we obtained cannot be regarded as providing unequivocal support for a planning component in decoding and comprehension.

It is not economical to explain reading, specifically word attack skills, by attributing it to either verbal ability or memory ability, as shown in the preceding research. Instead, in the next study we show that the coding and planning processes can be meaningfully related to individual differences in word reading (Das. Bisanz, & Mancini, 1984).

Average and backward readers from Grades 2, 4, and 6 were examined in this study for their performance on five cognitive tasks. The marker task for successive processing was Digit Span; for simultaneous processing, Memory for Designs; and for planning, Trail Making. In addition to these, we had also given the subjects a short-term memory test for confusable and nonconfusable consonant lists (consonants H, K, L, Q, R, S, W were used to construct lists for nonconfusable and B, C, D, G, P, T, V for the confusable material). The confusable and nonconfusable consonants were presented one at a time, every second, like the Digit Span test, starting with three items and going up to seven. Thus the tests were constructed as letter span tests for nonrhyming and rhyming letters.

Difference in the subject's performance as a function of reading competence within the same age and grade was examined. We had three hierarchical groups of Grade 4 children: average readers, a reading-disabled group which was 2 years behind the average readers, and a superior reading group which was 2 years ahead of average Grade 4 readers. A general increment was noted in all of the three span tasks; the reading disabled were the lowest, and the superior readers were the highest in Digit Span, Confusable Letter Span, and Nonconfusable Letter Span.

In a further analysis we wanted to compare the effect of reading competence on each one of the five tasks. On the basis of competence, the subjects were divided into two groups as follows: the Grade 2 normal readers and Grade 4 disabled readers, who were reading at the Grade 2 level, were combined; this group was contrasted to Grade 4 normal readers and Grade 6 disabled readers, who were reading at Grade 4 level. The contrasted groups, therefore, were 2 years apart in reading. The analysis of variance clearly showed the main effect for reading level for each one of the five tasks. It seems, then, that reading performance in a simple word recognition task, such as Schonell, is related to cognitive processes represented by simultaneous, successive, and planning tasks.

COMPREHENSION AND INFERENCING

In the next two studies, the focus was on different aspects of reading. A new feature of research in the first (McLeod, 1978) was to explore the generation of forward-looking and backward-looking inferences as they related to simultaneous and successive processing. McLeod also examined comprehension in relation to simultaneous and successive processing. The two types of inference had been proposed by Schank (1975) and are defined as follows. A *backward-looking inference* is required to establish the framework for each input conceptualization for which the necessary conditions have not been explicitly provided. In contrast, a *forward-looking inference* is a state that can be inferred from established conditions based on input conceptualization. The two concepts are discussed in relation to the role of the sentence within a paragraph, which is thought of as "tying of information" and setting the stage for the next sentence to follow.

In order to get backward- and forward-looking inferences, the subject is typically given a story to read and then asked to answer five forward-looking inference questions and five backward-looking ones. For example, the story "Scotty Becomes a Hero" was read by the child. Scotty was a pet dog who usually barked when there was a reason. One night he was barking too much in the middle of the night, and even though the father in the house asked him to be quiet, he did not listen. In fact, Scotty was warning the family about smoke in the house; so father, mother, and kids woke up and hurried out along with Scotty— the house was on fire.

The forward-looking inference question was, "Why did father not pay attention to Scotty's barking at first?" A backward-looking inference question was, "How did father feel towards Scotty at the beginning of the story?"

In terms of coding processes the children were divided into high-simultaneous–high-successive, high–low, low–high, and low–low groups as in the original Kirby and Das (1977) study. The answers to the comprehension questions were coded in terms of whether or not they were supported by the text of the story and also in terms of the type of inferencing. It was found that the high-simultaneous groups, irrespective of their status in successive processing, produced significantly higher numbers of inferencings supported by the text. In other words, both the high-simultaneous–high-successive and the high-simultaneous–low-successive groups significantly related their inferences to the textual-based information. In regard to the proportion of forward- versus backward-looking inference, no differences were observed between the four groups. High-simultaneous groups just produced more inferences.

In general reading proficiency, as measured by comprehension, the main effect for simultaneous processing came out to be highly significant, whereas successive processing was not found to contribute to reading comprehension. This was in variance with the Kirby and Das study. But consider that in the present research, all children had a vocabulary above the 70th percentile. Thus, reading comprehension was not limited by low vocabulary. It seems, then, that insofar as children with an adequate vocabulary are concerned, a significant difference exists between very proficient and less-proficient readers in terms of simultaneous processing.

Following up on both Kirby and Das (1977), and McLeod's (1978) findings that simultaneous and successive processes are involved in reading, Ramey (1985) included planning as the additional variable in a study on reading. In the first phase of his research, he gave junior high school boys and girls tests of simultaneous and successive processing (Progressive Matrices, Memory for Designs, and Figure Copying for simultaneous, and Digit Span and Serial Recall for successive) as well as Visual Search and Trail Making as planning measures. The reading test comprised vocabulary, and scores on level and speed of comprehension.

Factor analysis showed a strong reading factor; the three reading scores had high loadings on this factor. Both Progressive Matrices and Digit Span had substantial loadings on this factor too; the first, a marker test for simultaneous and the second for successive. For further analyses, the subjects were divided into high and low groups in reference to the median as before, except that planning was included. This resulted in eight groups. These groups were then compared on vocabulary and comprehension scores. It turns out that the main effects of both simultaneous and successive processing were significant for all three reading scores. But some unexpected results were also observed: the successive-processing main effect was significant for speed of comprehension, but neither simultaneous processing nor planning were. The level of comprehension scores, when analyzed, showed significant effects for simultaneous processing, as expected from previous studies, but planning, and not successive processing, also emerged as a variable which influenced comprehension. The implications for speed of comprehension are not clear except to state the obvious: good successive processing contributes to speed but is rather unimportant for level of comprehension among junior high students.

A subset of the sample was then identified as the top 15 "planners" and bottom 15 "planners" on the basis of their scores on Visual Search. (In an earlier study by Das & Heemsbergen, 1983, this test was also used to pick out top and bottom planners, and the results validated the selection by showing that the top planners were much better than bottom planners at a game involving hypothesis testing.) Do the top and bottom planners differ in intelligence? They do not, as the performance on the planning task was unrelated to Progressive Matrices, which is often used as an intelligence test. We do not think that the differences in various reading tasks can be discounted by invoking intelligence differences between top and bottom planners.

These subjects were tested 3 years later. Our main interest for this chapter is in their reading performance. The reading tests Ramey (1985) used were quite extensive—nine passages were read by each subject (by now, at least 17 years old and out of school), and the passages were of the narrative–emotive, expository/informative, and propositional–persuasive types; three of each type were read and recalled.

After a 3-year interval, 13 top planners and only 7 bottom planners could be located. The biographical data on the top planners showed successful adjustment to adult life; for the 7 bottom planners who could be traced, most had unsuccessful records.

The nine passages were read by these subjects silently and then were recalled; the recall was tape-recorded and later analyzed into the number of T-units, the "minimal" terminable units (Hunt, 1970). The *T-unit* is the shortest unit that is allowed grammatically to be punctuated as a sentence; a complex sentence may have two or more T-units or clauses which have pauses at their ends. Other types of responses, including number of inferences, were also noted in the analysis of the recorded variable (based on Visual Search). The top planners (high-planning–high-successive–high-simultaneous and high-planning–low-successive–high-simultaneous subjects were combined to give large enough numbers) were compared and contrasted to bottom planners (for large enough numbers, low-planning–low-successive–low-simultaneous and low-planning–high-successive–low-simultaneous subjects were combined). The results were as follows:

Top planners	*Bottom planners*
—had more T-units	—had fewer T-units
—made more inferential statements	—made fewer inferential statements
—questioned and evaluated the responses they made	—did not question or evaluate their responses
—tended to encapsulate the author's message in the text	—tended to be impulsive and easily frustrated (used expletives)
—were likley to modify the hypothesis	—stuck to incorrect hunches

Such qualitative analyses suggest that it will be profitable to carry out studies to examine the unique styles of high and low planners in learning and recall of text (Ramey, 1985). The Ramey dissertation distinctly ascribes an important role to planning in complex reading-related skills. In this regard, it is consistent with Das and Cummins' (1982) conclusion from another research project, which compared normal readers with disabled readers in elementary schools:

> The matter can be looked at broadly as a weakness in control processes . . . the RD [reading disabled] children had adequate vocabulary and comprehension . . . and coding skills, but they apparently need to adopt efficient strategies for utilizing these optimally. (p. 20)

No planning measures were included in the above study; one wishes they had been.

Kirby's research on reading has continued in Australia (see Kirby 1980; and Chapter 9, this volume). Two research projects supervised by him are reviewed here.

Comprehension was the focus of the study by Gordon (1982), who gave three kinds of passages to children from Grades 3 to 6. The passages were given either in a normal canonical format, or their presentation was altered by giving the passages in a mixed-up form—one word at a time, in inappropriate chunks, or in chunks that obeyed the rules of syntax. The children were also given two simultaneous-processing tasks (Raven's Coloured Progressive Matrices and Figure Copying) and two successive-processing tasks (Digit Span and Sentence Repetition). The groups were further divided into good, average, or poor on comprehension.

A multifactorial analysis of variance was then performed which yielded many significant and interesting results. As in previous studies, both simultaneous- and successive-processing factor scores contributed to the variance in comprehension; significant main effects were found for simultaneous and successive scores, indicating that the high-simultaneous group scored higher on the reading comprehension task than the low-simultaneous group, and likewise, the high-successive processors were better than the low. Did simultaneous processing have a closer relationship with comprehension than successive processing, as might be expected from previous research?

As reported by McLeod (1978), simultaneous processing did predict comprehension, and successive processing did not—but his subjects were fairly good in vocabulary. In Gordon's (1982) research, vocabulary was not considered. In light of this difference between the two studies, let us examine the analysis by Gordon. The significant interaction between simultaneous and successive processing showed that subjects who were high on both performed at a much higher level in the reading comprehension test than those who were low on either one of these processes or low on both, regardless of the manner of text presentation.

It seems, then, that no special relationship between simultaneous processing and comprehension was supported by the results, with both processes being important for comprehension. An examination of the correlation between reading comprehension for the normal text and simultaneous- and successive-processing factor scores across Grades 3, 4, 5, and 6 confirmed the results of analysis of variance. It was observed that for Grade 3 children, neither of the two coding processes could predict comprehension, but for Grades 4, 5, and 6, the correlation between comprehension and simultaneous or successive factor scores was significant (Gordon, 1982). Did the type of text presentation (canonical, word-by-word, inappropriate, or appropriate chunks) interact with simultaneous and successive processing? It did; children who were high-simultaneous but low successive processors performed better when the text was presented one word at a time but did poorly in the two-chunking conditions. The other three processing groups did better in the chunking conditions than in single-word presentations. The implications of the above results are not clear.

The next study from Kirby's group (Robinson, 1983) essentially tested the hypothesis that simultaneous processing is more important for semantic skills and successive processing for phonic and syntactical skills. The subjects were reading-disabled children, whose ages were between 7 and 15 years. On the basis of previous discussion and review in this chapter, it is reasonable to expect that a differential emphasis on successive processing for the acquisition of syntactic skills can be justiied. In clinical cases, Luria (1973, 1980) had observed that if a patient had difficulties in appreciating the rules that relate to how words are arranged sequentially into sentences, he or she had injuries that produced a dysfunction in successive processing. Our own research (Cummins & Das, 1978) may also support such a view, since we had found that lexical ambiguity ("He hit the girl with glasses"—eyeglasses or tumblers) was related to simultaneous processing, whereas the surface and deep structure syntactical ambiguities ("Flying planes can be dangerous"), related to successive processing. In a review article, we also discussed the association of successive processing with receptive and expressive syntactical skills (Das, Cummins, Kirby, & Jarman, 1979).

The results of the Robinson (1983) study are summarized. Simultaneous processing in this study was found to be associated with semantic aspects of language, as observed in language miscue analysis, language comprehension, and language expression. Successive processing was associated with the sequential analysis of language patterns as measured by language miscue analysis. Simultaneous processing was associated with prediction of language patterns in print and with the ability to recognize the meaning of whole words. Successive processing, however, was not associated with any reading-process factors. Thus, successive processing was involved in language miscue, and simultaneous processing contributed to reading miscue.

The shift from successive to simultaneous processing was explained by suggesting that lack of reading fluency of the reading-disabled subjects in his study made the indentification of sequential language patterns in print very difficult. It is, of course, unfortunate that Robinson did not have results from a group of normal readers to compare to the results for the learning disabled.

Reading achievement in the Robinson study was associated with simultaneous processing but not successive. Robinson explains this by stating that the results confirm the predisposition of the learning-disabled subjects in his study towards a simultaneous mode of processing; the reading-disabled subjects prefer to use simultaneous proecessing even when successive would be the more appropriate process.

The Robinson study dealt with quite complex variables in reading and language. Therefore, the relationship among those variables and simultaneous versus successive processing is not as straightforward as might be expected if the reading and language measures were simpler. To give an example of the complexity of relationships, the factor analysis of all the cognitive processing tasks and language and reading tasks showed that reading-disabled children used a more global, or simultaneous, strategy at early reading levels. This was supported further by dividing the subjects into reading age below and above 8 years and noticing that the more competent readers had a pattern of factor loadings which we expected because of results from previous studies. That is, the simultaneous and successive tasks had clearly higher loadings on the simultaneous and successive factors respectively. However, for the less-competent readers, two successive tasks had loadings on a simultaneous factor, reflecting a previous disposition among the learning-disabled children of low reading age towards a less-optimal global strategy of processing. We had noticed before (Krywaniuk & Das, 1976) that for the less-efficient readers, simultaneous and successive factor structures were not clear, and in fact, there was a mix-up of factor loadings, which was corrected following remedial training given to the subjects.

In a nutshell, the contribution of the Robinson (1983) study to our discussion is as follows: Reading-disabled children seem to be using simultaneous modes of processing at the expense of more optimal successive modes for early levels of reading skills, which mostly involve decoding. The observation is consistent with what we had found before in our own research.

FOCUS ON ARITHMETIC

Logico-mathematical and spatial are among the six intelligences proposed by Gardner (1983) in his influential book *Frames of Mind*. The logical and mathematical abilities are also considered to be one and the same by Piaget. Gardner agrees with Piaget, and gives this combined ability the status of a unique intelligence. He strengthens this further by reviewing the writings of some mathematicians, as for example, of Bertrand Russell who made the quotable statement: Logic is the youth of mathematics and mathematics is the manhood of logic. Luria's (1966, 1973) findings are not out of line with the hypothesized close relationship between logic and mathematics because the underlying process for both is simultaneous; any dysfunction of the parietal–occipital area disturbs logico-grammatical as well as mathematical abilities.

SIMULTANEOUS PROCESSING AND PIAGET'S TASKS

Following Luria's neuropsychological work, both logico-mathematical and spatial abilities should share the same underlying coding process, which is simultaneous processing. The occipital–parietal region is the appropriate functional unit for both of these abilities. Hence from the point of view of the information-integration model, we would consider the two abilities to share the same general process. Given below, first, is a discussion of the evidence relating Piagetian tasks—which may be regarded as requiring both logico-mathematical and spatial abilities— to measures of simultaneous processing. Then a direct relationship between arithmetic achievement and simultaneous processing is supported by some studies which are reviewed. Arithmetic achievement has two identifiable parts—ability to solve problems and computational ability. Some evidence is presented which links the first to simultaneous processing and the second to planning and executive functions.

Piagetian tasks such as class inclusion and transitive inference at the concrete operational stage may provide the best instances of measures of logico-mathematical operations in young children. How do these relate to simultaneous processing? Let us first look at the relationship between simultaneous and successive coding processes, and Piagetian tasks at the concrete operation level.

In two different projects, one in Canada and one in India, firm relationships between these tasks and simultaneous processing have emerged (Mwamwenda, Dash, & Das, 1985). The Canadian samples were in kindergarten to Grade 2; the Indian children were in kindergarten to Grade 5 classes. They were divided into the four groups of high-simultaneous–high-successive, high–low, low–high, and low–low, as in previous research. Analyses of variance were clear in showing simultaneous-processing main effects for both samples; the successive-processing effect was not significant at all.

How does one explain the basic operation in tasks, such as transitive inference and class inclusion, in order to demonstrate that common processes exist between logico-mathematical reasoning and these

Piagetian tasks? In *transitive inference*, for example, a simultaneous-processing strategy would enable children to look at objects symetrically rather than asymetrically. The children are able to examine each object in light of both direct and inverse relational operations, as conceptualized by Piaget. In other words, children are able to perceive that an object can be related to another object in more than one way at the same time. Similarly, in *class inclusion*, simultaneous processing should facilitate children to decompose classes from a superordinate level to a subordinate class, thereby indicating reversibility and mobility of thought. Such decompositions become possible because of the children's grasp of the relation between subclasses and their superordinate class. An understanding of part–whole relations becomes essential for the attainment of class inclusion concepts.

SIMULTANEOUS PROCESSING AND ARITHMETIC ACHIEVEMENT

As mentioned before, simultaneous processing is a major contributor to proficiency in arithmetic. We also expect that individual differences in successive processing will be at best a minor contributor.

The first study to be examined was conducted in Hong Kong on Chinese children who go to Western-style schoools. In this experiment (Leong, Cheng, & Das, 1984), we selected Raven's Progressive Matrices, Figure Copying, and Memory for Designs as the measures for simultaneous processing; Serial Recall, ITPA Auditory Memory, and Sentence Repetition, for successive; and Visual Search and Trail Making, for planning. The tests were given to Grade 4 and Grade 6 children.

Factor scores for simultaneous, successive, and planning processes were derived and used as predictors for standardized mathematics achievement. It was quite clear that the regression analysis showed simultaneous processing to be the best predictor of mathematics achievement. For example, in Grade 4 children the simultaneous component accounted for 16.7% of the variance, the successive component for only 5.7% of the variance, and planning for 2.5% of variance. The Grade 6 results were much more supportive of a special relationship between simultaneous processing and math achievement: the simultaneous component accounted for 18.6% out of a total variance of 21%. The other two components thus had negligible contributions to the prediction of math achievement (Leong, Cheng, & Das, 1985).

The next set of studies on simultaneous processing and arithmetic are taken from Kaufman and Kaufman (1983). Their measures for the two coding processes were different from the ones used by Leong, Cheng, and Das (1985). Thus the results are not entirely comparable to the previous study.

Kaufman and Kaufman (1983), in their interpretive manual, report correlations and factor loadings between their arithemtic achievement tests and the simultaneous and sequential tasks in their battery. Unfortunately, the correlational values given for arithemetic, reading decoding, and reading understanding do not seem to support the exclusive relationship between simultaneous processing and arithmetic achievement. For instance, the highest correlation on a group of 1,500 school-age children between arithmetic and simultaneous tasks is .55 (Photo Series), and the lowest is .35 (Gestalt Closure). Contrasting this to reading decoding, the correlations were .44 with Photo Series and .30 with Gestalt Closure. Then compare these to correlations with the sequential tasks. The highest one between arithemetic and Word Order, a sequential task, is .51, which is quite close to the correlation with the simultaneous task, Photo Series. Thus, it does not appear that the K-ABC simultaneous and sequential tasks are differentially related to arithmetic achievement. Decoding has previously been related more to successive (sequential) than to simultaneous processing, which seems to be true also in the case of K-ABC. The highest correlation between decoding and the K-ABC tasks is with Word Order (.53, a sequential task), compared to the best correlation with simultaneous tasks, which is .44 (Photo Series, triangles). These results are discussed again at the end of this section.

ARITHMETIC COMPUTATIONS AND PLANNING

Finally, I wish to present the results of a study done in Indiana by a researcher who has not been associated with our group. His study provides an independent examination of the relationship between the three processes and mathematics abilities (Garofalo, 1983). He used Raven's Progressive Matrices and Memory for Designs as target tasks for simultaneous processing, Digit Span and Serial Recall for successive, and Trail Making as well as the Wisconsin Card Sorting Task as measures of planning. Subjects were students in Grade 5. Factor analyzing the simultaneous, successive, and planning tasks, he found evidence for three clearly defined orthogonal factors. Then, he introduced math abilities test scores into the factor analysis, one at a time. The scores which have interest for us are on Problem Solving, which is the closest to mathematics achievement (Iowa test of basic skills), and Computation, a separate ability also measured by the Iowa test of basic skills. The factor loadings for these two abilities on the simultaneous, successive, and planning factors were as follows: Problem Solving had a loading of .51 on the simultaneous factor in contrast to .31 on successive and .28 on planning. The special relationship between simultaneous processing and solving mathematical problems is thus supported. Computation, on the other hand, had its highest loading on the planning factor (.56) and smaller loadings on simultaneous and successive factors (.34 and .22, respectively).

The researcher was looking at the old question of whether there is one arithmetic ability. In light of previous factor analytic studies which have found sometimes one and sometimes two abilities, Computation and Problem Solving, this research has certainly given a new interpretation to the old problem. Based on Garofalo's data, there appear to be two distinct processes which correspond to the two abilities.

A closer look at Garofalo's results suggests that whenever "math achievement" comprises arithmetic computation rather than problem solving, the ability can be predicted from scores on planning. It is thus important to separate computation from problem solving in order to understand each in terms of cognitive processes. In those studies in which arithmetic or math achievement tests include both components, as in K-ABC or in the standardized math test in Hong Kong, the size of the relationship between this achievement score and simultaneous or planning process will depend on the proportion of problem solving and computational skills required by the achievement test. In regard to K-ABC arithmetic achievement, the test questions contain many more questions on computation than on problems. This may be an important reason why the correlation between arithmetic and simultaneous tests were not high. The K-ABC does not provide a measure for planning; if it did, its relation to arithmetic computations could have been examined. But why was the correlation with successive processing significant at all? The K-ABC questions are read to the child, and thus there is the need to understand the succession of words as the child listens to the question. The correlation with successive (sequential) processing is thus expected.

Thus, a hypothesis has emerged for testing: if planning tests were given along with arithmetic computations, the two should yield a positive correlation. Computation requires the carrying out of calculations rather than understanding the logic of the problem. A study relating planning skills to math achievement (Kirby & Ashman, 1984) provides, I think, good support in favor of this hypothesis. In that research, Grade 5 children were given several tasks which were assumed to measure planning and a standardized Australian "operations" test, which was a test for arithmetic operations (add, subtract, multiply, divide). Factor analysis of the planning tasks yielded four factors; the one which had a correlation with arithmetic operations included Trail Making, Word Fluency, Matching Familiar Figures, and Mazes. These are the tests which have been used to measure planning in a previous study (Das, 1980). Incidentally, the other factors which did not show a significant correlation were defined by memory strategies such as rehearsal, clustering, and "metacognition" questions.

This study on planning and the previous one by Garofalo (1983) are certainly important in that they suggest a promising line of research for separating the two basic skills in mathematics achievement and then examining the processing requirements for each of those skills.

CONCLUDING REMARKS

This review suggests that abilities and processes can coexist. There are the well known primary mental abilities of Thurstone and the six intelligences proposed by Gardner (linguistic, musical, kinaesthetic, and personal, besides the two already mentioned, logico-mathematical and spatial). But abilities take us nowhere in establishing the diagnoses of cognitive difficulties which may then guide instructional and therapeutic interventions. Sometimes the assessment of abilities has been counterproductive. Consider the uses to which IQ tests have been put to segregate children of a low general intelligence. Largely because of such uses, we see the backlash and the total rejection of IQ tests in some quarters. Processes such as those in the information-integration model are recommended instead; both Biggs (1978) and Kirby (1980) have suggested that these processes would provide a preeminently superior basis for instructional designs. The aptitude–treatment interventions should benefit from a nonhierarchical diagnostic scheme of cognitive processing, such as ours, rather than a hierarchical written-in-stone typology of abilities.

We do not regard Gardner's to be one of the inflexible and immutable models of abilities. In fact, his reasons for choosing the six abilities to represent human cognitive functions are to a great extent based on neuropsychology, and so the reasons are the same as those for isolating the three functional blocks and their associated processes in the information-integration model derived from Luria. Perhaps, in our model, neuropsychological considerations play a major role, whereas both cultural and neuropsychological evidence are given equal weight by Gardner. Whatever may be the difference in orientations, the concepts of multiple abilities and processes are not mutually exclusive. Thus, in conclusion, it is suggested that abilities and processes are not incompatible; they coexist. Do the coding and planning processes coexist with cognitive styles and strategies?

The concepts of cognitive or learning styles and strategies have an unknown origin or, at least, undefined origins in comparison with the processes in the information-integration model and with Gardner's six abilities. But the manner in which these have been used by other authors in this book would suggest that the two concepts, style and strategy, together, are contained in the coding and planning processes. Further, the knowledge-base of the learner, toegther with his or her characteristic mode of processing information, determines proficiency in reading and arithmetic, as can be concluded from this review.

Process-related intervention has been tried successfully by me and my students (Brailsford, 1982; Kaufman, 1978; Krywaniuk, 1974) for improving performance in reading and arithmetic. The intervention program consists of training the coding and planning functions through selected tasks. For instance, the Matrix Numbers task is used for training in successive strategies. Children first look at five numbers arranged in a cross-pattern, then devise ways and means of remembering both the numbers and their spatial location on the matrix. The training program requires that they verbalize what they are doing and the reasons for their actions. The trainer or teacher discusses with the children several strategies for remembering the digits in order, and the child chooses the most appropriate one. Intentionality and purpose are thus brought to the foreground of training. Some remedial tasks are designed to train successive processing, while others are designed to improve simultaneous processing, and yet others lay equal emphasis on both coding processes. In all tasks, however, planning and organization are stressed.

In each of these previous studies in which the program has been tried out, the program produced the predicted improvement in successive and simultaneous processing. But, further, the effect of training was also carried over to performance in reading and arithmetic tests.

The intervention program emphasizes successive-processing training for children who have reading or decoding problems in early school years because of the dependence on successive processing for acquiring decoding skill; this was discussed earlier in the chapter. But simultaneous-process training as well as planning are not excluded from the program. Both of these obviously play a critical role in learning to read. Therefore, a strict separation of the two coding processes during training is not recommended.

Such procedures for process training could easily be accommodated in the framework of learning styles and strategies. The difference between the process and style approaches, however, lies in theoretical assumptions or their absence. One could easily proceed with training, in the case of a style and strategy approach, from a task-analytical scheme, which is devoid of theoretical underpinings. In fact, these theoretical ghosts accompanying processes could be considered by some as weighty baggage which interferes with the smooth movements of the mechanical steps of a task-analysis procedure.

But the question is, have we made significant progress in instructing the learning disabled, the poor performer in decoding or comprehension, or the inept essay writers among college students by following intervention programs within the context of atheoretical, antiprocess procedures? Given the best possible instructions available in schools and special reading–writing clinics in colleges, we may have improved the knowledge-base; but have we actually remedied the deficiencies so that the poor reader or writer, of equivalent IQ to his or her competent counterpart, can leave the crutches offered in the training program and walk independently in new terrains?

I leave the reader with the argument that the cognitive process approach is to be prefered, as proposed in this chapter, because it does three things: (a) enhances understanding of learned skills, such as reading and mathematics; (b) guides a rationally derived training procedure for removing difficulties which are experienced in learning; and (c) ensures transfer of learing, thus promoting broad generalizations (see, Das, 1985).

REFERENCES

Biggs, J. B. (1978). Genetics and education: An alternative to Jensenism. *Educational Research, 7*, 11–17.

Biggs, J. B. (1984). Learning strategies, student motivation patterns, and subjectively perceived success. In J. Kirby (Ed.), *Cognitive strategies and educational performance* (pp. 111–134). New York: Academic Press.

Brailsford, A. (1982). *The relationship between cognitive strategy training and performance on tasks of reading comprehension with a learning disabled group of children.* Unpublished master's thesis, University of Alberta, Department of Educational Psychology, Edmonton, Canada.

Cummins, J. P., & Das, J. P. (1977). Cognitive processing and reading difficulties: A framework for research. *The Alberta Journal of Educational Research, 23*, 245–256.

Cummins, J. P., & Das, J. P. (1978). Simultaneous and successive syntheses and linguistic processes. *International Journal of Psychology, 13*, 129–138.

Das, J. P. (1972). Patterns of cognitive ability in nonretarded and retarded children. *American Journal of Mental Deficiency, 77*, 6–12.

Das, J. P. (1973a). Structure of cognitive abilities: Evidence for simultaneous and successive processing. *Journal of Educational Psychology, 65*, 103–108.

Das, J. P. (1973b). Cultural deprivation and cognitive competence. In N. R. Ellis (Ed.), *International Review of Research in Mental Retardation, 6*. New York: Academic Press.

Das, J. P. (1980). Planning: Theoretical considerations and empirical evidence. *Psychological Research* (W. Germany), *41*, 141–151.

Das, J. P. (1984a). Aspects of planning. In J. Kirby (Ed.), *Cognitive strategies and educational performance* (pp. 13–31). New York: Academic Press.

Das, J. P. (1984b). Intelligence and information integration. In J. Kirby, (Ed.), *Cognitive strategies and educational performance* (pp. 35–50). New York: Academic Press.

Das, J. P. (1985). Remedial training for the amelioration of cognitive deficits in children. In

A. F. Ashman & R. S. Laura (Eds.), *The education & training of the mentally retarded* (pp. 215–244). London: Croom Helm.

Das, J. P., Bisanz, G. L., & Mancini. G. (1984). Performance of good and poor readers on cognitive tasks: Changes due to development and reading compentence. *Journal of Learning Disabilities, 17*, 549–555.

Das, J. P., & Cummins, J. P. (1982). Language processing and reading disability. In K. D. Gaddow & I. Bialer (Eds.), *Advances in learning disabilities, 1* (pp. 3–24). Greenwich, Conn.: JAI Press.

Das, J. P., Cummins, J., Kirby, J. R., & Jarman, R. F. (1979). Simultaneous and successive process, language and mental abilities. *Canadian Psychological Review, 20*, 1–11.

Das, J. P., & Heemsbergen, D. B. (1983). Planning as a factor in the assessment of cognitive processes. *Journal of Psychoeducational Assessment, 1*, 1–15.

Das, J. P., Kirby, J. R., & Jarman, R. F. (1975). Simultaneous and successive synthesis: An alternative model for cognitive abilities. *Psychological Bulletin, 82*, 87–103.

Das, J. P., Kirby, J. R., & Jarman, R. F. (1979). *Simultaneous and successive cognitive processes.* New York: Academic Press.

Das, J. P., & Snart, F. (1982, June). *Coding and planning functions of normal and disabled readers.* Paper presented at the Annual Meeting of the Canadian Psychological Association.

Das, J. P., Snart, F., & Mulcahy, R. F. (1982). Reading disability and its relation to information-integration. In J. P. Das, R. F. Mulcahy, & A. E. Wall (Eds.), *Theory and research in learning disabilities* (pp. 85–109). New York: Plenum.

Gardner, H. (1983). *Frames of Mind.* New York: Basic Books.

Garofalo, J. (1983). *Simultaneous synthesis, behavior regulations, and the factor structure of arithmetic performance.* Unpublished doctoral dissertation, Indiana University, Bloomington.

Gordon, C. G. (1982). *A comparative study of the role of word placed skills and processing strategies in the reading comprehension of primary school schildren.* Unpublished master's dissertation, University of Newcastle, New South Wales, Australia.

Hunt, K. (1970). Syntactic maturity in school children and adults. *Monographs of the Society for Research in Child Development, 35*, 134.

Kaufman, D. (1978). *The relationship of academic performance to strategy traiing and remedial techniques: An information processing approach.* Unpublished doctoral thesis, University of Alberta, Edmonton, Canada.

Kaufman, A. S., & Kaufman, N. L. (1983). *K-ABC, Kaufman Assessment Battery for Children* Minnestoa: American Guidance Service.

Kirby, J. R. (1980). Individual differences and cognitive processes. In J. R. Kirby & J. B. Biggs (Eds.), *Cognition, development and instruction* (pp. 119–143). New York: Academic Press.

Kirby, J. R., & Ashman, A. F. (1984). Planning skills and mathematics achievement: Implications regarding learning disability. *Journal of Psychoeducational Assessment, 2*, 9–22.

Kirby, J. R., & Biggs, J. B. (Eds.). (1980). *Cognition, development and instruction.* New York: Academic Press.

Kirby, J. R., & Das, J. P. (1977). Reading achievement, IQ and simultaneous-successive processing. *Journal of Educational Psychology, 69*, 564–570.

Krywaniuk, L. (1974). *Patterns of cognitive abilities of high and low achieving school children.* Unpublished doctoral thesis, University of Alberta, Edmonton, Canada.

Krywaniuk, L. W., & Das, J. P. (1976). Cognitive strategies in native children: Analysis and intervention. *Alberta Journal of Educational Research, 22*, 271–280.

Leong, C. K., Cheng, S. C., & Das, J. P. (1984). Arithmetic performance and cognitive processing. *Chinese University of Hong Kong Education Journal, 12*, 31–41.

Luria, A. R. (1966). *Human brain and psychological processes*. New York: Harper & Row.

Luria, A. R. (1970). The functional organization of the brain. *Scientific American, 222,*(3), 66–78.

Luria, A. R. (1973). *The working brain*. New York: Basic Books.

Luria, A. R. (1980). *Higher cortical functions in man* (2nd ed.). New York: Basic Books.

Luria, A. R., & Artem'eva, E. Y. (1970). Two approaches to an evaluation of the reliability of psychological investigations. *Soviet Psychology, 8*, 271–282.

McLeod, R. W. (1978). *An exploratory study of inference and cognitive synthesis in reading comprehension with selected grade four readers*. Unpublished doctoral thesis, University of Alberta, Department of Elementary Education, Edmonton, Canada.

Miller, G. A., Galanter, E., & Pribram, K. H. (Eds.). (1960). *Plans and the structure of behavior*. Holt, Rinehart & Winston.

Mwamwenda, T., Dash, U. N., & Das, J. P. (1985). A relationship between simultaneous–successive synthesis and concrete operational thought. *International Journal of Psychology, 19*, 547–563.

Ramey, G. (1985). Unpublished doctoral dissertation, University of Alberta, Department of Elementary Education, Edmonton, Canada.

Robinson, G. L. W. (1983). *Simultaneous and successive information processing, language, and reading processes in reading disabled children*. Unpublished doctoral dissertation, University of Newcastle, New South Wales, Australia.

Schmeck, R. R. (1983). Learning styles of college students. *Individual Differences in Cognition, 1*, 233–279.

Schank, R. C. (1975). The structure of episodes in memory. In D. G. Bobrow & A. Collins (Eds.), *Representation and understanding: Studies in cognitive science* (pp. 237–272). New York: Academic Press.

CHAPTER 6

Students' Self-Concepts and the Quality of Learning in Public Schools and Universities

PATRICIA McCARTHY and RONALD RAY SCHMECK

INTRODUCTION

This chapter focuses on theory and research concerned with the role of the self in learning. It is based on the assumption that the self-concept is the most significant cognitive structure organizing an individual's experience, while self-esteem is the most influential affective evaluator of this experience. The self-concept organizes all that we think we are, what we think we can do, and how best we think we can do it, while self-esteem is the extent to which we are pleased by that concept, or feel worthy (Hamachek, 1978; Wylie, 1974). Together, they comprise the self-theory or model of experience that helps us explain our past behavior and predict our future behavior. Like any theory, a self-theory can be a differentiated and valid interpretation of reality, or a vague, invalid one. Thus, it can both facilitate and bias information processing (Kuiper & Derry, 1980). it can also affect the degree of *stylistic* consistency present in an individual's behavior, including preferences for certain learning strategies.

PATRICIA McCARTHY • Department of Educational Psychology, University of Minnesota, 139 Burton Hall, 178 Pillsbury Drive S.E., Minneapolis, Minnesota 55455. *RONALD RAY SCHMECK* • Department of Psychology, Southern Illinois University, Carbondale, Illinois 62901.

ONE'S CONCEPTION OF ONE'S SELF

In this section, we will cover four aspects of one's self that seem to influence learning: self-reference, self-concept, self-esteem, and self-talk. The first aspect, *self-reference*, refers to the use of one's conception of one's self as a device for encoding information that is to be learned. The next two aspects, self-concept and self-esteem, both refer to conception of self, but *self-concept* is the informational part of the conception (what we know or believe about ourselves) and *self-esteem* is the emotional part (how we feel about ourselves). Reviews by Fleming and Watts (1980) suggest that the labels self-concept and self-esteem are often misused. In several places, we have used our own judgment and included a study that used the word *self-concept* in the section on self-esteem, because it appeared to us that the label was being misused. Finally, the last aspect, *self-talk*, deals with the internal dialogue that everyone carries on with themselves ("talking to ourselves").

SELF-REFERENCE

Rogers, Kuiper, and Kirker (1977) describe the self-concept as a consistent and uniform cognitive schema that can be used to encode, organize, and elaborate information. They use the term *self-reference* to describe the process and state that, "it is difficult to conceive of an encoding device that carries more potential for the rich embellishment of stimulus input than does self-reference" (p. 687). Rogers, Kuiper, and Kirker demonstrated the impact of self-reference by manipulating subject learning strategies. They used an incidental learning task and instructed subjects to rate adjectives under four conditions. In the structural condition, subjects rated the length of each word; in the phonemic condition, they rated the sound of the word; in the semantic condition, they rated the meaning of the word; and in the self-reference condition, they rated the extent to which the word described them personally. The subjects were then given an unexpected recall test for the words they had rated. In two different experiments the adjectives rated in the self-reference condition were recalled best. Rogers and his colleagues concluded that superior learning and memory result from self-reference.

Their findings have since been replicated by several researchers (e.g., Bower & Gilligan, 1979; Schmeck & Meier, 1984). Also, Bower, Gilligan, and Monteiro (1981) found that instructing subjects to relate information to actual personal events from their past significantly improved their retention of that information, and Schmeck and Meier (1984) demonstrated superior memory in individuals who habitually (stylistically) used self-reference as a learning strategy. McCarthy and

Schmeck (1982) showed that self-reference by a lecturer improved students' memory for the lecture, presumably by modeling self-referent processing for the students.

SELF-CONCEPT

There is some disagreement concerning the nature of the self-concept and its relationship to learning. Markus (1977) and Bower and Gilligan (1979) argued that the self-concept operates in the same fashion as any other cognitive schemata. However, Schmeck and Meier (1984) emphasize that the self-schema might be special, in that people invest more time and energy in processing information concerned with their identities. Thus, their self-concepts should be more distinct, elaborate, and stable than other schemata. They also noted that most theories of psychotherapy suggest that the schemata representing one's concept of self have considerably more affective components than other schemata.

Kuiper and MacDonald (1982) found that information congruent with one's self-concept was processed more efficiently than incongruent information. Also, MacDonald and Kuiper (1984) obtained reliability (consistency) data on individuals' self-reference ratings of adjectives and found that adjectives congruent with one's self-concept were rated more consistently. Information congruent with the self-concept is also processed faster (Kuiper & Olinger, in press) and remembered better (Derry & Kuiper, 1981).

In addition to demonstrating individual differences in self-concept integration or crystallization, the above studies suggest that one's initial concept of self can bias subsequent perception and encoding of self-referenced information in favor of information that is congruent with one's prior expectations. Further evidence of bias is provided by Rogers, Rogers, and Kuiper (1979). They presented subjects with adjectives to rate for self-reference, and they found on a recognition test $2\frac{1}{2}$ months later that adjectives most congruent with a person's self-concept were most likely to be mistakenly identified as members of the original list of adjectives.

Kuiper and Olinger (in press) reviewed research suggesting that both nondepressed and severely depressed individuals engage in self-reference more reliably and efficiently than mildly depressed individuals. This was true in spite of the fact that they focused on different aspects of the information, with severely depressed persons remembering negative and totally nondepressed persons remembering positive information. Mildly depressed individuals showed the least reliable and efficient self-reference and remembered equal amounts of positive and negative information. These findings imply that mildly depressed individuals have less crystalized self-concepts as compared with either severely depressed or totally nondepressed individuals, who apparently have "made up their minds" as to their identities.

We discuss this biasing effect in more detail below, but for now we would like to emphasize that the self-concept is a powerful cognitive prototype through which incoming stimuli are interpreted. When individuals actively use self-reference, they exhibit better learning and retention than when they engage in more literal memorization. Self-reference strategies apparently encourage the development of rich, detailed codings for material. However, there is a certain selectivity to choice of material. Individuals are more likley to actively perceive self-confirming data and recall successful and consistent aspects of their activities while avoiding discrepant information (Pervin, 1984). Furthermore, researchers (Bryan & Pearl, 1981; Gur & Sackheim, 1979; McCarrey, Edwards, & Rozario, 1982) have found that when individuals have poor self-concepts, or when their self-esteem is threatened, self-reference decreases (e.g., they avoid recognizing their own voice or looking into a mirror) and bias increases (e.g., they blame failure on external causes and take full credit for successes). Individuals who are dissatisfied with themselves typically find self-confrontation to be aversive. Thus, the specific nature of one's self-concept moderates the relationship between self-reference and learning, in some cases facilitating learning and in others biasing or misguiding it.

SELF-ESTEEM

A number of researchers have found a significant relationship between self-esteem and choice of learning strategies. Dean (1977) studied 48 preadolescent male and female gifted children who had either high or low self-esteem. He found that subjects with high self-esteem used more sophisticated learning strategies and performed better on free recall and nonverbal paired-associates tasks. When appropriate, they employed a recall order in reverse of that given them during paired-associates learning, and they used a clustering strategy on the free recall task. Subjects with low self-esteem, on the other hand, maintained an output order similar to that which they were given. These subjects were generally more rigid, employing a repetitive rehearsal strategy when a more complex strategy would have been more efficient. Dean's findings suggest that individuals with high self-esteem prefer to actively rework material, using deep, elaborative strategies, while individuals with low self-esteem prefer more shallow, repetitive strategies. We would suggest that deep and elaborative strategies are *self-assertive* in nature, while shallow strategies are more passive and dependent.

Schmeck and Meier (1984) examined the relationships between use of elaborative processing (which includes self-reference) and scores on measures of self-esteem, self-concept crystallization, and defensive self-perceptions (need for social approval) for 199 male and female college students. They found that subjects who preferred to elaborate on information when studying (rather than simply repeating it) also reported higher self-esteem and greater self-concept crystallization. The authors concluded that subjects with high self-esteem more readily involve their self-concepts in learning (assert themselves in their studies) through the use of self-reference. Recall that we noted above that others (e.g., Bryan & Pearl, 1981; Gur & Sackheim, 1979; McCarrey, Edwards, & Rozario, 1982) have found that individual's with low self-esteem actively avoid thinking about themselves. Additionally, Schmeck and Meier (1984) asserted that individuals who frequently employ their self-concepts in learning would more frequently perceive relationships between experience and self, leading to greater self-concept crystallization. The authors suggested that the relationship may be reciprocal, with self-reference leading to greater self-definition, which in turn increases the likelihood that more self-reference will occur.

Schmeck and Meier (1984) also found that defensive self-perception (need for social approval) in no way reduced the likelihood of elaborative processing. Furthermore, need for social approval was positively correlated with both self-esteem and self-concept crystallization. These findings suggest that a person can maintain self-esteem by fabricating an attractive self-concept, and this self-concept (although "false") can still be quite useful for organizing and encoding information. However, the authors note that individuals high on defensive self-perception will focus on and remember self-supportive information more than self-critical information, thereby introducing a bias into their contact with reality. The interested reader is urged to refer to Crowne and Marlowe (1964).

The latter analysis is supported by the findings of Markus and Sentis (1982), discussed earlier, and by Gaines, Fretz, and Helweg (1975), who examined the differences in subject self-reference as a function of need for approval (defensive self-perception). Their subjects viewed slides containing a variety of positive, negative, and neutral verbs, and in a later recall task they wrote a sentence containing the first verb they could remember from the slides and the first pronoun that came to mind. While all of the subjects used a large number of self-referent pronouns, high subjects with a high need for approval remembered the greatest number of positive verbs, while those with a low need for approval remembered the most negative verbs. Perhaps subjects with a low need for approval had a more balanced view of themselves, with less need to actively avoid critical self-reference (cf. Weiner, 1980). In this respect, the findings for subjects with a low need for approval are similar to those for the "mildly depressed" individuals studied by Kuiper and Olinger (in press, and discussed above).

Strassberg-Rosenberg and Gaier (1977) assessed the self-esteem of 23 learning-disabled male adolescents and 47 normally achieving male adolescents. The latter subjects generally reported higher self-esteem, as measured by the Coopersmith Self-Esteem Inventory (Coopersmith, 1967), but the differences were not as great as expected. The authors maintained that the differences were attentuated by the ego defenses of the learning-disabled subjects. For example, they repressed or denied failure experiences and avoided additional negative events by lowering their academic goals and substituting nonacademic ones. It would have been illuminating if the authors had included a measure of need for social approval in the study.

Similarly, Winne, Woodlands, and Wong (1982) found that self-esteem was significantly related to a child's interpersonal behavior patterns, self-attributions about success or failure, and academic achievement. They compared learning-disabled, normal, and gifted children and found that learning-disabled subjects had significantly lower academic self-esteem than normal and gifted children. However, there were no reliable differences among the three groups of children on other self-esteem subscales (e.g., home, general). If one assumes that the learning-disabled subjects did not overestimate or exaggerate their self-esteem in the home setting, then perhaps they were engaging in "compensation," that is, being successful at home as a way to protect themselves against their poor academic performance. These findings support Strassberg-Rosenberg and Gaier's (1977) hypothesis that learning-disabled children can substitute nonacademic goals to defend against poor performance. The findings also suggest that self-esteem can be situationally specific as well as cross-situationally (stylistically) consistent. And finally, the results suggest that specific aspects of the self-theory may take on more or less importance for different students; for example, gifted students might focus on academic domains, while learning-disabled students focus on social and physical–athletic domains.

Black (1974) found that the self-esteem of learning-disabled children identified as retarded readers was significantly lower than that of learning-disabled identified as normal readers. Furthermore, self-esteem was not significantly related to IQ. Perhaps the most important finding was that the magnitude of the negative relationship between self-esteem and reading increased with age and grade, suggesting a circular relationship in which low self-esteem contributes to school failure and school failure further lowers self-esteem. Since Boyle (1983) reported that feelings about one's self influence learning mainly under stressful conditions, perhaps the teacher can interrupt the circular relationship by maintaining less-stressful, less-competitive classroom conditions. Indeed, Margalit and Zak (1984) report that it is specifically individuals with low self-esteem who exhibit the highest general anxiety, suggesting that they are more vulnerable to *any* stressors present in the academic environment.

SELF-TALK

Meichenbaum (1980) discusses several studies illustrating relationships between positive and negative self-statements, affect, and performance. In one study, Henshaw (1978) used "think aloud" methods to study college students who were either high or low in creativity. He found during an experimental task that although both groups began with positive statements, the low-creativity subjects persistently moved toward negative statements over time. They expressed more detrimental ideas and negative affect about their personality and abilities, about the task, and about the whole experiment, while high-creativity students were more likely to express facilitative ideas and positive affect.

Meichenbaum (1980) concludes that poor intellectual performance is related to negative self-statements and associated negative affect in less-creative students, poor problem solvers, and children with learned helplessness. These negative internal processes are generally (a) oriented toward self rather than task; (b) catastrophizing—negative and self-defeating; and (c) automatic, run-on, and clichéd (as though they were nonnegotiable assumptions). Meichenbaum maintains that any time there is surprisingly low interpersonal and intellectual performance across tasks, it is likely that negative self-referent thinking is involved.

The view of the present authors is that core self-esteem consists of global feelings about self based on early experiences. Healthy esteem develops as a result of receiving unconditional positive regard from significant others, while unhealthy esteem is due to rejection or too much reliance upon conditional regard (Rogers, 1969). The core of esteem is a raw, preverbal, affective orientation toward one's self. This preverbal affect is subsequently "interpreted," or given meaning verbally (cf. Gazzaniga, 1985). In striving to understand themselves, children verbalize beliefs, assumptions, and interpretations which "make sense" of the fact that they feel good or bad about themselves. These interpretations form the basis of the self-concept and dictate the self-talk described by Meichenbaum (1980).

As mentioned earlier, Margalit and Zak (1984) examined the relationship between self-esteem and anxiety for 100 learning-disabled preadolescents and 118 nondisabled children attending regular school. As expected, there was a significant inverse relationship between anxiety and self-esteem for both subject groups. Furthermore, the learning-disabled children expressed the highest anxiety and the lowest self-esteem, apparent in their expressions of helplessness, self-dissatisfaction, and negative self-referent attributions (blaming themselves). These findings suggest that the learning-disabled children use task-inhibitive self-reference in the manner suggested by Meichenbaum. Furthermore, since Schmeck (1983) found that shallow, surface learning strategies are more prevalent in students with low esteem and high anxiety, it is likely that the emotions of learning-disabled students elicit strategies that lower their performance even further and reinforce the negative self-statements that are already so common in their internal dialogues (see Black, 1974).

As noted above, core self-esteem is a global feeling acquired very early, but it is also subject to interpretation. It is affected by subsequent successful or unsuccessful performance under conditions of social comparison and competition, that is, unconditional regard can be replaced by conditional regard. In other words, as development continues, esteem becomes increasingly contingent on the outcomes of performance, that is, it is "earned." This earning of esteem is related to Rotter's (1966) concept of locus of control ("Is success contingent upon my behavior?") as well as Bandura's (1977) concept of self efficacy ("Am I capable of the behavior upon which success is contingent?"). Beliefs about the locus of control and one's efficacy or competence become part of the self-concept, while the associated feelings become components of self-esteem.

These beliefs and feelings influence subsequent performance. For example, Meier, McCarthy, and Schmeck (1984) found that students' assessments of their self-efficacy with regard to writing were significant predictors of grades on actual compositions. Similarly, Prawer (1974) examined possible correlations between efficacy as a foreign language student and foreign language achievement. She found a strong positive correlation between feelings of efficacy and language grades. This relationship was greater than for global self-esteem and overall grade point average. She speculated that self-efficacy and experience affect each other reciprocally—experience with foreign languages raises evaluations of language ability which raise foreign language grades.

Muller and his colleagues (Muller & Spuhler, 1976; Sharp & Muller, 1978) studied the effects of experimentally raising or lowering academic self-efficacy on academic performance. In an initial study (Muller & Spuhler, 1976), subjects with lowered efficacy learned at a slower rate and made more errors than either subjects whose efficacy was raised or unmanipulated control subjects. The performance of these latter two groups was not significantly different, and a check showed that their efficacy did not differ either.

In a replication and extension, Sharp and Muller (1978) experimentally manipulated 270 college students' feelings of efficacy regarding their ability to learn a foreign language. The subjects had their expectations raised; lowered in a therapeutic, supportive manner ("it's O.K. to be myself, even if I am presently performing poorly"); lowered in a counter-therapeutic, nonsupportive manner ("low ability is unacceptable"); or they were part of a control group whose efficacy was not manipulated. The authors found that the subjects in the raised, therapeutically lowered, and control groups all performed equally well, and their performance was superior to subjects in the counter-therapeutically lowered group. They also found that the subjects whose self-efficacy was raised did show an increase in positiveness, but their absolute level following treatment was still statistically equivalent to the control group. This led the authors to conclude that students are generally more sensitive to negative feedback than positive.

They concluded, as did Margalit and Zak (1984), that the consequences of failure can be either positive (motivational) or negative (disruptive), depending on the students' perceptions of the failure and their subsequent self-statements. They believe that negative feedback given in a supportive way lowers expectations, but not performance, while punitive, rejecting feedback lowers both. Because punitive feedback threatens one's overall self-concept, it raises anxiety and leads to negative self-statements, in turn distorting actual ability.

In general, it seems that negative self-talk hinders performance. As we suggested earlier, individuals with low self-esteem tend to engage in task-inhibitive self-reference, which raises anxiety and leads to shallow, surface processing. Shallow strategies result in poorer performance, which confirms the feelings of inadequacy, weak efficacy, and external locus of control that may already be part of their self-theory. On the other hand, individuals with realistically high self-esteem, seem to have more academic and social success and use more task-facilitative self-reference. High self-esteem appears to be related to independence and versatility, since one can rely on internal judgments and intrinsic rewards when feeling less threatened. Although higher esteem will not overcome true deficiencies (e.g., brain damage, low IQ), it may help maximize potential and permit the flexibility necessary to select appropriate strategies.

DEVELOPMENT OF ONE'S CONCEPTION OF SELF

An infant is initially totally "egocentric" (Piaget, 1952), and experience of self is not differentiated from external reality. Information processing is literal, surface, or shallow, with very little symbolic (linguistic) interpretation of experience. However, as infants search out and actively manipulate new features of the environment, they organize increasingly sophisticated and differentiated theories of self and world. These early interpretations (theories) guide later processing of information about the self.

SECURE ATTACHMENT TO A CAREGIVER

Early emotional experience is critical in the child's development of a theory of self (Canfield & Wells, 1975; Pervin, 1984; Piaget, 1952; Santrock, 1986). Children learn to label internal states in response to their interactions with the environment and the feedback it provides. This labeling, or "naming," as Klein calls it (Kernberg, 1980), constitutes the beginnings of the self-concept (Ornstein, 1985).

Parenting is generally the most crucial component of early experience (see, Weininger, 1983). It appears that the development and maintenance of an integrated self-concept and positive self-esteem initially require a secure emotional attachment or bond between parent and child. Ainsworth and Bell (1970) and Ainsworth, Blehar, Waters, and Wall (1978) have done an excellent job of assessing this attachment process in humans. Also, Waters, Wippman, and Sroufe (1979) demonstrated that the quality of the initial attachment influenced development at least through the first $3\frac{1}{2}$ years of life.

Kohut (1971; 1977) describes this bond as one of idealized images through which self and parents are experienced as one. The parents are empathically in tune with and responsive to the child's needs for mirrorring and idealizing. They are responsive to their child's needs but are not overly protective or intrusive. Initially, they provide unconditional gratification of basic needs, including emotional ones such as contact-comfort (Bowlby, 1969), and then gradually and supportingly introduce contingencies and responsibility into the process. Ideally, these contingencies are introduced gradually enough that the child is left feeling competent, rather than excessively fearful or frustrated. These facilitative conditions lead to development of a self that integrates abilities through self-expression and goal striving; it is also a self that is restrained and sensitive to others.

On the other hand, if parents provide little unconditional early gratification, the child may associate negative feelings with its experience of self. Initially, this affect is "preverbal" or pure emotion, and it has been argued that it has its roots in innate fears of abandonment (see, Kernberg, 1980). As development continues, a cognitive base is built as the child interprets reality, including any preverbal, negative emotions that have been associated with self. Rychlak (1975) developed a theory of self-reference which states that during the very early stages of development we acquire basic feelings of liking or disliking toward ourselves, just as we do toward others. Affective evaluations of self as likeable during the early years leads one to favor storage of positive aspects of subsequent experience, while the reverse is true when individuals develop core feelings of dislike toward self. Rychlak (1975) and August and Rychlak (1978) report research in support of Rychlak's theory.

Similar to Rychlak, Natale and Hantas (1982) argued that emotion, or mood, is a basic node in the associative network for long-term memory, including memories that are part of one's self-concept (see also, Markus & Sentis, 1982; Rogers, 1981). They conducted an experiment in which they hypnotically induced either happy, sad, or neutral affective states. Those induced to experience depression recalled fewer positive self-descriptions and life experiences and tended to recall more negative self-descriptions and unpleasant life experiences. Subjects in the happy condition recalled fewer unpleasant life events and remembered more positive self-descriptions. Mood did not seem to affect the amount of self-reference, since subjects remembered approximately equal numbers of events in all conditions, but it did affect what was remembered. The authors hypothesized, similar to Bower (1981), that subjects retrieve experiences stored at times when their mood was the same as the current (induced) mood state.

Similarly, Derry and Kuiper (1981) reported a relationship between naturally occurring (unmanipulated) depression and the content of an individual's self-concept. They found that depressed individuals rated negative adjectives (depressed content) as significantly more self-referent, and they recalled more of those adjectives when given an unexpected test of recall. In contrast, nondepressed individuals rated positive adjectives (nondepressed content) as more self-referent and recalled more of them.

Object-relations theorists (e.g., Kernberg, 1980) suggest that individuals sometimes form two or more separate self-concepts in childhood, and these are organized around mood states, for example, one positive ("feeling good") and one negative ("feeling bad"). These self-concepts continue to develop separately throughout one's lifetime. When an individual is feeling rejected, the "bad self" and all related past experiences and behaviors are primed, while to some extent the neural circuits associated with the "good self" are suppressed and unavailable. On the other hand, when the individual is feeling accepted or successful, the "good self" and all related past experiences are available, and circuits related to the bad self are suppressed.

This cognitive process is called *splitting* (Kernberg, 1980), and the conditions that generate it are a perceived excess of neglect or aggression in the child's early family life. To obtain the minimal love (or "good feeling") necessary to avoid psychotic withdrawal, the child hesitates to ever "spoil" memories of the rare good times by simultaneously remembering the bad times. The result is a gradually increasing cognitive separation of memories organized around their affective investment (positive or negative). Theoretically, everyone has split his or her mental organization to some degree. The "good and bad moods" discussed in everyday parlance are often attributable to such a split cognitive organization. Likewise, the individual who "seems like a different person" under certain circumstances (e.g., when angry or when drinking) has probably had a history of splitting experiences according to his or her affective tone. In a sense, such an individual would have two separate, identifiable "styles." Gordon Pask (Chapter 4, this volume) accepts this possibility and refers to the separate styles, or persona, as "P-Individuals."

SEPARATION, SELF-CARE, AND SELF-EFFICACY

Kohut (1977) feels that even when a secure attachment is established between parent and child, a crucial element in the parent–child interaction is the inevitable, but hopefully infrequent, failures of perfect parental support and admiration. It is at these times that the child is gently forced to provide its own emotional support and admiration. Regardless of whether the child is given a sense of being unconditionally likeable, when negative emotions are associated with the introduction of self-care (e.g., the child feels suddenly abandoned), then the developing self-concept may be placed on a less-than-ideal developmental track. The possibilities are numerous, and so are the self-concepts or personalities that result. For example, the child may be left with the feeling that it was unconditionally cared for but that it is incapable of making it on its own in a conditional and competitive world. The child would feel uneasy whenever independence is called for. On the other hand, if unconditional love was scarce, but the child coped well when contingencies and self-care were introduced, then development might be guided by excessive need to prove oneself through repeated demonstrations of mastery (cf. descriptions of the achieving student in Entwistle's, Chapter 2, and Biggs', Chapter 8, this volume).

Santrock (1986) says that the feelings of autonomy that parents can give to a child are limited by the parents' own dignity and sense of personal independence. Similarly, Weininger (1983) argues that the mother's level of ego strength (including development of her own self-concept) is crucial to the child's healthy development. This influence is apparent during play. Weininger found that mothers with more-integrated self-concepts were warm and supportive, but less intrusive in their child's play. Their infants engaged in more frequent and relaxed in-depth investigations of toys. Weininger believes that these infants were able to process experiences in greater emotional and cognitive depth; they were freer to expressively explore, to take a longer time investigating situations, and to act independently. Children of less-integrated mothers were more dependent, showed poor attention, and seemed to expect to be guided. These findings are especially significant given that play also seems to be a major vehicle for the advancement of a child's general cognitive development (Piaget, 1962).

These early experiences are related to subsequent academic achievement. According to Weininger (1983), the most successful students tended to have parents who viewed themselves and their children as unconditionally valuable but who also expected them to be reasonably successful when competition was called for; their relationships with their children were generally warm and accepting, or at least the children perceived them as such.

Early parental rejection, neglect, and degradation are related to academic underachievement, while sensitivity, warm acceptance, and encouragement are related to achievement. Furthermore, subtle differences in parental attitudes and behavior may cause stylistic differences in children. For example, Bing (1963) found that mothers of children with high verbal ability were more controlling and pressuring, while mothers of children with high mathematical ability were less interfering and more tolerant of independence. Perhaps when children are forced to use verbal control to defend against excessive parental intervention, they may fail to develop (even reject) natural spatial–intuitive skills.

Rothbart and Posner (1985) reviewed studies that used either direct observation or videotaping of mother–child interactions. They report that the infant expresses its needs in the form of very subtle behavioral impulses that some mothers are sensitive to and others are not. The sensitive, empathic mother more frequently detects the infant's subtle behavioral expressions and implements them. The less-sensitive mother either ignores the childs inclinations or substitutes her own impulses for the child's due to feelings of insecurity regarding her own adequacy or control. These effects are extremely subtle and difficult to measure but are measurable nonetheles. This is the sort of process that Winnicott (1965) felt would force the child to develop a "false self" and lose touch with its "true self." In effect, the mother forces the child to substitute her impulses for its own and to reject its own impulses as unreal. It is important to note in the context of the present text that Dyk (1969) reports that the conditions Winnicott described as leading to development of a false self also lead to the development of extremely field-dependent cognitive styles.

To summarize, healthy development occurs when new ideas, feelings, actions, and beliefs can be flexibly integrated into the concept of self without an excessive experience of threat. Gratifying experiences in which the child's basic physical and emotional needs are satisfied promote the development of unconditional self-esteem. The infant develops a core reservoir of unconditional acceptance and valuing. In addition to providing unconditional positive regard, it is also crucial that parents gradually allow children to develop competencies and confidence to do tasks for themselves. For example, by the age of 2, children begin to perceive of themselves as problem solvers. They also begin to show a concern with organizing or integrating activities toward a goal and with standards and personal competence (Ornstein. 1985). Independence, creativity, and self-reliance, essential characteristics for self-concept formation and reorganization, can only develop when children are supported at an early age in these attempts to make their own judgments and to evaluate the consequences (Rogers, 1969).

SELF-CONCEPT CRYSTALLIZATION

Like all theories or models, one's conception of self is not equal to reality; it is an interpretation of reality. Thus, identity is to some extent an illusion, and some disillusionment is certain to occur as one encounters life experiences that do not fit one's interpretations of oneself. A crucial determiner of development is what children do with potentially disillusioning experience. Do they experience the disillusionment (including the feelings involved) and revise their self-concepts, or do they ignore or distort experience to avoid the pain.

Self-concepts are always changeable but become more and more crystallized with age and use (see, Marton, 1981). Crystallization occurs, in part, because of built-in bias toward assimilating data into existing interpretations (confirming them) rather than revising interpretations to accommodate data. This bias is probably related to an inherited aversion to cognitive inconsistency (see, Festinger's, 1957, discussion of cognitive dissonance; Kelly's, 1963, discussion of construct permeability; or Kohut's, 1977, "fragmentation"). Experiences that are incongruent with the self-concept are a source of discomfort and are often distorted or denied to achieve consistency (Rogers, 1969). If we change one cognitive component of the self-concept without realigning all of the others to maintain consonance, we experience discomfort which Kohut (1977) calls *fragmentation* and Festinger (1957) calls *cognitive dissonance*.

Because the system strives for consistency, later conceptions tend to form so as to be consonant with preexisting ones. At times, this leads to a sort of compounding of errors which Kernberg (1980) refers to as *condensations*. Children "tag" themselves at an early age as worthy or unworthy and competent or incompetent, and they start to view reality as friendly or hostile. Then, they tend to act in ways that verify these early tags, perceiving situations and emitting behaviors based on preexisting assumptions and encoding resulting new experience wherever possible to be consistent with those assumptions. Thus, they develop crystallized matrices of cognitions resulting in stylistic consistency at a behavioral level.

Beck (1967) argued that a predisposition to depression begins in childhood and adolescence, when individuals develop a habit of thinking negatively about themselves. Beck argues that the self-concept of depressed individuals, when engaged under stressful conditions, distorts perception such that "instead of a schema being selected to fit the external details, the details are selectively extracted and molded to fit the schema" (Beck, 1967, p. 286). It is as though they automatically accept the dislike that they feel for themselves and go on to interpret this dislike and its causes without question. In Piaget's (1952) terminology, cognitive "assimilation" wins out over "accomodation." One can always provide data to substantiate a self-fulfilling prophecy. This is similar to Rychlak's (1975) views regarding the effect self-esteem has on later learning (discussed previously).

Rogers (1969) argued that the extent to which new experience threatens to change an individual's self-concept profoundly affects the quality of learning, that is, what the person learns from the experience. Sometimes it is who we are that is threatening, and at other times, it is who we could be, that is, the recognition that we might be able to develop certain latent behavioral or cognitive abilities. Change is frightening since, "If I *can* do this, then what does it say about who I am, and what would be the implications of this new conception of self with regard to the future?" We fear a domino effect leading to changes in the entire personality, including life-style, worldview, and long-term goals.

If the individual restricts learning outcomes to memorization of atomized bits of information, there is less threat to the self-concept. Compartmentalization of thought helps guarantee that the domino effect will not occur, since keeping isolated bits of information from "bumping into one another" ensures that we won't be forced to revise or integrate them to produce consonance. It is possible to hold two entirely opposite points of view if we simply don't think about the two of them at the same time. On the other hand, the deep approach to learning, discussed elsewhere in the present text (e.g., Chapter 2 and 3), poses the greatest threat to self-concept, since "deep strategies" (and those that Schmeck and Meier, 1984 call "elaborative") tend toward information integration (Das, Chapter 5, this volume) and thus shun compartmentalization.

This may be one of the reasons why these more meaningful learning processes are often rejected in favor of rote memorization. Unless our self-esteem is securely established, deep and elaborative strategies are more likely to occur in learning contexts where threat to the personality is low, for example, with regard to the content of a chemistry class, although competition for grades in such classes can still threaten the self-concept.

Under ideal conditions, dissonant experiences (disillusionments) will be slight and gradual, so that the cognitive system can slowly and nondefensively revise conceptions of reality, keeping viable assumptions and replacing others. However, if disillusionments are traumatic or sudden, it is possible that individuals will use what psychologists call defense mechanisms to deal with a fear that the whole system will fragment (see Kohut, 1977). Defense mechanisms often block natural developmental changes. Also, defense against traumatic experience in early childhood might mean that some experience will leave a "trace" in the nervous system but be refused admission to the linguistic system that most of us recognize as "consciousness" (cf. Gazzaniga, 1985, and Kernberg, 1980). These "traces" may affect the individual's behavior by affecting motives and yet not be subject to normal revision (see the discussion of self-awareness in the next section).

SELF-AWARENESS AND THE DEVELOPMENT OF COGNITIVE STYLE

With regard to reading comprehension, Kirby (Chapter 9) maintains that cognitive functioning changes developmentally from "global" to "analytic" to a synthesis of the two. Pask (Chapter 4) refers to this latter synthesis as "versatile," and Torrance and Rockenstein (Chapter 10) call it "whole-brained." Likewise, Entwistle's (Chapter 2) "meaning orientation to studying" requires a synthesis or integration of global and analytic functioning. Kirby's analysis suggests that "cognitive style" could result from excess focus or dependence upon one of the two earlier modes of functioning, prior to integrating the two. Theoretically, this could result in the learning pathologies, globetrotting and improvidence, discussed by Pask (Chapter 4). If an individual does not develop much beyond global functioning. we have a global style (and perhaps "globetrotting"); movement to and fixation at the phase of analytic functioning would give rise to an analytic style (and perhaps "improvidence"); and a reinstatement of the global along with the analytic would give rise to Kirby's synthetic style ("versatile").

Based upon numerous psychophysiological investigations, Gazzaniga (1985) theorized that the human brain is organized into "modules" which operate separately but in parallel fashion. One of these modules is a seat of consciousness which is predominantly a linguistic interpreter that can coordinate many of the other modules. All of the modules can act "on their own," without interpretation or coordination, but under some circumstances coordination requires that "the interpreter" be aware of, or in communication with, the other modules. Many of the defense mechanisms discussed by psychoanalysts could be viewed as cognitive processes that interfere with communication between Gazzaniga's "interpreter" and other modules of the brain.

Similarly, proponents of a brain hemisphericity model of human functioning (e.g., Ornstein, 1985; or Torrance and Rockenstein's Chapter 10, this volume) believe that the left hemisphere specializes in language, logical activities, and things that generally happen in a sequential order. The right hemisphere is then theoretically involved in simultaneous, spatial, and artistic activities, maintains literal images of past experiences, and specializes in part–whole relations (Ornstein, 1985). Ornstein argues that, with satisfactory developmental experiences, the two ways of knowing specific to the hemispheres will be coordinated and complementary rather than competitive. For example, he reports that when healthy subjects are asked to switch from spatial to logical processes on an experimental task, recorded brain activity indicates that there is a shift in the focus of neurological activity from the right to the left hemisphere. Cooperation or communication between the hemispheres would also seem to promote maximum flexibility (Pask's "versatility"), allowing individuals to perceive differentiated contextual cues before choosing appropriate strategies. However, traumatic developmental experiences could theoretically lead to excessive hemispheric dominance, with a fixedness and propensity to prefer certain modes of processing regardless of task demands.

An alternative model of cognitive functioning is described by Tulving (1985). Based upon extensive research in the area of human memory, he posits three distinct memory systems: (a) procedural, in which information is prescriptive; (b) episodic, which carries information about prior events and their relation to the individual's personal identity as it exists in subjective time and space; and (c) semantic, in which information is restructured to describe the world with abstract principles. Tulving characterizes procedural memory as anoetic, or nonknowing; semantic memory as noetic, or knowing; and episodic memory as autonoetic, or self-knowing. Procedural memory can only be expressed directly in behavior, while semantic and episodic memory can be expressed more flexibly (e.g., linguistically). Although research has shown that episodic memory can be lost without imparing everyday behavior, effective long-term functioning requires coordination of all three systems. Self-concept formation would involve the use of semantic memory to draw abstract generalizations from the experiential data stored in episodic memory, including knowledge of one's procedural memories experienced previously as behavior.

It is important to include some mention of emotion in this discussion of integration, coordination, and flexibility. According to de Bono (1983), emotions influence thinking in three ways. Prior to encountering a situation, a person may experience a strong emotion such as fear or anger which channels perceptions of the situation. Second, there may be a brief period of undirected perception, until a situation is classified, and then emotion may channel subsequent perception. Third, perception may explore a situation as widely as possible, taking in all information including emotion, and then decisions can be made using cognition and affect in integrated, complimentary fashion. The main point, for our present purposes, is that de Bono emphasizes coordination of emotional, spatial, and verbal analyses of situations.

One theme that is common to these varied models of the brain's functioning is the necessity for integration or open communication between modules or processes if maximum potential is to be achieved. Carl Jung felt that such open communication, and fully integrated functioning, could be accomplished only by increasing awareness of one's own thoughts, memories, and motives (Campbell, 1971). Jung believed self-awareness would stimulate what he called the "transcendental function," involving the development of cognitions about cognitions and feelings about feelings, permitting an integration of cognitive elements that might otherwise be resistant to integration. Similarly, object relations theorists (e.g., Kernberg, 1980) use the term *observing ego* to refer to the *experience* of oneself at the same time one is in the process of *being* oneself.

The term *metacognition* is also relevant in the present context (e.g., Biggs, in press; Bobrow, 1975). Bobrow delineated two types of metacognition, one pertaining to facts and one to process. Knowledge about facts refers to knowing what we know. Knowledge about process involves awareness of one's capabilities, knowing which strategies work best in a situation, and being sensitive to the benefits of efficient cognitive resource allocation. A number of researchers (Biggs, in press; Cavanaugh & Perlmutter, 1982; Flavell & Wellman, 1977; Meichenbaum, 1980) have shown that metacognition is as important as task and strategy variables to overall performance.

Phenomenology offers yet another perspective on self-awareness. Husserl (1960) said,

> The self establishes both understanding and meaning. Meaning does not inhere in immanent or transcendant things; it is a dynamic relationship between self and its experiences. . . . Fulfilled meaning derives from a reflective self turned towards its past experiences. (p. 42)

The self lives in its continuous reflections, memories, fantasies, and other intentional acts. "Lived experiences, then, are not only 'mine', but quite literally 'me'" (Husserl, 1960, p. 44). Husserl argued that the prepotent cognitive process is "prereflective or prepredicative experience," pretheoretical awareness whereby the ego "lives its experiences" without reflecting on them. Active interpretations of everyday prepredicative experiences, then, are "predicative." According to Husserl, individuals seek consistency, with their ultimate goal being the development of a consistent, valid, and unified self. Ideally, predicative experience presupposes simple experience, then actively and intentionally goes beyond it. However, predicative experience is "founded" as directly as possible upon prepredicative experience, less so upon other predicative experience. In other words, if we build interpretations of reality upon other interpretations of reality, we are in danger of drastically losing contact with that reality.

In the same regard, Rogers (1983) argues that reality can never be known independent of self-consciousness, and all acts of consciousness are (or should be) interconnected. Furthermore, the more aware we are that our present behavior is highly related to past experiences and to expectations for the future, the more integrated and consistent we should be (see Das' discussion of "planning," Chapter 5). The development of meaning in general runs parallel with making conscious meaning of ourselves. A high level of consciousness exists when people can think about their thinking and have feelings about their feelings. When consciousness accumulates separated experiences, there can be no synthesis in which an identity is formed of the external experiences.

> Progress in knowledge . . . involves more than the accumulation of objectively valid cognitions; it means the growth of a subject progressively better equipped to know and to be the validating source of the knowledge it has or acquires. (Rogers, 1983, p. 44)

Our point is this: the integration and coordination of a person's various cognitive functions might be linked to the integration of a unified self-concept which is founded upon raw (prepredicative) experience rather than fabricated on the basis of selective perception, biased memories, and avoidance, that is, defense mechanisms. Phrasing this differently: it may be the case that placing limits upon self-knowledge (i.e., "not wanting to know" something about oneself) may be what places limits upon overall cognitive integration. If this is so, then increasing self-acceptance will permit greater self-awareness and lead ultimately to a cognitive style characterized by greater versatility, flexibility, and adaptation in overall functioning.

PROMOTING DEVELOPMENT OF SELF IN THE CLASSROOM

We believe that the educational system should encourage more than the acquisition of pieces of information in separate academic disciplines; it should encourage development of the whole person, and that requires (to use Das' terms, Chapter 5) information integration. We recommend that aspiring teachers be taught a qualitative conception of learning. The term *qualitative conception* is used elsewhere in the present text to refer to the idea that learning includes understanding, changes in point of view, and self-actualization. This is in contrast to a *quantitative conception*, which holds that learning is the accumulation of compartmentalized memories such as descriptions, rules, formulas, and other procedural algorithms.

From the quantitative perspective, grades should be assigned on the basis of a count of something, such as number of correct answers, number of pieces of information remembered, and the like. From the qualitative view, learning includes basic changes in the person, and grades are assigned on the basis of the teacher's judgment of such things as the degree of differentiation and integration present in externally observable indicators of student thought.

Following Luria's (1982) conception of brain functioning, Das (Chapter 5) distinguishes between the coding and integrating of information. We are advocating greater emphasis on information integration in the classroom, but in so doing we are not disregarding basic coding of experience, which must occur prior to integration (see Das, 1980). However, most of the coding that occurs in school is secondhand; students memorize someone else's descriptions of life rather than experiencing and coding life for themselves. In the language of phenomenology, interpretations are frequently based upon other interpretations rather than being founded upon experience. We are aware that teachers can rarely provide elaborate life experiences for students, but they certainly can encourage them to combine the personal experiences they've already coded with the interpretations presented in textbooks and lectures to reach conclusions through integration. These would be conclusions for which students could take responsibility and which they could actively evaluate and reevaluate through acquisition of additional experience.

As Husserl (1960) said, "Fulfilled meaning derives from a reflective self turned towards its past experiences" (p. 42). Self-reflection, self-awareness, and self-expression are the keys to encouraging integration, while the chief stumbling blocks are shame, self-doubt, feelings of helplessness, and general fear and avoidance of evaluative or comparative situations. The learning environment should include a warm teacher who communicates some unconditional positive regard. The teacher should also demonstrate a bit of respect for the fact that students have been nurtured to different degrees before entering the classroom and thus bring with them differing vulnerabilities which can make them seem slow, dumb, or, to use a more gentle label, "learning disabled" (Hamachek, 1978). Many of their stumbling blocks are related to a self-concept characterized by low self-esteem. Teachers cannot of course "reparent" every student who finds his or her way into the classroom, but they can develop a learning environment that is conducive to self-expression and that is less likely to "key into" vulnerabilities related to low self-esteem.

As noted earlier, feelings about one's self influence learning mainly under stressful conditions (Boyle, 1983). It was also noted that corrective feedback given in a supportive manner accomplishes its objective far better than the same feedback given in a nonsupportive manner (Sharp & Muller, 1978). Thus, teachers need to consider all forms of motivation (not just competition) and all forms of social influence (not just punishment and criticism). The basic difference between supportive and non-supportive settings is acceptance of the student. It is critical, when all is said and done, that the student feels respected as a human being who has rights, even if he or she gives the "wrong" answer.

In the present volume, Torrance and Rockenstein (Chapter 10) maintain that there are two forms of creativity: creating by inventing and creating by improving. The first requires a safe, noncritical environment for generation of ideas and self-expression. The second requires a critical environment where errors are noted and corrected. Our fear is that too many schools and too many teachers place most of their emphasis upon improving—upon "catching" students in the act of making errors. We feel that school systems and teachers need to permit and reward some of the self-expression that is implicit in creating by inventing, the kind of self-expression that leads to self-discovery, self-awareness, and ultimately to integration and adult cognitive functioning.

Furthermore, we noted at the outset that self-expression while learning course content can improve immediate performance. Rogers *et al.* (1977) said that "it is difficult to conceive of an encoding device that carries more potential for the rich embellishment of stimulus input than does self-reference" (p. 687). Some types of content are more amenable to self-reference than are others, for example, a course in psychology versus a course in mathematics. However, even if content cannot be self-referenced, the teacher can still deal with the students' feelings about their performance and about how their performance relates to their personal identities. The importance of attending to feelings was illustrated by Powell (1981), who content-analyzed course evaluations of 18 students and related their comments to performance in the course. He found that strong negative feelings were systematically linked to poor learning in such a manner as to suggest that bad feelings in a course start a downward spiral; perceptions are altered and performance is lowered, creating more bad feelings in the manner of a vicious circle.

Teachers can evaluate the learning environments that they present to students by asking themselves questions such as the following: To what extent do I encourage the individual student to develop a sense of self-worth and dignity by asking his or her opinion under conditions where it is clear that there is no single correct answer? To what extent do I repeat, and thereby reward, what is interesting and unique about the student's response? On the other side of the coin, to what extent do my students feel that they have to "cover up" to avoid criticism or avoid feeling foolish or "being wrong" in my classroom (Weiner, 1980)? To what extent do my students feel that, in the final analysis, I respect them and accept them in all of their humanness and vulnerability (Hamachek, 1978).

Teachers can periodically ask students, "What does that mean to you," or "How would you describe what happened," or "What do you think about that, and why?" They can more frequently answer questions with other questions or ask students for their opinions about other students' comments, rather than always having the last word themselves. They can share their wonder and concern, occasionally admit ignorance, respect others' opinions, and demonstrate that learning to live with some ambiguity and confusion is vital if we are to discover less-obvious conclusions and find our own unique perspectives.

These suggestions may seem a bit vague and a bit emotional, but that is the main point with regard to self-esteem and self-efficacy; they are primarily emotional experiences. It is emotion that may interfere when a student is encouraged to integrate information and express a conclusion. It is emotion that drives students to try to second-guess teachers in order to come up with "right" answers, telling teachers what they think they want to hear rather than what they, the students, personally believe. That is why making classrooms more nurturant and "safe" aids development. Teachers cannot make students grow up; they cannot make them develop. However, they can make it safe for students to involve themselves and integrate information to reach a few personal conclusions.

Anything the teacher can do to permit human variation, such as validating more than one answer to a question and more than one path to an answer, has the potential to aid development. We admit that it's difficult to maintain a nonjudgmental atmosphere in school systems that are obligated to compare in order to produce grades. Some of the more radical solutions proposed for this problem (e.g., Rogers, 1969) have not been implemented because societies (e.g., the corporations that hire graduates) place great emphasis upon comparing and rank-ordering people. However, we would argue for compromises, even little ones.

REFERENCES

Ainsworth, M. D. S., & Bell, S. M. (1970). Attachment, exploration, and separation: Illustrated by the behavior of one-year-olds in a strange situation. *Child Development, 41,* 49–67.

Ainsworth, M. D. S., Blehar, M. C., Waters, E., & Wall, S. (1978). *Patterns of attachment.* Hillsdale, NJ: Erlbaum.

Bandura, A. (1977). Self-efficacy: Toward a unifying theory of behavioral change. *Psychological Review, 84,* 191–215.

Beck, A. T. (1967). *Depression: Clinical, experimental, and theoretical aspects.* New York: Harper & Row.

Bing, E. (1963). The effect of child rearing practices on development of differential cognitive abilities. *Child Development, 34,* 631–648.

Black, F. W. (1974). Self-concept as related to achievement and age in learning-disabled children. *Child Development, 45,* 1137–1140.

Bobrow, D. G. (1975). Dimensions of representation. In D. G. Bobrow & A. Collins (Eds.), *Representation and understanding: Studies in cognitive science.* New York: Academic Press.

Bower, G. H. (1981). Mood and memory. *American Psychologist, 36,* 129–148.

Bower, G. H., & Gilligan, S. (1979). Remembering information related to one's self. *Journal of Research in Personality, 13,* 420–432.

Bower, G. H., Gilligan, S. G., & Monteiro, K. P. (1981). Selectivity of learning caused by affective states. *Journal of Experimental Psychology: General, 110,* 451–473.

Bowlby, J. (1969). *Attachment and loss* (Vol. 1). London: Hogarth. (New York: Basic Books.)

Boyle, G. J. (1983). Effects on academic learning of manipulating emotional states and motivational dynamics. *British Journal of Educational Psychology, 53,* 347–357.

Bryan, T. H., & Pearl, R. A. (1981). Self-concepts and locus of control of learning disabled children. *Educational Horizons, 59,* 91–96.

Campbell, J. (1971). *The portable Jung.* New York: Viking Press.

Canfield, J., & Wells, M. C. (1975). Self-concept: A critical dimension in teaching and learning. In D. A. Read & S. B. Simon (Eds.), *Humanistic education source book* (pp. 460–468). Englewood Cliffs, NJ: Prentice-Hall.

Cavanaugh, J. C., & Perlmutter, M. (1982). Metamemory: A critical examination. *Child Development, 53,* 11–28.

Coopersmith, S. (1967). *The antecedents of self-esteem.* San Francisco: Freeman.

Crowne, D. P., & Marlowe, D. (1964). *The approval motive.* New York: Wiley.

Das, J. P. (1980). Planning: Theoretical considerations and empirical evidence. *Psychological Research* (W. Germany), *41,* 141–151.

Dean, R. S. (1977). Effects of self-concept on learning with gifted children. *Journal of Educational Research, 70*, 315–318.

de Bono, E. (1983). The direct teaching of thinking as a skill. *Phi Delta Kappan, 64*, 703–708.

Derry, P. A., & Kuiper, N. A. (1981). Schematic processing and self-reference in clinical depression. *Journal of Abnormal Psychology, 90*, 286–297.

Dyk, R. B. (1969). An exploratory study of mother–child interaction in infancy as related to the development of differentiation. *Journal of the American Academy of Child Psychiatry, 8*, 657–691.

Festinger, L. (1957). *A theory of cognitive dissonance*. Stanford: Stanford University Press.

Flavell, J. H., & Wellman, H. M. (1977). Metamemory. In R. V. Kail, Jr. & J. W. Hagen (Eds.), *Perspectives on the development of memory and cognition*. Hillsdale, NJ: Erlbaum.

Fleming, J. S., & Watts, W. A. (1980). The dimensionality of self-esteem: Some results for a college sample. *Journal of Personality and Social Psychology, 39*, 921–929.

Gaines, L. S., Fretz. B. R., & Helweg, G. C. (1975). Self-referent language and need for approval. *Psychological Reports, 37*, 107–111.

Gazzaniga, M. (1985). *The social brain: Discovering the networks of the mind*. New York: Basic Books.

Gur, R. C., & Sackheim, H. A. (1979). Self-deception: A concept in search of a phenomenon. *Journal of Personality and Social Psychology, 37*, 147–152.

Hamachek, D. E. (1978). *Encounters with the self* (2nd ed.). New York: Holt, Rinehart & Winston.

Henshaw, D. (1978). *A cognitive analysis of creative problem-solving*. Unpublished doctoral dissertation, University of Waterloo.

Husserl, E. (1960). *Cartesian meditations: An introduction to phenomenology*. The Hague: Martinus Nijhoff.

Kelly, G. (1963). *A theory of personality*. New York: Norton.

Kernberg, O. (1980). *Internal world and external reality: Object relations theory applied*. New York: Jason Aronson.

Kohut, H. (1971). *The analysis of self: The psychoanalytic treatment of narcissistic personality disorders*. New York: International Universities Press.

Kohut, H. (1977). *The restoration of the self*. New York: International Universtities Press.

Kuiper, M. A., & Derry, P. A. (1980). The self as a cognitive prototype: An application to person perception and depression. In M. Cantor & J. Kihlstrom (Eds.), *Cognition, social interaction, and personality*. Hillsdale, NJ: Erlbaum.

Kuiper, N. A., & MacDonald, M. R. (1982). Self and other perception in mild depressives. *Social Cognition, 3*, 223–239.

Kuiper, N. A., & Olinger, L. J. (in press). Dysfunctional attitudes and a self-worth contingency model of depression. In P. C. Kendall (Ed.), *Advances in cognitive–behavioral research and therapy, Vol. 5*. New York: Academic Press.

MacDonald, M. R., & Kuiper, N. A. (1984). Self-schema decision contingency in clinical depressives. *Journal of Social and Clinical Psychology, 2*, 264–272.

Margalit, M., & Zak, I. (1984). Anxiety and self-concept of learning disabled children. *Journal of Learning Disabilities, 17*, 537–539.

Markus, H. (1977). Self-schemata and processing information about the self. *Journal of Personality and Social Psychology, 35*, 63–78.

Markus, H., & Sentis, K. (1982). The self in social information processing. In J. Suls (Ed.), *Psychological perspectives on the self*. Hillsdale, NJ: Erlbaum.

Marton, F. (1981). Phenomenography—Describing conceptions of the world around us. *Instructional Science, 10*, 177–200.

McCarrey, M., Edwards, H. P., & Rosario, W. (1982). Ego-relevant feedback, affect, and self-serving attributional bias. *Personality and Social Psychology Bulletin, 8*, 189–194.

McCarthy, P. R., & Schmeck, R. R. (1982). Effects of teacher self-disclosure on student learning and perceptions of teacher. *College Student Journal, 16,* 45–49.

Meichenbaum, D. (1980). A cognitive–behavioral perspective on intelligence. *Intelligence, 4,* 271–283.

Meier, S. T., McCarthy, P. R., & Schmeck, R. R. (1984). Validity of self-efficacy as a predictor of writing performance. *Cognitive Therapy and Research, 8,* 107–120.

Muller, D., & Spuhler, R. (1976). The effects of experimentally induced changes in self-concept on associative learning. *Journal of Psychology, 92,* 89–95.

Natale, M., & Hantas, M. (1982). Effects of temporary mood states on selective memory about the self. *Journal of Personality and Social Psychology, 42,* 927–934.

Ornstein, R. (1985). *Psychology: The study of human experience.* New York: Harcourt Brace Jovanovich.

Pervin, L. A. (1984). *Current controversies & issues in personality* (2nd ed.). New York: Wiley.

Piaget, J. (1952). *The origins of intelligence in children.* New York: International Universities Press.

Piaget, J. (1962). *Play, dreams, and imitation in childhood.* New York: Norton.

Powell, J. P. (1981). Helping and hindering learning. *Higher Education, 10,* 103–117.

Prawer, F. H. (1974). The self-concept as related to achievement in foreign language study. *American Foreign Language Teacher, 4,* 7–10.

Rogers, C. R. (1969). *The freedom to learn.* Columbus, OH: Merrill.

Rogers, M. F. (1983). *Sociology, ethnomethodology, and experience.* Cambridge: Cambridge University Press.

Rogers, T., Kuiper, N., & Kirker, W. (1977). Self-reference and the encoding of personal information. *Journal of Personality and Social Psychology, 35,* 677–688.

Rogers, T. B., Rogers, P. J., & Kuiper, N. A. (1979). Evidence for the self as a cognitive prototype: "The false alarm effect." *Personality and Social Psychology Bulletin, 5,* 53–56.

Rothbart, M. K., & Posner, M. I. (1985). Temperament and the development of self regulation. In L. C. Hartlage & L. F. Telzrow (Eds.), *The neuropsychology of individual differences.* New York: Plenum.

Rotter, J. B. (1966). Generalized expectancies for internal versus external control of reinforcement. *Psychological Monographs, 81* (1 Whole No. 609).

Rychlak, J. F. (1975). Affective assessment, intelligence, social class, and racial learning style. *Journal of Personality and Social Psychology, 32,* 989–995.

Santrock, J. W. (1986). *Life-span development* (2nd ed.). Dubuque, IA: Brown.

Schmeck, R. R. (1983). Learning styles of college students. In R. Dillon & R. R. Schmeck (Eds.), *Individual differences in cognition.* New York: Academic Press.

Schmeck, R. R., & Meier, S. T. (1984). Self-reference as a learning strategy and a learning style. *Human Learning, 3,* 9–17.

Sharp, G. L., & Muller, D. (1978). The effects of lowering self-concept on associative learning. *Journal of Psychology, 100,* 233–241.

Strassberg-Rosenberg, B. S., & Gaier, E. L. (1977). The self-concept of the adolescent with learning disabilities. *Adolescence, 12,* 489–498.

Tulving, E. (1985). How many memory systems are there? *American Psychologist, 40,* 385–398.

Waters, E., Wippman, J., & Sroufe, L. A. (1979). Attachment, positive affect, and competence in the peer group: Two studies in construct validation. *Child Development, 50,* 821–829.

Weiner, I. B. (1980). Psychopathology in adolescence. In J. Adelson (Ed.), *Handbook of adolescent psychology.* New York: Wiley.

Weininger, O. (1983). Play of mothers with babies: Some relationships between maternal personality and early attachment and development processes. *Psychological Reports,* *53,* 27–42.

Willerman, L. (1979). *The psychology of individual and group differences.* San Francisco: Freeman.

Winne, P. H., Woodlands, M. J., & Wong, B. Y. L. (1982). Comparability of self-concept among learning disabled, normal, and gifted students. *Journal of Learning Disabilities,* *15,* 471–475.

Winnicott, D. M. (1965). *The maturational process and the facilitating environment.* New York: International Universities Press.

Wylie, R. C. (1974). *The self-concept.* Lincoln: University of Nebraska Press.

PART II

Applications of the Concepts of Strategy and Style

CHAPTER 7

Context and Strategy

Situational Influences on Learning

PAUL RAMSDEN

INTRODUCTION

This chapter focuses on contextual aspects of learning. Its special concern is with understanding higher education students' learning in terms of the teaching and evaluation environment in which it takes place. The question posed is this: How does this environment, defined by institutional practices, assessment methods, the skills and attitudes of faculty, and the kinds of learning tasks encountered, influence the ways individual students learn?

The argument advanced here is that learning in realistic educational settings involves students in adapting to those settings. It is necessary to understand the process of adaptation in order to understand the process and outcome of learning academic content. Consider the simple dichotomies between the context of learning for the doctoral student and the undergraduate; between problem and discipline-based curricula; between a threatening, punitive method of teaching and a supportive, empathetic one; between a learning task requiring no more than the application of the correct algorithm and one demanding insight and creativity; between clinical problem solving and respiratory physiology; between science and humanities subjects; between evaluation by multiple-choice questions and by term papers. Context differences impose on or suggest to students different strategies of learning; individuals try to

PAUL RAMSDEN • Centre for the Study of Higher Education, University of Melbourne, Parkville, Victoria 3052, Australia.

adapt to the demands and opportunities presented by the content of what is to be learned and its institutional setting.

The next section of the chapter enlarges on this idea of adaptation by outlining a model of situational influences on learning. From this model, a number of expectations are derived concerning approaches to and strategies of learning in different contexts. These are examined against some evidence from empirical studies of upper secondary and, especially, higher education. Issues of the relative influence of individual stylistic differences and the context of learning are considered against this background. Finally, we look at some implications of our knowledge of learning-in-context for intervention aimed at improving learning in higher education.

A MODEL OF SITUATIONAL INFLUENCES ON STUDENT LEARNING

Our model of situational influences (learning-in-context) maintains that three related contextual domains constitute influences on students' deployment of strategies of learning in the institutional settings of higher education. The three domains are the teaching (the method of transmission of what is learned), the assessment (the method of evaluation of what is learned), and the curriculum (the content and structure of what is learned).

The point of contact between the context and student experience is defined as the student's perception of assessment, teaching, and curriculum (see Figure 1). This experiential link is one mechanism that explains how the context influences learning. However, contextual effects operate directly as well as indirectly. The three contextual domains directly constrain the use of strategies. For example, learning material may lack a structure which can be meaningfully grasped; it is not possible to use a learning process other than memorizing or imposing meaning through a mnemonic strategy to learn such material (Dahlgren, 1978). To take another instance, poor teaching of basic concepts may prevent a deep approach from being realized in relation to more complex subject matter that *does* have an internal structure that can be grasped.

The context influences student learning indirectly through students' perceptions of the requirements of learning tasks. Perceptions of tasks describe a relation between the student's experience and the three domains. Each time an individual begins a realistic learning task, whether it is reading a scientific paper, trying to solve a problem in engineering, or writing an essay in history, numerous decisions about its requirements have to be faced. The student's perception of a task's

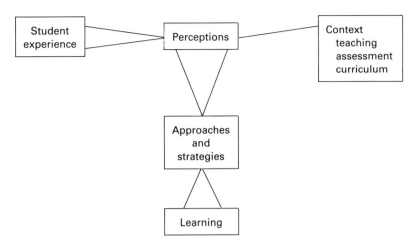

Figure 1. A model of learning in context.

demands is partly a function of his or her previous experiences of learning, partly a function of the characteristics of the context.

Learning tasks are always tackled in context, but the way in which a student engages with the task is only partly explained by the relationship between context and experience. A complete model would need to include many diverse elements, such as chance, determination to succeed, and the motivational factors discussed by Entwistle (Chapter 2, this volume). According to the present model, different strategies of learning will be adaptive in different contexts. It is assumed that students strive to adapt to the context, although there is no assumption that their efforts will be successful or that successful adaptation implies that learning will occur. The educational import of this model is that in so far as contextual variables are in the control of instructors, it is possible to structure the environment of learning in such a way that adaptive responses are congruent with instructors' aims.

The following expectations flow from our model. Observation of different teaching and evaluation contexts will reveal that different learning strategies are used in differently structured environments. For example, some learning tasks will be seen to require reproductive approaches, while others will require meaningful ones. There will be within-student variation depending on the nature of the task. There will be similar variation depending on the student's perception of the adequacy and range of the teaching experienced. General effects of learning contexts at the level of programs and institutions should also be observable. For example, notwithstanding within-group variation in deep or surface approaches to learning, students encountering problem-based curricula in professional education should be expected to adopt meaningful approaches more consistently than those experiencing discipline-based curricula. Interventions to change approaches to learning will be more or less successful depending on the student's perception of the demands of the learning context in relation to the intervention. There will also be consistency in strategies within students; students' previous experiences will shape the decisions they make to adopt different approaches.

LEARNING TASKS AND LEARNING STRATEGIES

A fundamental concept for describing how students learn is that of *approach*. The dichotomy between deep and surface approaches, as we have seen elsewhere in this book, is applicable to many different types of learning tasks. Approaches have both a referential and a relational component. The *referential* component is concerned with the student's intention—whether he or she focuses on the meaning of the numbers, words, or sentences in the learning material or on the components themselves, to the exclusion of what they signify. The *relational* component is about process, or cognitive approach, that is, whether the student is oriented toward (a) manipulating the task in such a way that its underlying structure is retained (deep or "holistic" approach) or (b) tinkering with the components of the task so that its content structure is distorted (surface or "atomistic" approach; see Marton, Chapter 3, this volume). A nontrivial educational question is how to present tasks so as to engage the student at a deep level.

The emphasis in this chapter, as in Marton's, is on learning which is aimed at improving the understanding of a phenomenon by taking part in a symbolic representation of that phenomenon. People's ways of learning represent relations between them and aspects of the world around them. The perception of a task describes a relation between context and student experience. Deep and surface approaches describe a relation between student perceptions and learning (Laurillard, 1984). This definition of approach makes it clear that approaches, as originally defined by Marton (1976) are both context dependent and student dependent. The Gothenburg studies and the subsequent work of Laurillard (1979, 1984) entail the assumption that approaches, defined as *relations*, are not *characteristics* of students. The empirical studies of Säljö (1975) and Laurillard lend some support to this position. In an investigation of university students' approaches to reading chapters from textbooks (Marton & Säljö, 1976), subjects were divided into two groups. One group was asked questions of a highly factual and specific nature, while the other was asked questions that focused on relations between conclusions and evidence and required judgment. It was clear that the first group of students were induced to adopt surface approaches. However, not all of the second group used deep approaches. It would seem that students in this group interpreted what was demanded of them in different ways and adapted to the assessment context in unexpected ways. This is a good example of the difficulties that arise in trying to structure the learning context to encourage appropriate adaptive responses. We return to this issue later.

While Marton and Säljö were originally interested in reading tasks, Laurillard looked at science students' approaches to their most common form of assignment—problem solving. The majority of students in her study exhibited both surface and deep approaches, supporting the interpretation that they perceived the requirements of problems differently and adjusted their intentions accordingly. Two descriptions of different approaches by the same student illustrate the dichotomy and its contextual referents.

Deep approach:

This has to be handed in—it's an operation research exercise, a program to find a minimum point on a curve. First I had to decide on the criteria of how to approach it, then drew a flow diagram, and checked through each stage. You have to think about it and understand it first. I used my knowledge of O.R. design of starting with one point, testing it and judging the next move. I try to work through logically. . . . I chose this problem because it was more applied, more realistic. You can learn how to go about O.R. You get an idea of the different types of problem that exist from reading.

Surface approach:

This problem is not to be handed in, but it will be discussed in the lecture because the rest of the course depends on this kind of thing. I knew how I'd do it from looking at it; it practically tells you what equation to use. You just have to bash the numbers out. I knew how to do it before I started so I didn't get anything out of it. There's not really any thinking. You just need to know what you need to solve the problem. I read through the relevant notes, but not much because you don't need to look at the system . . . in this sort of situation you've got to get through to the answer. (Laurillard, 1984, pp. 134–135)

Laurillard's discussion of the contextual variability of comprehension and operation learning styles within her sample of students is also important. Pask's identification of these two styles has frequently been confused with Marton's deep-surface dichotomy, but these two ways of describing learning are best seen as lying within separate dimensions. Operation learning concerns the manipulation of entities within the subject matter domain and the use of rules and procedures; comprehension learning involves their description, or meaning, and the search for analogies. All students in Laurillard's investigation were found to use both styles of learning, but the proportion of one to the other varied depending on the task. On a stereographic projection task, all used operation learning to a high degree; on an equilibrium diagram task, half were biased more towards comprehension learning (Laurillard, 1979, 1984). It ' seems clear that tasks influence the choice of learning style. An extension of this line of reasoning leads us to expect that styles will vary in different subject areas.

Perceptions of learning tasks are partly determined by students' previous experiences. It is often difficult to separate context and previous experience in describing learning in normal studies. Background knowledge and interest in the material of the task, both of which are in turn related to contextual factors such as experiences of teaching and curriculum structure, are particularly important influences on approach. Intrinsic interest in the subject matter—learning out of interest and a desire to find something out—is, not surprisingly, associated with an intention to impose meaning. In his study of reading, Fransson (1977) demonstrated that intrinsic motivation, absence of threat, and absence of anxiety, as perceived by students (although not always as intended by the experimenter), were associated with a deep approach. Failure to perceive relevance was related to surface approaches. Ramsden (1984) described similar relationships between interest and approach in the normal setting of students' course work. It is also apparent that inadequate background knowledge in a field may influence both the student's intention and the process used to carry out that intention (Entwistle & Ramsden, 1983).

STUDENT ASSESSMENT AND APPROACHES TO LEARNING

We now turn to the relation between student experience and the evaluation domain. Several investigations have identified methods of student assessment as the most critical situational influence on learning strategies. The evidence constitutes a serious indictment of many of the current ways in which student learning in higher education is evaluated. Yet the potentially debilitating effects of inappropriate assessments have been known about for many years, even if the mechanisms by which they operate have not been fully understood. As long ago as 1876, Pattison complained of an Oxford assessment system in which "memory is really almost the only faculty called into play" (Pattison, 1876). Much later, Snyder (1971) identified a disjunction between the aims of the formal curriculum as defined by faculty staff, which emphasized independence of thought and analytic skills, and a "hidden" curriculum perceived by students, whose message was that rote memorization of theories and facts considered important by teachers was required in college.

As we saw above, questions designed to encourage students to use surface approaches to reading succeed in their intention (Marton & Säljö, 1984), while methods of problem solving are functionally associated with students' perceptions of grading schemes (Laurillard, 1984). Fransson's investigation (1977) illustrated the important point that perceived anxiety, created by a threatening assessment situation (whether thus manipulated by the experimenter or not), increased the probability of surface approaches. Research carried out by other Swedish workers (Dahlgren, 1978; Johansson, Marton, & Svensson, 1985) makes it clear that higher education students' misapprehensions of fundamental concepts in economics and physics may remain undisturbed by the questions they are asked in assessments. If the evaluation of students' learning does not go beyond what can be unreflectively retained in the memory, then misunderstandings may never be revealed, despite the fact that students have successfully negotiated examinations. Dahlgren's study of economics students showed that, although the results of end-of-first-year examinations implied that students had developed an understanding of such basic concepts as the mechanism of price determination in a free market, in fact:

> If a more thorough understanding is required in order to answer a question, the number of acceptable answers is very low. . . . In many cases, it appeared that only a minority of students had apprehended basic concepts in the way intended by teachers and textbook authors. Complex problems seem to be solved by application of memorized algorithmic procedures. . . . In order to cope with overwhelming curricula, the students probably have to abandon their ambitions to understand what they read about and instead direct efforts towards passing examinations . . . which reflect the view that knowledge is a quantity. (Dahlgren, 1978)

Investigations of British students have revealed similar connections between excessive workloads, inappropriate forms of assessment, and surface approaches (Entwistle & Ramsden, 1983). A physics student spoke of how his learning was geared solely to examined topics; his revision was "purely and simply aimed at passing the exams without bothering too much about studying the subject" (p. 153). A geology student talked of "just memorizing a few facts" to get credits for courses he needed but did not enjoy; while "for some coursework you can get it straight out of the textbook and you give them a result, just copying down something if you're lucky—which lots of people do" (p. 152). It seems clear that inappropriate assessment methods and an excessive amount of curricular material may both encourage surface approaches and hide the inadequate understanding which such approaches inevitably lead to. The evaluation process provides a signal to students about the kind of learning they are expected to carry out; they adapt by choosing strategies that will apparently maximize success.

A combination of high perceived workload and limited choice over study methods was strongly associated with high scores on surface approaches in a survey of British university undergraduates (Ramsden & Entwistle, 1981); this evidence is discussed in more detail below. If the evaluation domain is such a strong influence, as these various studies suggest, we would expect intervention consisting of changes to assessment methods to influence students' approaches dramatically.

An excellent example of how relatively small changes in evaluation methods may have a quite disproportionate impact on learning comes from the experience of the School of Medicine at Adelaide University, Australia (Newble & Jaeger, 1983). In 1971, final-year assessment was modified to emphasize the importance of clinical skills. Ward-based assessments replaced the traditional clinical *viva*. However, the new ward-based assessments proved to be less critical than expected—few students failed them. Students responded by spending less time in the wards and more in library study for the more hazardous theoretical component of the clinical assessment, based on multiple-choice questions. The effect of the change was thus exactly opposite to that intended, but precisely as our understanding of learning-in-context would suggest. There was a disjunction between the faculty's goals and the goals perceived by the students to be expressed in the new scheme. The students' response was a rational adaptation to circumstances. When faculty responded by introducing a more innovative and demanding form of practical clinical assessment, the effect was to improve student learning: students' study habits were less influenced by the theory test, and the form of assessment was seen to be relevant to subsequent practice.

Some recent evidence indicates that closed-ended and open-ended assessments in higher education tend to elicit different types of learning strategy (Thomas & Bain, 1984). A transformational approach, involving some restructuring of material to afford a better understanding of it and bearing some similarity to a holistic approach, was more common in relation to written assignments than a reproductive approach. Similarly, the reproductive approach, having some resemblance to an atomistic approach, although also including the use and understanding of terminology and facts, was more often used in association with multiple-choice and short-answer examinations. There was also some cross-situational consistency in students' preferred approaches, which is congruent with Marton's original conception of approach and the arguments advanced by Entwistle, Biggs, and Schmeck in this volume. Another series of Australasian studies (Crooks & Mahalski, 1985) has linked study strategies to the cognitive demands of different types of university examination. Three investigations of note taking and performance revealed that students adapted to examinations which were seen to test low-level skills by narrowing their attention to material presented in class. Surface approaches, involving students in collecting large quantities of notes which were later reproduced in the examinations, were effective—as far as grades were concerned—in the tests which focused on the lower cognitive levels.

TEACHING AND APPROACHES TO LEARNING

We have seen that certain assessment methods encourage surface approaches, and in some situations, other assessment methods may help to elicit meaningful strategies. Effective teaching and greater freedom to choose content and ways of learning also appear from recent research findings to be important positive influences on the use of deep approaches.

From our perspective, effective teaching in higher education is teaching which enhances the facilitators or mediators of task performance (see Messick, 1982). Effective teaching places students in situations where they are encouraged to develop more complex conceptions of learning and practice the use of deep, holistic approaches. There is surprising unanimity about the characteristics which are linked to such enhancement. Factor analytic studies of students' ratings of instructors (see e.g., Kulik & McKeachie, 1975) and of departmental environments (see Entwistle & Ramsden, 1983; Gaff, Crombag, & Chang, 1976; Jones, 1981) have identified dimensions of good teaching, such as skill in lecturing, choice of content and method, reasonable workload, clear goals, and a recurring factor variously labeled "student-centeredness," "respect for students," or "individual guidance." The latter factor probably reflects the teacher's capacity to feel and demonstrate empathy. Brennan and Percy (1977) reported that British students distinguished between good and bad instructors chiefly in terms of the concern the teachers showed for student learning and their awareness of communication difficulties between themselves and their students. The Lancaster study (Entwistle & Ramsden, 1983; Ramsden & Entwistle, 1981; see also Chapter 2, this volume) revealed similar factors. Especially important in defining good teaching was help with students' learning problems. The scales of the course perceptions questionnaire developed in this study (Table 1) summarize the main dimensions of effective learning contexts as seen by students.

Until recently it has been difficult to see how these several con-

Table 1. *Categories Describing Students' Perceptions of Courses and Academic Departments*

Good teaching	How much help faculty give students with study problems; how competent and well-prepared faculty are perceived to be
Freedom in learning	How much discretion students have over choice of curriculum content and methods of learning
Openness to students	How friendly and adaptive to student needs faculty are perceived to be
Workload	How crowded the curriculum and how heavy the pressure to submit or prepare for assessed work is
Social climate	The quality of academic and social relationships between students
Formal teaching	The importance placed on class teaching relative to individual study
Clear goals and standards	How clear the standards of assessed work and the goals of study are perceived to be
Vocational relevance	The perceived relevance of the content studied to students' careers

Note. Adapted from Ramsden, 1984.

textural variables connect with learning. It is remarkably hard to demonstrate that teaching in higher education influences learning outcomes. What was missing from the earlier attempts was an understanding of the important indirect effects that operate through the process of students' adaptation to different types of teaching. The recent work, especially that which has employed rigorous qualitative analysis of interview data, clearly outlines the steps by which the higher education teaching context influences student learning outcomes by connecting students' perceptions of what instructors do with their approaches and orientations to learning.

Hodgson (1984) has examined students' experiences of lectures in a British university. Two categories of engagement with the lecture were identified which were analogous to deep and surface approaches: an intrinsic experience of relevance of the lecture and an extrinsic one. However, relevance could also be experienced vicariously, an intermediate category between extrinsic and intrinsic which stresses the quality of the relationship between teacher and student. It appears that teaching which helps students to perceive relevance through the teacher's use of vivid illustrations and enthusiasm can help students to see the content as having meaning in the real world. Hence, vicarious experience of relevance provides a bridge between extrinsic experience (surface approach) and intrinsic experience (deep approach), and it appears that such experience is fostered by good teaching. Hodgson's investigation clarifies the connection between the skills identified in studies of lecturing as "lecturer–student rapport" or "maintenance of student interest" and approaches to learning. Her findings also fit well with Jones's (1981) description of a general factor in New Zealand university students' definitions of good teaching, as noted above—student-centeredness or the structuring of a course in such a way that it encourages perceptions of relevance and independence in learning.

Research at Lancaster also demonstrated functional connections between students' perceptions of teaching quality and their approaches to learning. In an extensive interview study (summarized in Ramsden, 1984), the teaching context was shown to influence the adaptive behavior of students in a number of ways. Links were revealed between previously identified aspects of good teaching in higher education—such as interest in undergraduate students, commitment to a speciality, help with difficulties in understanding, teaching at a level appropriate to the student's current knowledge, regular feedback on performance—and students' methods of tackling particular tasks. Similar findings emerged from replication studies in Australia (e.g., Watkins, 1982).

Instructors in higher education typically have a great deal of say over the degree of structure and the balance between teacher and student direction in their courses. Students' perceptions of choice over content and method of study are associated with deep approaches. It appears likely that there are at least two mechanisms by which student choice may influence approaches to learning. First, if there is a degree of discretion over methods of teaching and learning (group work, formal instruction, individual study, etc.), students may self-select study environments which suit their preferred habits of learning, or at least if a variety of methods is used they stand a greater chance of encountering a personally stimulating one. Second, and more obvious, interest in a learning task is likely to be greater if it has been chosen by the student rather than imposed by an instructor, and interest in performing learning tasks for their own sake tends to evoke deep approaches. Conversely, restriction in choice over assessed work (e.g., a high proportion of compulsory examination or assignment questions) tightens the focus of studying to essentials and suggests to students that they ought to pay special attention to the external form in which the material to be learned is presented rather than its content. Successful strategies are likely to involve verbatim note taking and the rehearsal of expected answers.

PROGRAMS, DEPARTMENTS, AND INSTITUTIONS

What general effects of different types of courses and programs undertaken in different institutions or taught within different academic departments can be observed? If teaching and assessment policies in academic units vary, what influence does this have on students' adaptive behavior and hence on their approaches to learning? Over the last few years an impressive body of evidence has been accumulated which unambigously demonstrates such general effects at higher and upper secondary educational levels.

In Chapter 2, Noel Entwistle described the development and use of an Approaches-to-Studying Inventory in Britain. In the national survey (Entwistle & Ramsden, 1983; Ramsden & Entwistle, 1981), from Marton's characterization of approaches to learning as relationships between perceptions and study methods it was predicted that approaches to learning would vary directly with students' perceptions of academic units (which in this case were British academic departments). That is to say, under conditions in which surface approaches would be adaptive, scores on the inventory's reproducing orientation scale would be high. Conditions for surface approaches to be adaptive would be situations of high workload combined with a lack of discretion over method and content of study. Conversely, though less certainly, meaning orientation scores would be high under conditions perceived to consist of choice over method and content together with good teaching.

The results of the analysis gave strong support to this predicted pattern. The relationships between course perceptions (as measured by the course perceptions instrument described above; see Table 1) and the two principal orientations remained firm in different academic areas and were not influenced by differences in student attainment. Two other findings made sense in the context of the earlier qualitative work and Marton's theories. First, students in the condition of good teaching and choice were more likely to report positive attitudes to academic work; in the low-choice–high-workload condition, the opposite response (cynical and disenchanted attitudes) was more common. Second, it was easier to predict which departments would score higher on reproducing orientation than on meaning orientation. This was consistent with Marton and Säljö's finding (Marton & Säljö, 1976) that surface approaches could be induced in students relatively easily, while changes to the types of questions asked did not necessarily lead to the use of deep approaches. It is perhaps the case that some students perceive the environment as one demanding shallow memorization, even when the instructor intends for the reverse to be true.

Subsequent studies of different institutions and departments have revealed differences in students' orientations which are hard to explain except in terms of contextual effects. In Australia, Clarke and Newble (1985) examined characteristic patterns of approaches to studying in two contrasting medical schools, using a slightly modified version of the

Approaches-to-Studying Inventory. In the Newcastle school, which has a problem-based curriculum similar to that at McMaster University, students scored consistently higher on meaning orientation than students in the more traditional school. These differences were not explicable in terms of the different approaches used by students before entry to their medical courses. Again in Australia, differences are apparent between students' learning strategies in different tertiary education sectors consistent with the educational policies of those sectors (Biggs, 1982). Cross-sectoral differences in approaches, apparently associated with the differing curriculum and teaching practices, have been observed in undergraduate students in English universities and polytechnics (Ramsden, 1983).

There is evidence that different types of high school environment influence the deployment of approaches to learning. This chapter does not examine the large corpus of research on public school learning environments, although the main dimensions identified in such studies bear a strong resemblance to those discovered in the research on higher education students. Selmes' (1985) research suggests that senior high schools employing different teaching methods would be expected to elicit different approaches in their students. A recent study of British sixth-form students which made use of a modified version of the Approaches-to-Studying Inventory (Martin, 1985) has revealed differences in approaches which conform to the expected pattern. Both schools in the investigation taught the English A-level curriculum (the main, externally examined qualification for entry to tertiary education), to students of similar ability, but in different ways. One school tried to encourage independence in learning by stressing the development of information-using strategies and the use of small-group teaching methods. The other adopted more traditional, didactic approaches to teaching aimed directly at ensuring success in the external examinations. The inventory results showed that students in the first school scored significantly higher on meaning orientation and lower on reproducing orientation than students in the second school. However, they were also more likely to show evidence of the learning pathology of *globetrotting* (see Chapter 2)—a tendency to jump to unsubstantiated conclusions. This may explain why students in both schools gained similar examination results on average.

At the more general level of high school learning contexts in different countries, Entwistle and Kozecki's work on Scottish and Hungarian school students' approaches to learning (Entwistle & Kozecki, 1985) has produced findings consistent with those summarized above. Within Hungarian schools in recent years the greater emphasis on imaginative thinking and the *use* of factual material, rather than on its rote learning, was reflected in students' higher scores on meaning orientation. The Scottish students, in a context of learning in which external examinations played a major part, scored higher on reproducing. However, they were also less likely to display the failure to support imaginative thinking by evidence and logic which characterizes globetrotting. Entwistle and Kozecki suggest that in both countries the emphasis in teaching may be unbalanced.

THE CONTEXT OF LEARNING IN DIFFERENT SUBJECT SPECIALISMS

We have already considered several ways in which the content and structure of what is learned in higher education may influence learning strategies. A direct curriculum constraint, and an obvious one, is the specialism (or major) being studied. Learning physics at college is different from learning history. But why? Intuitively, one is a "hard" specialty: cumulative, paradigmatic, replicable, structured, capable of being summarized in terms of general laws. The other is "soft": particularistic, idiographic, reinterpretive, and not amenable to broad generalizations. Other distinctions between specialties rest on differences between life systems and nonlife systems (e.g., biology vs. computing; Biglan, 1973a, 1973b; Schwab, 1964) and between pure and applied fields of knowledge—the former being concerned more with achieving understanding and the latter more with improving practice.

The question we address here is, how do these differences influence the strategies higher education students adopt? This is a complex issue. Students entering most tertiary education systems have already developed interests and loyalties to specialisms—in an extreme case, England, decisions about science versus arts specialization are often made early in high school. Students begin college with a good deal of tacit knowledge of the disciplinary culture in which they study. Moreover, there are systematic differences between faculty attitudes and teaching methods in different subjects areas which are part of a complicated system of culturally defined norms and rituals. These influences make it impossible to isolate purely subject-dependent contextual features.

However, a clear picture of disciplinary cultures emerges from a number of studies. Faculty in scientific and professional fields are more likely to use formal, didactic teaching methods and are less permissive in their attitudes towards students and student learning. Humanities and social science teachers are less likely to see the evaluation of students as a method of classifying and motivating students (Wilson, Gaff,

Dienst, Wood, & Bavry, 1975). It is hardly surprising that students' perceptions of different specialisms reflect faculty's methods and attitudes (Gaff *et al.*, 1976), with applied and scientific fields being seen to demand more time and commitment, to offer fewer opportunities for self-direction, to have clearer goals in their courses, and to be more vocationally relevant.

Recent work reveals that students have implicit theories about how subject specialties impose constraints on learning strategies (Ramsden, 1984). To oversimplify the findings somewhat, science and arts students have consistent views about the types of learning these two broadly defined subject areas demand; they also agree on what the differences are. Learning tasks in science are typically described as hierarchical, logical, heterogeneous, and rule and procedure governed; humanities and social science tasks are seen to require interpretation, comparison, generalization, and self-direction. The constructs mirror with remarkable accuracy the distinction between operation and comprehension learning described by Pask (1976). Manipulation of concepts and objects within the subject matter domain and an emphasis on procedure building, rules, methods, and details are characteristic of operation learning styles and the science approaches described in these students' implicit theories. General description and interpretation of relations between topics defines comprehension learning and is related by students to typical approaches in arts and social science disciplines. The two types of strategy map neatly on to the different teaching and assessment practices of the two cultures.

These strategy stereotypes tell us a lot about the typical pattern of learning tasks set in different subject specialisms. If they reflect the reality of how the context of learning affects strategies, we would expect that systematic differences in styles of learning should be apparent in professional, science, and humanities students. Of course, self-selection of students for different fields will play an important part, but in any case, differences among specialisms do occur. Entwistle and Ramsden (1983) reported that, in a survey of 2,200 British college students, science and engineering students scored highest on operation learning measures, and arts and social science students scored highest on comprehension learning measures. However, high combined operation and comprehension learning scores—in Pask's terms, versatility in strategies—were also more common in science students.

We noted above that different tasks within a specialism appear to elicit different strategies in the same student. If strategies are context dependent, do deep and surface approaches themselves differ in academic specialisms? The conclusion of current research is that while the general distinction is applicable to tasks as diverse as reading academic articles and solving engineering problems, the meaning of the concepts has to be reinterpreted in relation to different subject areas. The descriptive category of deep approach needs to be redefined somewhat to include, in some science tasks especially, an *initially* narrow concentration on detail, which taken on its own is empirically hard to distinguish from a surface approach. In contrast, deep approaches in the humanities seem more likely to involve the student in stressing, right from the start, an intention to reinterpret material in a personal way. In describing surface approaches, science students are more likely to emphasise over-concentrating on techniques and procedural details. Arts students tend to report a more generalized, vague approach, which typically includes oversimplification of the main ideas in reading and essay writing or memorizing unrelated generalities in their preparation for assessments (Ramsden, 1984).

CONTEXT AND STYLE CONTROVERSIES

To what extent are the ways in which students learn determined by individual differences in learning style and to what extent by students' responses to environmental demands? Are approaches to learning stable attributes of students, or are they alterable? Are strategies of learning consistent across situations? These closely related questions do not permit any straightforward answers. One source of confusion arises from the research questions asked in different studies. Studies which have concentrated on comparisons between distinct tasks have tended to provide evidence of variability; those concentrating on general approaches or orientations reveal consistency. However this is not the whole story.

The first issue to examine is the consistency or variability of deep–holistic and surface–atomistic approaches, or more generally, meaning and reproducing orientations. It is true beyond any reasonable doubt that individual students in higher education display variability in their approaches to learning tasks. Deep and surface approaches to learning are highly responsive to the context of learning, as the evidence which has documented within-student variation across contexts clearly indicates. Indeed, the definition of *approach* as a relation between a person's perception and learning rather than an individual characteristic entails contextual variation. However, it also permits approaches to be seen as partly dependent on students' preferences. The critical experiment was that of Säljö (1975). Säljö found that if two groups of students expect different kinds of questions after reading, they will adopt different approaches to a reading task. But he also found variation both in process and outcome of learning within the group that was given questions intended to elicit a deep approach. Differences within the same treatment group must have had their origins in differing perceptions which the students brought with them to the experiment (Marton & Säljö, 1984; see also Chapter 3, this volume). In other words, some students used surface approaches even though deep approaches were called for; these individuals must have interpreted the context as requiring a different method of study from the subjects who used deep approaches. According to Säljö, their interpretation was a function of their previous experiences with similar learning tasks.

In fact, there is a persuasive evidence of consistency in approaches over time and tasks. Such evidence is entirely in accord with common sense and does not disturb the relational character of the concept of approach. It is not surprising that individual students develop habitual ways of approaching study tasks. The concept of study orientation (meaning orientation, reproducing orientation, achieving orientation— or in Biggs's terminology, internalizing, utilizing, achieving; see Biggs, 1978, and Chapter 8, this volume) is one attempt to capture such relatively stable preferences. The fact that students are able to respond meaningfully to questions about their general learning orientations as well as their approaches to particular evaluations or other tasks (see e.g., Biggs, 1978; Entwistle & Ramsden, 1983; Pask, 1976; Schmeck, 1983) supports the idea of consistency. Numerous investigations, including those by Biggs (Chapter 8, this volume), Säljö (1981), Svensson (1976), and Ramsden (Entwistle & Ramsden, 1983), have described consistencies in approaches arising from qualitative and quantitative data and shown that consistent tendencies to use meaningful or reproductive strategies are associated with several indices of learning outcome.

However, it is important to grasp that stability of orientations does not imply fixity. Orientations to studying are changeable and responsive to the context of teaching, evaluation, and curriculum. It is not easy to explain the findings of studies which have controlled for differences in groups of students at entry to their programs and still discovered systematic variation in meaning and reproducing orientations without postulating context effects on orientations. It seems that approaches to learning have to be understood as being both variable and consistent. As Thomas and Bain (1984) have discovered, absolute changes in students' approach scores from one assessment context to another can coexist with replicable relative positions of individuals on such scores in each assessment context.

Investigations of individuals' conceptions of learning reinforce this conclusion of stability coexisting with variability. Students' conceptions of learning, particularly whether they construe learning as a quantitative increase in knowledge or as a process aimed at interpreting reality, influence their approaches to particular tasks (Van Rossum & Schenk, 1984). A sophisticated conception of learning by no means guarantees that a student will use a deep, holistic approach to a particular task (see Säljö, 1982; Marton, Chapter 3, this volume). However, a view of learning as consisting of memorizing discrete pieces of knowledge prevents a student from extracting meaning from an academic task. Whatever the context, a surface approach is inevitable. Students' conceptions of learning reflect their previous experiences of learning in scholastic settings. Like approaches, conceptions are relational in nature and typify educational settings rather than individual characteristics. There is evidence that the learning tasks set in the early elementary school are influential in developing a quantitative and unreflective conception of learning (see Bennett, Desforges, Cockburn, & Wilkinson, 1984). Changes in conceptions of learning, in some cases related to changes in students' epistemological frameworks, can be documented over time as well as over tasks, and this evidence further strengthens the argument for consistency and variability (Gibbs, Morgan, & Taylor, 1984; Perry, 1970). A further complication is that the concepts of deep–holistic and surface–atomistic approach have both an idiographic and a nomothetic component. That is to say, while deep and surface are universally applicable descriptions of how students in higher education relate to complex learning tasks, they differ in the way they are realized in different academic specialisms.

If approaches to learning need to be seen as both stable and contextually dependent, what of styles and strategies of learning? *Cognitive styles* are characteristic modes of thinking, remembering, and problem solving conceived as varying across individuals, developing in congenial ways around underlying personality differences (Messick, 1982). Defined thus, they are deliberately seen as stable, even unchangeable, individual characteristics which partly control and organize more-fluid cognitive strategies. Strategies and approaches are amenable to change through intervention, and an educational problem is how to help students, within the limits imposed by their styles, to adopt flexible strategies.[1]

[1]A source of confusion in commentaries of the research on deep and surface approaches is the attempt to understand approaches or orientations as cognitive styles. While styles can be seen as bipolar (each pole having positive aspects in adapting to different situations) and fixed, approaches are the opposite: unipolar and variable. There is an explicit value assumption that learning should involve the learner in changing his or her way of thinking about a phenomenon. In relation to academic material that has a recognizable structure capable of being understood, deep approaches are the only way of understanding such material. Approaches are more reminiscent of cognitive strategies than styles, but they are conceived of at a more abstract level, as relations between learning and perception of a task. A related difficulty arises if no distinction is made between the logical and the empirical description of association between approaches and learning outcomes. The logical association is inevitable; the empirical association is not (see Marton, Chapter 3, this volume).

It is beyond the scope of this chapter to consider more than one example of cognitive styles and strategies in relation to the issue of variability and consistency. It is clear that individual students have different styles of learning (in Pask's (1976) understanding of style). The Lancaster research offered support for the notion of consistency of learning style in that it revealed associations between fundamental personality differences and students' self-reported stylistic preferences (significantly, it failed to find such personality associations with orientations to studying). On the other hand, comprehension learning and operation learning can also be conceptualized as contextually dependent strategies. Empirical work, such as Laurillard's investigations described earlier, has lent support to this view. Pask's own idea of versatility—the flexible use of differing mixtures of comprehension and operation learning in different circumstances—allows for this dual conception of these types of learning as being both consistent and variable.

The position advocated here, then, is that both approaches and styles–strategies need to be seen as consistent *and* context dependent (although in somewhat different ways). Our idea of learning-in-context helps to explain this apparently conflicting evidence of consistency and variability. Learning is a function of the individual's engagement with the learning context. The pattern of engagement is incompletely determined by the context's characteristics, as perceived by the student— incompletely because many other variables, including luck and determination, influence it. The student's perceptions are partly determined by previous experiences (in which the individual will have developed characteristic modes of thinking and perceiving as responses to educational tasks) and partly by the characteristics of the context. As long as experiences and contexts differ, as in "natural" learning settings, and as long as students strive to adapt to the learning environment, an observer will note elements both of consistency (differences between individuals on different tasks) and of variability (differences within an individual between task contexts). It is fruitless to ask which side of the consistency–variability argument is right; they are looking at the phenomenon from different points of view. They are complementary rather than conflicting explanations. The focus on approaches and conceptions as relations provides a way of looking at learning which is superordinate to personological or situational explanations.

The study of the context of learning paradoxically highlights the importance of individuals' decisions and previous experiences, educational or otherwise, in the explanation of learning processes and outcomes. Some individuals reveal a capacity to adapt to or shape the environment of learning more effectively than others; this capacity appears to be learnable and, indeed, is one of the outcomes of learning an academic discipline or profession. Variability in strategies to suit contexts is an important component of this capacity. Students who are aware of their own learning strategies and the variety of strategies available to them, and who are skilled at making the right choices, can be said to be responding intelligently (or in a different terminology, metacognitively) to the context (see Sternberg, 1985).

One way in which these skills manifest themselves is through the use of highly strategic approaches to assessment demands—such as the tactics used by Miller and Parlett's cue-seeking undergraduate students, who went out of their way to impress faculty and to discover, subtly, the forms of questions to be asked in unseen examinations (Miller & Parlett, 1974). In the investigations carried out at Lancaster, individual differences in strategic study methods paralleling Miller and Parlett's categories were identified; the more strategic students gained significantly better grades (Entwistle & Ramsden, 1983). It is important to note that in this investigation, the form in which strategic studying manifested itself differed in different courses. In other words, the context influenced the strategy used. In one department where formal student–faculty relationships were the cultural norm, the highly strategic students did not spend time trying to make a favorable impression on faculty; in the less formal departments, they did.

While flexibility in learning strategies is educationally desirable, such "strategic" study behaviors are less so, perhaps because a strategic focus is extrinsic, even if practical. The underlying value assumption of the position adopted here is that an answer to the question, How much is stable style and how much is flexible strategy in this situation? is trivial compared with an answer to the question, How can we enhance an individual's flexibility in dealing with future situations? Yet attempts to convert cognitive styles into cognitive strategies, by teaching students to be selective and aware, run a risk of increasing surface approaches as students respond strategically to contexts which seem to require them.

CONCLUSION: INTERVENTION MUST TAKE THE CONTEXT INTO ACCOUNT

The analysis of the context of learning in higher education which we have attempted here has implications for interventions aimed at improving the quality of learning outcomes and processes. It has previously been argued (see Entwistle & Ramsden, 1983) that intervention strategies need to be aimed both at students—involving programs designed to increase metalearning capability and awareness of different strategies—and at faculty—implying the need to develop more appropriate evaluation methods and professional skills in curriculum design and teaching. The recent evidence suggests that such interventions need to be planned with extreme care. A necessary condition for improved student learning, by which we mean aligning the strategies students use more closely with the aims of faculty, is attention to the three contextual domains of evaluation, transmission, and curriculum. Of these three domains, the most critical is evaluation. As Eriksen (1983) has put it, "An examination is a revealing statement by a teacher about what is important in the course. . . . As God looks down on Ann Arbor or any other college town, He or She sees more sin relating to testing and grading than to classroom teaching" (p. 135). Students never receive teachers' instructions completely passively, whether in university courses or elementary school; they adapt to the context by trying "to deliver what the teacher is predicted to reward" (Desforges, Bennett, Cockburn & Wilkinson, 1985, p. 168).

Changes to aspects of the other domains may be inescapable if assessment is to be perceived as requiring deep approaches. Among these changes are the clear display of faculty goals to students in the structure of the curriculum and an emphasis on teaching principles, concepts, and their derivation. Eizenberg (1985) offers one useful description of how this approach has been applied in a medical curriculum; Marton (Chapter 3, this volume) suggests some additional ways.

It should be clear from what we have said above that variation in approaches and strategies is a result of an interaction between the student and the context of learning. If this model of learning-in-context is a reasonable representation of reality, then it is useless to seek generalizable principles for improving student learning in the characteristics of students, teaching, subject matter, assessment formats, and learning tasks taken singly. It follows that attempts to intervene directly in student learning by teaching general learning skills stand a limited chance of success. Such interventions are themselves a part of the context of learning. Interventions do not exist separately from the remainder of the student's experience; they are interpreted, just as learning tasks are interpreted, in their educational context. In adapting to the context, students make decisions about how to use what an intervention offers.

That such decisions may run counter to the intentions of the organizers of the intervention is predictable from our knowledge of situational influences on student learning. Students actively and critically extract from intervention programs, as from other aspects of teaching, what is useful to them. In this case, what is useful is a function of their perceptions of the requirements of the remainder of their programs as well as a function of their styles and personalities. An example of this process in practice comes from a recent attempt to introduce learning skills programs in the University of Melbourne (Ramsden, Beswick, &

Bowden, 1985). It was hypothesized that attendance at learning skills programs which were not separated from the normal teaching in first-year courses would increase students' use of deep approaches and decrease the use of surface ones. Yet in comparison with a control group, the learning skills students actually increased their surface scores during the year. Interview data supported the interpretation that students derived useful advice from the learning skills sessions, which enabled them to deploy surface approaches successfully as a means of fulfilling perceived assessment demands. If this result seems puzzling, readers may care to look back at Laurillard's student's description of deep and surface approaches (in the section "Learning Tasks and Learning Strategies") and ask themselves whether enhanced metalearning capability would decrease the probability of a surface approach being used in the second task. Teaching students to become more strategic cannot ensure that faculty goals are met. Teachers need to be aware that the student's interpretation of the advantages of a learning skills intervention may well be different from their own.

Do we enter a relativistic hall of mirrors when we argue that interventions are themselves context constrained? Not necessarily. If the student–context interaction is the source of variation in approaches, then practical educational solutions must tackle both individual and contextual aspects of student learning concurrently. Improving learning must focus on the relation between the person and the world around the person. The intervention problem inheres in both teachers and students. The important component of good teaching (in students' perceptions), that is, help with improving approaches to learning, points the way to this integrated approach. If attempts to improve student learning consider faculty and students at the same time, teachers will need to be involved, as part of their professional development, in systematic analyses of their students' perspectives on learning tasks and in studying how subject matter is conceptualized and understood by their students (see Baird & White, 1982; Svensson & Hogfors, 1984; Whelan, 1985; Marton, Chapter 3, this volume). A strength of recent phenomenological approaches to explaining student learning processes is that they provide the tools to make such analyses possible (see Marton, Hounsell, & Entwistle, 1984). Laurillard (1985), for example, has outlined a teaching methodology which, by taking account of a student's existing conception of a topic and giving him or her direct access to the manipulation of its content (perhaps through a computer simulation), is intended to maximize the probability that students will be engaged with subject content at a deep level.

Teaching students to become more aware of their own motives and resources and to select and use them appropriately is a component of such activity by faculty. It involves teaching subject content in ways which directly address the general structures that students use to interpret specific content. Instead of the development of skills in structuring and of flexibility in strategy-use being seen as a by-product of learning content, or alternatively, as desirable ends which require special interventions, they become direct teaching goals (see Weinstein, Chapter 11, this volume). It is on the interaction between content and process, the *genre* of a learning task (see Biggs, Chapter 8, this volume), that teachers should focus in order to improve performance.

In their turn, these activities on the part of faculty sharply outline for them deficiencies and inadequacies in their assessment methods. As Gibbs (1985) has illustrated, participating in teaching sessions that focus on the process of carrying out realistic tasks in a subject specialism can demonstrate to faculty for the first time how their assessment demands may be distorting the types of learning they wish their students to adopt.

An increased commitment to understanding and intervening in the student learning process cannot of course guarantee that teachers devise problems and other assessments which have the potential to engage students at an appropriate level. Formidable skill is needed to plan and carry out changes to curriculum and teaching successfully—especially if the changes involve interventions aimed at placing more responsibility on students for their own learning. Yet even a high level of individual teaching skill may not be enough. Changes to teaching to maximize the probability of faculty aims being met may not be practicable without substantial revision of the management of academic units and without major alterations to traditional disciplinary boundaries and reward systems in some undergraduate courses, especially professional programs. Teachers in higher education are not immune to the same sorts of situational effects that so finely shape their students' learning.

REFERENCES

Baird, J. R., & White, R. T. (1982). Promoting self-control of learning. *Instructional Science,* 11, 227–247.

Bennett, N., Desforges, C., Cockburn, A., & Wilkinson, B. (1984). *The quality of pupil learning experiences.* Hillsdale, NJ: Erlbaum.

Biggs, J. B. (1978). Individual and group differences in study processes. *British Journal of Educational Psychology, 48,* 266–279.

Biggs, J. B. (1982). Student motivation and study strategies in university and college of advanced education populations. *Higher Education Research and Development, 1,* 33–55.

Biglan, A. (1973a). The characteristics of subject matter in different academic areas. *Journal of Applied Psychology, 57,* 195–203.

Biglan, A. (1973b). Relationships between subject matter characteristics and the structure and output of university departments. *Journal of Applied Psychology, 57,* 204–213.

Brennan, J. L., & Percy, K. A. (1977). What do students want? An analysis of staff and student perceptions in British higher education. In A. Bonboir (Ed.), *Instructional design in higher education.* Louvain, Belgium: European Association for Research and Development in Higher Education.

Clarke, R., & Newble, D. I. (1985, August). *Students' approaches to learning: A comparison between two medical schools.* Paper presented at the Annual Conference of the Australasian and New Zealand Association for Medical Education, Melbourne.

Crooks, T. J., & Mahalski, P. A. (1985, August). *Relationships among assessment practices, study methods, and grades obtained.* Paper presented at the Conference of the Higher Education Research and Development Society of Australasia, Auckland.

Dahlgren, L. O. (1978, September). *Qualitative differences in conceptions of basic principles in economics.* Paper presented at the Fourth International Conference on Higher Education, Lancaster, U.K.

Desforges, C., Bennett, N., Cockburn, A., & Wilkinson, B. (1985). Understanding the quality of pupil learning experiences. In N. J. Entwistle (Ed.), *New directions in educational psychology: 1. Learning and teaching* (pp. 161–172). London: Falmer.

Eizenberg, N. (1985, November). *Applying student learning research to practice.* Paper presented at an invited symposium on student learning and learning skills, Marysville, Victoria, Australia.

Entwistle, N. J., & Kozecki, B. (1985). Relationships between school motivation, approaches to studying, and attainment, among British and Hungarian adolescents. *British Journal of Educational Psychology, 55,* 124–137.

Entwistle, N. J., & Ramsden, P. (1983). *Understanding student learning.* London: Croom Helm.

Eriksen, S. C. (1983). Private measures of good teaching. *Teaching of Psychology, 10,* 133–136.

Fransson, A. (1977). On qualitative differences in learning. IV—Effects of motivation and test anxiety on process and outcome. *British Journal of Educational Psychology, 47,* 244–257.

Gaff, J. G., Crombag, H. F. M., & Chang, T. M. (1976). Environments for learning in a Dutch university. *Higher Education, 5,* 285–299.

Gibbs, G. (1985). Teaching study skills. In N. J. Entwistle (Ed.), *New directions in educational psychology: 1. Learning and teaching* (pp. 153–160). London: Falmer.

Gibbs, G., Morgan, A. R., & Taylor, E. (1984). The world of the learner. In F. Marton, D. J. Hounsell, & N. J. Entwistle (Eds.), *The experience of learning* (pp. 165–188). Edinburgh: Scottish Academic Press.

Hodgson, V. (1984). Learning from lectures. In F. Marton, D. J. Hounsell, & N. J. Entwistle (Eds.), *The experience of learning* (pp. 90–102). Edinburgh: Scottish Academic Press.

Johansson, B., Marton, F., & Svensson, L. (1985). An approach to describing learning as change between qualitatively different conceptions. In L. H. T. West & A. L. Pines (Eds.), *Cognitive structure and conceptual change* (pp. 233–257). New York: Academic Press.

Jones, J. (1981). Students' models of university teaching. *Higher Education, 10,* 529–549.

Kulik, J. A., & McKeachie, W. J. (1975). The evaluation of teachers in higher education. In F. N. Kerlinger (Ed.), *Review of Research in Education 3* (pp. 210–240). Itasca, IL: Peacock.

Laurillard, D. M. (1979). The process of student learning. *Higher Education, 8,* 395–409.

Laurillard, D. M. (1984). Learning from problem-solving. In F. Marton, D., J. Hounsell, & N. J. Entwistle (Eds.), *The experience of learning* (pp. 124–143). Edinburgh: Scottish Academic Press.

Laurillard, D. M. (1985, November). *A teaching methodology as an answer to issues raised in phenomenographic research.* Paper presented at an invited symposium on student learning and learning skills, Marysville, Victoria, Australia.

Martin, E. (1985). *Information skills and approaches to learning in contrasting sixth forms.* Unpublished doctoral dissertation, University of Lancaster, England.

Marton, F. (1976). What does it take to learn? In N. J. Entwistle (Ed.), *Strategies for research and development in higher education.* Amsterdam: Swets & Zeitlinger.

Marton, F., & Säljö, R. (1976). On qualitative differences in learning: II. Outcome as a function of the learner's conception of the task. *British Journal of Educational Psychology, 46,* 115–127.

Marton, F., & Säljö, R. (1984). Approaches to learning. In F. Marton, D. J. Hounsell, & N. J. Entwistle (Eds.), *The experience of learning* (pp. 36–55). Edinburgh: Scottish Academic Press.

Marton, F., Hounsell, D. J., & Entwistle, N. J. (Eds.). (1984). *The experience of learning.* Edinburgh: Scottish Academic Press.

Messick, S. (1982). Style in the interplay of structure and process. *Educational Analysis, 4,* 105–121.

Miller, C. M. L., & Parlett, M. (1974). *Up to the mark: A study of the examination game.* London: Society for Research into Higher Education.

Newble, D. I., & Jaeger, K. (1983). The effect of assessment and examinations on the learning of medical students. *Medical Education, 17,* 25–31.

Pask, G. (1976). Styles and strategies of learning. *British Journal of Educational Psychology, 46,* 128–148.

Pattison, M. (1876). Philosophy at Oxford. *Mind, 1,* 84–97.

Perry, W. G. (1970). *Forms of intellectual and ethical development in the college years: A scheme.* New York: Holt, Rinehart & Winston.

Ramsden, P. (1983). Institutional variations in British students' approaches to learning and experiences of teaching. *Higher Education, 12,* 691–705.

Ramsden, P. (1984). The context of learning. In F. Marton, D. J. Hounsell, & N. J. Entwistle (Eds.), *The experience of learning* (pp. 144–164). Edinburgh: Scottish Academic Press.

Ramsden, P., & Entwistle, N. J. (1981). Effects of academic departments on students' approaches to studying. *British Journal of Educational Psychology, 51,* 368–383.

Ramsden, P., Beswick, D. G., & Bowden, J. A. (1985, July). *Effects of learning skills interventions on first year university students' learning.* Paper presented at the British Psychological Society (Cognitive Psychology Section)/Society for Research into Higher Education Conference on Cognitive Processes in Student Learning, Lancaster, U.K.

Säljö, R. (1975). *Qualitative differences in learning as a function of the learner's conception of the task.* Gothenburg: Acta Universitatis Gothoburgensis.

Säljö, R. (1981). Learning approach and outcome: Some empirical observations. *Instructional Science, 10,* 47–65.

Säljö, R. (1982). *Learning and understanding: A study of differences in constructing meaning from a text.* Gothenburg: Acta Universitatis Gothoburgensis.

Schmeck, R. R. (1983). Learning styles of college students. In R. Dillon & R. R. Schmeck (Eds.), *Individual differences in cognition.* New York: Academic Press.

Schwab, J. J. (1964). Structure of the disciplines: Meanings and significances. In A. W. Ford & L. Pugno (Eds.), *The structure of knowledge and the curriculum.* Chicago: Rand McNally.

Selmes, J. P. (1985). *Approaches to learning at secondary school: Their identification and facilitation.* Unpublished doctoral thesis, University of Edinburgh.

Snyder, B. R. (1971). *The hidden curriculum.* New York: Knopf.

Sternberg, R. J. (1985). *Beyond IQ: A triarchic theory of human intelligence.* Cambridge: Cambridge University Press.

Svenson, L. (1976). *Study skill and learning.* Gothenburg: Acta Universitatis Gothoburgensis.

Svensson, L., & Hogfors, C. (1984, August). *On science learning.* Paper presented at the Sixth International Conference on Higher Education, Lancaster, U.K.

Thomas, P. R., & Bain, J. D. (1984). Contextual dependence of learning approaches: The effects of assessments. *Human Learning, 3,* 227–240.

Van Rossum, E. J., & Schenk, S. M. (1984). The relationship between learning conception, study strategy, and learning outcome. *British Journal of Educational Psychology, 54,* 73–83.

Watkins, D. (1982). Factors influencing the study methods of Australian tertiary students. *Higher Education, 11,* 369–380.

Whelan, G. (1985, August). *Fourth year medical students' approaches to clinical problem-solving.* Paper presented at the Annual Conference of the Australasian and New Zealand Association for Medical Education, Melbourne.

Wilson, R. C., Gaff, J. G., Dienst, E. R., Wood, L., & Bavry, J. L. (1975). *College professors and their impact on students.* New York: Wiley.

CHAPTER 8

Approaches to Learning and to Essay Writing

JOHN BIGGS

The terms *learning styles* and *learning strategies* would seem to refer to two different aspects of student learning. *Styles* are stable ways of approaching tasks that are characteristic of individuals, while *strategies* are ways of handling particular tasks: styles are focused on the person, strategies on the task.

It is interesting and valuable to ask if, in considering performance on any particular task, there is any interaction between styles and strategies: Do students with certain enduring personal characteristics accept and deploy optimal strategies more readily than do other students? Such interaction is implied by the term *approach,* as used by the present author (Biggs, 1987), which refers to the learning processes that emerge from students' perceptions of the academic task, as influenced by their personal characteristics. This concept of approach thus has both situational and personological elements, and the present focus of this chapter is on the interaction between these two elements with respect to the particular task of essay writing.

An *essay* is defined here as a response in continuous prose to a specific question, for which the student has received advance notice, which is to be prepared in the student's own time, and which is to be subject to some kind of summative evaluation. The *genre* of an essay is the structure, within a content area, that satisfactorily meets the require-

JOHN BIGGS • Department of Education, University of Hong Kong, Hong Kong.

185

ments of a class of questions, such as "compare and contrast" or "explain the causes of," and the like.

APPROACHES TO LEARNING

Certain broad approaches to student learning may be distinguished, and a reasonable degree of consensus exists as to their general characteristics (e.g., Entwistle, 1981; Schmeck, 1983; Entwistle, Chapter 2 and Marton, Chapter 3, this volume). The particular conceptual framework and terminology used here, however, derive from the present author's model of student learning (Biggs, 1987). Three major approaches are postulated: *surface, deep,* and *achieving.*

Students adopting a surface approach are instrumentally or pragmatically motivated; for example, they are at university in order to obtain a qualification with minimal effort. A task, such as an essay, is then seen as a demand to be met, a necessary imposition if the longer-term goal is to be achieved. This set of aspirations is frequently accompanied by worries about the time the task is taking, and the inverse of that, worries about failure in the event that too little time is spent on task. The general strategy to which this orientation gives rise is to focus on what are seen to be "essentials"—usually factual data and the ways they are represented symbolically—and to reproduce them as accurately as possible. In the case of reading from text, Marton and Säljö (1976) state that this strategy focuses on the *signs* of learning, the words and sentences used by the author, rather than what is signified, that is, meanings the author intended to convey. The reproductive nature of the surface strategy thus omits or avoids the interrelations that may exist between components of the task, so that it is not seen as a unified whole.

The affective orientation of students adopting a deep approach starts with an intrinsic interest in the task and the expectation of enjoyment in carrying it out. Consequently, they adopt strategies that are likely to help satisfy their curiosity by searching for meanings inherent in the task. It may be appropriate to personalize the task, by making it coherent with their own experience, to integrate it with existing formal knowledge, or to theorize about it, forming hypotheses. In Marton and Säljö's (1976) terms, they focus on what the text signifies, on what meanings the author intended to convey, which requires that the parts of the task are seen as making up a whole.

The affective orientation of students adopting an achieving approach is based on mainfesting one's excellence relative to other students, specifically in obtaining grades that are as high as possible. The associated strategy is rather different from the deep and surface ones in that it is not concerned with how the task content is engaged so much as with self-organization, particularly on the matter of time management (e.g., allocating fixed time slots for studying related activities, assiduously submitting assignments on time, etc.). The achieving approach may therefore be used in conjunction with either of the other two: the deep-achieving composite is in fact characteristic of many high-achieving students.

A self-conscious and planful approach to learning thus requires. first, that students are *aware* of their motives and intentions, of their own cognitive resources, and of the demands of academic tasks; and second, that they are able to *control* those resources and monitor their consequent performance. Being aware of one's own cognitive and affective states, and controlling and monitoring one's own cognitive processes, are the defining attributes of *metacognition* (Brown, Bransford, Ferrara, & Campione, 1983), and the specific application of metacognition to the area of student learning is referred to as *metalearning* (Biggs, 1987; cf. Kirby, Chapter 9 and Das, Chapter 5).

Metalearning may be realized in varying degrees in the approaches to learning described above, being most evident in deep and least in surface. These approaches to learning stem from the interaction, mediated by metalearning, between the general orientations that an individual displays across particular learning situations and over time, on the one hand, and the current task and situational demands, on the other. For example, an individual who is typically predisposed toward meaningful learning may nevertheless so interpret immediate situational demands that a particular task is rote learned.

Performance variables in student learning research have mostly been quite general, such as grade point average, or in studies of specific learning situations, restricted to reading from text. With the exception of the work of Hounsell (1984), very little has been done on the creation of text in academic contexts, in particular essay writing, despite the fact that writing generally has recently and deservedly become the focus of a great deal of research activity.

The aim of the present chapter, then, is to review some of the research concerned with approaches to learning as it bears upon that most typical of academic tasks, writing the essay assignment, and to integrate the two areas. A model of writing is synthesized from the literature, and its "goodness of fit" is tried out on data derived from student interviews. It will be shown that a close parallel exists between students' general orientations to learning and their particular approaches to essay writing.

THE ROLE OF WRITING IN THINKING AND LEARNING

The essay assignment and its many variants have for years, and in many content areas, provided the most used, and most important, medium for the summative evaluation of learning and student thinking. It is possible that this use of writing has impeded other, more important functions. Currently, as a result largely of increasing interest in sociolinguistic models of language, writing is being seen as the tool par excellence for clarifying and extending thought in most content areas (e.g., Halliday, 1974). This is a function that is frequently if not necessarily degraded by emphasis on summative evaluation.

Prima facie there are several reasons why writing might serve such a clarifying function with respect to learning and thinking (Applebee, 1984):

1. Writing externalizes thought, thereby allowing the thinker–writer the opportunity of reconsidering, clarifying, or revising what has been proposed.
2. The fact that writing is disembedded from an immediate context that is rich in nonverbal cues means that the writer, unlike the speaker who may rely on paralinguistic supports, needs to be particularly clear and explicit.
3. Writing usually requires more activity than simply "thinking" about the topic, and so the writer tends to be more actively involved in the process of creating meaning.
4. Proper attention to the audience will force the writer to consider different perspectives on the message content from that of the writer's own.

This list appears to provide a compelling case for the role of writing in learning. Applebee concludes from a review of the empirical evidence that while the more a writer manipulates new material in writing about it the better it appears to be understood, writing activity promotes only the type of thought cognate to that activity. For example, writing lists and catalogues will help a person remember lists; writing to explore novel relationships between data will help the writer develop an integrative conceptual framework.

Given this very important qualification, Applebee notes it as particularly unfortunate that writing in schools emphasizes skills at the word and sentence level only, being used largely to convey previously organized content to an audience that is better informed on the content than is the writer. Schools typically do not require writers to elaborate their thoughts or create new meanings, and thus to concentrate their skills at the level of *discourse*, or discourse structure, that is, on the meaning of the message as a whole. As it is only when planning, revising, and clarifying at the discourse level that writing may become a heuristic activity that extends the knowledge of both writer and reader, schools are thus typically underselling the power of writing. Also, by emphasizing the role of writing in summative evaluation, educators have probably contributed to lowering students self-efficacy with regard to writing and thereby diminished the *formative* contribution of writing activity (cf. Meier, McCarthy, & Schmeck, 1984).

Applebee's distinction between word–sentence and discourse levels of concentration strongly recalls Marton's point of departure for surface and deep levels of reading text, that is, the distinction between the signs used (surface concentration) and what they signify (deep concentration). It is seen below that this distinction vis-à-vis writing can be discerned in several accounts of skilled and unskilled writing.

Levels of Approach to Essay Writing

Several writers have noted how the writing processes, and the resulting products, differ between competent and incompetent writers. Many parameters in the growth of competence may be distinguished, but an important one, occurring at the first level at which reasonably clear written communication takes place, involves a linear structure. Biggs and Collis (1982a) place writing that displays this characteristic at the unistructural level of their SOLO Taxonomy (discussed later) and call it simply "linear" writing; Bereiter (1980) refers to "associative" writing, in which the content is presented in the order received by the writer; Graves (1983) refers to "bed-to-bed" writing in the narrative genre, when children's stories tend to relate all the events of the day from getting up to going to bed at night. This simple linear structure thus appears early on in the growth in writing competence over a variety of genres, yet it persists to some extent in the work of many otherwise sophisticated writers.

Flower (1980) distinguishes "writer-based" and "reader-based" prose: the former uses an inappropriate narrative genre to relate what the writer knows rather than concentrating on what the reader needs to know. Hounsell (1984), from an entirely different conceptual framework, investigated the "conception" of writing demonstrated by the student writer when asked to define an essay. He interviewed several history and psychology students and distinguished two basic kinds of conception of what an essay is (some history students also held an intermediate conception): One group saw essay writing as the presentation of relevant facts and ideas "in an ordered form," the other group as an integrated argument (in psychology), or as a viewpoint (in history), supported in both cases by evidence or argument. Not surprisingly, students who held these conceptions planned and wrote their essays accordingly. In the first group, interpretation "takes the form of a loose collection of thoughts and ideas" (Hounsell, 1984, p. 286), and in the second, data and organization are subordinated to the overall interpretive stance adopted by the writer.

Another very similar distinction is made by Scardamalia and Bereiter (1982) when they refer to a *knowledge-telling* (as opposed to reflective) strategy, which consists of reducing essay assignments to a list of topics, and then telling what one knows about each topic. The main concern of the writer in this case is simply what to say next, and how to put that in suitable language. There is little evidence of any *reflective* activity, involving interpretation and integration of components, or the production of higher-order knowledge from lower-order inputs. Knowledge-telling allows the writer to reduce the process to a sentence-by-sentence routine, and as Applebee noted, that routine suffices for most of the writing tasks that are required of school students.

Scardamalia and Bereiter propose a "dual problem space of reflection" comprising a *content* space, consisting of beliefs and opinions, and in which one works out decisions and explanations; and a *rhetorical* space, consisting of mental representations of actual or intended text that gives written expression to semantic contents. The content space is concerned with the question "What do I mean?" and the rhetorical space with "What do I say?" (see Figure 1).

Figure 1A indicates that in knowledge-telling, students move in one direction only, from content to rhetorical space, and what emerges is the final text, with perhaps minor revision at the word–sentence or surface

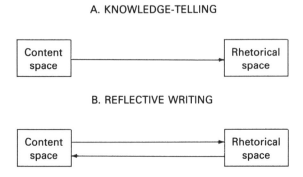

Figure 1. Knowledge-telling and reflective writing strategies. (After Scardamalia and Bereiter, 1982.)

level (i.e., spelling and punctuation, within-sentence grammar, word choice, and the addition of a sentence here or there).

Reflective writing (Figure 1B), on the other hand, is cyclical: the product itself adds to the content space—"Is what I have written really what I mean?"—so that revision in this case involves a more fundamental examination and molding of basic meaning and structure. Planning, monitoring, and revising one's thought in this way is essentially a metacognitive process (see Brown *et al.*, 1983; cf. Das, Chapter 5, this volume) in that one treats one's own thought as an object of further thought. The basic questions of reflective revision—"What do I really intend to say?" "Does this say what I mean?" "How else might it be put for a reader who doesn't know what I know?"—involve a level of metacognitive sophistication parallel to that in metalearning and which is absent in knowledge-telling.

This parallelism between reflective activity in writing and metalearning may perhaps be traced in the development of each. Burtis, Bereiter, Scardamalia and Tetroe (1984) report that reflective activity is "completely absent" from the think-aloud protocols of elementary school writers. These authors, as did McCutchen (1984), found that "planning" in young writers simply foreshadows the words that are written down. Burtis *et al.* found that it wasn't until the age of 18 or so that students were generally capable of planning, in the sense of thinking and talking *about* the text, in words quite different from those ultimately written down.

By a similar token, Biggs (1987) found that the control aspect of metalearning typically did not develop until the end of senior high school; earlier, in the case of highly motivated and internally controlled students; later, if at all, in unmotivated or externally controlled students. Being aware of and controlling one's own thought, envisaging alternative expressions of that thought, and revising its written expression may well involve similar processes; and to the extent that they do, one would indeed expect to find a parallel between approaches to learning in general and to writing in particular.

In the above review, we have seen that Flower's (1980) distinction between writer-based and reader-based prose, Hounsell's (1984) distinction between different conceptions students hold of what an essay is, and that of Scardamalia and Bereiter (1982) between knowledge-based and reflective strategies of writing all imply two basic approaches to writing, which derive from the level at which the writer's attention is focused; a surface level consisting of the words and sentences used, or a deep level consisting of the discourse itself. This distinction closely parallels—in its nature, in its focus, and in its terminology, if we so choose—that made by Marton in his description of deep and surface approaches to learning (see Marton, Chapter 3). Beyond that, it seems plausible to describe reflective approaches to writing as metacognitive in much the same way as metalearning is evoked to characterize effective approaches to learning. The development of these metacognitive aspects of both learning in general and writing in particular indeed seem to unfold in a similar time scale.

A MODEL OF ESSAY WRITING

If one is to take the parallel between writing and learning seriously, one should use the general approach to learning as the format for the application to writing. In that event, the next step would be to identify motivational and cognitive components in an approach to writing, just as a motive and a related strategy comprise an approach to learning. In the case of writing a particular essay, the motivational component might better be expressed as "intentional", that is, the sort of experience the student intends or expects writing the essay to be, and the sort of grade aspired to.

The cognitive component of the approach to writing has in fact been well researched, particularly from the point of view of writing as a problem-solving task (Burtis *et al.*, 1984; Flower, 1980; Hayes & Flower, 1980; Humes, 1983; Smith, 1982). Several stages or activities may be distinguished: a common classification referring to *prewriting* (e.g., planning, updating relevant content knowledge), *writing* (composing the ideas, and transcribing or putting those ideas on paper), and *postwriting* (reviewing and revising). There is, however, considerable overlap and interaction between activities so defined. Nold (1981), for example, argues that revising cannot be a postwriting stage as it itself involves writing, in that existing text is replaced by freshly composed text. Similarly, composition is a process that commences during planning and controls writing, but it can also occur retroactively, from the written word to replanning (McCutchen, 1984). Thus, while planning is in one sense a "pre"-writing activity, it may occur temporally speaking during writing, so that it would be more accurate to speak of planning as a parawriting, rather than a prewriting, activity.

In the present model, then, the following aspects of writing may be distinguished:

1. *Intentional*, including affective and aspirational aspects prior to writing.
2. *Parawriting* activities, including planning and knowledge updating.

3. *Writing* activities, including composing and transcribing, reviewing, and revising.

It remains to describe these aspects in more detail. In so doing, it will help to clarify the nature of each by illustrating with data obtained by interviewing members of a freshman English class who were in the process of planning and/or writing their second essay assignment.

INTENTIONAL ASPECTS

These aspects refer to the feelings the students have about the prospect of essay writing. The freshmen English students were asked if they saw the forthcoming essay as "a learning experience" or "a chore to be done," what sort of grade they expected, and in general how they felt about the essay.

Responses were of two general kinds, which reflected a basic deep–surface distinction. The first class of response emphasized a high degree of personal involvement and enjoyment, anticipation of an enriching and personally meaningful experience, and—usually—the expectation of a high grade. These characteristics appear to reflect the motivational or affective component of a deep approach, and in the case where students endorsed the expectation of a high grade, a deep-achieving approach. Sample deep, and deep-achieving, responses are given below by Maryanne and Emma respectively (all names are fictitious):

> *Maryanne:* It's not a chore, I'm looking forward to it. Yes, I think it will be a way of learning. . . . You tend to know the material better when you write it out yourself, not like material you've only been lectured on.
>
> *Emma:* I want to get into things a lot more deeply than I should in (freshman) year. That's my problem. I've got to stop myself getting too engrossed in it. . . . I hope to get a High Distinction. Actually I'd like to get one or two marks more than a basic High Distinction.

The second kind of response indicated that the essay is perceived as a necessary hurdle in the course, rather than as a desirable activity in itself, and some apprehension is felt at the prospect, with frequently little desire for anything more than a minimal pass. Such responses seem clearly parallel to the affective component of a surface approach:

> *Jane:* I just write to get it finished . . . because I've got to write it. . . . I'll be lucky if I just pass. . . . I'd be pleased with a pass.

These responses reveal two quite different orientations to the essay, and ensuing parawriting and writing activities would be expected to differ accordingly.

PARAWRITING ACTIVITIES

The major parawriting activities all relate to planning. Planning has been extensively studied (e.g., Das, Chapter 5). A great deal of planning research exists in the general problem-solving area (Brown *et al.*, 1983; Hayes-Roth & Hayes-Roth, 1979) and in the area of writing (Burtis *et al.*, 1984; Hayes & Flower, 1980; Smith, 1982), although not for essay writing in particular. It is possible to put this work together to synthesize a model of parawriting activities in particular reference to the essay: The Brown *et al.* discussion is particularly helpful in this as it emphasizes the role of metacognition in planning. The steps are illustrated as far as possible by the student interview material.

1. *Interpret the question.* This step overwhelmingly determines what follows; it is also likely to be the greatest source of difficulty. Assuming that the question itself is clear, and reflects the instructor's intentions, the student needs to be satisfied as to the meaning of the question and any unclear words checked out.

2. *Form global intentions.* This is Smith's (1982) term for, in effect, pegging the claim before working it ("I intend to handle the question in this way and to make the points that . . .") and corresponds closely with metaplanning in general problem solving (Brown *et al.*, 1983). These intentions may be quite broadly stated at first, or even withheld; "I need to find out a lot more yet before I can even interpret the question adequately." On the other hand, a knowledgeable writer could move at this point to a detailed outline, in either mental or note form. In essence, either explicitly but normally implicitly, the genre is decided: This is a compare-and-contrast, an evaluate, or an outline kind of essay. That question is implicitly and satisfactorily answered once the student correctly understands and acts upon an appropriately worded question.

3. *Summon knowledge, define lacunae, obtain further knowledge.* As the question is interpreted, the writer's existing knowledge about the topic is summoned, and a decision made about where the gaps in knowledge are, and how to go about finding out further needed knowledge, as in "world knowledge decisions" (Brown *et al.*, 1983). Lecture notes, prescribed readings, other students, instructors, and guided browsing in the library are some of the sources of such knowledge.

4. *Decide on a particular structure, prioritize, and organize.* Some students methodically outline the main points in note form prior to writing, while others have a less-detailed mental listing of topic priorities. Nevertheless, at some level most writers have a hierarchy of items in semantic space, arranged according to level of importance, and this hierarchy guides their subsequent composing of the text. Indeed, without some such hierarchy it is difficult to see how the writer could decide how to

put any words down at all. This hierarchy derives from the *discourse structure* of the final plan for the essay: this structure may be mapped in terms of the SOLO Taxonomy (discussed later).

5. *Opportunistic planning.* This is the term given by Hayes-Roth and Hayes-Roth (1979) to describe planning that alters shape and direction at any point. For example, when carrying out further reading, or later when writing the essay, it is possible and even likely that a new tack will occur to the student. This new angle may or may not be incorporated into the growing or hitherto completed essay plan.

6. *Monitoring criteria.* Implicit in the planning process is the establishment, conscious or otherwise, of criteria that will guide both composition and transcription and subsequent review. Such criteria include:

a. Audience: To whom does "the fact beneath the page" belong (Britton, Burgess, Martin, McLeod, & Rosen, 1975)? What prerequisite knowledge is the reader expected to have to understand the treatment or a particular sentence? What sort of thing is the presumed reader likely to be irritated by or be partial toward?

b. Originality: Is the writer striving to be original or conventional in either form or content?

c. Aesthetics and style: What importance does the writer give to stylistic aspects of the text?

d. Compatibility with intentions: Is what-is-about-to-be-written, or what-has-been-written, in accordance with *what*-was-intended-to-be-written, *how*-it-was-intended-to-be-written?

7. *Form focal intentions.* Focal intentions (Smith, 1982) are the final refinement of the as yet unspoken thoughts, before their translation–transcription–publication into the external medium of written text. The process of *composition* might be seen as a long wedge, beginning with the formation of global intentions, culminating in the sharp edge of focal intentions. The formation of the latter are in a sense preverbal, thus giving rise to the mystique surrounding composition (Salgado, 1980).

These seven activities are not meant to imply a necessary sequence that is followed by all writers, or that all activities are engaged by all writers irrespective of sequence. Many activities are revisited at any point in the writing process, while others may not be heeded at all: the list simply provides a convenient reference for looking at essay planning activities.

From Interpreting the Question. Many students move straight from interpreting the question to a knowledge update, before deciding on a particular structure. To Emma (below), this movement makes her believe she doesn't plan anything, despite the fact that she engages in intense mental activity prior to writing:

> *Emma* As soon as I get the assignment I read what I can find. Race down to the library madly the minute the lecture finishes and get there first to get all the stuff and then read it and then I just think about it while I'm going about whatever I'm going about. And then I leave it as long as I can before I write anything except for the odd thought that I have . . . so you see, I don't plan anything. I just go around thinking about it all the time when I'm driving my car and in the garden and thoughts just spring to mind . . . you know, the light bulb flashes and I think, ah yes, that's great. I keep these little exercise books and I write down thoughts that may be useful when I come to the essay.

Jim, on the other hand, is more deliberate and, when commenting on his sources for updating knowledge, he makes an important point about arriving at an essay plan:

> *Jim:* Obviously notes and books are important. Then there are the critics in the various journals. That gives a broad outline and you can always agree with them or disagree; it gives a starting point from where to work. . . . I always try to include at least one reference I've dug out for myself; it's nice to have that as a focus. It's more "mine." Then I mull it all over until a structure emerges.

Both by their affective involvement and by their immersion in content, Emma and Jim seem clearly to be planning in a deep sense. Their approaches, while different from each other, are both radically different from those of Bill and Anne.

Bill derives his essay plan from his lecture notes:

> *Bill:* The lecturer tells us the basic points are in the lecture notes. Then it's a matter of matching those up with selections from one or two of the recommended critiques. I go on from there.

Anne tries "grabbing ideas here and there" and, when that fails, turns to a previous English teacher:

> *Anne:* I try to plan but I usually go straight into it. As soon as I think of an idea I write it down. I write bits and pieces . . . just sit there grabbing ideas here and there, trying to see what I can do with them. . . . If I have a lot of trouble I go to my old English teacher. She helps me get my ideas together.

Both these last two students show, in various degrees of desperation, the need to turn to external resources to structure their work—to, as it were, tell them what to say.

Already, then, in the early stages of planning, we can see deep and surface approaches emerging, with the reflective and knowledge-telling strategies coming into play. Emma and Jim are reflective and intent on finding a suitable discourse structure, while Bill and Anne simply want a prompt to put their ideas in order.

Discourse Structure and Genre. The deep approach, then, shows a strong awareness of an underlying structure to the essay, which is another way of saying that the students realize the genre implicit in the question. Despite the fundamental importance of selecting the essay genre, however, no student referred to genre as such, although several were aware of the generalized essay structure: introduction, body, and conclusion. Barbara's response shows the close interconnection between the interpretation of the question, content, and structure:

> *Barbara:* When I am writing I want to refer back to the question because actually the question in this case is quite general but there are two layers of meaning: there is the reality, and the underlying sort of metaphor that Pinter uses. So as I write, I keep the two levels in view. . . . If I have a plan or blueprint at all it is just that there is an introduction, and the body of the essay, and the close. I don't know whether that's the way it should be, but it works for me. I have only a very basic structure and then let the rest of it just sort of happen.

Barbara, like Jim, immerses herself in content, with the question in mind, until "a structure emerges."

It is possible to map the planned discourse structure (as well as the observed discourse structure as it appears in the final essay) with the aid of the SOLO Taxonomy (Biggs & Collis, 1982b). SOLO (the *s*tructure of the *o*bserved *l*earning *o*utcome), deriving from a study of learning outcomes in the classroom, is based on the assumption that learning quality is reflected in the level of complexity with which the learning outcome is structured, regardless of whether the item learned is a skill, a concept, or a problem. Five such levels may typically be identified.

The original application of SOLO was to the outcome, and creative writing tasks have been used for such an analysis (Biggs & Collis, 1982a). SOLO analysis may, however, apply to the planned discourse structure as well as to the observed discourse structure, so that discourse structure refers either to planning or to outcome.

SOLO analysis hinges on the *level of abstraction* of the contents discussed. The middle three levels—unistructural, multistructural and relational—deal with content at the level of abstraction sought in the question, but with differing degrees of effectiveness. Prestructural writing is at an inappropriately low level of abstraction (e.g., an academic case addressed by narrating personal experience), and extended abstract is at a level higher and more general than that which would suffice. These levels of discourse structure (discussed below) are outlined in Table 1, showing their relationship to genre and to the approach to writing that both stems from the discourse structure proposed at the planning stage and contributes toward creating the structure finally emerging in the outcome.

Table 1. *Discourse Structure, Genre of Essay, and Approach to Writing*

Discourse structure	Essay genre	Writing approach
1. Prestructural: structure inadequate; question addressed at too low a level of abstraction.	Unformed.	Surface-subjective: associative, word-based.
2. Unistructural: one major relevant line of argument.	Partial listing.	Surface-restrictive: partial knowledge-telling; focus on words and sentences.
3. Multistructural: several major relevant arguments developed but independently with little interrelation.	Listing.	Surface-elaborative: knowledge-telling, focus on words–sentences; incorrect perception of whole
4. Relational: evidence and/or argument integrated to make a case that satisfies the question within the context set.	As appropriate to question, e.g., causal explanation, compare–contrast, evaluate, etc.	Deep-integrative: focus on the whole, so that discourse structure is integrated with the question.
5. Extended abstract: more than answers the question; raises issues and possibilities beyond the set context; e.g., "questions the question," hypothesizes at higher level of abstraction.	As above, but may use a different and better genre than that intended in the question.	Deep reflective: focus on discourse, and on implications beyond the question, so that higher-order knowledge results.

It is seen that these considerations linking structure with approach modify and extend the basic deep and surface distinctions already outlined. At this stage, these links between structure and approach are hypothetical, although there is a good deal of analogous evidence from the student learning literature which closely links approach, structural complexity, and outcome (Biggs, 1987; Marton & Säljö, 1976; Schmeck & Phillips, 1982; Van Rossum & Schenk, 1984; Watkins, 1983). Table 1 extends the link to the field of writing and includes structure of the intended outcome as well as that of the actual outcome. Kirby (see Chapter 9) makes a similar application to reading comprehension.

1. *Prestructural.* The question here is not properly addressed so that the discourse structure is necessarily inadequate, and the genre is there-

fore unformed or insufficiently developed to meet that required by the question. The writing approach is *surface-subjective:* attention is focused on words and sentences that either refer (inappropriately) to personal experiences that are linked by subjective associations or to a case that is put with linguistic tools that are inadequate to the task, so that words are linked by a "grammar" that is subjective and associative. In either event, the product emerges as incoherent and inadequate (Biggs & Collis, 1982a).

2. *Unistructural.* The question is addressed by only one relevant line of argument, so that it is unlikely to satisfactorily address the question. The genre might be called "partial listing." The writing approach is *surface-restrictive,* involving partial knowledge-telling, and attention is focused on stringing together sentences that make the point that is chosen. The surface-restrictive approach is based on the mistaken belief that the one point or argument answers the question. For example, the question "What caused the Declaration of Independence?" might be answered by starting off: "Because the British charged tax on the tea sold . . ." and then describing, however accurately or interestingly, the Boston Tea Party.

3. *Multistructural.* The question is addressed by a more complete listing than in the previous case, but—unless the question called for such a listing—the genre is still inappropriate. For example, following the previous example, one might give a detailed account of all the main events leading up to the Declaration of Independence but still without explaining why independence was declared. Narration, however elaborate, does not explain causes, and the latter was the point of the question. The approach is thus called *surface-elaborative,* which is a fuller form of knowledge-telling. Attention is still focused in fact on sentences and elaborating with more sentences, in the belief that more detail makes the case: this is simply a misunderstanding of the genre. This point is made tellingly by Forster (1968) in distinguishing between a story and a plot:

> We have defined a story as a narrative of events arranged in their time sequence. A plot is also a narrative of events, the emphasis falling on causality. "The king died, and then the queen died," is a story. "The king died, and then the queen died of grief" is a plot. (p. 93)

In writing essays, as in writing fiction, the writer's concern needs to exceed the span of a sentence: it is necessary to see how those sentences hang together to form a discourse structure.

4. *Relational.* The requirements implicit in the question are satisfied for the first time. A case is made; a plot is created. The approach to writing is *deep-integrative:* a deep approach because attention is properly focused on the discourse structure as a whole and how that relates to the

question put; and integrative because the arguments and points made, which at the multistructural level were left as loose ends, are integrated and balanced, one with the other, so that a genuine conclusion to the question is possible. The case itself, however, is strictly within the bounds of the question: There is at this level no extension of the argument, no answering hitherto unasked but pertinent questions.

5. *Extended abstract*. The question is answered at a higher level of generality and abstraction than the case strictly needs. Issues and possibilities are raised that are beyond the set context: The question may be questioned ("What one should really be asking is . . ."), so that the genre implied in the question may not be used and a different (and arguably better) one used instead. The approach is *deep-reflective*, in the sense originally implied by Scardamalia and Bereiter (1982) in that higher-order knowledge is derived from lower-order inputs. The deep-reflective approach, in other words, is that used in research, either critical or creative; something new emerges as a result. In answering essay questions, the deep-reflective approach might even be seen to lead to irrelevance: An exasperated teacher might well argue that the student wasn't asked or expected to reply at a higher level of abstraction or to question the question. Be that as it may, in cognitive terms this level of response is at a higher level, even if educationally speaking it may be taking the student beyond the boundaries assumed by the teacher.

To summarize, then, the elements of the final discourse structure exist at the planning stage and can be categorized into the five SOLO levels of complexity. In so doing, the two basic surface and deep approaches may be seen to incorporate the knowledge-telling and reflective approaches already described by Scardamalia and Bereiter, and they may be elaborated into the following approaches:

1. Surface-subjective, leading to unorganized and irrelevant outcomes.
2. Surface-restrictive, leading to a limited, unistructural outcome.
3. Surface-elaborative, leading to complex and detail-rich outcomes, but which are likely to miss the genre required by the questions.
4. Deep-integrative, leading to a well thought-out outcome that satisfied the question.
5. Deep-reflective, leading to higher-level and more generalized outcomes than those sought in the original question.

Opportunistic Planning. This is a "wild" activity that may occur at any time or not at all. Basically, it amounts to the readiness with which the writer is led by research, or the emerging text, into hitherto unplanned directions. Such a readiness seemed to be more characteristic of deep, especially deep-reflective, writers:

> *Jim:* Yes, I do get sudden inspirations. That happens a lot. It makes the essay more exciting because that's where originality comes in. But you've got to be careful. You've got to work out how it will all come back together in the end.

The emphasis here is upon the writer working out an original structure, but remaining in control of it: Jim's reply shows a strong sense of internal locus of control, which is an important component of metalearning and of a deep approach (Biggs, 1987).

Surface responders, on the other hand, need some external prop to guide their planning. Anne, it will be remembered, simply tried "grabbing ideas here and there," and when that failed, went to a previous English teacher. It is perfectly compatible for her, then, to reject opportunistic planning:

> *Anne:* No, I ignore sudden inspirations. That'd make things too messy. I'd get right off the track. When I get an off-beat idea, I think "No. He wasn't asking for that. Forget it."

McCarthy and Schmeck (Chapter 6, this volume) suggest that the rejection and avoidance of opportunistic planning by a surface responder might stem from a generally poor self-concept with its attendant lack of self-respect and confidence.

Monitoring Criteria. Throughout planning, composing, writing, and reviewing, the writer works within certain criteria by which the various stages of the production of text will be subject to concurrent evaluation.

1. *Audience.* Is the writer addressing someone whose knowledge of the topic is more, or is less, than the writer's own? Does the writer recognize that certain sorts of statements, or the way they are made, will be particularly irritating, or particularly pleasing, to the presumed reader? Does the writer "empathize" with the anticipated audience? The question of audience is particularly interesting in the case of an essay, which should be written in "grapholect," a dialect used in formal text that is written to address a wide or educated audience (Hausen, 1968). One consequence of writing in grapholect is that the writer does not have to envision the needs of a particular audience (Nold, 1981); the fact beneath the page is not that of a particular individual, but an identikit reconstruction from the community of scholars, in which the writer includes himself or herself as a member. This apparently "audience-free" aspect of essays comes out in some of the student replies. Emma, for instance, says:

> *Emma:* Funny, I've never thought of an audience. The whole process of writing seems to me to be such a strangely personal one that it's not as if it's for an audience. Now Philosophy essays are much more for an audience because with them I have to keep telling myself, well, this is what he wants . . . it's an important way of being able to even write the wretched thing.
>
> *Margaret:* I'm my own audience. I write it as if it's making sense to me to reread to myself. It's different to writing speeches because they are for a specific audience but you don't know who you are writing for in essays.

Both Emma and Margaret were classifiable, in their other responses, as using a deep approach to writing. Anne, classifiable in other responses as surface approach, makes it clear she does try to please a particular lecturer:

> *Anne:* I've got to look at it from the lecturer's point of view because it seems that what the lecturer thinks is the most important thing rather than what you think. . . . You really try to make it really sophisticated and complicated because you think you will be impressing the lecturer. It's what the lecturer thinks is what matters. I've found that if you don't give back what you've been given it's not accepted.

Anne here recognizes the "academic style" but misunderstands it: writing in grapholect does not mean making it "really sophisticated and complicated" in order to please a particular person. It is interesting and important to note that Anne and Emma had the same marker, yet only Anne felt under pressure to conform to his *presumed* biases. Her need to "give back what you've been given" thus reflects rather the inadequacy of her own inner resources and the need therefore to latch on to any cues to define the boundaries of the knowledge she is to *retell*. Not surprisingly, Emma obtained a higher grade for the essay than did Anne, despite the fact that it is Anne's thinking that is dominated by the function of summative evaluation that the essay is to serve.

2. *Originality.* In discussing his sources, and how he sowed the conditions for his structure to emerge, Jim referred to selecting an off-the-track reference which then became "more mine." This sense of proprietoriality likewise stems from an internal locus of control, in "integrating the task with oneself" (Entwistle & Ramsden, 1983, p. 137; cf. McCarthy & Schmeck, Chapter 6, this volume) and is characteristic of a deep approach. Judith expresses the same thing:

> *Judith:* I find in the novels as they relate to this question that I can see something of my own life experience in it so that I feel as though it's relevant to me and therefore I can associate myself with the novelists and the people they are writing about. I end up writing from my own understanding. I look at various critiques . . . but it's what I think is the main thing and these others just come in and modify my thinking a bit.

Jenny and Debbie, on the other hand, see originality as the pre-rogative of the expert or of the rebel, and they see themselves as neither (see McCarthy & Schmeck, Chapter 6):

> *Jenny:* No, I don't try to be original at all; . . . I don't know very much about any of the works we're dealing with. This is my first introduction to any intellectual sort of reading. Most of my reading has been light and Harold Robbins type of thing and so this is all very new to me. It's very hard to form your own opinions. I haven't got enough background yet.
>
> *Debbie:* I've no intentions of being original or different at all. I just thought of a combination of the lecture material and the other material you've got to use. I don't want to be provocative or difficult.

3. *Aesthetics and Style.* While concern with style might be expected to characterize all good writers, such concern might particularly be expected among English students. This was true of only some of the inter-viewed students; those who gave deep-style responses on other items tended to enrich their composing with this dimension (one is reminded of Pask's "redundant holist," see Chapter 4):

> *Emma:* Another thing I don't like about Philosophy essays is that there isn't any joy in creating a lovely essay. They don't really care if it's a clumsy sentence as long as the point you are making comes across. So the crafting of an essay for itself alone doesn't have the enjoyment that I get from English ones. I am not able to look at a beautiful sentence and find some lovely words to go into it that are really expressive of the right feeling and exactly the right sort of emotion. . . . I think Philosophy is so boring having to do away with things like beauty, joy, and pleasure.
>
> *Judith:* Yes, words and language fascinate me.

The concerns of the other writers are simpler:

> *Bill:* No, I don't worry about style. I write to say what I think is wanted, what they're looking for. I'm not a poet (laughs).

4. *Compatibility with Intentions.* This criterion is something of a cov-er-all—for the deep writer in particular—in that the emphasis is upon how well the product, at various stages of its emergence, realizes the initial intentions the writer had. The point is that all parawriting and writing activities should be constantly monitored in terms of the global intentions originally formed or as may later be modified opportunis-tically.

WRITING ACTIVITIES

Parawriting and writing activities merge at the stage of forming focal intentions (see Figure 2). Composition may be regarded as com-

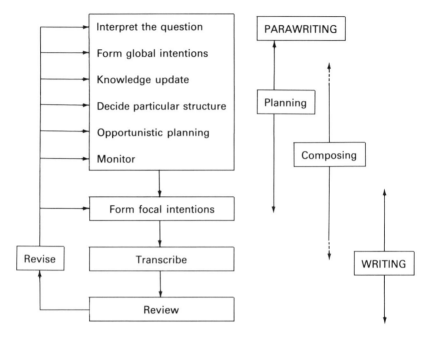

Figure 2. Interactions between parawriting and writing activities.

mencing with that long series of activities that are triggered by interpreting the question and culminating in that final act—forming focal intentions—of foreshadowing written words with unspoken thoughts.

Writing proper begins with transcription—putting down in written
form the focal intentions—and then continues with review in terms of
the monitoring criteria mentioned above. If change is necessary, then
revision will commence at whatever parawriting activity or activities
require reactivating; the question might be seen to have been misread,
or the global intentions might be inappropriate, or more knowledge
necessary, with consequent restructuring or reprioritizing.

At all events, the act of composing is very difficult to pin down; its
very nature calls up conflicting theories of the relationship between
thought and language. In general, researchers seem to fall into two
schools of thought. There are those who see writing as "translating"
thought into text, as if the thought preexists in some preverbal, possibly
nonverbal, form. The Scardamalia and Bereiter model (see Figure 1) is
basically of this nature: the content space providing the substance and
the rhetorical space, the translation service. Others see the act of writing
as the creation of meaning, so that Britten *et al.* (1975) describe writing as

"shaping at the point of utterance"; or as Forster (1968) asks, "How can I know what I think until I see what I say?" (quoted in Salgado, 1980, p. 70).

Clearly, both models address some aspect of the truth. We do not have to write a note to the milkman before we know how many bottles of milk we might need (Steinberg, 1980); on the other hand, a deep approach to writing clearly does clarify meaning.

The interaction between *immediate text* and composing is emphasized by McCutchen (1984), who was concerned that the heavy emphasis on writing as a cognitive problem-solving process had led researchers away from the real problem in writing, which is the generation of extended coherent language: "Well planned text is not necessarily well written text" (p. 229).

McCutchen examined think-aloud protocols of a professional journalist and of an elementary school student to illustrate the importance of bottom-up or text-based processes in good writing. The journalist paid a good deal of attention to the "feel" or "cadence" of a particular word, which often stimulated a new substantive angle to the text (in this case a wine column). Text-based considerations are even more clearly evident in literary writing, when the length, sound, and even sight of the word interact with the word's connotative meaning to play a large part in the final audience effect. Coleridge's phrase, "the prop'rest word in the prop'rest place," refers precisely to this balance between textual and semantic demands: that complex interaction between what-is-meant, what-is-said, and how-else-it-might-be-put. The elementary school student, on the other hand, could only write what she had written; being unable to distinguish between what-is-said from what-is-meant, revision of text was a pointless procedure (see below).

It could be that the processes of composing and revising are in principle inexplicable. Certainly, writers themselves emphasize the mystique of writing. Salgado's (1980) comments about the creative process in novelists seem applicable to the more mundane but equally mysterious composing processes of essay writers:

> But after we have learned what there is to learn about a novelist's methods, routines, and outlook, there is still a core of mystery about the art of fiction which does not yield up its secrets; . . . Most novelists admit they do not know just how they produce their work. One of the simplest and most straightforward statements on the subject came from one of the best of living novelists, Saul Bellow. "Well I don't know exactly how it's done," he said. "I let it alone a good deal." (p. 70)

If one wished to explain why composing is such a mysterious business, one might refer to studies of hemispericity which indicate different levels of involvement between the cerebral hemispheres (cf. Torrance &

Rockenstein, Chapter 10). Rico and Claggett (1980) argue that creative ideation is a right hemisphere and essentially nonverbal process, quoting C. S. Lewis's claim that all his novels began with "seeing pictures in my head," which Sagan (1977) claims to be true of all composing. Glassner (1980) took measures of hemispherical activity during writing and found what we would call parawriting activities to be right dominant, and transcription-related activities to be left dominant. Torrance and Rockenstein argue that creativity in general involves both hemispheres, with "inventing" being right dominant and "improving" being left dominant. Following through with Jaynes' (1976) highly speculative argument on the rise of "consciousness" as a left-hemisphere task, it could be that the only way we can describe the right-to-left shift (from composition to transcription) is allegorically. Hence, perhaps, the mystery: the need to invoke a demon to explain what cannot in principle be explained in words. On the other hand, Beaumont (1983) would suggest that the concept of hemisphericity in this context may be misleading and invalid.

The matter is obviously too complex to discuss any further here. We need merely note that, through a mysterious interfacing of thought with transcription processes, text emerges.

The transcription processes include those activities that are involved in the creation of text, independent (as far as may be) of purely semantic considerations. They may be listed as a series of skills in order of increasing generality: orthographics (spelling and punctuation), syntax, lexicon (a vocabulary of technical terms), grapholect (the ability to write in "academese"), and to realize the genre of the essay in question.

Review and Revision. Review is undertaken in terms of the monitoring criteria mentioned at the planning stage: audience, originality, aesthetics and style, and global intentions. There nevertheless appear to be strong differences between surface and deep approaches to writing at this point, depending in part on the size of unit for review.

Writers tend to fall into two groups: those who review regularly and frequently, choosing review units of a sentence or so, sometimes more, sometimes less; and those who delayed review until a whole thought sequence has been written out, in a few paragraphs, or even pages. For example, Rose (1984) found that students who "blocked" reviewed frequently and in small units, whereas fluent writers reviewed in large units. Similar findings were found in the present study: students endorsing a surface approach tended to review frequently, with respect to words and sentences, while those using a deep approach reviewed relatively infrequently. When the latter did review, they separated review of discourse features from review of surface features such as orthographics (spelling and punctuation), word choice, and syntax.

Revision itself is not a separate process from writing (Nold, 1981); it involves rethinking, composing, and transcribing again to replace old text with new text and is not a "post"-writing phase. Torrance and Rockenstein (as noted above) regard revision as "improving," a left-hemispheric process which is integral to the total creative act.

The following statements by students, in answer to questions about their procedures of reviewing and revising text, show the focus students had and how this differs between deep and surface approaches. Those using a deep approach showed that their primary aim is to revise at the level of discourse, mechanics being a matter that may be attended to later:

> *Joanne:* I do check spelling and grammar but that's really no problem at all. No, it's repetition, redundancy . . . and the contradictions that I have made somewhere, because you go off a tangent and think of another angle. They're my real concerns when editing.

Surface responders were concerned almost exclusively with words and sentences:

> *Bill:* Oh I just reread the draft, check that it's clear to read, haven't left out words, if the spelling's OK. I try and turn in the first draft or maybe the second go at it, so I don't want to alter too much.

There is an intimate link between revision and planning that may be illustrated by reference to McCutchen's example mentioned earlier; the interaction between what-is-meant, what-is-said, and how-else-it-might-be-put. Whereas her wine correspondent continually refined his text—thus showing an awareness of all three—the elementary school student only saw identity between what-is-said and what-is-meant. What-is-said *must* be what-is-meant, otherwise she would have said something else![1]

CONCEPTUALIZING APPROACHES TO ESSAY WRITING

The intentional, parawriting, and writing activities elucidated above need to be represented in such a way that student approaches to writ-

[1] The lack of relation between planning and revising in young children is beautifully illustrated in a story told by Lauren Resnick. Her 10-year-old son showed her a story he had "edited." The original story was a well-structured one about an animal. The editing, however, transformed this story into nonsense: words were crossed out that already made perfectly good sense; lines and arrows linked appropriately embedded sentences to obviously inappropriate sections of the text. He was asked why he changed an already good story into one that wasn't nearly as good. He replied, "Oh, that isn't *writing* the story. I've done that. This is editing it, you know, like you always do when you have written something!"

ing—the variants of surface and deep—may be mapped easily. The basic notions of Scardamalia and Bereiter (see Figure 1) of a "content space" and a "rhetorical space," and a unidirectional knowledge-telling strategy and a bidirectional reflective strategy, are retained but considerably modified and relabeled. The "content" space is referred to as "semantic," and contains long-term as well as updated knowledge, while the "rhetorical" space is subdivided into planning (essay-specific) and transcription (general linguistic) activities. These activities and their interrelationships are shown in Figure 3.

With this as guide, we can trace the five approaches in terms of intention, parawriting, and writing, using the above and other student interview material paradigmatically.

1. *Surface-subjective approach.*
Intention. To answer the question (unelaborated).
Parawriting and Writing. Planning is minimal, with no knowledge updating, and the structure is nonexistent. Prioritizing is in terms of subjective criteria. Monitoring during planning, and reviewing of either discourse or surface features, is unlikely. The approach amounts to a

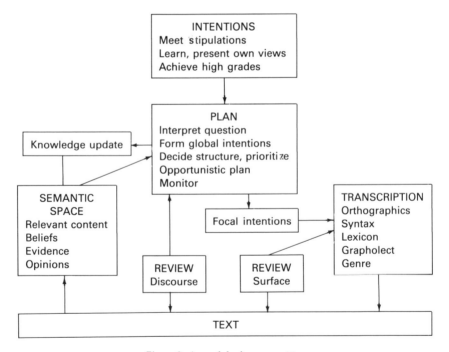

Figure 3. A model of essay writing.

direct "emptying" of unsupported opinion onto paper, usually transcribed with minimal skill.

2. *Surface-restrictive approach.*

Intention. To answer the question with minimal involvement and trouble.

Parawriting. The question is interpreted in such a way that a simplistic response is seen—or hoped—to satisfy the question. There is little knowledge updating; the content is chosen which the student already knows most about. The structure is a simple retelling of the details surrounding the chosen aspect in a simple time sequence, either as they occurred to the writer or chronologically. As the structure and shaping comes from a linear time sequence, there is little modification of this to suit an audience: the style is bland and impersonal. There is little or no opportunistic planning, and no current monitoring in terms of style or originality.

Writing. During composition, transcription, and review, the focus is on words and word sequences of no greater than a sentence in length. The criteria for review are almost exclusively orthographic and within-sentence grammar.

3. *Surface-elaborative approach.*

Intention. To write as full an account as possible and to do a reasonable job, but a feeling of pressure is usually present. The essay is essentially a hurdle to be cleared, notwithstanding some possible interest in the subject.

Parawriting. Interpretation of the question varies widely, especially according to subject, but in history it frequently becomes a tension between "tell as much as you know about . . ." consistent with time available, other course demands, and the perceived predilections of the presumed marker. Realizing this interpretation often means considerable knowledge updating, which is organized into independent segments (multistructural). Prioritizing, deciding what to say and in what order, is more a matter of reading the presumed marker's predilections or of telling a story chronologically rather than assembling points in a structure and order that are intrinsic to the case being put. There is some room for opportunistic planning, but of a restricted kind—for example, "where can I best put this extra information I've just come across?"—rather than involving a fundamental rethinking of the essay itself. Monitoring is often with respect to audience prejudices but at a sentence level, for example, selection of words, phrases, and sentiments that might please.

Writing. The sentence level basically remains the unit size for composing, review, and revising. Review tends to be fairly frequent, sentences often being inspected immediately after completion for orthographics, word choice, and grammar, which tends to have a disruptive effect on concentration (Rose, 1984). There are, however, the rudiments of a global sense of structure that transcends sentences; sentences can be added, and more importantly subtracted, with a view to overall effect, but without a sense of true genre, that is, each component is not linked inevitably as an integral part of the case. This approach makes most use of knowledge-telling as such: saying as much as one conveniently and plausibly can, in the belief that in so doing one is making a case. The text is not "recycled" by being reentered into semantic space.

4. *Deep-integrative approach.*

Intention. To use the assignment as a learning experience and (possibly) to achieve as high a grade as possible.

Parawriting. The question is interpreted by implicitly or explicitly recognizing the required genre (e.g., "As a compare–contrast essay, I'll need to examine both sides first. For that I'll need to . . ."), which then guides the knowledge update. The particular points to be made in the essay will then be balanced and refined, the structure and essay plan is clarified, and then it is time to prioritize. There is some chance for opportunistic planning, but basically the structure is constrained by the original interpretation. Monitoring is concerned with all aspects: audience, particularly the generalized audience of scholars to whom grapholect is addressed, style, and, up to a point, originality.

Writing. Deep writers, both integrative and reflective, seem to keep the two levels of discourse and surface features separate, with their prime attention on discourse, on the case being put. They typically then produce relatively long passages of text before stopping for review and revision, and typically leave surface review of syntax and orthographics until last, so that their attention is not arbitrarily diverted from the level of discourse. Deep writing follows for the first time a cyclical pattern: plan—transcribe—discourse review—plan, and so forth, until time or personal satisfaction decrees an end to the process. There is also a symmetry from planning to product in the discourse structure, which is at the relational level and specifically designed around the genre and which becomes progressively clearer at each cycle of write—review—revise—rewrite. The text itself becomes part of the semantic space, which it does not, in the surface approaches.

5. *Deep-reflective approach.*

Intention, parawriting, and *writing* are all much the same as for deep-integrative, except that there is much stronger emphasis here upon originality, especially with respect to genre. In particular, the discourse structure does not necessarily follow that expected in the question, and the level of abstraction will be correspondingly higher than that of the deep-integrative approach.

The surface and deep approaches differ in two main ways: in their processes and in their outcome. The deep processes involve metacognition in a way that the surface ones do not; review and revision at the discourse level involve the reexamination and frequently the restatement of one's thought. The surface writer, on the other hand, simply states what is already known. Those process differences determine the outcome differences. The outcome of a deep approach is a fresh way of looking at the matter at hand, whereas the outcome of a surface approach is at best a new accretion of known data. To put it another way, a deep approach leads to outcomes that are *qualitatively* different from the prior inputs, whereas a surface approach leads only to quantitative rearrangements of previously existing data.

In this section, three surface and two deep approaches to writing are described in terms of intentions, parawriting, and writing activities. The approaches are described in terms of a model of writing synthesized from a variety of sources, including aspects of writing research and student learning research, and they are illustrated with excerpts from student interviews. Finally, it remains to apply the model to case studies. Unfortunately, space forbids selecting cases illustrating all five approaches. The two cases reported below illustrate the best of each of a deep and a surface approach—deep-reflective and surface-elaborative.

TWO CASE STUDIES

The two students were enrolled in the Australian history class of the Open Foundations Course (OFC), which is designed for mature age students who do not possess the necessary qualifications for direct entry into the university. They may do so after passing two subjects in the OFC, of which the present course in Australian history is one.

The essay in question was the second and final assignment in the course, and the students were interviewed after the essay had been marked and handed back with comments. The students were asked previously to keep any notes and early drafts and to bring them and the final essay, after it had been marked, to the interview.

The essay question was the following: *Identify the basic causes of the Eureka Stockade, and try to establish which were the most important. Explain whether you think that this revolt was inevitable.* (About 1,500 words.)

[2]I am grateful to Stephanie Moylan for collecting the data on the case studies.
[3]The Eureka Stockade was the nearest thing to a civil war in Australian history. It occurred in 1854, when the goldminers in the Victorian goldfields rose in armed revolt against the government and rallied under their own flag. However, it rapidly fizzled, and the leader, Peter Lalor, later became a respected member of the Victorian Parliament.

Syd

Syd, aged 57, finished school over 40 years ago after completing the Intermediate Examination (roughly Grade 9). He was currently employed, and his previous employment included clerical and industrial (foreman) experience. He was taking the course for personal satisfaction. He claimed to have no difficulties with essay writing and had in fact written book reviews for the local newspaper.

On the Study Process Questionnaire (SPQ) (Biggs, 1987), Syd's profile showed him to have scored in the bottom decile on the Surface Approach scale, and within the top deciles on both Deep and Achieving Approaches, according to national norms for male arts undergraduates. In other words, he scored as high on Deep and Achieving, and as low on Surface, as it is possible to do.

The following is heavily edited and abridged from the interview transcript, and is divided into intention, parawriting, and writing phases.

Intention:

I write to produce something that I like, within the constraints of having to present an acceptable and reasonable essay to the lecturer that set the topic. I want to do well, but I am fairly confident of my ability and am not unduly concerned about the particular mark that I get. Basically, I like writing and have no difficulty.

Parawriting:

Normally, I find several reference books which I think have something relevant in them, and read the relevant parts, taking notes of the various points that crop up. I like to get a fairly wide coverage. Various points of view all differ to some extent, even if it is only slightly, but sometimes that slight difference can be the interesting twist you can put into the essay. In this case, I read all the suggested references and five additional ones. I took notes from all the readings and from them just let things evolve. I correlated them together and they fit a structure, whether it is chronological or something else. Then I give it a twist that has emerged from my reading. Now in this case, soon as this topic came up, I had in mind that the slant would be that it was part of the rise of the middle class in the nineteenth century.

This essay was to put this point of view, this twist sort of, and support it with references. But it's a compromise. You are in a position where you have to provide a point of view and back it up with references but you can't diverge from the official point of view because of what is required in the essay by the lecturer. You have to take into account your own point of view and what is actually being sought by the person setting the essay. So you have to compromise a bit.

Writing:

My first draft is done by collating the rough notes and what else I want to say. Once I have the outline, based on my own twist, the rough draft didn't take long to do. The rise of the middle classes in the nineteenth century is how I started. The Eureka Stockade is just part of that: that was my case, my twist. I then selected the reference notes to support that, the details, etc. But I can't diverge too much from the official view that's likely to be supported by the lecturer. At least, so I think—I don't really know his views. I really write to suit myself. I try and produce something that *I* would like to read. I can't really write for the lecturer; I can't read his mind. When editing, I look for spelling mistakes, badly expressed things, verbosity, if it's convoluted. I try to keep it as straightforward as possible and as direct as possible. Repetition—none of that sort of thing. I edit to keep it coherent, logical, and as orderly as possible. I keep a dictionary beside me and check meanings and spellings while I'm writing when I'm in doubt. I worked in three stages. A rough outline from the notes, then the rough draft from the outline. I edited that as far as I went and changed the weighting I gave to something. Then I corrected and edited the final draft from that.

The essay is reproduced in the Appendix.

Comments. Syd's essay is an example of deep-reflective writing, despite the fact that he does not appear to spend much time in planning or redrafting. He also says that he is prepared to "compromise" his own views with what he imagines to be the "official" view, but this is really overstated in the event, as he also says of his lecturer, "I can't read his mind."

The structure is highly appropriate, a strong example of causal explanation. The discourse structure is extended abstract: the particular event, the Eureka Stockade, is hypothesized as an example of a wider phenomenon, the rise of the middle classes in Europe at that time. The details and events surrounding the rebellion—the personal backgrounds of the miners, their "small business" rather than working-class value system, the roles and values of the police officers and of the government officials—are all highly relevant to that structure and illustrate the thesis well. The marker commented: ". . . you are perhaps the only student who is capable of fitting both into a broad political/historical framework. . . ." All the other students used a structure that was at best relational, in which the details and surrounding events were discussed only with respect to the rebellion itself. The SOLO analyses thus clearly back up the lecturer's own view of the quality of Syd's thinking as revealed in his essay.

In short, although Syd does not produce many drafts as evidence of reflective activity, the reflection is nevertheless present. It is possibly fortuitous that the topic fitted so well into a matter that Syd was already interested in and had devoted much thought to. It was not so much then a matter that the essay gave him an opportunity to clarify his meaning, as one to test an already formed hypothesis. The essay, then, is strongly top-down, possessing a coherence and unity in which the components clearly relate to each other and to the thesis.

GEOFF

Geoff, aged 34, left school nearly 20 years ago, and like Syd, he completed the Intermediate Examination (Grade 9). He is a clerk and is taking the course to discover his capacity for university work. He doesn't enjoy writing, finding it an "involved process." Nevertheless, he felt at the time that he had done a "pretty fair job" on his first essay, but barely passed. He attributed that disappointing result to his writing style, following a comment the marker made. He liked the present topic better than the first one, and said that he was genuinely interested in the Eureka Stockade and felt confident about the essay. However, he started work a month after the topic was given out, put off attempting it several times, and then found he had a problem with time to complete.

His SPQ profile showed him to be scoring in the top 30% of the male arts undergraduate population on the Surface Approach scale (in the top decile for the Surface Strategy itself), the bottom decile for the Deep Approach, and the bottom 30% for the Achieving Approach scales.

Intention:

I like to present the facts, you know, what I have read and try to present a point of view. . . . I just cover the story right through and then say why I think it happened. . . . I more or less cover the whole thing from beginning to end and put a summary on it.

Parawriting:

I read the main three recommended texts and sort of got a more detailed version than just the general history. I got the actual full volume on that section to try to get more information . . . jotted down sentences and quotes where I thought quotes might be helpful to the points I had mentioned and put them together. After reading the books, I had my reasons why I thought it was caused.

Writing:

I made up a bit of a guideline of what I was going to do. I did it in stages and started off with the different causes and then worked through. I took the quotes and tried to rearrange the words and substitute my own words: break it down a little. If they [the sources] do a couple of paragraphs I try and combine it together, just with a couple of sentences myself. Bring in my own words, type of thing. I did a paragraph on each point. I knew who was going to mark it but I just try to present my own sort of version. I didn't really have anyone in mind reading it; I just tried to cover the topic and answer the question as best I could. I had no problem with grammar and spelling and I felt I had no difficulty in presenting what I wanted to say. My style of writing isn't truly historical but, I sort of said what I wanted to, more or less a narrative coverage of it rather than an an analytical approach [this was also a reflection of the marker's comments on his first essay]. I just sort of covered the topic . . . yes, I felt I had answered the question. I found the first and last paragraphs the hardest, explaining why you thought it happened, type of thing. The middle part was more or less covering the topic, which I found easy. I did six drafts altogether and improved each draft [this is arguable, on viewing the drafts]. I edited grammar and spelling each time and made sure I didn't use the same words all the time. I changed a few paragraphs around, I thought I might have had it a bit out of sequence, a bit disjointed, so I changed a couple, reorganized the structure. No, I didn't change the orientation at each draft [response to a specific question].

The essay is reproduced in the Appendix.

Comments. Geoff might appear at first to be adopting a deep approach to writing: he says that he does not attempt to please a particular marker, he presents his own point of view supported by evidence, and he edited and revised six drafts. Despite what he says, however, he does not present a unified point of view supported by evidence: the structural complexity of the essay is multistructural at best, and his approach is surface-elaborative. He takes a series of events and lists them as possible causes and then selects the most likely, in his view. The events are not integrated into a causal sequence, each implicating the other. Put otherwise, the genre is inappropriately realized.

Something of this is indicated in the comments "I like to present the facts. . . . I more or less cover the thing from beginning to end." This is straight knowledge-telling, and as the marker comments, his essay reads more like narrative than historical analysis. The first draft is in fact a paraphrase of his notes: "My sort of version" is "his" at the word–sentence level only; the semantic content is second hand.

He draws on his not inconsiderable knowledge to list the causes and then says what he knows about each cause, independently of the other. His conclusion is to settle for the one cause that seems most salient (governmental actions). Knowledge-telling traps him into giving far too much irrelevant detail, such as depth of mining shafts, the exact dates of various events, even repetition of bibliographical details in the text as well as in the reference list. Typically surface-elaborative, he appears to believe that the case is made by weight of detail.

His diligent attempts at revision amounted to little more than surface editing. Revision at the level of discourse involved reordering some paragraphs which were "out of sequence," but such revision is of only marginal relevance to the causal explanation genre, which is that required here. As the marker also notes: "You did not have to give an account of the rebellion, merely discuss its causes." It will not do to dismiss Geoff's problem as being due to his having misunderstood the question. Whether he understands what historical causes are or not, his approach to writing is one that precludes the causal genre; it does not permit him to argue a case. In this, his approach to writing is mostly in keeping with his general approach to learning itself, as indexed by his SPQ responses, which characterize him as relying heavily on the surface strategy and avoiding the deep.

SUMMARY, CONCLUSIONS, AND IMPLICATIONS

Deep and surface approaches to learning in general have been distinguished by a variety of researchers. Marton's original work referred to reading text, and an important distinction he noted in that context was that students adopting a surface approach focused on the word–sentence level, while those using a deep approach focused on the level of meaning. This distinction leads to another: a deep approach involves metacognition, in that the search for meaning involves one in monitoring and reshaping one's own thought, whereas a surface approach is simply reactive.

Writing researchers have made similar distinctions. Applebee (1984) refers to the use of writing in summative evaluation as forcing student concentration on the word–sentence level of processing, with the result that writing in school contexts has not been able to fulfill its function as a means of discovering or clarifying meaning. This is a serious charge, given the role of essays in higher education particularly. Further, Scardamalia and Bereiter (1982), in distinguishing knowledge-telling and reflective writing strategies, draw out the metacognitive nature of reflective writing, as opposed to knowledge-telling, in that in the former the writer's thinking is reexamined and progressively clarified.

Such obvious parallels between surface and deep approaches to learning in general and to writing in particular led to the formulation of a model of essay writing, based on intentional, parawriting, and writing activities. Several activities were distinguished within each category, and excerpts from student interviews provided concrete illustrations of the activities so distinguished.

Further parallels were noted between discourse structure (both during planning and as it finally emerged in the product), genre, and approach to writing. The SOLO Taxonomy was used to operationalize discourse structure, and on the basis of findings from student learning research relating process and outcome structure, three surface and two deep approaches to writing were distinguished.

Surface. Intentional aspects are all dominated by the instrumental (summative evaluational) function of the essay rather than the opportunity it provides for a learning experience. Planning activities are virtually nonexistent in the surface-subjective approach and only slightly more evident in surface-restrictive, which involves a time-structured sequence of relevant but limited data. The surface-elaborative approach may involve much knowledge updating and apparent thought given to structure, but that which emerges is in the listing genre, which is usually inappropriate. In none of the surface approaches is a more complex genre realized, although in the surface-elaborative there is the nascent awareness that the case put is somehow more than the sum of the sentences comprising the text. Otherwise, the focus during planning, composing, transcribing, reviewing, and revising does not exceed sentence length. The last two processes do not occur in surface-subjective, are restricted to orthographics in surface-restrictive, and may involve addition and even deletion of sentences in surface-elaborative. Discourse structures are pre-, uni-, and multistructural, respectively.

Deep. Intentional, parawriting, and writing activities are similar in the deep-integrative and deep-reflective approaches. The essay is seen in both cases as a learning experience in its own right and is anticipated with pleasure. Considerable planning, knowledge updating, and care for style, audience, and addressing the question is exerted. The focus is on the substantive question of discourse structure. Main differences between the two are on the degree of originality present, the level of abstraction, and the discourse structure itself, which in the deep-integrative case is relational (staying within the context and the genre defined by the question) and in the deep-reflective case, extended abstract (defining its own genre, and by virtue of the reflective activity itself producing a product at a higher level of abstraction than that demanded). In both cases, review and revision of surface features—orthographics, syntax—is usually considered apart from review and revision of discourse and may be left until the penultimate draft.

Two case studies were presented to illustrate two approaches to essay writing and to note any agreement with each student's general approach to learning. Syd, classified by his SPQ responses as an extreme deep achiever, showed a deep-reflective approach to writing. He had thought about the topic before writing, and he used the essay topic as a means of testing a hypothesis. He did not, however, need to "discover" his meaning (like Steinberg, 1980)—his hypothesis was clear enough already—and so most of his thinking had been outlined, and the details tested to his satisfaction, in the first draft. His essay shows evidence of a high degree of conceptualization, as seen in the extended abstract structure and in its originality.

Geoff's SPQ profile indicated a high surface approach in general, and his approach to this particular essay confirmed this. While he often seemed to have deep-sounding intentions and made multiple drafts, his focus was essentially at the word–sentence level, for example, when paraphrasing his sources into "his" version. Basically, he saw only one way of structuring his essay, that of telling everything he thought relevant about the topic in chronological order; he then selected one subtopic as "the" cause of the rebellion. It is worth commenting that in some respects Geoff's is the more interesting essay to read—he reports more concrete detail and his images are sometimes quite vivid—whereas Syd's expression is often dull and ponderous. Nevertheless, as a history essay, the latter realizes the genre most effectively, as indicated both by the independent marking by the instructor and by the present analysis.

It is dangerous to generalize from an N of two, but these cases seem clearly to demonstrate the possibility, and hopefully the utility, of describing approaches to essay writing and aligning them to approaches to learning. At least in these two cases, the approaches to writing were very compatible with their general approaches to learning at university.

Assuming that further research substantiates the general thrust of the model outlined above, certain implications for the setting, writing, interpreting, and evaluating of essays would follow.

1. The essay has functionally and historically two major aspects: a heuristic and an evaluative one. Students can too easily concentrate on the one to the exclusion of the other. Usually the latter dominates, and this leads to a surface approach to writing. This tendency is greatly exacerbated if teachers, overtly or in their teaching behaviors, overemphasize the evaluative function.

2. While a student's approach to writing a particular essay may be constrained to some, or even to a large, extent by that student's general learning style, there are some points at which the writing process might be steered in a more academically and linguistically appropriate direction. Certain contextual conditions—for example, teacher comments that focus on orthographics and grammar—encourage students to focus primarily if not exclusively on the word–sentence level, which all but precludes original substantive learning.

3. A good essay, that meets both heuristic and evaluative criteria, is one that results from a deep approach and in which the genre is appropriate to the question. It is thus a complex amalgam of a sound knowledge base, deep thought, and rhetorical skill in transcribing—an interaction between content and language that transcends attempts to improve essay writing by concentrating on either one. "How-to" courses in essay writing in general necessarily avoid issues of content structure, and so tend to restrict focus to the word–sentence level, while concentration on more content further confounds the writer already embarrassed by the riches of fact and detail.

4. The interface between content and language is *genre*, in particu-

lar, the specific genre required by the question. Many students, particularly those whose only approach to writing is a version of knowledge-telling, are either uncaring or unknowing of the range of genres in their subject discipline. It is possible that in this respect many teachers are as functionally ignorant as their students and by their setting and marking of questions blur the distinction between *what* are the relevant points to be made and *how* do the relevant points make the case in question. In fact, there are not all that many cases in question; teachers should be aware of their general structure, and so should their students. If teachers are not so aware, it is likely that they will encourage knowledge-telling in their students. It seems that teachers should explicate and illustrate these genre structures in their subject disciplines, and they should be at the basis of any planning and writing activities.

A crucial difference between surface-elaborative and the two deep approaches to writing is in the structural complexity of planning, composing, and reviewing. It is important, therefore, that future research look into the range of factors—for example, the wording of questions, the time limitations and other conditions of essay submission, perhaps in interaction with the learning styles of the students concerned—that facilitate or inhibit the development and deployment of structure in writing.

It may then become possible explicitly to develop the role of writing as a tool for clarifying and extending thought. What has happened instead, ironically enough, is that writing has become the medium that, to paraphrase Anne above, constricts thought to a shopping list that apes grapholect: "You try to make it really sophisticated and complicated because you think you will be impressing the lecturer. It's what the lecturer thinks is what matters."

APPENDIX

Syd's Essay

The Eighteenth century is regarded as the Age of Enlightenment, a period that brought the flowering of new scientific and philosophical thought and a stronger concept of individual freedom for the common man. It saw the slow, but steady, spread of ideas as communications and education gradually improved and extended their influence down the social scale. This century came to its close with two notable events; the American War of Independence with its avowed goal of freedom, and the later, and more drastic, French Revolution with its rallying cry of "Liberte, Egalite and Fraternite." Europe entered the Nineteenth century on a rising tide of liberalism.

This Nineteenth century was to be a period of remarkable contrasts, an age both of turbulence and of long periods of conservative calm, that saw the tide of liberalism and democracy fostered largely by the growing middle class which owed much of its growth and increasing influence to the effects of the Industrial Revolution. This middle class of mainly mercantile, commercial and industrial origins was, in itself, basically conservative but, in securing its own aims, managed to spear-head most of the revolutionary movements in Europe, and elsewhere, during the Nineteenth century. It enthusiastically spread the credo of liberalism and democracy for its own purposes and this credo was just as enthusiastically taken up by those further down the social scale. While this is to overly simplify a very complex process, it is in light of this that the Eureka incident must be examined (Ayerst, Littlefield).

From the Paris revolution in 1830, through to the "Year of Revolutions" in 1848—with uprisings in France, Italy, Germany and Hungary—Europe was in a state of considerable turmoil and ferment. So much so, that even staid, insular Britain, largely isolated from Europe by the shield of her naval power and by inclination, found herself troubled by unrest and incipient uprisings as typified in the Chartist movement. It was from this background of stirring ideas and emotions that many of those who took part in the gold rushes, came.

The diggers on the gold-fields were something of a special breed. The majority had traveled considerable distances to get there and, in the process, had undergone varying degrees of hardship which had tended to weed-out the weak, the timid, and the less resolute. As Blainey suggests, "conditions favored the more robust." They had in common too, the fact that they were largely either small capitalists, or would-be small capitalists and their main aim was to improve their own lot, as is clearly indicated by Irving (Crowley), Shaw, and Ward. Many of them were well educated men (i.e., Peter Lalor, a graduate of Trinity College, Dubin) and of liberal out-look. Most appear to have been politically and socially conscious to some degree, and they were further "politicized" by the attitude of the Authorities, a body administered by mainly upper-class appointees with little or no understanding of, or sympathy for, middle class or working class aspirations. It was these middle class elements among the diggers that gave impetus to the reform movements, which, in turn, largely reflected middle class values—values often regarded by the Authorities as radical and subversive in nature.

During the California gold rush of 1849 the Australian Colonies had suffered a serious loss of population to California. Now that the gold rushes were taking place in Australia, the fear was that there would be a similar loss, particularly of agricultural workers, to the gold fields. The Master and Servant Act having proved ineffectual in stemming this loss, the expensive Gold License was introduced (originally in New South Wales) in an attempt to drive the unsuccessful diggers back to their former employment, though in this aim, it was no more successful than the Master and Servant Act had been. This may have seemed a sensible course in 1852, but it was the cause of the crisis in 1854 (Blainey). By then, gold was becoming increasingly difficult to win, and the per capita take had declined from three hundred and ninety Pounds in 1852 to one hundred and forty eight Pounds in 1854, so that the license fee of thirty Shillings per month became a heavy burden (Ward).

Also, as Blainey points out, the Ballarat field was unique in some ways in that it tended, by its nature, to favor the few at the expense of the majority. For one thing, the claims were very small and, as the gold tended to be concentrated in small, rich pockets, a few struck it very rich, while most made little or nothing. Also, the alluvial gold, which was what was being sought, was quite deeply buried in old, overlain stream beds and this necessitated "deep" mining with its increased and strenuous work, its attendant risks of cave-ins and problems with both gases and water.

The Government saw the diggers as mostly, temporary migrants, who would leave taking their money with them, if successful—and, probably, even if they were not successful—and who were imposing great strains on the fabric of Society. The cost of administering the gold fields was involving the Government in an annual deficit of over one hundred and thirty thousand pounds which made them all the more determined to collect the license money, which by now, had become an economic necessity (Shaw, Ward).

The diggers, particularly the less successful among them, while increasingly resentful of the license fee and bitterly opposed to the high-handed, often brutal, means used to collect it, were most strongly interested in obtaining social and political reforms, particularly the unlocking of the land, for many of them, having failed at mining, were increasingly inclined to take up farming, if they could. The Government, viewing them as transitory migrants, refused to see that such matters as male suffrage, parliamentary representation, vote by ballot, payment of Members of Parliament, land reforms and so on, were any concern of the diggers. However, the diggers did see these things as their concern. particularly as desirable ways of improving their lot, and it was these aims that were the basis of the various reform movements among them.

The diggers' aims were largely based on Chartist ideas, and their approach to the matter too was largely Chartist and non-violent, reformist rather than revolutionary. This is largely borne out by the role played by John Basson Humffray in the affair and the moderating influence that he exercised. While it seems obvious from this that the majority of the diggers as a whole, were more concerned with social and political reform than with the irritant of the Gold Licence, it was, nonetheless, the Gold Licence that became the fuse to the powder keg.

The spark that lit the fuse was undoubtedly the riot that lead to the burning down of Bentley's hotel after he had been acquitted, by magistrate D'ewes, of the murder of Scobie. This, and the subsequent clash with the troop reinforcements sent up from Melbourne, and the harsh reactions of the Authorities in both instances, brought the diggers resentment to the flash point. Hothams' out-of-hand rejection of the diggers delegation only added more heat to what was already an incendiary situation (Serle).

What happened at Eureka had obviously been coming for some time and, had long been seen as inevitable by many observers. Problems on the gold fields were not new and there had been an increasing polarization of feelings going on since the gold rushes began. Hothams' predecessor, La Trobe, had, due to unrest and the Red Ribbon Movement in Bendigo in 1853, reduced the Licence fee to eight Pounds per annum temporarily. And the restiveness was not confined to the Victorian fields either, for also in 1853 there had been the "roll-up" on the Turon River in New South Wales, when over four hundred armed, and angry miners had confonted thirty two police with the situation becoming tense enough to require troops being rushed up from Sydney. So, it was increasingly obvious that an outbreak of some sort was inevitable somewhere on the gold fields. Bendigo, on the basis of the unrest there in 1853, was considered by most to be the likely venue, but it was to be at Ballarat that the matter came to a head.

Eureka and the Castle Hill rebellion of 1804 are two exceptional aberrations in a very notable aspect of Australian social and political development which is the remarkable lack of violence and disorder with which these developments have been accomplished. Nowhere has this been more evident than on the gold fields where, if anywhere, conditions were such as to promote disorder and violence. Yet there was no evidence of "lynch law" such as had been seen in California and in Australia, in areas where nearly every man went armed, there appears to have been little or no bloodshed and violence. Everything seems to have been remarkably peaceful and the diggers—and others—seem to have displayed a high level of self-discipline and responsibility, often in the face of considerable provocation. Most historians tend to attribute this to the fact that the great majority of the diggers were of British (not just English) stock—which, at that time, included the Irish—and that most of the gold fields were adjacent to centers of firmly established governments (i.e., Sydney and Melbourne at this period). Also, there was no large foreign element among the diggers, nor was there any aggressive indigenous race in any of the areas to cause friction. The only racial troubles were to come later when tension reached a high pitch with the arrival of numerous Chinese on the various diggings.

There is about the Eureka affair a melancholy similarity to the ill-fated Castle Hill rebellion of 1804, particularly the Irish involvement. However, the large part played by the Irish at Eureka can be seen as being largely co-incidental, in that the Eureka Lead, where the stockade was sited, happened, by chance, to be a predominantly Irish area and proximity did the rest (ref: Ward, Irving/Crowley). It is worth noting too, that of all the diggers in the Ballarat area, only some fifteen percent took up arms, while those actually involved in the Stockade battle were but a fraction of one percent. It seems obvious too that the diggers, particularly the English and Welsh Chartists, were moderates who were loath and reluctant to in any way espouse armed rebellion as a solution to their problems. It was only a few of the "fire-brands" like Frederic Vern that seriously propounded revolution as a solution, and they all seem to have run away when the action started (Irving/Crowley).

The Royal Commission into the Eureka affair concluded that it had been inevitable, "even had there been no foreigners present," thus adopting the old Anglo-Saxon ploy of blaming it all on the foreigners if possible! In retrospect it is difficult, given the attitude of the Victorian administration, to seriously disagree with this assessment. Had Hotham and Rede, particularly, been a little less autocratic and a bit more tactful in their approach, a little less nervous about what was largely, just loud talk initially, on the part of the diggers, then a happier outcome might have resulted. That this could have been so is strongly suggested by the successful dealings with the diggers after the event by Major-General Sir Robert Nickle and Colonel Edward MacArthur (Serle).

It would seem that much of the blame for the causes of the uprising can be seen in the bungling and unduly autocratic handling of the situation by the ill-informed and badly advised Hotham, and by the uncompromising stand taken by his subordinate, Gold Commissioner Rede. Hotham failed to appreciate that he was no longer on the quarter-deck of a man-of-war and that the diggers were not prepared to be treated as surly lower deck ratings. In this, he displayed a failing noticeable among other naval officers who became Colonial Governors.

That Eureka did happen is fairly convincing proof that it was inevitable. As it turned out, although the diggers lost the battle, they seem to have won the war, in that most, if not all, of their demands were met within a very short time of the uprising. The Gold Licence was abolished and replaced by the much more sensible export tax on gold, they were given the vote and eventually, representation, and, probably most important, they were given the control and administration of their own mining Courts. Eureka Stockade, the Australian revolution that never really got off the ground, faded quickly into memories shortly after the event as other rushes carried the diggers to new fields and dispersed them across the continent. It has never been completely forgotten and lingers uneasily in the folk-memory even today. It has become a symbol, of sorts, to the mild mannered left of Australian politics and to the trendy, if tepid, would-be republicans.

GEOFF'S ESSAY

There were several basic causes of the Eureka Stockade. These included the three great grievances of the diggers which were the payment of a licence fee, the purchase of squatters' land and the right to vote. Other basic causes were the way government officials and police administered the law on the goldfields and how they mistreated the diggers who already had to overcome difficult conditions to mine the deep leads of Ballarat. Also the acquittal by a local magistrate of the murderer of a miner accelerated a confrontation between the diggers and the government.

Diggers began returning to Ballarat early in 1853 when they heard that large nuggets of gold had been discovered at a depth of sixty feet at Canadian Gully. The type of mining had changed from alluvial on the eastern side of Ballarat to sinking deep shafts on the western side. Geoffrey Blainey stated in *The Rush that Never Ended* that "Ballarat diggers became deep miners. They had found the amazing systems of deep leads, the buried rivers of gold." To reach the deep leads the diggers had to overcome many problems. Initially they formed into small syndicates of four or six men to cope with the heavy workload and to help with the high cost of supplies. While digging the shaft the miners had to contend with water flooding and shifting sand. If the water became too heavy men from other shafts had to help bale water out by order of the gold commissioner or they would forfeit their claim. Other problems they faced were from cave-ins, escaping gases from the river beds, and from the heat and humidity deep underground caused by a hot north wind blowing and shafts not being connected. Also there was no guarantee they would "strike it rich." Most diggers did not find the rich veins of gold. Geoffrey Blainey in *The Rush that Never Ended* quoted a Ballarat digger, H. W. Silvester who said to a parliamentary committee in 1853 that "Deep sinking is nothing more nor less than a species of lottery." Despite all these problems the most annoying thing for the diggers at Ballarat was to be ordered to the surface from about one hundred feet down the shaft by the police just to show their licence for about thirty seconds. Their digging could be delayed half an hour or more for the inspection of a piece of paper.

The major grievance of the diggers was the licence fee of thirty shillings a month. It was introduced into Victoria by Governor La Trobe on the 1st September, 1851. This very high fee was partly to help pay for the administration of the gold fields but mainly to discourage people from flocking there. During 1852 the fields were fairly quiet. However opposition to the licence fee grew as diggers found it harder to obtain good returns because the alluvial finds were decreasing. From the middle of 1853 a well organized and widespread movement of protest against the licence system began in Bendigo, where almost half of the Victorian diggers were working at the time, when news was received that thousands more people were due to arrive in the colony. At one meeting the diggers adopted a petition which was to be taken by a delegation to the Governor in Melbourne.

The petition opposed the monthly licence tax levied on the goldfields because it was unconstitutional, excessive and penalized the unsuccessful digger the same as the successful. The petition also asked for the right to vote and to buy squatters' lands. The Government was worried by this campaign especially when the diggers on some fields offered only ten shillings for their licences in September, 1853. Governor La Trobe then waived the fee but a week later it had returned in a different form. The licence fees were reduced to 1 for the month, 2 for three months, 4 for six months and 8 for twelve months. Soon after the diggers held meetings to discuss the new regulations. At one meeting on the 21st November, 1853, A.H.M. (Manning) Clark stated in *A History of Australia IV* that a huge number gathered at Eureka on the Ballarat field to hear Dr. Carr tell them that the new regulations would lead to armed rebellion.

By June 1854 goldfields had declined even more and diggers were less able to pay the licence fee. Government officials knew the diggers' situation needed careful handling. Into this tense situation came a new Governor Sir Charles Hotham. After a visit to Ballarat in August he was convinced the diggers were loyal and prosperous. But he also noted that they avoided paying a licence fee. As the Government was then facing a financial crisis, Hotham decided that by a more regular collection of licence fees the government would increase revenue. In mid-September he ordered the police to make licence inspections twice a week instead of the usual once a month. The diggers were immediately angry and resentful at the Governor's action but the licence raids continued up until the building of the Eureka Stockade.

Other grievances of the diggers were the right to vote and to buy squatters' land. Although the vast majority were not concerned with politics, an important minority always demanded the diggers be given the right to vote. Manning Clark stated in *A Short History of Australia* that "As they saw it they had contributed to the wealth and greatness of the colony without enjoying any voice whatever in its administration." The diggers also complained about the lack of opportunity for them to buy land on reasonable terms. Those who wanted to invest their gold earnings in land found they could not do it because the squatters held the lands.

Another cause of the Eureka Stockade was the way the Government and its officials administered the goldfields. A chief commissioner, his assistant and a police force controlled each field. The commissioners appointed were usually young and too inexperienced for such a position. The diggers referred to them as "boy commissioners." They visited the diggings daily to settle arguments over the boundaries of rich strikes which were deep underground. Their decisions were often unfair and inconsistent which annoyed the diggers.

The police on the goldfields were called "Joes" by the diggers after the Lieutenant Governor of Victoria Joseph La Trobe. They would arrest anyone not carrying his licence and would not allow a digger to return to his tent if he had it there. Their behavior was arrogant and cruel. Licence inspections became known as "digger hunts" and the miners opposition grew as their raids continued. A. G. L. Shaw stated in *The Story of Australia* that "The police became more and more unpopular as they tried to collect the miners' licence fee of one pound per month. This had to be paid by successful and unsuccessful alike. It was comparatively easy to evade and the police inexperienced often only accustomed to controlling the convicts of Van Dieman's Land, and sometimes convicts themselves, were tactless if not ruthless in their methods. Ill feeling between them and the miners grew, accentuated by corruption, bias and brutality."

The situation between the government and the diggers had reached a very tense stage. All that was needed was one incident to accelerate their inevitable confrontation. That incident occurred on the night of the 6th October, 1884, when a miner named Scobie was murdered outside the Eureka Hotel. James Bentley, an ex convict who owned the hotel, his wife Hanacea and John Farrell were tried and acquitted of the murder charge. The diggers were incensed by Bentley's acquittal and that the local magistrate was bribed. After a mass meeting on October 17, the hotel was burned down by some drunken miners, three of whom were charged with riot. From then on the diggers held a series of mass meetings. At one such meeting of about 10,000 diggers the Ballarat Reform League was founded. A series of demands were made including release of the rioters, the abolition of licence fees and some political reforms. The diggers were in an angry mood because the rioters were given long sentences.

Governor Hotham responded to the diggers' demands by ordering more licence hunts and dispatching further troops to Ballarat. At the same time the diggers began to turn from 'moral force' leaders to the more radical type. On the 29th November a mass meeting of diggers at the Bakery Hill was addressed by their leaders including Peter Lalor, an Irish engineer who was eventually to become a respectable Victorian politician. Also over the speakers platform flew a new flag the Southern Cross. After the meeting many of the diggers burnt their licences.

The next day saw the government deliberately looking for trouble by organizing a general licence hunt. It was a hot windy day and diggers began to rebel. Geoffrey Blainey in *The Rush that Never Ended* stated that "the day was made to try tempers and send men up the shafts. And the Government officials chose that day to make another raid for licences. On the flats hundreds of men defied the police." That afternoon a huge gathering of diggers assembled at Bakery Hill and with Peter Lalor as their leader they took an oath of loyalty under the Southern Cross.

The dedicated men moved to the Eureka Section of the hill fields where they built a rough stockade. They were marched and drilled and reinforced the stockade in preparation for the attack they believed must soon come but it did not. By Saturday night the enthusiasm of the diggers was disappearing and the numbers in the stockade began dwindling. On Sunday morning 3rd December, 1854 when the troops attacked just before dawn there were only 150 men in the Eureka Stockade. The fighting lasted less than half an hour and about 150 diggers were either killed or wounded. The troops suffered about 15 casualties. After the fighting they destroyed the stockade, burnt the tents and tore down the flag. Martial law was introduced for a few days and then the captured rebels were taken to Melbourne to be tried for high treason. They were subsequently acquitted. Although the diggers lost the battle they won the fight for their rights.

The most important causes of the Eureka Stockade were the introduction of the licence free and how the government officials and police enforced it without any consideration for the diggers of the Ballarat goldfields. I think that this revolt was inevitable because the diggers after years of petitioning, protesting and voicing their grievances to the authorities without result had no alternative left for them except rebellion.

The following writings are discussed in the essay:

1. Geoffrey Blainey—*The Rush that Never Ended.* 3rd edition, published 1978 (1st published 1963).
2. A. G. L. Shaw—*The Story of Australia.* 2nd edition, published 1960.
3. C. M. H. Clark—*A History of Australia IV, The Earth Abideth Forever,* 1851–1888. Published 1978, reprinted 1980.
4. Manning Clark—*A Short History of Australia.* 2nd edition, published 1963.

REFERENCES

Applebee, A. N. (1984). Writing and reasoning. *Review of Educational Research, 54,* 577–596.
Beaumont, J. G. (1983). How many brains for how many minds? Hemisphericity and education. *Educational Psychology, 3,* 213–226.
Bereiter, C. (1980). Development in writing. In L. Gregg & E. Steinberg (Eds.), *Cognitive processes in writing.* Hillsdale, NJ: Lawrence Erlbaum.

Biggs, J. B. (1978). Individual and group differences in study processes. *British Journal of Educational Psychology, 48,* 266–279.

Biggs, J. B. (1987). *Student approaches to learning and studying.* Hawthorn, Victoria: Australian Council for Educational Research.

Biggs, J. B., & Collis, K. F. (1982a). The psychological structure of creative writing. *Australian Journal of Education, 26,* 59–70.

Biggs, J. B., & Collis, K. F. (1982b). *Evaluating the quality of learning: The SOLO Taxonomy.* New York: Academic Press.

Britton, J., Burgess, T., Martin, N., McLeod, A., & Rosen, H. (1975). *The development of writing abilities (11–18).* London: Macmillan Educational.

Brown, A., Bransford, J., Ferrara, R., & Campione, J. (1983). Learning, remembering and understanding. In P. H. Mussen (Ed.), *Handbook of Child Psychology, Vol. III: Cognitive development.* New York: Wiley.

Burtis, J., Bereiter, C., Scardamalia, M., & Tetroe, J. (1984). The development of planning in writing. In B. Kroll & C. G. Wells (Eds.), *Exploration of children's development in writing.* Chichester: Wiley.

Entwistle, N. J. (1981). *Styles of learning and teaching.* Chichester: Wiley.

Entwistle, N., & Ramsden, P. (1983). *Understanding student learning.* London: Croom Helm.

Flower, L. (1980). *Problem solving strategies for writing.* New York: Harcourt Brace Jovanovich.

Forster, E. M. (1968). *Aspects of the novel.* Harmondsworth, Mdx.: Penguin Books.

Glassner, B. M. (1980). Hemispheric relationships in composing. *Boston University Journal of Education, 162,* 24–95.

Graves, D. H. (1983). *Writing: Teachers and children at work.* Exeter, NH: Heinemann Educational.

Halliday, M. A. K. (1974). *Language and social man.* London: Longmans.

Hausen, E. (1968). Linguistics and language planning. In W. Bright (Ed.), *Sociolinguistics.* The Hague: Mouton.

Hayes, J., & Flower, L. (1980). Identifying the organization of writing processes. In L. Gregg & E. Steinberg (Eds.), *Cognitive processes in writing.* Hillsdale, NJ: Lawrence Erlbaum.

Hayes-Roth, B., & Hayes-Roth, F. (1979). A cognitive model of planning. *Cognitive Science, 3,* 275–310.

Hounsell, D. A. (1984). Learning and essay-writing. In F. Marton, D. Hounsell, & N. Entwistle (Eds.), *The experience of learning* (pp. 103–123). Edinburgh: Scottish Academic Press.

Humes, A. (1983). Research on the composing process. *Review of Educational Research, 53,* 201–216.

Jaynes, J. (1976). *The origin of consciousness.* Boston: Houghton Mifflin.

Marton, F., & Säljö, R. (1976). On qualitative differences in learning: I. Outcome and process. *British Journal of Educational Psychology, 46,* 4–11.

McCutchen, D. (1984). Writing as a linguistic problem. *Educational Psychologist, 19,* 226–238.

Meier, S., McCarthy, P., & Schmeck, R. R. (1984). Validity of self-efficacy as a predictor of writing performance. *Cognitive Therapy and Research, 8,* 107–120.

Nold, E. (1981). Revising. In C. Frederiksen & J. Dominic (Eds.), *Writing: The nature, development and teaching of written communication.* Hillsdale, NJ: Lawrence Erlbaum.

Rico, G. L., & Claggett, M. F. (1980). *Balancing the hemispheres: Brain research and the teaching of writing.* Berkeley: University of California.

Rose, M. (1984). *Writer's block: The cognitive dimension.* Carbondale, IL: Southern Illinois University Press.

Sagan, C. (1977). *The dragons of Eden*. New York: Random House.

Salgado, G. (1980). The novelist at work. In M. Seymour-Smith (Ed.), *Novels and novelists* (pp. 66–70). New York: St. Martin's Press.

Scardamalia, M. & Bereiter, C., (1982). Teachability of reflective processes in written composition. Assimilative processes in composition planning. *Educational Psychologist, 17*, 165-171.

Schmeck, R. R. (1983). Learning styles of college students. In R. F. Dillon & R. R. Schmeck (Eds.), *Individual differences in cognition, Volume 1*. New York: Academic Press.

Schmeck, R. R., & Phillips, J. (1982). Levels of processing as a dimension of difference between individuals. *Human Learning, 1*, 95–103.

Smith, F. (1982). *Writing and the writer*. New York: Holt, Rinehart & Winston.

Steinberg, E. (1980). A garden of opportunities. In L. Gregg & E. Steinberg (Eds.), *Cognitive processes in writing*. Hillsdale, NJ: Lawrence Erlbaum.

Van Rossum, E. J., & Schenk, S. M. (1984). The relationship between learning conception, study strategy, and learning outcomes. *British Journal of Educational Psychology, 54*, 73–83.

Watkins, D. (1983). Depth of processing and the quality of learning outcomes. *Instructional Science, 12*, 49–58.

CHAPTER 9

Style, Strategy, and Skill in Reading

JOHN R. KIRBY

Reading is typical of a variety of complex cognitive performances which involve a large number of discrete but interdependent mental processes. The processes which are brought to bear in any particular instance of reading are a function of the task difficulty, the reader's general and specific skills, and the reader's purpose in performing the particular task. Each of these factors is in turn subject to extensive (and so far interminable) subdivision and elaboration. Thus while a comprehensive theory of reading can be outlined, it is not yet possible to specify sufficient detail to prescriptively guide instruction or to understand the entire reading behavior of individual subjects. This chapter briefly examines the outline of what appears to be a consensus theory of reading but then concentrates upon a particular class of reading processes, those loosely within the domain of styles and strategies. A feature of this analysis, and an important conclusion from it, is that the effects of this domain must be understood in conjunction with the effects of a second domain, which can equally loosely be termed *skills*.

This chapter is composed of four sections. In the remainder of this first section, a framework is described for understanding the two domains mentioned above, and some research and measurement problems discussed. Section two outlines a general theory of reading, underlining its hierarchical and interactive aspects. The third section selects potential

JOHN R. KIRBY • Faculty of Education, Queen's University, Kingston, Ontario, Canada K7L 3N6.

areas of strategic involvement and reviews some evidence regarding each area. The final section elaborates implications for instructional applications and questions for future research.

THEORETICAL FRAMEWORK

Two Domains of Cognitive Processes

Recent psychological theory and research has tended to divide cognitive processes into two domains which can loosely be termed those of strategies and skills. The basic distinction between these is not hard to grasp at first, but terminological confusion obscures much work in the area, and detailed examination of any instance of either class seems to lead unavoidably to recognition that the other is also involved. Neither of these forms of confusion eliminates the heuristic value of the basic distinction, but they do recommend caution.

The distinction between strategies and skills is based on the argument that *skills* are existing cognitive routines for performing specified tasks, and *strategies* are the means of selecting, combining, or redesigning those cognitive routines. Skills range from *knowledge skills,* the accessing by stimulus patterns of stored representations and associations (e.g., knowing that "7" says "seven") to *action skills,* the transforming of input information to obtain desired results (e.g., adding numbers). Skills can also be either specific (knowing that 2 + 2 equals 4) or general (knowing how to add numbers). Skills are fundamentally related to *abilities,* to the extent that the latter sets some sort of upper limit to the development of the former. In this sense abilities represent some preexisting level of "potential" (the product of constitutional and experiential factors), which limits the level which skills can attain or the speed with which those levels can be attained (see Figure 1).

Strategies, on the other hand, involve choice or decision making. The strategy domain consists of tactics, strategies, and styles (see Figure 1). A *tactic* is the decision to employ a certain skill (e.g., deciding to add two numbers). A *strategy* is a combination of tactics, or a choice among

Figure 1. Terminology within skills and strategies domains.

tactics, that forms a coherent plan to solve a problem (e.g., deciding to use algebra and arithmetic to solve a word problem). *Styles* refers to the habitual use of a class of similar strategies; for example, an analytic style could include the use of strategies such as breaking the problem into sections, writing down known information, using algebra and arithmetic, and so on.

Neither the skill domain nor the strategy domain precedes the other, and neither exists without the other, at least not in any reasonable task performance. The two domains constantly interact, strategies determining which skills are employed, and skills (e.g., knowledge) influencing which strategies are likely to be employed. To emphasize this last point, the strategies we select are a function of what we think will work to meet our purposes, and that in turn is a function of what we know about both the task and our own skills (metacognitive knowledge).

One further distinction is necessary, that between the *executive* (i.e., control) aspects of the strategy domain (which are properly part of it) and the *knowledge* on which those executive processes are based. My argument would be that these knowledge aspects, which some term *metacognitive* knowledge, are still essentially part of the skills domain. Other authors tend to combine these two aspects (e.g., see Lawson's 1984 review), but there seems little theoretical or empirical reason for doing so (e.g., Cavanaugh & Perlmutter, 1982; Kirby & Ashman, 1984). The crucial feature of the strategies domain is that it *controls* processing; knowledge has the potential to be used to control processing, but does not do so itself.

STRATEGIES AND SKILLS IN READING

While precise definitions of the two domains in reading are not as easy as they are, for instance, in mathematics, it is possible to make the distinction between strategies and skills reasonably clear. In this and much of what follows I am using the word *strategy* in the general sense, to refer to the entire domain which consists of styles, strategies, and tactics. For example, skills in reading would include the recognizing of words, the encoding of words' meanings, the encoding of the meaning of sentences, and so on. Skills would also include, for example, the construction of inferences, once it had been decided that an inference was to be constructed. On the other hand, the strategy domain would consist of the decision processes that lead one to carry out those skills. For example, there may be several possible ways of encoding or recognizing words or several ways of constructing the meaning of a sentence or larger segment of text. To choose among these alternatives would be to use strategies in reading, and if these strategies were habitual, then they would be examples of styles in reading. In the section entitled "Outline of a Theory of Reading," I examine reading and various levels of processes within reading in order to identify several areas in which strategies and styles could have a major impact upon reading performance.

One of the benefits of the strategy approach to reading, or at least the approach that recognizes that strategies could be important, is that it identifies another potential source of reading problems. Traditional approaches to reading tended to emphasize that poor readers either lacked specific skills (e.g., they don't know particular words or how to pronounce certain letter combinations), or they weren't trying hard enough (in other words, a question of motivation). The implication of either of these views was that what poor readers needed to do was to try harder and to practice the skills in which they were poor, such as word recognition. Two crucial assumptions behind these traditional approaches were that there is only one correct path toward competent reading and that the steps along this path consist of skills. Thus, those experiencing reading problems merely need extra practice in the next higher level skill areas. An approach to reading and reading problems that recognizes the importance of strategies does not necessarily deny the importance of skills, practice, and motivation, but rather it allows that there may be different ways of approaching the reading task and suggests that some crucial strategy learning may be required. Furthermore, it may be that some poor readers are not able to approach the reading task in the optimal way, and therefore they have to be taught a way around their disability—in a sense, using a strategy to overcome a skill-level problem.

One of the consequences of the strategic approach to reading is that reading problems are no longer conceptualized as necessarily requiring extensive drill and practice to be overcome. If the reading problem is due to a skill problem, then practice will still be necessary, as all methods to overcome skill problems essentially involve extensive practice. This can be a time-consuming process and is usually not terribly interesting to the learner. Many practitioners find that drill with poor readers is ineffective, though the reasons for this are not yet clear. In contrast, the strategic approach suggests that the poor reader either already possesses the required skills to be a good reader or could develop them relatively easily if he or she were taught to adopt the correct strategy for reading. For example, a common suggestion is that poor readers are paying attention at the word level, at the level of recognizing or pronouncing the words on the page before them, when they should be attending to the meaning of these words and of the sentences. The strategic approach suggests that these readers should in a sense learn to relax, to let the words flow around them, and pay more attention to the broader and deeper aspects of the text rather than to the relatively superficial and narrow level of words (e.g., Goodman, 1967; Smith, 1971).

It is worth noting that we should be cautious of the seductive appeal of the strategic approach to reading. After all, it suggests that many reading problems, and perhaps problems in other academic areas as well, are not that major after all and can be solved relatively quickly and efficiently. While this is appealing to those who feel that traditional educational methods have been restrictive and unimaginative and have constrained students' thinking powers, those who have been involved in remediating children's learning problems know that the problems are major and very resistant to brief remedial efforts. In that most children with reading problems have spent at least 3 or 4 years acquiring those reading problems, and have failed to benefit from at least several years of attempts to overcome those problems, it seems highly unlikely that a simple strategic answer is sufficient.

In other words, while strategies may be involved in reading problems, it is unlikely that they are the complete answer. It is one of the conclusions of this chapter that, in general, one must work at both the strategic and skill levels if reading problems are to be overcome or if reading is to be significantly improved. If skill practice in the absence of strategic awareness is unnecessarily sterile, strategic instruction in the absence of appropriate skill levels is equally overoptimistic and unrealistic. A similar argument has been posed by Schmeck (in press) with regard to learning strategies training (cf. Schmeck Chapter 1, this volume).

It should be noted at the outset that the most sophisticated current descriptions of reading and of reading problems emphasize skill-level problems far more than they do strategy-level problems (Perfetti, 1983; Perfetti & Lesgold, 1977, 1979). These descriptions emphasize that the bottleneck in reading occurs more at the word recognition or word-encoding level and also involves working memory space. These theories argue that observed strategy problems are most likely by-products of skill-level problems or, in fact, that strategy-level problems have not yet been successfully detected. In the present chapter I present some evidence that strategy-level problems can be seen, though strategy problems may indeed be secondary for many poor readers. I emphasize that several or many different types of poor readers exist, or could exist, and that strategic problems may be more central to some types than to others.

I also argue that strategies and skills are in a sense opposite sides of the same coin, that what can be seen from one point of view as a strategy problem can be seen from another as a skill problem. For example,

Perfetti and his colleagues describe the crucial bottleneck in reading as the encoding of words, clearly a skill factor. Inefficient encoding of words results in inefficient use of working memory space and, therefore, in insufficient space to process the meaning of phrases, sentences, and paragraphs. This description is clearly from the point of view of skills.

The same situation can be described from the point of view of strategies. Instead of beginning with an inefficient skill of word encoding, this description would posit an inefficient or inappropriate strategy, such as either attention to an inappropriately general or vague level of the text or attention to an inappropriately narrow or superficial level of the text. The inefficient strategy would result in inappropriate skills being employed, which in turn would result in inappropriate information, or at least incomplete information, being retained in working memory. The result would be the same as if the skill itself were inefficient, but the causal description would be quite different. Furthermore, the implications for remediation would also be different. If the problem is seen to be at the skill level, it is still not clear how an inefficient word-encoding process should be remediated. One suggestion is that extensive vocabulary-building drill is required (Beck, Perfetti, & McKeown, 1982). However, if the actual word-encoding process itself is slow or inefficient, it is not clear that this can be overcome. On the other hand, if the problem is largely or even partly due to the use of an inappropriate strategy, it would seem much more simple to reorient the reader to the correct approach to the task. In this case, as Schmeck (in press) has argued, a newly learned strategy may lead individuals to the appropriate skills on their own.

MEASUREMENT AND CONCEPTUAL ISSUES

Before beginning the description of skilled reading it is necessary to outline one characteristic of the present approach to styles and strategies. When describing styles or strategies in relation to a particular area of performance such as reading, it is possible to describe styles and strategies in ways that are relatively close to the reading task, that is, from measures taken during reading, or to describe them in ways that are relatively remote from the reading task, that is, from measures which have essentially nothing to do with reading itself.

This second approach has been the more traditional approach to styles and strategies and is best seen in what has been referred to as cognitive style research. In this research, questionnaire-type measurements or other types of measurements quite remote from the task of interest are taken to determine how a person generally approaches any sort of task, not specifically the task in question. This approach assumes the existence of cognitive styles that are akin to personality types that are very pervasive in their influence. Unfortunately, because these styles are so remote from, for instance, the reading task, it is unlikely that very powerful (or useful) relationships between styles and performance areas will ever be found. Thus, for example, readers of a particular style may in general tend to process information in a certain way, but there is no reason why those same readers couldn't learn to process information in a different way if they saw that as useful. For example, a particular type of reader may be *inclined* to ignore the details of what is read but willing to attend to those details in a task in which they are clearly important. What in theory should have been a strong relationship between style and performance, or perhaps between style and strategy, disappears due to subjects' perceptions of such situational variables as the demand characteristics of a particular task.

While there is nothing specifically wrong with the use of correlated tasks (e.g., questionnaires) to study styles and strategies in reading, it will not be the approach adopted in this chapter. Instead, I discuss styles and strategies as derived from measures taken more from the reading task itself. Styles and strategies will refer more precisely to how individuals go about the reading task, rather than how they go about the world in general. Measures taken during the actual task of reading relate better to what is actually being done by the subjects, and so it is more likely that such measures will yield strong relationships with reading performance.

Furthermore, it is also likely such measures and such findings will have stronger implications for what should be done to assist poor readers. While it may be true to say that poor readers evidence an inappropriate cognitive style such as field dependence, it is not clear how teachers should go about remediating this problem. First of all, should a general cognitive style such as this be changed just to improve reading? Second, how does one go about changing such a broad cognitive style? One could conclude that an alternative form of reading instruction must be devised that is more appropriate to readers of that particular cognitive style, but this immense curriculum development problem does not seem to be about to be solved, nor is it clear how two or more curricula would exist simultaneously in the classroom. My conclusion is not that the broad approach of cognitive styles is wrong, but rather that it may not be terribly helpful in remediating educational problems.

OUTLINE OF A THEORY OF READING

In order to conceptualize how reading takes place, it is necessary to recognize a variety of different hierarchical levels at which reading can be analyzed. In the description which follows, eight different hierarchical levels are identified. Most of these have been identified by other authors, though many authors would disagree with the actual ones identified, some preferring to add levels, some preferring to combine levels. Much of what follows is either based upon or at least is consistent with work presented by Gibson and Levin (1975), LaBerge and Samuels (1974), and Kintsch and van Dijk (1978).

The eight levels are presented in Figure 2. The lowest level presented there is that of features. *Features* are the lines or curves of which letters are composed. Each letter is composed of a different set of features which the brain must learn to recognize. The second level is that of *letters*, visual patterns composed of features and which in turn are components of higher-level units. The third level is the level of *sounds*, which are associated with letters or letter combinations. This level appears in some ways to be optional, in that while sounding out words is common and very helpful early in learning to read, it seems to be less likely to occur later on when reading skill has developed. As we see below, there seem to be two possible routes to take from letters to words. One involves a phonological analysis, that is, going through the sounds level, whereas the other relies more upon a visual analysis, in a sense going

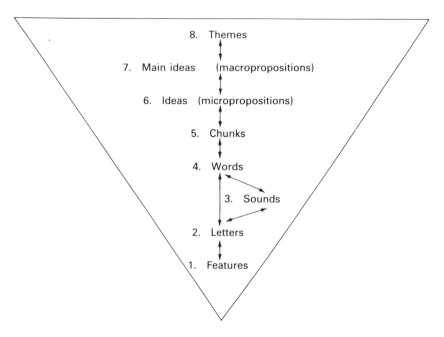

Figure 2. Eight hierarchical levels of information processing in reading.

directly from letters to words. This choice of phonological or visual routes represents the first potential area of strategic impact.

The fourth level of analysis is the *word* level. Words are stored in long-term memory and must be accessed by their visual or phonological features. To access a word may mean to visually recognize it, to pronounce it, or to recognize its meaning. Skilled readers are seldom conscious of working at levels below the word level. Strategic factors have a role to play in word identification in that two different sources of information can be employed to identify words. One source of information, described above, is the visual information contained on the printed page. This information can be analyzed either visually or phonologically and can be referred to as "bottom-up" information. The second source of information is "top-down": this is information that comes from what has been read previously or what is understood about the text which is being read. Thus, top-down information leads the reader to expect certain words or classes of words, or perhaps only words that mean certain things or are consistent with certain interpretations. This choice of bottom-up or top-down approach constitutes the second area in which strategies are involved in reading.

The fifth level of analysis has been referred to in Figure 2 as the chunk level. In this case a *chunk* refers to a syntactic phrase or syntactic grouping of words such as "the tall boys," "we went fishing," and so on. In order for the meanings of sentences to be constructed, a relatively large number of words must be interpreted, a number which usually exceeds the amount of space available in working memory. Syntactic chunking provides a mechanism whereby large numbers of words can be subdivided into a more manageable number of higher-level units. Thus, a sentence may consist of 15 or 20 words but only four or five chunks, each of which contains a "unit of meaning."

Construction of sentence meaning is the sixth level of analysis, the idea level. Alternatively this can be termed the *microproposition* level (Kintsch & van Dijk, 1978). An *idea* is a basic statement usually involving at least a subject and a predicate. Unlike the previous levels, ideas are no longer exact replicas or direct associations of what is on the page; instead, they are abstractions of meaning. The set of ideas in a text represents all of the meaning expressed in that text. In contrast, the seventh level of analysis, that of *main ideas*, represents a distillation of what has been presented in the text. The mean ideas of the text provide a summary of what it says, that is, the gist of the text, and have to be constructed from the micropropositions or ideas which are presented in the text. The main ideas are often referred to as the macropropositions of a text.

Levels six and seven involve the *generation* of meaning from a text. Strategies can be important in the generation of meaning at either or both of these levels. As seen below, strategies at these levels can relate to questions as simple as whether any meaning at all is generated or to questions as complex as how does the student summarize a difficult text. A further question within these levels is the degree to which comprehension is assessed or monitored. This is a question of awareness. Again it seems that some readers continue reading without assessing whether they have understood adequately what they have read. In contrast, more skilled readers carry out this assessment procedure as they are reading, and they carry out appropriate actions to correct any comprehension failures.

The final level of reading analysis is referred to in Figure 2 as the *thematic* level. It is even further removed from the surface structure of the text; just as main ideas represent abstractions from ideas, themes can be seen as abstractions from main ideas. Themes are interpretations of what the text is trying to say and often are not stated explicitly in the text. Themes are not common in expository text because those texts tend to say explicitly what it is that they mean. On the other hand, narrative or literary texts often involve an important implicit thematic level, for example, to convey a moral. Again, strategies are important at this level because, for example, many readers may not even recognize that a thematic level exists.

Information processing can be occurring at all of these levels simultaneously, though the reader is usually only consciously thinking or working at one level. In order to work at a particular level smoothly, it is necessary for the lower levels to function automatically. For example, if the reader is having difficulty identifying words (level 4), then chunking or simple comprehension (levels 5 or 6) can become very difficult. Expenditure of conscious effort at any level is likely to inhibit effective functioning at any higher level. To the degree that the level at which one works is determined by styles or strategies, then these will have a major impact upon performance. If, for example, the reader decides that working at the word level is what he or she should be doing, then it is unlikely that much comprehension or thematic analysis will take place. On the other hand, if the reader decides to work at a higher level, such as at the level of thematic interpretation, then subtle distinctions at lower levels may be missed or glossed over. In this way a reader may have an expectation of what a text is saying and therefore be working at a higher level. However, the text might present information which is contrary to this interpretation; because the student is working at the higher level, this conflicting information is not recognized, and therefore an incorrect interpretation is proceeded with. Editors are well aware of the importance of level of analysis and often read text several times, each time focusing upon a different level.

It is important to recognize that control or conscious processing can shift back and forth from level to level. Thus, a skilled reader may be reading at the idea or micropropositional level, processing the meaning of each sentence as it is read. In this case words and chunks would be recognized automatically. As Kintsch and van Dijk (1978) indicate, these micropropositions themselves would be periodically processed to generate macropropositions. If, however, two micropropositions were encountered, in proximity to each other, which appeared to state contradictory or at least incompatible facts, processing would probably slow down and control would shift back from the macropropositional level to the micropropositional level, or even lower. Similarly, macropropositional processing could come to a halt when an unknown word was encountered. The meaning of what unknown word may be determined by visual or phonological analysis, or it may be inferred on the basis of the general meaning of the text so far. An important strategic question, of course, is how much compatibility or confusion must exist in the reader's mind before processing is stopped or returned to a lower level. Again, some readers appear not to assess contradiction or confusion at all, and just proceed, whereas others may stop processing far too quickly.

POTENTIAL INFLUENCES OF STRATEGIES AND STYLES

As was foreshadowed in the preceding section, four areas of information processing in reading have been selected for deeper analysis regarding the potential influences of strategies and styles. This is not to imply that strategies and styles have no influence in other areas of reading but rather that these are four areas in which considerable research evidence shows that they do have an influence. Theoretically, of course, strategies and styles are involved in all aspects of information processing in reading, in that information processing is always being guided by some sort of strategy (or plan) and some sort of style (cf. Das, Chapter 5). While other aspects of information processing in reading require the involvement of a strategy or style, differences in strategies and styles in those areas are not so obviously related to differences in performance. The first two areas of potential strategy influence concern the level of word analysis or word identification (level 4 in Figure 2). The third concerns the generation of meaning at the micropropositional or macropropositional levels (levels 6 or 7), and the fourth area relates to level 8, the generation of thematic meaning.

Visual versus Phonological Word Analysis

There are essentially two ways in which words can be analyzed or identified. One of these has been termed the *visual* method, in which the visual patterns of the letters are linked directly to the overall sound of the word and/or its meaning. (The term *visual* is somewhat misleading because *all* reading is necessarily visual in nature.) This method could also be described as "direct," because no intermediary step of phonological analysis is involved (see Figure 2). The key aspect of this method is that the word to be read is taken as a whole, not as a combination of letters or phonemes each with its own sound. The sounds or the meaning associated with the visual stimulus are accessed in memory just as the name or meaning of a person's face is, as a single unit.

The second method of word analysis or identification is the *phonological* method. In this method, the phonemes or syllables that compose the word are "sounded out" and blended; that is, the visual stimuli lead to the sounds, which then lead to the word's name and/or meaning (thus the alternative path through level 3 in Figure 2 is taken). Again the term *phonological* is misleading, because both methods involve accessing the word's "name," the sound of it read aloud. The distinction is whether those sounds are accessed holistically (visual method) or one-by-one (phonological or indirect method).

This dichotomy was the basis of the traditional distinction between the whole word and phonetic approaches to reading instruction (Chall, 1967). In the past this distinction has been discussed in terms of which is the better way of reading or the better way of learning to read. Recent research, however, seems to indicate that both methods of word identification are involved and both are possessed by skilled readers. In fact, it now seems obvious that both methods of word identification are valuable skills and that what is important is not whether one or the other is used, but rather whether both are possessed and are able to be used in a flexible manner (e.g., Crowder, 1982).

The phonological method of word identification seems to be the more logical and systematic way of approaching the task. It also seems ideal for the identification of words that have not been encountered before or at least not very often before. Phonological skills allow the reader to pronounce virtually any word that roughly conforms to normal orthographic regularity. In contrast, however, the visual approach is defended by the argument that skilled readers seldom revert to a phonological analysis of a word. This is true, in terms of most readers' intuitions of not being conscious of sounding out all the words they are silently reading, but it is also confirmed by experimental evidence which indicates that the phonological stage is bypassed in much skilled reading (e.g., Healy, 1980). Nevertheless, considerable evidence exists that poor readers have a particular difficulty with phonological analysis (e.g., Liberman & Mann, 1981; Perfetti & Lesgold, 1979; Stanovich, 1981). On the other hand, there seems relatively little evidence that a lack of visual skills is associated with reading disability (e.g., Vellutino, 1979). However, the lack of evidence showing visual skills related to reading disability does not mean that visual skills are not involved in normal reading. It merely suggests that most children master these basic visual skills so that they are not a source of individual differences observed in reading. In any case, for the present purposes, it is only necessary to acknowledge that both phonological and visual skills are involved in skilled reading.

Phoenicians and Chinese. A stylistic or strategic interpretation of word analysis problems has been studied by Jonathan Baron and his associates (e.g., Baron, 1977; Baron, Treiman, Wilf, & Kellman, 1980). They have identified what are referred to as two styles of spelling or reading. One is referred to as the Phoenician style and relies heavily upon phonological word analysis. The style is termed *Phoenician* because the Phoenicians were the first people to invent the phonologically based alphabet. Baron referred to the second style as "Chinese." Persons using this style relied heavily upon a visual analysis of words, supposedly similar to the approach used in reading written Chinese. (Chinese orthography has subsequently been recognized to consist in the main of phonograms, or phonologically based, characters; e.g., Hung & Tzeng, 1981.) Baron's so-called Phoenicians and Chinese, therefore, differ in the types of errors they made in reading and in spelling. For example, in reading, a Phoenician will tend to pronounce all words as though they are phonologically regular, whereas a Chinese will pronounce words on the basis of the recognition of visual elements which are similar to visual elements found in other words. Thus a young Phoenician may pronounce the *s* in island or the *g* in sign. A young Chinese may recognize both of these words correctly, if he or she knows them, but on first encountering the word *signify,* may inappropriately transfer the pronunciation of *sign* to pronounce *signify* as *sine-ify.* In spelling, Phoenicians again tend to spell words as though they are phonologically regular, whereas the Chinese tend to spell words on the basis of isolated visual components. Thus, a Phoenician might misspell *sign* as *sine,* and a Chinese may misspell it as *sgin,* knowing that it has a *g* in an odd position.

In the discussion that follows the terms *Chinese* and *Phoenician* are not used, not because of the potential ethnic slur that one anonymous reviewer pointed out, but rather because the Chinese label in particular seems inappropriate. Instead the two styles are referred to as the *phonological* and *visual* approaches to reading and spelling, recognizing that these refer to the method of word identification and that they do not suggest that it is possible to read without visual input or sound output. It would seem that these approaches are strategies, which could become habitual and, therefore, styles. Each of these strategies would involve a separate array of tactics, which would in turn draw upon various knowledge and action skills.

It would be expected, though it is not necessarily so, that a subject's relative tendency to employ one strategy or the other would be to some degree dependent upon that subject's skills and, ultimately, abilities in appropriate areas. Thus, it would be expected that a subject with low phonological skill, that is, someone who had great difficulty in analyzing the sound components of words, would be unlikely to employ a phonological approach in reading or spelling. In theory, it is equally possible that a subject lacking visual skills (e.g., skill in discriminating between similar complex visual displays) would similarly avoid the visual approach to word identification. Existing research, however, has tended to identify the former type of student as the one more likely to develop reading problems. In fact, there has been a relative lack of evidence regarding subjects who fit the latter characteristic.

Existing research is consistent with the interpretation that normal skilled readers employ both visual and phonological strategies in a flexible manner (e.g., Crowder, 1982), whereas many children who are characterized as reading disabled rely heavily upon the visual strategy and appear to have great difficulty with the skill underlying the phonological strategy (e.g., Liberman & Shankweiler, 1979). The only evidence to date of reading problems originating from use of the phonological strategy and in the absence of the visual strategy comes from research based upon brain-damaged subjects (see Hung & Tzeng, 1981, for a review of this literature, particularly with respect to speakers and readers of Japanese).

Skilled readers would appear to have well-developed visual representations of a large number of relatively small and common words, such as *the* and *he*, and use phonological analysis for relatively long or new words (McCusker, Hillinger, & Bias, 1981). If a particular long or unfamiliar word is encountered regularly in a particular instance of reading, such as the word *phonological* in this section of this chapter, then it would be transferred to the visual representation list as well. Presumably words which are on the visual list at any point in time are recognized more quickly and with less effort than are words which require phonological analysis. Thus, a good reader can read quite quickly, relying heavily upon visual recognition for the highly predictable words and only dropping back to phonological analysis when the material becomes difficult. On the other hand, it seems that poor readers have a great deal of difficulty with the sequential, phonological analysis and therefore attempt to rely more heavily upon global understanding of what words and sentences mean.

Phonological Coding. Several lines of evidence shed some light upon how these different word identification strategies develop and also upon the question of whether or not the inappropriate overreliance upon the visual approach can be overcome through instruction. Liberman, Shankweiler, Camp, Blackman and Werfelman (1980) demonstrated that children who at age 7 were able to segment words according to their number of phonemes were more likely to be skilled readers one year later than were those children who had been unable to segment phonemes. While this suggests that phonological skills are a prerequisite for success in reading, research by Morais, Cary, Alegria, and Bertelson (1979) has suggested otherwise.

The latter authors studied the phonetic coding skills of adult illiterates before or after learning to read. Those who had not yet learned to read had low levels of phonological coding skill, but those who had learned to read showed greater phonological skill. Rather than acting as a prerequisite for reading skill, it may be that phonological coding skills normally develop during reading instruction or even as a result of reading instruction. Those who do not normally develop phonetic coding skills, that is, those who are normally identified as the reading disabled, are more unusual and may fail to do so because of a low level of *ability* in phonological coding. An important question for research is whether low phonological coding ability can be overcome by instruction.

Word Encoding. A second line of evidence relating to the visual versus phonological approaches to word identification comes from research which has shown that poor readers take longer to access the long-term memory representations of seen words, at least in the sense that they take longer to name or vocalize them. For example, Stanovich (1981) presented his subjects, first-grade children who were divided into skilled and less-skilled readers, with a variety of stimuli which they had to name as quickly as they could. The stimuli were of five sorts: colors, line drawings of common objects, numerals from 1 to 10, letters, or words. The amount of time between presentation of the stimulus and the child's response was measured. Considering only stimuli which were correctly named, Stanovich found that good and poor readers did not differ in the amount of time they took to name colors, line drawings, numerals, or letters, but did differ greatly, by over one-third of a second per word, in the amount of time taken to name words.

Perfetti and Lesgold (1977) have made use of results such as these to develop their bottleneck hypothesis of reading, that poor readers take longer at the word identification level and, therefore, for example, over the course of a normal sentence are taking several more seconds just to identify the words. This then results in less likelihood that the required word meanings exist in working memory after a certain length of time and, therefore, comprehension is hindered. While this research does not specifically identify inefficient phonological analysis as the cause of the increased reading times, this explanation would be consistent with the results of researchers such as Liberman and Shankweiler (1979).

Phonological coding is thought to be important for several reasons. First, while direct visual access should in principle be faster, because a step is eliminated, this will not be so when stimuli are difficult to discriminate holistically. Second, phonological coding produces a more durable working memory trace, ensuring that the words are still available for further processing after several seconds. In early reading, phonological encoding of words is the strategy associated with success.

Information Processing Skills. The third approach to looking at visual versus phonological word identification strategies investigates the nature of the information processing skills which underlie these two strategies. Das, Kirby and Jarman (1979) have elaborated the theory of simultaneous and successive cognitive processes (see Das Chapter 5, this volume). Briefly, *simultaneous processing* involves the coding of a set of information into a unitary representation which is gestaltic or quasi-spatial in nature, whereas successive processing involves the coding of information into a sequence or temporally dependent series. While both forms of information processing can take place with visual or auditory input, it can be seen that simultaneous processing is more congruent with visual input and successive processing with auditory input. It would seem clear that simultaneous processing underlies visual word identification and that successive processing underlies phonological word identification.

A number of studies have shown that both simultaneous and successive information processing skills are required for skilled reading (e.g., Kirby & Das, 1977), and other studies have demonstrated that poor readers are particularly poor at successive processing (Kirby & Robinson, 1987; Krywaniuk & Das, 1976; Leong, 1980). Krywaniuk and Das (1976) and Kaufman and Kaufman (1979) have conducted remedial studies in which successive processing has been trained and word identification skills thereby improved. The results of these experiments are consistent with the bottleneck hypothesis and also with the hypothesis that phonological skills can be trained, even in children with reading problems. What these studies do not reveal, however, is whether the children's original problem was with the *skill* of phonological coding or whether it was with the *strategy* of phonological coding or both. It is not clear from the studies of Krywaniuk and Das, and Kaufman and Kaufman, whether it was phonological coding skill that was being improved or whether training had simply reoriented the children towards using the more successive phonological coding strategy which drew upon the phonological skills they already possessed.

Because neither of these experiments employed reading materials in the training program, it seems unlikely that a narrow skill improvement interpretation is valid. However, it does seem reasonable to suggest that a combination of strategy reorientation and skill improvement was involved. In other words, the children previously may not have had the phonological coding skills and, therefore, didn't know how to use them and didn't try to use them. The simultaneous–successive processing point of view suggests that they didn't have these skills because they lacked appropriate successive processing skills or at least an orientation towards using successive processing. Accordingly, once successive processing had been trained, and the children had been shown its usefulness in a range of tasks, it was possible for them to transfer the successive processing approach to word identification via phonological coding. Future experiments employing successive processing training, but specifically attacking phonological skills, should show even greater improvements in word recognition skills. (See Das, Chapter 5 for more on simultaneous–successive processing.)

Conclusions. These studies raise a number of issues which recur throughout this chapter. The first issue is the relative contribution of strategies and skills in affecting reading performance. The most likely interpretation is that a combination of strategy and skill factors is involved and that remediation should make use of both. The second question which was not addressed by Krywaniuk and Das, or Kaufman and Kaufman, was whether there exists a group of severely disabled readers who are *unable* to effectively learn phonological coding. Aside from those with acquired brain damage, the existence of such a group has not been conclusively demonstrated and in fact would be difficult to demonstrate. If such a group of children does exist, the important question is whether or not an alternative form of instruction can be devised to allow them to acquire a normal level of reading skill without acquiring phonological coding skills. While many reading instructors have favored the whole-word reading approach as the alternative to the phonetic approach, it is not yet clear that one can learn to read entirely by the whole-word approach without acquiring phonological skills in some way. If a visually based reading instruction system could be developed, then the existence of an aptitude–treatment interaction could be demonstrated, whereby some children might learn to read more effectively with phonological instruction and others with visual instruction. However, at the moment, the most reasonable interpretation is that both strategies are required for skilled reading performance. Overreliance upon either strategy results in distinctive styles of reading, neither of which is very successful. Thus, in contrasting good and poor readers, we are not contrasting one style with another but rather contrasting two partial styles with an integrated one. In this regard, the learning pathologies that Pask discusses in (Chapter 4, this volume) may be relevant to reading.

USE OF CONTEXT TO DETERMINE MEANING

In the previous section we have seen how two different types of bottom-up information can affect word identification in reading and how subjects' use of these two types of information could be due to both strategic and skill factors. In the present section we see another such dichotomy in respect to word identification, that between the use of bottom-up information in general as opposed to top-down information. These various effects are illustrated in Figure 3.

Use of Top-Down Information. One of the basic facts of life in reading research is that skilled readers can read words in coherent text far faster than they could read the same words in random order or individually (e.g., Cattell, 1886). This occurs because readers, as they read, develop expectations about what subsequent text is likely to say. In other words, prior context helps them identify, or at least restrict, the possibilities regarding what is to come, and therefore much less effort has to be devoted to identifying subsequent words. In order to understand reading, therefore, it is necessary to include not only the bottom-up pro-

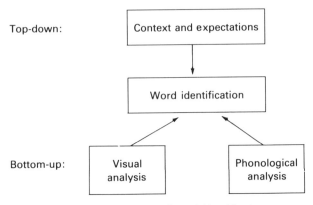

Figure 3. Determinants of word identification.

cesses of visual and phonological analysis but also the top-down processes that involve context.

The importance of context in determining word identification was strongly promoted by a group of reading researchers who came to prominence in the late 1960s (Goodman, 1967; Smith, 1971). These researchers termed their approach to reading the "psycholinguistic approach" and emphasized that reading is essentially a language task. In other words, even though a different set of skills is involved in the input of information (i.e., visual rather than auditory), the most important determiners of reading success are the same determiners of language success. Furthermore, they argued, since most 5- and 6-year-olds are very competent in both receptive and expressive oral language, reading should really not present a great difficulty to any child. One of their central beliefs was that children will develop the appropriate phonological and visual analysis skills spontaneously and that, in fact, overemphasis on these skills by teachers can actually harm reading performance rather than help it. They perceived reading as a natural activity and stressed that the extraction of meaning and the use of context to predict and determine subsequent text were the most important aspects of reading.

These researchers had a dramatic impact upon both theory and practice in reading, an impact which could be argued to far exceed the quality of the research upon which they based their theories. Much of this impact was beneficial, however, in that it made teachers think about the nature of reading and about how it could be taught. In that they have influenced many teachers to change their instructional goals and methods, away from a traditional bottom-up approach to encompass more top-down factors in their teaching, the psycholinguistic researchers have made a positive contribution.

It might be fair to say that they overstated their case, overemphasizing the importance of context at the expense of visual and phonological skills, in order to shift many conservative researchers and teachers away from an overly simplistic point of view. Unfortunately, it can also be argued that, in their overstatement, they produced an equally simplistic view, which ignored many of the difficulties that some children have in learning to read and overestimated the "naturalness" of reading. Unfortunately, it now appears that many teachers were influenced by this simplistic view and altered their teaching to eliminate especially instruction in phonological skills, changes which were also consistent with the then-prevalent emphasis upon child-centered education and meaningful learning.

One of the major results of the psycholinguistic approach to reading was the development of the technique known as miscue analysis (Good-

⸤e, 1972). This technique analyzes the errors or miscues that
⸤e in oral reading and attempts to infer the determinants of
_. For example, miscues are assessed for their graphic accept-
aɒility—that is, the degree to which the word that was said visually
resembles the word that was on the page—their phonological acceptability, their syntactic acceptability, and their semantic acceptability.
One of the premises behind this research was that errors or miscues
differ in their quality. Errors which were largely due to a focusing upon
the graphic or phonological information were seen as less good than
errors which were more determined by the syntactic and semantic context. For example, skilled readers when reading aloud make many errors, almost all of which are consistent syntactically and semantically
with the text as it is printed. Miscue analysis has been used by numerous researchers to investigate the development of reading skills (e.g.,
Leu, 1982).

Three Phases of Reading. Research centering upon top-down factors
can be interpreted as indicating that reading skill development proceeds
in three phases. The first phase is virtually a prereading phase and can
be characterized as *global* in nature. In this phase the "reader" treats the
text as a whole rather than as a set of words (Barr, 1972; Biemiller, 1970).
The reader responds on the basis of what he or she thinks the text is
about rather than what it actually says. Readers in this phase will often
say that pictures can be read, that they themselves can read, that books
could be read even though the pages are upside down, and so forth
(e.g., Johns, 1980). This appears to be the normal beginning point in
reading and is not necessarily bad, because the child is oriented toward
the extraction of meaning from text. As is argued below, however, this
phase can have negative effects. If it persists, even in a subtle form,
children's learning to read can be seriously disrupted.
    The second phase could be termed the *analytic* phase. At this point,
the child begins to "crack the code," to learn the association between
visual symbols and sounds (Biemiller, 1970). In a sense this is a less
"intelligent" phase than the preceding one, in that the child is not
primarily attending to meaning but to a relatively artificial code. Again,
this phase is not bad in itself, for in it the child learns the crucial phonological skills that will enable him or her to attack unknown words in
the future. However, if this phase persists as the general orientation to
reading, reading problems can result.
    The third phase, which can occur after the first few years of reading,
could be termed the *synthetic* phase; in it the reader assembles the best
parts of the preceding phases, being oriented towards the extraction of
meaning but highly constrained by the printed text. In other words, the

reader attempts to read at the word, chunk. or idea levels (see Figure 2), with all of the prior levels functioning automatically. However, when difficulties arise, due perhaps to an unknown word, the synthetic reader quickly transfers control to the appropriate visual or phonological processes and smoothly integrates the resultant information with information derived from the preceding context.

These three phases of reading skill development are analogous to three different reading styles, all with respect to the identification of word meaning. The global phase represents a style which is overly context driven. This style is characterized by what could be termed an overly intelligent approach to reading, relying far more on expectations and predicted meanings than is wise. This style is also characterized by a disinclination to analyze the printed word carefully and systematically. In particular, the successive–processing-based phonological skills referred to in the preceding section are either absent or not employed. This holistic approach to reading has been observed in many children who are termed reading disabled (e.g., Kirby & Robinson, 1987). For example, such children are likely to guess at the identity of words, perhaps on the basis of the first letter or two. For these reasons such children are often termed impulsive, in that they leap to the identity of words or the meanings of sentences without sufficient analysis (Kagan, 1965; cf. Pask's discussion of the globetrotting pathology, Chapter 4, this volume). As is seen in the next section, a comparable reading style can be observed in more-skilled readers, with respect to the extraction of passage meaning rather than word identification.

The analytic phase corresponds to a style of reading which is overly bottom-up in nature, that is, too much data driven. This corresponds to Pask's improvidence pathology. Readers adopting this style focus on the identification (naming) of words rather than the extraction of meaning (cf. Marton, Chapter 3). Such children may be able to read a text accurately, and perhaps even fluently at the syntactic level, but then be unable to report its meaning. Persistence with use of the analytic style can also result in reading problems. Some children may be using this style because they are not skilled in the processes which it requires, that is, phonological analysis. For example, one can imagine the child who has great difficulty with phonological coding, and yet whose parents and teachers insist upon practicing the very skill which causes the problem. (In fact, this is the very sort of problem that the psycholinguistic theorists were reacting most against, e.g., Smith, 1971). In this case, reading would be painfully slow and word-by-word, if not letter-by-letter. On the other hand, it is also possible for a child to be reading in an analytic manner because he or she has mastered the analytic, phonological skills but has not seen any reason for going beyond this level.

In this case, the problem is related more to strategy than to skill. Such children would be able to read fluently but without much comprehension. In such cases, teaching has most likely not been adequate; children with good phonological skills should be able to be led toward the extraction of meaning by the posing of appropriate tasks and challenges. The suggestions which Marton offers for improving education are also relevant here (see Chapter 3).

Both the global and analytic styles can be due to the lack of appropriate skills, to a disinclination to use those skills, or to both. The synthetic style, on the other hand, requires adequate levels of both sorts of skills and an inclination to use them appropriately. (It is similar to the versatile style discussed by Pask in Chapter 4.) These three reading styles are not equivalent in value. The global and analytic styles may be approximately equal in value, if success is measured by a gross score such as reading age. The synthetic style is clearly superior to both in that it is required for competent reading.

Context-Using Strategies. One difficulty in assessing children's reading styles or strategies is that there can be a large discrepancy between what they say they would do in a particular situation and what they actually do. For example, Moore and Kirby (1981) presented evidence of children reporting that they used either global or analytic strategies, when in practice it was clear that they employed a more synthetic strategy. Grade 2 and Grade 6 children were asked what they would do if while they were reading they encountered a word which they did not know. The second-grade sample supplied a variety of global and analytic solutions, primarily the former. These included skipping the word, guessing, or asking somebody else. Analytic solutions were more often provided by the sixth graders. These included sounding the word out and looking it up in a dictionary. No second graders and very few sixth graders said that they would use context to determine the meaning of the unknown word (similar findings had been obtained by Myers & Paris, 1978).

Moore and Kirby then presented the same subjects with a reading passage of several sentences with one word missing. The children were asked to decide what the missing word was and to justify their answer. The majority of children obtained the correct answer and all children justified whatever answer they gave on the basis of context. While this task is not exactly the same as the one referred to in the previous question, that is encountering an unknown word, it is similar. Whereas the children provided a variety of global and analytic responses to the metacognitive question, their performance in the actual task was far more related to the synthetic style of reading.

Use of context in reading has also been studied by Kirby and Teasdale (1987). They provided a group of Grade 3 and Grade 4 children with cloze tests (passages in which blanks replace some words) that had supposedly been completed by other children. The experimental subjects were asked to go through the cloze tests and judge whether the previous children had actually supplied the correct words. In fact that words had been handwritten in the blanks by the experimenters, and the words inserted had been carefully chosen to represent different types of errors. The errors differed in the amount of context which was required to be processed to recognize them as errors.

Some inserted words in the Kirby and Teasdale (1987) experiment were incompatible with the preceding portion of the sentence in which they appeared. In this case subjects would only have to process the meaning of the first part of each sentence to recognize the error. Another type of inserted error was compatible with the first part of the sentence but incompatible with the following portion of the sentence. In this case subjects would have to read on, that is process following context to detect the error. Another type of inserted error was consistent with both the preceding and following portions of the sentence in which it appeared but inconsistent with parts of the text beyond that sentence. In this case sentence-by-sentence reading would not result in error detection. Successful detection of any of these errors requires synthetic strategies, in that the inserted word must be correctly identified and compared with the word predicted from appropriate context. The different error types require different tactics or strategies within the synthetic category. In this study Kirby and Teasdale found that the less-able readers were able to identify errors which were inconsistent with preceding context within the sentence, but they were far less able when following context had to be used and less able still when extra-sentence context was required. Better readers also easily employed preceding context and had difficulty with extra-sentential context, but they far exceeded the poor readers on the use of intra-sentential following context.

This discrepancy between good and poor readers can be interpreted as due to an interaction of skill and strategy. The less-able readers were probably less efficient in identifying words (cf. Perfetti & Lesgold, 1977), and therefore, their working memories were less likely to contain the meanings of all the words of a sentence simultaneously. Thus while they could process the meaning of the first half of a sentence to determine whether the inserted word was acceptable, they were unable to go beyond the inserted word to process the meaning of the entire sentence to retroactively assess that inserted word's adequacy. This is basically a skill interpretation of the poor readers' behavior. However, this skill difficulty could result in a strategic difference: being unable to consider following context very easily, poor readers would probably choose to approach the task with a strategy which did not involve the assessment of following context. It is not surprising for individuals to avoid activities that they perform poorly. However, as Kirby and Teasdale pointed out, failure to attempt to employ such a strategy would prevent the subjects from obtaining sufficient practice in the skills to become more adept at them. Thus, in the manner of a vicious circle, an initial skill problem could produce a strategy problem, or an initial strategy problem could produce the corresponding skill problem, the result being poor performance in the task in either case.

Use of context beyond the sentence is characteristic of neither good nor poor readers. Again, this is most likely due to a combination of skill and strategy factors. At the skill level, even the better readers would have difficulty in retaining enough information from the context beyond the sentence to be able to employ it to detect errors in the sentence. With respect to strategies, it seems likely that neither good nor poor readers would spontaneously expect use of extra-sentential information to be required in the task. This strategic difficulty may well be due to prior experience with cloze tests, in which the words required can be supplied on the basis of intra-sentential context.

Conclusions. Obvious questions concern the degree to which appropriate word identification strategies can be trained and how that training should take place. The vast majority of children seem able to learn to use synthetic strategies, at least some of the time, so there should be considerable optimism that synthetic skills and strategies can be trained. At the same time, a variety of inappropriate teaching practices seem able to result in adoption of either the global or analytic strategies, to the exclusion of the more appropriate synthetic strategy. It also seems likely that children differ in their ability to employ certain skills effectively. Just as some children may be less able than others to employ phonological coding effectively, others may be less able to employ context in determining word meaning. The inferring of word meaning from context is clearly a reasoning skill related to intelligence; it would not be surprising if less-intelligent children were less able to carry out more complex inferences. However, while individual differences in effectiveness should be anticipated, only in the most extreme cases (e.g., brain damage) should an inability to employ a strategy be anticipated.

Beck, Perfetti and McKeown (1982) have presented an elaborate and clear example of how to teach synthetic word identification. Their long-term vocabulary instruction program concentrated simultaneously upon the visual, phonological, and semantic aspects of the words to be learned. They encouraged children not to process new words as only collections of letters or sounds but as semantic units related meaningfully to other semantic units. Such instructional approaches not only teach children appropriate knowledge skills but also encourage the more appropriate synthetic strategies, in that they imply that that is how adults approach the learning of new words.

THE GENERATION OF TEXT MEANING

The two preceding sections have concerned strategic variables which affect reading during the early years of reading acquisition. Once basic reading skills have been acquired, typically by age 9 or 10, those strategic variables have less and less impact upon reading performance. In this and the next section I consider two strategic factors which have more impact upon skilled reading, that is the type of reading done by high school students or adults.

In terms of the eight levels of reading processes presented in Figure 2, skilled reading normally takes place at the levels of micropropositions and macropropositions. Skilled readers are seldom aware of identifying specific words or of forming syntactic chunks and are very seldom aware of processes below the level of word identification. Normally they generate the meaning for most or all micropropositions in an automatic fashion.

However, not all of this meaning can be retained for very long due to working memory limitations. Factors such as the number of times that a proposition or chunk is stored in working memory (Miller & Kintsch, 1980) determine which propositions are likely to be retained and reprocessed in the form of macropropositions. The generation of macropropositions is also determined by what Kintsch and van Dijk (1978) have termed *macro-operators*, such as deletion (whereby a proposition is recognized to be unimportant) or construction (in which two propositions are combined). Kintsch and van Dijk and others have shown that skilled readers, reading texts which are well within their reading abilities, regularly generate and retain most of a text's macropropositions or macrostructure.

If most readers generate the macrostructure consistently, style and strategy factors would appear to have little impact at this level. However, this statement needs to be qualified in at least two ways. First of all, there is a suggestion in some data that while most readers may remember a similar number of macropropositions, readers may differ in the number of micropropositions that they remember (e.g., Tyler, Delaney, & Kinnucan, 1983). In normal text, micropropositions or details are relatively unimportant. Once they have been processed to obtain the main ideas or macropropositions, they can be safely discarded. However, when texts are more challenging, it is not always clear which details are necessary to be retained and which are not. In fact, when texts become more complex or longer, often details must be retained if later sections of the text are to be comprehended. It is at least possible that good readers are more able to retain as-yet-unintegrated facts or details more efficiently than poor readers, thus giving them an advantage in later text processing.

As we have seen in preceding sections, this advantage for good readers is probably due to a combination of strategy and skill factors. At the skill level good readers are more able to efficiently encode word meanings and microproposition meanings and therefore have more working memory space left over for retaining additional propositions. At the strategy level, this surplus working memory space allows good readers to be more planful or farsighted in their text processing, allowing them to recognize that some details might be useful in the future. Thus, one potential area of reader differences in generation of meaning concerns the amount of detail which is retained for later processing.

The second qualification that needs to be added to the statement that readers regularly retain macropropositions concerns the nature of texts themselves. Much research has been done with texts which are quite simple, quite short, or have a quite straightforward or standard structure. If a text consists of the normal story grammar segments of setting, complication, attempted resolution, successful resolution and ending, it is not surprising that most skilled readers can retain its main ideas. In such cases, as Schank and Abelson (1977) have pointed out, readers already have the "scripts" of such stories before they begin reading. The qualification that needs to be added here is that all readers probably do not process and retain all of the macrostructure when texts are difficult or are structured in a more-complex manner. The narrative texts which are used with beginning readers for the purposes of teaching reading *per se* are typically simple in content and structure. However, once readers have attained high school level or above, teachers and authors appear to lose any sympathy for the reader's problems. Texts at these levels not only contain difficult content but are often structured in what would today be termed "user unfriendly" ways. In contrast to the elementary school texts, whose purpose was learning to read, secondary and tertiary texts instead concern reading to learn. Accordingly, skill and strategy differences in handling complex and difficult text material are possible and are very relevant for educational purposes.

In the remainder of this section, I examine three aspects of styles and strategies which affect the generation of meaning from text. These three aspects are (a) whether meaning beyond the sentence level is generated and retained, (b) how important ideas are selected for further processing, and (c) to what degree and in what way strategies are selected for different purposes.

Meaning Generation. Most teachers of adolescent and adult students have had the experience of instructing their class to study a chapter for homework, only to discover subsequently that the students have relatively little understanding of the meaning of that text, even though they claim that they did study it. This problem is highlighted when students are requested to present an oral summary of what a chapter was about or to say what it was that the author was trying to say. A common student response to this request is "I didn't realize you wanted us to learn *that*," or "I thought you just wanted us to read the chapter." In other words, there is a discrepancy between what the instructor means by "study" and what the students often mean by "study" (cf. chapters by Entwistle, Marton, & Ramsden, this volume). Usually students are quite sincere in believing that they have actually studied the text. In fact, if there had been any major within-sentence syntactic or semantic problems, they probably would have noticed them, indicating that meaning (at the sentence level) was being processed. In many ways such students are performing like Kirby and Teasdale's (1987) third- and fourth-grade subjects, though admittedly, with much more difficult material.

Whether or not comprehension is assessed has been studied in recent years under the title of *comprehension monitoring* (e.g., Wagoner, 1983). Many initial studies of oral communication (e.g., Markman, 1977, 1979, 1981) demonstrated that many listeners, especially younger children, fail to assess the adequacy of oral communications which they receive. Similar if not stronger findings are obtained when reading is the medium of communication. Findings to date indicate that younger or less-able readers are less likely to detect inconsistencies or errors in text or oral communication, that inconsistencies relating to main points are more likely to be detected than inconsistencies relating to details, and that instructions alerting subjects to the possibility of an error increase the likelihood of such errors being detected, though not always (Wagoner, 1983). Three general conclusions seem valid from this literature: First, considerable effort must be expended by experimenters to make subjects recognize the presence of errors or inconsistencies; second, whether an error is detected or not must be dependent upon the difficulty of the text and the subject's ability to comprehend that text easily; and third, most subjects seem capable of comprehension monitoring but appear to choose not to do so in standard reading situations (Kirby & Teasdale, 1987).

The second point above concerns a skill effect and restates the bottleneck hypothesis: if considerable effort is being expended by subjects at the word recognition level, then little comprehension and certainly little reflection upon comprehension is likely. However, the first and third points are clearly strategy and style factors. Subjects seem unlikely to challenge the adequacy of print, assuming that any comprehension fault must lie within themselves. Alternatively "fix-up" strategies may be employed by subjects during reading such that inconsistencies within the text are glossed over. Frequently, although on-line reading time measures indicate that subjects have noticed inconsistencies, subsequent comprehension or interview data reveal no awareness on subjects' parts that inconsistencies were noticed or that some sort of repair work was done upon the text's meaning (e.g., Baker & Anderson, 1982).

This type of reading seems characterized by a degree of passivity with respect to the text's meaning. Little attempt is made to attack the text to determine what its meaning is and to assess potential contradictions or inconsistencies (Biggs, e.g., 1984, has termed this a reproducing strategy; Entwistle, Chapter 2, a reproducing orientation; and Schmeck, 1983, shallow processing). Other characteristics of this ineffective form of reading, especially in studying, would probably include either failure to make notes or the making of ineffective notes and a lack of self-testing. The difficulty seems to be that many students do not realize that they should be engaging in active comprehension at the main idea level, and this difficulty is enhanced by the failure of secondary and tertiary instructors to teach students how to do this (see Marton's suggestions at the end of Chapter 3).

Selection of Important Ideas. A first step toward active comprehension is the identification of important ideas. Brown and Smiley (1977) examined the developmental course of the ability to select important ideas in text and found that children in Grade 5 were able to identify the most important ideas in text but were unable to separate more than two levels. With age, more and more levels if importance were differentiable, their results showing four separate levels of being differentiated by adulthood. This research was based upon relatively standard or straightforward texts (Grade 5 difficulty level) and was conducted in the context of instructing subjects to select important ideas.

That Grade 5 children *can* select the most important ideas does not necessarily mean that they *will* select the most important ideas in their own reading. Furthermore, what is deemed to be important when texts are nonstandard remains a question. Hidi, Baird and Hildyard (1982) compared children's memory for various sorts of text normally encountered in elementary schools. They found, with normal narrative texts and normal expository texts, that children were most likely to recall the important ideas. However, the most interesting results of Hidi *et al.*

concerned a composite form of text which was expository in nature but which used narrative-like material, supposedly to enhance interest. For example, in an otherwise expository text on the development of submarines, a fanciful description of an encounter between Alexander the Great and an immense fish occurred. Subsequently, this salient but unimportant information was as likely or more likely to be recalled than was more-central information. This study indicated that the ability to identify what is most important does not necessarily imply that the ability will be used to determine depth of processing and subsequent recall (cr. Marton, Chapter 3).

Further evidence regarding children's ability to select the important features of text is provided by studies of children's metacognitive knowledge about reading (e.g., Kirby & Moore, in press; Moore & Kirby, 1981; Myers & Paris, 1978). In these studies children were asked how they would read if they had to read quickly. Most children below the Grade 6 level indicated relatively inappropriate skimming strategies. For example, many children indicated that they would "read the little words" and "skip the big words" because that would be easier. While such responding may reflect children's inability to reflect metacognitively upon what they would actually do in a concrete situation, it also demonstrates an immature approach to reading which is not oriented towards the extraction of meaning. In response to other questions, children showed little recognition that the first and last sentences of passages contain more valuable information.

Another way of examining how readers select important features in text is to examine how they make use of instructional aids provided with the text. These aids may include organizers, summaries, lists of objectives, figures, tables, and maps. For example, Kirby and Cantwell (1985) presented both good and poor readers at the high school level with advance organizers to a narrative text. The organizer helped good readers to identify deeper meanings in the text, but the poor readers were either unaffected or harmed by the organizer. The poor readers seemed to treat the organizer as yet more to read rather than as something which would facilitate the reading that they were about to do.

A less-commonly studied aid to reading is the inclusion of geographical maps with the text. A series of studies (e.g., Dean & Kulhavy, 1981; Kirby, Jurisich, & Moore, 1984; Schwartz & Kulhavy, 1981) has found that readers benefit from the inclusion of maps, but that the benefit is mainly in terms of the recall of information that had been contained on the maps. In other words, subjects use the instructional aid to assist their memory for geographical details, but not to assist their comprehension of more abstract text content, for example, as a cognitive anchor for the recall of event information. In a more recent study (Kirby,

1985), I have found that readers make use of maps not only to learn just geographical information but geographical information of the lowest sort. The adult subjects were presented with a text in which they had the option to inspect a map after each sentence. The results indicate that subjects inspect the map when a new place name is mentioned but less often when a more useful geographical relationship is mentioned, such as an overview of the terrain about to be encountered or a description of the relationship between two or more geographical entities. This style of reading and map inspection is focused at the micropropositional level rather than at deeper levels.

Taken as a group, these studies indicate that readers have some difficulty, particularly if they are young or if the texts are difficult, in identifying the most important parts of the text if asked to do so and that they are even less likely to do so in the course of normal reading. When the importance of a text feature is made apparent with, for example, the inclusion of an organizer or map, readers are still unlikely to use them; or if they do use them, they are likely to use them in the least powerful way. Skill levels are clearly a factor here, in that asking poor readers to read instructional aids is likely to accentuate their problem. Perhaps nonverbal reading aids would be more helpful (see, e.g., Tyler, Delaney, & Kinnucan, 1983). However, reading style and strategy factors are also operative. While children may have difficulty in selecting the most important elements of the text and using instructional aids, it is also clear that more often they do not attempt to select the more important elements of text or to make maximal use of instructional aids. This would seem to be an area where skill- and strategy-oriented instruction could begin to have an impact.

Selection of Strategies. The third and final aspect of the generation of text meaning that I consider concerns which strategies are used in extracting meaning and whether strategies are used at all. In our study of metacognition in reading, Moore and I found that the great majority of children in Grades 2, 4 and 6 admitted no awareness of the usefulness of a variety of strategies, such as imagery, for reading (Kirby & Moore, in press). Only the more able readers in Grade 6 deviated from this pattern, appearing to approach the reading task in a qualitatively different way. We suggested that whereas the other children were engaged in the process of comprehension, these high-ability sixth-grade children had mastered that process (i.e., it had become automatic) and could therefore devote their attention to what could be termed *metacomprehension.* Unlike their less-able colleagues, these children were able to step back from the text and consider various ways of approaching it. The fact that these children were able to verbalize an appreciation for more-advanced reading strategies does not imply that they would necessarily employ those strategies in actual reading tasks. Furthermore, as the task grows more difficult and therefore more needing of a complex strategy, the complexity of strategies actually employed should decrease, due to the probable breakdown of automatic comprehension.

The strategies of poor readers, or more generally poor students, can be characterized as erring in one of two directions (cf. Pask, Chapter 4, and Schmeck, Chapter 12). One strategic error is to process the text at too global, or general, a level. Thus while the meaning of microproposi- tions is presumably processed in passing, few of these are retained for deeper processing and relatively few macropropositions are either con- structed or retained. The student reading in this manner can tell you roughly what the chapter set for homework was about (e.g., it was about how people learn), but little else and in no greater detail. "It was about Russia" one such student must have said at some time about Tolstoy's *War and Peace*.

The second erroneous strategy goes too far in the opposite direc- tion. Such students may devote considerable effort to study, aiming to memorize as much as possible of what they have to read. These students pay attention to the surface level of text, to the micropropositional level, but fail to attain deeper levels of interpretation. Biggs (e.g., 1984; cf. Chapter 8) has characterized this as a reproducing strategy of learning, and has shown that it is associated with text anxiety. Unfortunately, rote memory is a fragile form of learning and most fragile in the presence of anxiety. Therefore, it is not surprising to find such students failing. Biggs and Rihn (1984) showed that university students requesting help with their study method were characterized by an excessive concern with rote memory and the surface aspects of text. They also showed that following an appropriate study skills course these students shifted to a more balanced combination of deep and surface strategies (cf. the con- trast between deep and surface learning styles, e.g., Marton & Säljö, 1976; Schmeck, 1983).

Conclusions. Styles of meaning generation can be characterized in the same terms used to describe styles of word identification: global, analytic, and synthetic. The global style pays insufficient attention to the details of text and to the extraction of an appropriate level of meaning. This style skips the hard work of identifying the middle level of meaning and jumps too quickly to the broadest level of interpretation. The analyt- ic style also pays too much attention to the wrong level of meaning in text, in this case to too superficial a level, and is characterized by an attempt to remember the details or micropropositions of the text via the only means possible, rote memory.

Neither of these styles by itself is an adequate method of reading, and both are components of the more appropriate synthetic style, in which details are processed but are only retained if the text or the reader's purpose indicates that they are important. Synthetic reading requires automatic comprehension processes, so that the reader can carry out the metacomprehension tasks of determining how to process information and assessing whether the results achieve the current purpose. Although reading should be oriented towards the highest level of interpretation, it should also seek to ensure that this interpretation is as elaborate as possible and as accurate as possible. In other words, there must be a rather careful balancing and cross-checking of evidence and interpretations, with the details constituting evidence for the more abstract propositions, or interpretations.

THE GENERATION OF THEMATIC MEANING

The final area considered in which styles and strategies affect reading performance concerns level 8 in Figure 2, the extraction of thematic meaning. This level requires readers to go beyond the information given on the page, in fact, to go beyond the first level of abstraction from the information given on the page, the macrostructure. This requires them to consider the implications of what has been read and to consider the relationship of what has been read to what was previously known. This is what Marton (Chapter 3) labels the "deep" approach to reading. When one considers the difficulties that many readers have in working at the lower levels in reading, it is not surprising that so little thematic interpretation occurs. In fact, to date, little interest in this level of reading has been shown in the reading literature. To some degree this may be a circular problem in that little thematic interpretation is commonly done by readers and, therefore, it is difficult to study. However, reading researchers are also guilty because they frequently employ either texts which cannot have any thematic superstructure at all (e.g., many expository texts) or texts that are so straightforward and standard in nature that they do not have a thematic superstructure of any complexity.

This represents another vicious circle, in which teachers and researchers expect little thematic interpretation from students, who do their part by not producing much. My point is that thematic interpretation is important, and most or at least many students are capable of it. From the researcher's point of view, the implications are that more complex and ambiguous texts need to be studied. For the teacher, the needs are to define what thematic interpretations should (or could, as there may be several) be drawn from a text and to design techniques for eliciting thematic interpretation from students.

Kirby and Cantwell (1985) employed a relatively complex and ambiguous text with a group of high school students. This text told the story of a man who butchered frogs for a living and of the great hate which he had for his job and the despair that he felt. At a superficial level, this text can be seen as a description of a man's job and of his reaction to it. However, it also contains paragraphs describing his religious doubts, which arose from his unhappiness with his life and with his job, his doubts about his own sanity, and the possibility of his committing suicide. The story concludes with a fantasy trial in which, thematically at least, he atones for the guilt he feels over the death of the frogs. Thematically, the text is quite complex, describing what one man must do in order to survive and his psychological and spiritual reactions to that necessity. The main ideas of the text, that the man butchers frogs, that he doubts the existence of God, that he thinks he might commit suicide, that he hates his job, and that he and his family imagine they are on trial, do not explain how these main ideas are linked in the text. The links are implicit and are left to the reader to generate. As such, this text is more representative of the literature which high school and university teachers encourage their students to read.

We presented the text as a normal high school task: study the story because we're going to ask you questions about it later. The subjects were not aware that they would be asked to recall as much of the text as they could remember, but all seemed to realize that comprehension was the goal.

In general, we found that high school students' thematic interpretation of this text in their free recalls was disastrous. Readers of below-average reading ability were likely to remember some of the main ideas but not those that couldn't be easily integrated into an "I hate my job" script. Better readers tended to remember more main ideas, those which did not fit the simple script, but they did not integrate them. At the thematic level, under standard reading conditions, neither type of reader was likely to remember or produce anything. In other words, regardless of what main ideas were recalled, there was no tendency for even the good readers to integrate them into a thematic structure. One wonders what these readers thought some of those main ideas were doing in this text.

We contrasted the performance of this control group with a variety of groups which received experimental advance organizers. The organizers had no effect upon the thematic recall of the poor readers. There was no thematic interpretation with or without an organizer. The good readers on the other hand responded slightly to the presence of the organizers: no thematic recall without an organizer became a modest amount of thematic recall with an organizer. However, the performance of the good readers was nonspecific in nature, in that it did not depend upon the type of organizer employed. We interpreted these results as indicating that the poor readers had a skill-level problem, that the organizers were difficult for them to comprehend, and merely added to the amount of material which they had to read. If anything, the poor readers processed the organizers at the same level at which they processed the regular text. We saw the good readers, on the other hand, as having more of a strategic problem. They took the organizers as an indication of the level at which they should be processing the text and were able to rise to a slightly higher level of recall.

Good readers clearly needed more practice and training in thematic interpretation, but there seemed little doubt that they were capable of it. Poor readers too are undoubtedly capable of thematic interpretation, at least with much simpler texts; after all, most young children seem able to draw thematic interpretations, for example, morals, from texts such as Aesop's Fables. However, it is not yet clear that poor readers can become capable of extracting thematic meaning from complex texts. The problem is that as texts develop deeper thematic structures, they also generally develop more difficult surface structures. To take an example common in secondary schools, Shakespeare's plays may indeed foster profound thematic interpretations for the very best readers, but the words and syntactic structures employed, as well as the unfamiliarity of the content, render these texts incomprehensible to the below-average reader at level 4, much less level 8 (see Figure 2).

Thematic interpretation as described here appears to require what Biggs (1980; Biggs & Collis, 1982; see also Chapter 8, this volume) terms *extended abstract* processing. The student is required to examine the relationships between relational concepts themselves and between relational concepts extracted from the text and other relational concepts stored in long-term memory. This requires that the student disembed the meaning of the current text and generate from it principles of greater generality. If, as Biggs suggests, this type of processing is akin to late formal operations, it is not surprising that it is so rare in secondary school children. However, it also seems rare in more mature students of above-average mental ability. I would suggest (as does Marton, Chapter 3) that what is at fault here is instruction. Under normal circumstances a small proportion of students succeed in developing some, if not many, of the skills of thematic interpretation, and these students go on to excel in literary subjects. Good students who do not develop these thematic skills go on perhaps to excel in subjects which do not require them, that is, the more scientific and analytic subjects. A far greater number of students might be able to develop these thematic skills if more consistent efforts were made to teach these skills.

Conclusions. Thematic interpretation clearly involves one or more strategies to generate this sort of meaning from what is read. It is equally clear that a variety of skills are also required, both skills in automating processing at lower levels so that attention can be devoted to the thematic level and skills in working at the thematic level. I seem to recall from my own high school days being told what the themes of various texts were, but I never knew how to generate them for myself. As in preceding sections it is possible to see how global, analytic, and synthetic styles could be involved. The global style would correspond to the premature generation of a vague thematic interpretation, one which hardly deserves the name. The analytic style would concentrate upon the accurate extraction of meaning at a lower level, perhaps at the main idea or micropropositional levels. Again, neither of these styles is adequate for proper performance at the thematic level. Aspects of each must be combined to generate the synthetic style of appropriate thematic interpretation.

FINAL CONCLUSIONS AND IMPLICATIONS

It should be clear that what I have attempted to do in this chapter is present a broad overview of as many aspects of reading as possible to examine the potential influences of styles and strategies. I chose this approach, rather than a more narrow attempt to defend one or more particular definitions of style or strategy in one or more particular instances of reading, because I fear that not yet enough is known with respect to any particular instance of reading to be able to present a very comprehensive picture of it. If nothing else, this review has highlighted what we do not know about the effects of styles and strategies upon reading. The conclusion that "more research is needed" is unfortunately all too close to the conclusion (regarding *War and Peace*) that "it was about Russia." However, it is also feasible at this point to draw more precise conclusions regarding the effects of styles and strategies in reading. I discuss five such conclusions, or themes, from this review, the first four related to instructional issues and the fifth to research goals. These themes are presented as five questions, thereby illustrating the ambiguous nature of many such themes.

SKILLS VERSUS STRATEGIES?

Questions of this nature inevitably arise when a new domain of cognitive functions (e.g., strategies or styles) is being proposed as operating in an area where previously only another type of cognitive function (e.g., skills) were seen to operate. Although challenging pretenders to the theoretical throne with Occam's razor is a good thing, it can result in the wrong sorts of questions being asked.

One of the most hardheaded versions of this question is, "which accounts for more achievement variance, strategies or skills?" If the appropriate study were performed, the simple answer to this simplistic question would probably favor skills, as reading is heavily knowledge- and skill-dependent. However, it seems more useful to decide *a priori* that this question is a poor one. Both skills and strategies are involved, and they are so inextricably linked that it would be difficult to disentangle their effects.

There is no firm dividing line between skills and strategies as categories of cognitive activity. What might be a strategy early in one's reading career must often become a skill, and then an automatized skill, if one is to progress beyond that level. For the early reader, whether or not phonological coding is employed is largely a function of a strategic decision (which may also be related, of course, to whether or not phonological skill is present). But later in one's reading career the use of phonological coding becomes automatic and thus independent of any strategic choice. In a sense, the habitual and automatic use of phonological skills becomes a style at this point. In this situation it is difficult to see any specific, independent effect of reading strategies (i.e., conscious choices), and it is certainly difficult to disentangle their influence from the influence of skills.

As we see in the next two sections, this issue is further complicated by the fact that the strategies and styles identified to date do not appear to be equivalent in value with regard to achievement. Use of particular styles or strategies seems to result in more success than use of others; this suggests that we may have to do away with the idea that different strategies or styles are alternative means to the same ends.

How Many Reading Styles Are There?

Much of the research reviewed above was interpreted as indicating three qualitatively different styles of approaching reading tasks, the global, analytic, and synthetic styles. These reading styles were identified at different levels within the reading hierarchy, that is, at the word identification, meaning, and theme generation levels. Consistent labels were employed for these styles across the levels of the reading hierarchy because at each level the strategies employed within a given style share a crucial characteristic. For example, at the various levels a global style was identified, making use of strategies to avoid dealing with the details of the words to be identified, especially their phonological details, or the details of the micropropositions, macropropositions, or themes to be identified. The basic characteristic of the strategies employed in this style are to rely too much upon prior contextual knowledge and to rely upon too small a subset of information presented in the reading task. In contrast, the analytic style, which normally follows on from the first in developmental terms, is characterized by strategies which orient the reader to the details of the task, whether it be word identification or meaning generation. This style relies too much upon the information on the page and not enough upon either prior knowledge or the generation of deep new knowledge. The third style identified was termed synthetic, in that it integrated the more appropriate aspects of the two former styles. In this style the strategies have become more flexible, in that control is able to be shifted from one to the other during task performance. In other words, the synthetic style is not just the *combination* of preexisting strategies, but rather the *integration* of them. The progression from global to analytic to synthetic means a reasonable developmental sequence within each of the reading levels. The sequence can be described as first, a general orientation towards the task; second, the learning of specific skills required in the task; and third, the integration of the general orientation with the specific skills.

The development of reading skill would seem to proceed from global to analytic to synthetic within a given level, and then to global at the next level, and so on in a spiral fashion. Thus, a person engaging in global word identification is not necessarily engaging in global meaning generation. However, the spiral is not quite as neat as this, in that the beginnings of meaning extraction do not have to wait for the attainment of synthetic word identification skills. Thus, it is possible for two or more global (or analytic or synthetic) styles to coexist in one person at the same time. Also possible is the tendency for a person who was "stuck" in a given style at one level to become similarly stuck in this style at higher levels.

Are there other reading styles? I certainly hope so. The three reading styles identified so far are quite general, perhaps too general to be of much specific use. However, these three stylistic descriptions are useful in categorizing general reading development and in categorizing reading development within specific task areas. If other reading styles are to be identified, then they must be either substyles within the three identified above, or styles based on an entirely different analysis of the reading task. For example, there may well be a reading style which is based upon formation of spatial images. Aspects of this style could be seen in each of the three styles identified above. However, it seems more appropriate to term this a reading strategy rather than a reading style, as it could likely be used only in particular instances of reading.

At the strategy level many more candidates become available. For example, a variety of strategies can be described for handling particular

reading problems. If the problem is what to do about a piece of information which contradicts something either known or just read, possible
strategies would include rereading the previous statement, rereading
the current statement, reading quickly on to following statements to see
if they resolve the conflict, deciding not to worry about the conflict, and
also not processing the information to the point where a conflict is
recognized. Alternative strategies within particular reading tasks have
considerable interest to educators because they are so deeply related to
what readers are actually doing while reading and because the more
appropriate strategies seem logical goals for instruction. For our present
purposes, these particular reading strategies are most interesting in that
they can be at least roughly categorized into the three reading styles
identified above. Thus some are more concerned with the keeping of
information in discrete bundles (analytic) while others are more concerned with the integration of those discrete bundles (global).

Just as the different styles call upon different strategies, the styles
and strategies call upon different clusters of information processing
skills. Though this is not the place to develop this argument more fully, I
would hypothesize that the global style and its strategies employ simultaneous processing, while the analytic style and its strategies employ
successive processing (see Das *et al.*, 1979; Kirby & Robinson, 1987; Das,
Chapter 5, this volume). The synthetic style consists of the integration
and orchestration of these clusters of styles, strategies, and skills, suggesting much interesting future research concerning simultaneous and
successive processing.

Not surprisingly, these three styles resemble those studied by other
researchers as well. I have noted above that the analytic style of meaning
generation has much in common with the surface style (cf. Biggs, Entwistle, Marton, and Schmeck, this volume); presumably the deep style
corresponds to that described here as synthetic. The present analysis
adds the global style, which does not appear to have been examined by
those investigating the surface–deep dichotomy; to some extent it may
be a primitive form of the deep style. The global style may also be
employed by those referred to by Biggs (1984) as "idealists," who are
oriented towards meaningful learning but who lack appropriate achieving motives and strategies. A further theoretical parallel should be noted
with the work of Pask (e.g., Pask & Scott, 1972; Chapter 4, this volume):
the global and analytic styles resemble, respectively, his holist and serialist styles.

Are There Alternative Styles of Equal Value?

Part of the seductive appeal of strategies in psychology is that they
suggest there are alternative ways of approaching the same task that

make use of different skills or abilities and yet yield equivalent success. This description is akin to that of the *Tibetan Book of the Dead* describing alternative religions: that they are like rivers, all following different paths but all flowing to the same sea. The even more seductive conclusion from this description is that many of the individual differences we observe, and which our education system is intended to overcome, only exist because we are attempting to fit all people to the same mold. More recent research, perhaps reflecting the spirit of the times, seems instead to point to some styles as being inappropriate or ineffective (e.g., the surface approach to learning), whereas other styles are effective approaches to learning (e.g., the meaningful or deep approaches to learning).

In the present chapter I have identified two of the ineffective approaches, the global and analytic styles, and one effective type, the synthetic style. Neither of the first two styles is equivalent in value to the third style by definition, because each of them is subsumed by it. Nor is it accurate to say that either of the first two styles is equal to the other, because each would accomplish some aspects of reading successfully and others unsuccessfully. The two perhaps might appear equivalent if some very general characteristic such as reading age was being measured, but they would certainly not be equivalent in any more precise measure of reading competency. At this point then, it seems that the sad conclusion is that there are not alternative styles of equal value. This partially accounts for the intimate connection between skills and strategies and their joint relation with overall success. Perhaps some future edition of the *Tibetan Book of the Dead* will recognize that while some rivers lead to the sea, others become lost in swamps and bogs.

What Is to Be Taught?

The description of reading provided in this chapter can act as a basis for the design of reading instruction. Three general principles can be emphasized as well as several more specific ones. The first principle is that skills and strategies should be taught together, not independently. A second principle has been referred to by others (e.g., Biggs & Telfer, 1981) as the plus-one teaching strategy, whereby one aims instruction at the level above the one at which the student is currently working comfortably. Thus, if a student seemed able to work at the sentence or micropropositional level but had difficulty going beyond it, instruction would be better aimed at the next level, the macropropositional level, rather than at the thematic level at which one might ultimately be aiming. This also increases the students' chances of achieving success (cf. Entwistle, Chapter 2). Instruction at too high a level instead increases the likelihood that what is taught will be interpreted at a lower level, as when high school students memorize the four themes in Shakespeare's *Macbeth* without any clear conception of what a theme is or how one would go about identifying a theme in another work. A third general principle, which is often overlooked in practice, is that teaching must aim to automate lower levels, not just to attain them. Thus, it is not enough for children to be able to identify words, they must be able to identify them smoothly or automatically if deeper processing is to occur. For this reason drill, or what used to be termed *overlearning*, is valuable even after the "pass" level of skill has been attained.

More-specific suggestions relate to particular instances of teaching or to attempts to overcome particular reading problems. As was suggested by the miscue theorists, it is important to recognize the basis of errors that readers make. In terms of the present chapter it is important to recognize what strategy was being employed to produce the errors observed. Strategies may relate either to the eight different levels of reading identified in Figure 2 or they may relate to the three stylistic orientations, global, analytic, and synthetic. In each case the method of instruction should be to follow the plus-one teaching strategy to proceed to the next level of processing or stylistic orientation.

A second specific recommendation with respect to reading concerns how to change children's strategies. Strategies would seem to have been acquired over a period of time and thus can be relatively entrenched. Because of this, children are unlikely to change them merely because a teacher has said they should. In fact, if children are currently not using a particular strategy, it is unlikely that they will comprehend any instruction to do so. The trick seems to be to get children to recognize that they are using an inappropriate strategy and to design a task in which they spontaneously use a strategy comparable to the appropriate one (cf. Marton, Chapter 3). In reading, for example, it has been found that children normally perform little comprehension monitoring while reading (see Wagoner, 1983). However, when the task is one which intuitively involves comprehension monitoring, such as the checking of another child's work, considerable comprehension monitoring seems to be performed, even by the poorer readers (Kirby & Teasdale, 1987). Case (1980) has presented a number of examples of this from areas other than reading.

A final issue regarding instruction concerns the possible cultural value of particular stylistic orientations. While it is not my intention to review this literature here, it has been observed in the past that different ethnic and cultural groups do adopt different cognitive styles and, presumably, learning styles. The education of minority or third world students often raises the problem of whether such different cognitive styles exist, and if they do and are linked with achievement problems, whether they should be altered. While few could disagree with the morality of teaching a child to read, many more would argue that it is not right to interfere with another cultural group's preferred mode of thinking. For example, some cultures have been said to possess relative strengths in the areas of visual and spatial information processing (e.g., Australian aboriginals; see Klich & Davidson, 1984). If this is the case, then children of such cultural groups could be more oriented, for instance, to visual information in word identification, and thus have greater difficulty in acquiring phonological skills. If this is the case, does one threaten their cultural integrity by attempting to teach them the phonological skills which we see as necessary for learning to read? It would seem preferable to develop an alternative means of teaching such children to read, that is, a more-visual, whole-word approach. This also, unfortunately, raises several difficulties, not the least of which is that a successful and comprehensive whole-word approach has not yet been shown to succeed in the absence of phonological skills. Other problems concern how alternative teaching methods could be made available within the same school, much less the same classroom. Furthermore, the ethics of teaching one group differently, in a manner which may or even probably will produce differences, are not at all clear. If cultural styles are firmly linked to academic styles and strategies, neither alternative appears attractive.

However, there may well be a way out of that particular cultural maze. The solution, as suggested by Davidson and Klich (1984), is to find examples from the particular cultures of the use of the more appropriate cognitive strategies, use these situations as means for training those strategies, and then transfer them to the achievement context. This line of reasoning suggests that all cultures should have access to the variety of cognitive strategies, even though they may in general prefer certain subsets of these and thus adopt a certain cognitive style. A novel task, such as learning to read, may be initially approached with these preferred, inappropriate strategies, but this does not mean that the more appropriate strategies are not potentially teachable. Thus the suggestion is that particular cultural groups, if they wish, may retain a preferred stylistic orientation but still learn to use other strategies in particular situations, just as we see no difficulty if a person, who in general is logical and scientific in orientation, is also emotional in other situations. If instruction does go this way, that is towards the increased differentiation of styles and strategies, then many interesting questions are raised about how distinct general styles and particular strategies may be.

What Do We Need to Know?

The basic requirement for future research is to attain a better conceptualization of the strategy domain and to investigate the relationships between this domain and that of skills. We have seen in this chapter that it is often not clear whether a strategy or skill is being discussed, or, if there is a problem, which should be attacked first. In fact, it is not clear whether one can attack either in the absence of the other.

A primary goal must concern the measurement of strategies and styles. Even though this paper has argued that styles, strategies, and skills are inextricably linked, it still seems worth attempting to measure styles and strategies in ways that are distinct from skills and achievement performance. The literature reviewed above has pointed to connections between particular styles or strategies and levels of achievement and thus to the conclusion that there are not distinct styles of equal achievement value. However, the possibility remains that this has been due to the ways in which styles and achievement have been measured. Only further attempts to measure styles independent of performance will alter the conclusion that styles of equal value do not exist.

A second question which needs to be addressed concerns the relative independence of styles and strategies. It was suggested in the preceding section that it would be possible for a person to retain a particular general style while making use of strategies which would otherwise be associated with a contrary general style. Expressed in different terms, this suggests that people are capable of being flexible, that is, acting in one way in one situation and in another way in other situations. Perhaps because of measurement difficulties or the desire to simplify, we often lose sight of the likelihood that people can behave in quite different ways in different situations. For example, I have suggested above that many reading-disabled children react in a global manner to reading materials and that this is a crucial component of their reading disability. Academics, on the other hand, are skilled readers and therefore, presumably, not likely to engage in a global style of processing. However, if academics were assessed on the basis of their performance in situations related to problems with their automobile or with their home life, much more global processing would be observed. We need to know more about how styles and particular strategies can exist independently.

The most important research needs, however, concern instruction. Considerable efforts are needed to develop instructional programs which are comprehensive in nature and yet teach the required strategies and skills. Too many research efforts to date have been piecemeal, aimed only at relatively narrow instances of instruction. In these cases it is difficult for the practitioner to see what generalizations should be made and what inferences should be drawn for other teaching questions. Other research can be faulted for being too general in nature, aimed at designing a comprehensive program or identifying general learning styles but paying insufficient attention to the cognitive processes involved and how they would be taught. Do these two approaches to research sound like the analytic and global approaches? If so, then what is really required is the development of a synthetic approach to research on styles, strategies, and skills.

REFERENCES

Baker, L., & Anderson, R. I. (1982). Effects of inconsistent information on text processing: Evidence for comprehension monitoring. *Reading Research Quarterly, 17,* 281–294.

Baron, J. (1977). Mechanisms for pronouncing printed words: Use and acquisition. In D. LaBerge & S. J. Samuels (Eds.), *Basic processes in reading: Perception and comprehension.* Hillsdale, NJ: Erlbaum.

Baron, J., Treiman, R., Wilf, J., & Kellman, P. (1980). Reading and spelling by rules. In U. Frith (Ed.), *Cognitive processes in spelling.* New York: Academic Press.

Barr, R. C. (1972). The influence of instructional conditions on word recognition errors. *Reading Research Quarterly, 7,* 509–529.

Beck, I. L., Perfetti, C. A., & McKeown, M. G. (1982). Effects of long-term vocabulary instruction on lexical access and reading comprehension. *Journal of Educational Psychology, 74,* 506–521.

Biemiller, A. (1970). The development of the use of graphic and contextual information as children learn to read. *Reading Research Quarterly, 6,* 75–96.

Biggs, J. B. (1980). Developmental processes and learning outcomes. In J. R. Kirby & J. B. Biggs (Eds.), *Cognition, development, and instruction* (pp. 91-118). New York: Academic Press.

Biggs, J. B. (1984) Learning strategies, student motivation patterns, and subjectively perceived success. In J. R. Kirby (Ed.), *Cognitive strategies and educational performance* (pp. 111-134). Orlando, FL: Academic Press.

Biggs, J. B., & Collis, K. F. (1982). *Evaluating the quality of learning: The SOLO Taxonomy.* New York: Academic Press.

Biggs, J. B., & Rihn, B. A. (1984). The effects of intervention on deep and surface approaches to learning. In J. R. Kirby (Ed.), *Cognitive strategies and educational performance* (pp. 279-293). Orlando, FL: Academic Press.

Biggs, J. B., & Telfer, R. A. (1981). *The Process of Learning.* Sydney, Australia, Prentice-Hall.

Brown, A. L., & Smiley, S. S. (1977). Rating the importance of structural units of prose passages: A problem of metacognitive development. *Child Development, 48,* 1–8.

Case, R. (1980). Implications of neo-Piagetian theory for improving the design of instruction. In J. R. Kirby & J. B. Biggs (Eds.), *Cognition, development, and instruction* (pp. 161-186). New York: Academic Press.

Cattell, J. M. (1886). The time it takes to see and name objects. *Mind, 11,* 63–65.

Cavanaugh, J. C., & Perlmutter, M. (1982). Metamemory: A critical examination. *Child Development, 53,* 11–28.

Chall, J. (1967). *Learning to read: The great debate.* New York: McGraw-Hill.

Crowder, R. G. (1982). *The psychology of reading.* New York: Oxford University Press.

Das, J. P., Kirby, J. R., & Jarman, R. F. (1979). *Simultaneous and successive cognitive processes.* New York: Academic Press.

Davidson, G. R., & Klich, L. Z. (1984). Ethnography, cognitive processes, and instructional procedures. In J. R. Kirby (Ed.) *Cognitive strategies and educational performance* (pp. 137-153). Orlando, FL: Academic Press.

Dean, R. S., & Kulhavy, R. W. (1981). Influence of spatial organization in prose learning. *Journal of Educational Psychology, 73,* 57–64.

Gibson, E. J., & Levin, H. (1975). *The psychology of reading.* Cambridge, MA: MIT Press.

Goodman, K. S. (1967). Reading: A psycholinguistic guessing game. *Journal of the Reading Specialist, 6,* 126–135.

Goodman, Y. M., & Burke, C. L. (1972). *Reading miscue inventory: Procedure in diagnosis and evaluation.* New York: Macmillan.

Healy, A. F. (1980). Proofreading errors on the word *the:* New evidence on reading units. *Journal of Experimental Psychology: Human Perception and Performance. 6,* 45–47.

Hidi, S., Baird, W. & Hildyard, A. (1982). That's important but is it interesting? Two factors in text processing. In A. Flammer & W. Kintsch (Eds.), *Discourse processing.* Amsterdam: North-Holland.

Hung, D. L. & Tzeng, O. J. L. (1981). Orthographic variations and visual information processing. *Psychological Bulletin, 90,* 377–414.

Johns, J. L. (1980). First graders' concepts about print. *Reading Research Quarterly, 15,* 529–549.

Kagan, J. (1965). Reflection-impulsibity and reading ability in primary grade children. *Child Development, 36,* 609–628.

Kaufman, D. & Kaufman, P. (1979). Strategy training and remedial techniques. *Journal of Learning Disabilities, 12,* 416–419.

Kintsch, W. & van Dijk, T. A. (1978). Toward a model of text comprehension and production. *Psychological Review, 85,* 363–394.

Kirby, J. R. (1985). Map inspection during reading. Paper presented to the First Joint Conference of the Australian and New Zealand Psychological Societies, Christchurch, New Zealand.

Kirby, J. R. & Ashman, A. F. (1984). Planning skills and mathematics achievement: Implications regarding learning disability. *Journal of Psychoeducational Assessment, 2,* 9–22.

Kirby, J. R. & Cantwell, R. H. (1985). Use of advance organizers to facilitate higher-level text comprehension. *Human Learning, 4,* 159–168.

Kirby, J. R. & Das, J. P. (1977). Reading achievement, IQ, and simultaneous-successive processing. *Journal of Educational Psychology, 69,* 564–570.

Kirby, J. R., Jurisich, R. & Moore, P. J. (1984). Effects of map processing upon text comprehension. Paper presented to the American Psychological Association, Toronto, Canada.

Kirby, J. R., & Moore, P. J. (in press). Metacognitive awareness about reading and its relation to reading ability. *Journal of Psychoeducational Assessment.*

Kirby, J. R., & Robinson, G. L. W. (1987). Simultaneous and successive processing in reading disabled children. *Journal of Learning Disabilities, 20,* 243–252.

Kirby, J. R., & Teasdale, W. R. (1987). Children's monitoring of another's comprehension: Effects of reading ability and context. *Australian Journal of Education, 31,* 73–85.

Klich, L. Z., & Davidson, G. R. (1984). Toward a recognition of Australian Aboriginal competence in cognitive functions. In J. R. Kirby (Ed.), *Cognitive strategies and educational performance* (pp. 155-202). Orlando, FL: Academic Press.

Krywaniuk, L. W., & Das, J. P. (1976). Cognitive strategies in native children: Analysis and intervention. *Alberta Journal of Educational Research, 22,* 271–280.

LaBerge, D., & Samuels, S. J. (1974). Toward a theory of automatic information processing in reading. *Cognitive Psychology, 6* 293–323.

Lawson, M. J. (1984). Being executive about metacognition. In J. R. Kirby (Ed.), *Cognitive strategies and educational performance* (pp. 89-109). Orlando, FL: Academic Press.

Leong, C. K. (1980). Cognitive patterns of "retarded" and below-average readers. *Contemporary Educational Psychology, 5,* 101–117.

Leu, D. J. (1982). Oral reading error analysis: A critical review of research and application. *Reading Research Quarterly, 17*, 420–437.

Liberman, I. Y., & Mann, V. (1981). *Should reading instruction and remediation vary with the sex of the child?* (Status Report on Speech Research SR-65.) New Haven, CT: Haskins Laboratories.

Liberman, I. Y., & Shankweiler, D. (1979). Speech, the alphabet, and teaching to read. In L. B. Resnick & P. A. Weaver (Eds.), *Theory and practice in early reading, Vol. 2* (pp. 109-132). Hillsdale, NJ: Erlbaum.

Liberman, I. Y., Shankweiler, D., Blackman, B., Camp, L., & Werfelman, M. (1980). In P. Levinson & C. H. Sloan (Eds.), *Auditory processing and language: Clinical and research perspectives.* New York: Grune & Stratton.

Markman, E. M. (1977). Realizing that you don't understand: A preliminary investigation. *Child Development, 50*, 643–655.

Markman, E. M. (1979). Realizing that you don't understand: Elementary school children's awareness of inconsistencies. *Child Development, 50*, 643–655.

Markman, E. M. (1981). Comprehension monitoring. In W. P. Dickson (Ed.), *Children's oral communication skills.* New York: Academic Press.

Marton, F., & Säljö, R. (1976). On qualitative differences in learning. I. Outcome and processes. *British Journal of Educational Psychology, 46*, 4–11.

McCusker, L. X., Hillinger, M. L., & Bias, R. G. (1981). Phonological recoding and reading. *Psychological Bulletin, 89*, 217–245.

Miller, J. R., & Kintsch, W. (1980). Readability and recall of short prose passages: A theoretical analysis. *Journal of Experimental Psychology: Human Learning and Memory, 6*, 355–354.

Moore, P. J., & Kirby, J. R. (1981). Metacognition and reading: A replication and extension of Myers and Paris in an Australian context. *Educational Enquiry, 4*(1), 18–29.

Morais, J., Carey, L., Alegria, J., & Bertelson, P. (1979). Does awareness of speech as a sequence of phones arise spontaneously? *Cognition, 7*, 323–331.

Myers, M., & Paris, S. G. (1978). Children's metacognitive knowledge about reading. *Journal of Educational Psychology, 70*, 680–690.

Pask, G., & Scott, B. C. E. (1972). Learning strategies and individual competence. *International Journal of Man–Machine Studies, 4*, 217–253.

Perfetti, C. A. (1983). Cognition and reading. In R. Dillon & R. R. Schmeck (Eds.), *Individual differences in cognition.* New York: Academic Press.

Perfetti, C. A., & Lesgold, A. M. (1977). Discourse comprehension and sources of individual differences. In M. A. Just & P. A. Carpenter (Eds.), *Cognitive processes in comprehension* (pp. 141-183). Hillsdale, NJ: Erlbaum.

Perfetti, C. A., & Lesgold, A. M. (1979). Coding and comprehension skill in reading and implications for reading instruction. In L. B. Resnick & P. A. Weaver (Eds.), *Theory and practice of early reading, Vol. 1* (pp. 57-84). Hillsdale, NJ: Erlbaum.

Schank, R. C., & Ableson, R. (1977). *Scripts, plans, goals, and understanding.* Hillsdale, NJ: Erlbaum.

Schmeck, R. R. (1983). Learning styles of college students. In R. E. Dillon & R. R. Schmeck (Eds.), *Individual differences in cognition, Vol. 1.* New York: Academic Press.

Schmeck, R. R. (in press). Individual differences in learning strategies. In C. E. Weinstein, E. J. Goetz, & P. A. Alexander (Eds.), *Learning and study strategies: Issues in assessment, instruction, and evaluation.* New York: Academic Press.

Schwartz, N. H., & Kulhavy, R. W. (1981). Map features and the recall of discourse. *Contemporary Educational Psychology, 6*, 151–158.

Smith, F. (1971). *Understanding reading: A psycholinguistic analysis of reading and learning to read.* New York: Holt, Rinehart & Winston.

Stanovich, K. E. (1981). Relationships between word decoding speed, general name-re-trieval ability, and reading progress in first-grade children. *Journal of Educational Psychology, 6,* 809–815.

Tyler, S. W., Delaney, H., & Kinnucan, M. (1983). Specifying the nature of reading ability differences and advance organizer effects. *Journal of Educational Psychology, 75,* 359–373.

Vellutino, F. R. (1979). *Dyslexia: Theory and research.* Cambridge, MA: MIT Press.

Wagoner, S. A. (1983). Comprehension monitoring: What it is and what we know about it. *Reading Research Quarterly, 18,* 328–346.

CHAPTER 10

Styles of Thinking and Creativity

E. P. TORRANCE and Z. L. ROCKENSTEIN

In this chapter the authors review and synthesize literature in the areas of creativity, learning styles, brain studies, teaching technologies, learning strategies, and evaluation. Our position on the topic of thinking styles and creativity is a holistic one. While learning styles and strategies may differ from person to person, creativity is maximized in the use of the fully functioning brain.

CREATIVITY

Creativity is defined as

a process of becoming sensitive to or aware of problems, deficiencies, and gaps in knowledge for which there is no learned solution; bringing together existing information from the memory storage or external resources; defining the difficulty or identifying the missing elements; searching for solutions, making guesses producing alternatives to solve the problem; testing and retesting these alternatives; perfecting them and finally communicating the results. (Torrance, 1978, p. 146).

The creative process has been described by Wallas (1926) as occurring in four stages: preparation, incubation, illumination, and verifica-

E. P. TORRANCE • University of Georgia, 183 Cherokee Ave., Athens, Georgia 30606 . Z. L. ROCKENSTEIN • Department of Human Services, Western Carolina University, 211 Killian, Cullowhee, North Carolina 28723.

tion. Both Torrance's definition and Wallas' stage model describe creativity as a whole-brain process. As such, it involves the cognitive domain (Bloom, Englehart, Furst. Hill, & Krathwohl, 1964), the intuitive domain (Rockenstein, 1988), and the affective domain (Krathwohl, Bloom, & Masia, 1964; Torrance, 1978), and their physiological correlates in the brain.

Expressed another way, Taggart and Torrance (1984) delineate creative behaviors associated with left-hemisphere and right-hemisphere thinking.

Left-Dominant Creativity
You tend to be a *conforming* person
Who prefers *structured assignments*
In which you can *discover systematically*
By *recalling verbal material*
In order to *look for specific facts*
Which will *sequence ideas*
In the form of an *outline*
From which you can *draw conclusions*
To *solve problems logically*
So that you can *improve something.*

Right-Dominant Creativity
You tend to be a *nonconforming* person
Who prefers *openended assignments*
In which you can *discover through exploration*
By *recalling spatial imagery*
In order to *look for main ideas*
Which will *show relationships*
In the form of a *summary*
From which you can *produce ideas*
To *solve problems intuitively*
So that you can *invent something new.*

With the preceding comments on creativity in mind, the following review of the literature on learning styles is presented.

LEARNING STYLES

Learning styles have been categorized by Kolb, Rubin, and McIntyre (1979), Lotas (1979), Fischer and Fischer (1979), McCarthy (1980), Gregorc (1982), and Taggart and Torrance (1984). Each is reviewed in turn.

Kolb *et al.* (1979) define perceiving and processing as two dynamics of learning style. They describe four types of people based on their learning styles: divergers, assimilators, convergers, and accomodators. The divergers take in information concretely and process it reflectively.

They generalize from what they see. Assimilators, according to Kolb, begin with an idea or abstraction and process it reflectively. They think and watch. The convergers take in experience abstractly and process it actively. They start with an idea and then test it through experimentation. Accomodators perceive experience concretely and process it actively. They are sensor/feelers and doers.

Based on Jung's (1921) *Psychological Types*, Lotas (1979) classifies four types of learners: The affective one learner, the cognitive two learner, the cognitive one learner, and the affective two learner. The affective one learner learns best in a group. This person is sensitive to others and makes decisions based on the group's feelings. The cognitive two learner uses facts to build and/or understand theories. The cognitive one learner is concerned about the practical aspects of life and makes decisions based on accuracy of information. The affective two learner is concerned with the meaning and purpose of life. Decisions are based on moral or aesthetic considerations.

Fischer and Fischer (1979) classify learners as (a) emotionally involved (two types), (b) incremental, (c) sensory generalist–specialist, or (d) intuitive. The first type of emotionally involved learner needs an emotionally colorful learning atmosphere. The second type of emotionally involved learner requires dynamic interplay of ideas and activities. The incremental learner wants a logical–sequential structure. The generalist is a multisensory learner, while the specialist prefers one dominant sense (usually sight or hearing). The intuitive learner has sudden insights and makes meaningful and accurate generalizations based on information and experience gathered unsystematically.

McCarthy (1980) combined the findings of the preceding theorists and formed a new synthesis of the following four styles of learners: innovative, analytic, commonsense, and dynamic. The innovative learner seeks meaning through personal involvement and learns through discussion. He or she perceives information concretely, processes it randomly, and is a divergent thinker. The analytic learner values facts and the opinions of experts. Information is perceived abstractly and processed reflectively. This learner thrives in the traditional classroom. The commonsense learner wants to know how things work and seeks relevance. The dynamic learner is a risk taker who is interesting in hidden possibilities. This person is a good problem solver and likes to make things happen.

Gregorc (1982) developed the Gregorc Style Delineator, a self-report instrument designed to identify an individual's learning style as (a) concrete sequential, (b) abstract sequential, (c) abstract random, or (d) concrete random. Gregorc describes the concrete sequential person as objective, persistent, and careful with detail. The abstract sequential person is evaluative, analytical, logical, and oriented to research. The abstract random person is sensitive, aesthetic, aware, and spontaneous. The concrete random person is intuitive, experimenting, creative, and risk taking.

Torrance's instrument, Your Style of Learning and Thinking (SOLAT; Torrance, Reynolds, & Ball, 1977), is based on knowledge about thought processes which are identified with the functions of the left and right hemispheres of the brain. Research on brain hemisphericity indicates that the left cerebral hemisphere is specialized primarily for verbal, analytical, abstract, temporal, and digital operations (Ornstein, 1972). The same researchers have found the right cerebral hemisphere to be primarily specialized for nonverbal, holistic, concrete, spatial, analogic, creative, intuitive, and aesthetic functions. The SOLAT describes people as right, left, or integrated in their learning styles. Right and left styles reflect their corresponding brain hemisphere dominant characteristics. The integrated learner uses both hemispheres equally. Of the styles previously reviewed, the integrated style most resembles Gregorc's concrete random style.

THE LEARNING STYLE DILEMMA

In the previous section we examined a total of 23 learning styles claimed by various researchers in this field. When we examine the implications this research has for classroom teachers, a dilemma arises.

On the one hand, teachers may find it impossible to teach every lesson from 3 to 23 different ways. The more reading a teacher does on learning styles, the less pragmatically applicable the information becomes. On the other hand, the application of one or more learning style theories may impose limitations on the learner.

A learning style may become a learning disability if cultivated at the expense of other ways of learning. Following learning style assessment, teachers may come to view individual students as being certain "types" of learners. Using Torrance's classifications, for example, teachers may begin to see students as right-brain, left-brain, or integrated learners. Teachers may feel that they are helping students by presenting materials in a way that complements individual learning styles. McCarthy (1980) recommends this approach. By teaching each lesson four different ways, corresponding with the four different learning styles she identifies, McCarthy claims that each student will shine 25% of the time. For the student who rarely shines in the traditional classroom, this may appear to be an improvement. Conversely, the student who responds well to the teacher's usual approach may become bored and exhibit undesirable behavior. Either way, all students are at a learning disadvantage 75% of the time.

Another possible danger in the application of learning style theory is that students will form self-limiting views as a result of being informed of learning style assessment. For example, if a student is told that he or she is a left-brain learner and given a list of corresponding learning behaviors, the student may assume that he or she is incapable of learning in right-brain ways.

This approach is particularly unsuitable for the development of creative thinking. As previously stated, creative thinking of a high quality involves the whole brain. It requires a variety of learning styles and strategies.

TEACHING METHODS THAT ENHANCE CREATIVITY

Earlier in this chapter, left-brain dominant and right-brain dominant styles of creative thinking were reviewed. Traditional teaching methods that seek to develop logical, sequential thinking and problem solving are fairly successful at developing left-brain creativity. Lessons based on Bloom's (1964) taxonomy are excellent for this purpose. Since these methods are so widely used, they will not be covered in this chapter.

Teaching technologies that facilitate right-brain and integrated, or whole-brain, creative thinking styles are less widely known and used. Some of these methods are briefly described in this section.

RIGHT-BRAINED CREATIVITY

When we refer to certain abilities or creative characteristics as right-brain, it is important to realize that many parts of the brain are involved. The right cerebral hemisphere, or "right brain," may operate simultaneously with other areas of the brain (e.g., limbic system, reticular activating system, and left cerebral hemisphere). As Reynolds and Torrance (1978) suggest, teaching methods designed to develop right-brain abilities may enhance left-hemispheric abilities as well.

Original thinking is a product of right-brain creativity. It can also result from an integrated or whole-brain approach if the right-brain abilities are sufficiently developed.

Research indicates a positive corelation between fluency and originality scores on the Torrance Tests of Creative Thinking (TTCT). Special attention will be given to the enhancement of these abilities.

Fluency. Fluency is the ability to consider large numbers of alternatives. While fluency does not guarantee originality, the two abilities seem to work together.

Torrance (1979a) designed activities to facilitate fluency in producing (a) alternative explanations, (b) alternative consequences, and (c) alternative solutions. One example of each is given in Table 1.

Originality. The ability to produce original ideas goes beyond the other creative abilities of fluency, flexibility, and elaboration in ways that are yet to be fully understood. Torrance (1979a) suggests:

> the emotional, nonrational, and motivational factors are especially important in the production of original ideas. The original thinker must be comfortable with being different (or a minority of one) to be able consistently to produce original ideas. (p. 40)

Some characteristics of experiences that facilitate original thinking include:

1. Adequate time for the production of alternatives
2. "Playing with" ambiguities and uncertainties
3. Heightening concern about the seriousness or importance of a problem
4. Making original thinking legitimate (Torrance, 1979a, pp. 46–47)

Teachers can facilitate creative thinking by:

1. Being respectful of unusual ideas and solutions
2. Showing that unusual ideas can be useful
3. Providing practice time when there is no evaluation (Torrance, 1979a, p. 40)

Torrance provides several examples of activities that enhance originality (Table 2).

WHOLE-BRAIN CREATIVITY

The whole-brain methods proposed are designed to activate all parts of the brain that are known to contribute to the creative process.

Table 1. *Activities that Enhance Fluency in Creative Thinking*

Producing alternative explanations	Why might your highly creative daughter be earning low grades in grade school?
Producing alternative consequences	What are the possible consequences of your sister becoming an alcoholic?
Producting alternative solutions	How could we get more people to want to be scientists?

Table 2. *Activities that Facilitate Originality*

Improbable situations:	What might happen if it was against the law to sing?
Producing similies:	Complete the following—happy as a . . . crazy as a . . . smooth as a . . .
Making-up titles:	What would you call a greaseless sunburn lotion that you can also use to flavor hamburgers?

These include, but are not necessarily limited to, the cerebral hemispheres, cerebral cortex, prefrontal cortex, limbic system, and reticular activating system (Rockenstein, 1988).

In the traditional application of learning style research, traits are often contrasted to describe differences among people (e.g., logical–intuitive, verbal–visual, right-brain–left-brain). The realization that every person with a normal, healthy brain has the potential for developing the abilities inherent in every learning style leads to different implications of learning style theory (Taggart & Torrance, 1984).

Learning style assessment can be used to describe differences within people at given points in time. Instruments like the Human Information Processing Survey, which was developed from the SOLAT (Taggart & Torrance, 1984), can be repeated to assess progress toward a whole-brain style. We need all of our mental abilities. We could be more proficient if we could draw at will on the processing style appropriate to the situation.

Experiences designed to facilitate whole-brain learning can be used both at home and at school. Torrance and Frasier (1983) report that personal experiences outside school also influence information processing.

As Williams points out, teaching to the whole brain of each student does not alter what is taught. The same skills can be taught in a different way, resulting in a more holistic understanding of the subject matter and higher scores on standardized tests (Forston, 1970). In the process of introducing, explaining, reviewing, and testing material, the cognitive, affective, and intuitive domains can all be activated singly or in any combination. The following brief descriptions of learning activities illustrate how the different domains vital to whole-brain thinking may be developed simultaneously.

The Creative–Aesthetic Approach. The creative–aesthetic approach to reading and math readiness in the kindergarten was developed by Forston (1970). The model is further described in Torrance and Fortson (1968) and Aaron and Fortson (1978).

The activities in Fortson's model are designed to introduce and teach basic skills in reading, writing, and mathematics through the original thoughts and creative productions of children.

In one of the activities, children use their original songs as reading text. They sing their songs into a tape recorder in a one-on-one interaction with the teacher. The teacher writes the songs on large chart paper. Children first learn to read their own songs and then the songs of their classmates. The songs, illustrated and prominently displayed, are used to teach both sight-reading and phonetic approaches to reading.

In Fortson's classroom original, creative production gives birth to cognitive learning and understanding. Children's emotions are freely and beautifully expressed. The creative, affective, and cognitive aspects of the child are facilitated, activated, and appreciated simultaneously.

Future Scenario Writing. Future scenario writing is a technology used by futurists to forecast events. Gifted students, ages 9–18, have also been involved in future scenario writing through state, regional, national, and international contests held as part of a Future Problem Solving competition. Students are given instructions resembling these:

> At various times during your life you have doubtless thought a great deal about what you want to accomplish in life—your mission. You have thought about the kind of work you want to do in the future, what you want to produce; about the kind of knowledge and skills you want to acquire during your life. You have thought about what you want to accomplish in regard to your family, your community, society, and the like.
>
> Now, it is the year 2005 and you are thinking about what you have accomplished. Record your thinking in a soliloquy. In a soliloquy, one reminisces not only about what one has done but also about how one has felt and now feels about these accomplishments and world events, those secret feelings, hopes, and dreams. Your soliloquy should reflect not only what you are doing and have done, but also what is happening in the world at the time, how you have changed, and how the world has changed.
>
> You may focus your soliloquy in whatever way you like. if you are a parent, you might want to soliloquize about your family. If you are a business person, you could soliloquize about your business. If you are a professional person, you could soliloquize about your professional career and its contribution. (Torrance, 1979a, pp. 113–114)

A future scenario is an original production involving whole-brained creative thinking. It requires the higher-level cognitive skills of analysis, synthesis, and evaluation. As students merge their own imagined future with the future of the world and universe, the scenarios often become emotionally laden. This emotional expression activates other parts of the brain and is one of the creative strengths identified by Torrance (1979a).

The opportunity to predict future events gives students an opportunity to engage in precognition—one of the advanced intuitive abilities proposed in Rockenstein's (1988) Taxonomy of Educational Objectives for the Intuitive Domain. While gifted students will probably write superior scenarios, future scenario writing can be done by average students. It is the type of activity that employs whole-brain creative thinking while still emphasizing traditional basic skill development.

Future Problem Solving. Another activity that encourages whole-brain creative thinking is future problem solving (FPS). Like future scenario writing, FPS was developed as a competition for gifted students. State and national future problem-solving bowls are held each year.

FPS can be adapted for regular classroom use. It is a group process that involves

> practice in the skills of putting things together into a larger or universal context. These include the development of problem-solving skills, the improvement of teamwork skills, the enlargement and enrichment of images of the future, and the mastery of skills in interdisciplinary thinking. (Torrance, 1979a, pp. 110–111)

The future problem-solving program was designed to last throughout the school year. Students work on three practice problems. Torrance (1979a) describes the process:

> . . . three sets of practice problems, each including the statement of a fuzzy future problem, a list of suggested readings, and reference materials, and a problem-solving guide. The first of these practice problems calls only for: brainstorming the problems involved, stating the problem for creative attack, and brainstorming alternative solutions. The second practice problem extends this to include the formation of criteria, the evaluation of alternatives, decision making, and polishing the best alternative to make it better. The third problem adds the stages of selling and implementing the best solution. (pp. 110–111)

The benefits that students report from FPS activities are a tribute to the principles of whole-brain learning. The five most frequently mentioned benefits are

1. Learned more about the future and to anticipate it
2. Worked more effectively as a group
3. Acquired a new technique to produce ideas/solutions
4. Learned how to increase my own ideas/solutions
5. Learned how to think and solve problems (Torrance, 1979a, p. 112)

In the first benefit named, students value developing the intuitive ability of precognition. In the second, students refer to both the intrapersonal (affective) and interpersonal lessons that must be learned for good group interaction. The new technique that students learn from FPS for producing new ideas and solutions aids them in right-brain originality.

An increase in ideas and solutions reflects an increase in fluency. Cognitive ability is expanded as students report learning to think and solve problems.

Like future scenario writing, future problem solving encourages whole-brain learning and creative thinking. The first method is a short-term, individual project, while the second is a long-term group project.

Sociodrama. The purpose of sociodrama is to examine a group or social problem by dramatic methods. Many of the production techniques employed in sociodrama are described in Torrance (1975, 1979c). Although sociodrama is highly spontaneous in nature since the scenes are not rehearsed in advance, it can be as disciplined as any other problem-solving approach. The eight steps in the problem-solving process in sociodrama are described by Torrance (1979c).

Step 1: Defining the problem. The teacher explains that the group is going to participate in an unrehearsed skit in order to explore some ways of solving a problem that is of concern to all of them. The teacher then asks a series of questions to help define the problem and establish the conflict situation. A wide range of responses is encouraged and accepted in order to broaden understanding about the conflict.

Step 2: Establishing a situation or conflict. Drawing from the responses in Step 1, the teacher states a conflict situation in understandable, objective terms. The problem is defined.

Step 3: Casting characters. Participation in roles should be voluntary. Frequently, the teacher gets a "feel" for which students would like to play certain roles by their verbal responses and body language during Step 1. Many students may play the same role, if desired. This brings a variety of perspectives to the situation.

Step 4: Briefing and warming up of actors and observers. Actors should be given a few minutes to meet and plan their setting and direction. During this time, the teacher may suggest possible alternatives to the audience. Members of the audience may want to choose a character to identify with.

Step 5: Acting out the situation. The actual skit may take only seconds or 10 to 20 minutes. This will depend partially on the variety of techniques the teacher uses to help the actors explore the problem in depth.

Step 6: Cutting the action. If the actors are unable to continue, or if the conflict is resolved, the teacher should stop the performance. The teacher may also want to cut the action in order to substitute other actors or change direction.

Step 7: Discussing and analyzing the situation, the behavior, and the ideas produced. The teacher helps the group redefine the problem, if necessary, and/or identify possible solutions indicated in the action.

Step 8: Making plans for further testing and/or implementing ideas for new behavior. Possible solutions or directions may be tried in or out of the sociodramatic context as deemed appropriate.

One of the great advantages of sociodrama is that it encourages the acting out of feelings simultaneously with the analysis of a problem. By taking the role of a character in the conflict, the personal risks involved in sharing one's feelings are reduced.

Torrance (1975) hypothesizes that, through the use of certain production techniques, different states of consciousness may be activated during sociodrama. These states may help the brain to process information in different ways, through offering a wider variety of insights and solutions.

THE IMPORTANCE OF INSTRUCTIONS

Regardless of the activities chosen to stimulate whole-brain creative thinking, the instructions for the activities should contain a common element: students should be directed to consider problems creatively whenever possible.

Torrance and Harmon (1961) conducted research involving three different types of instructions and their effect on students' abilities to see implications and applications of new knowledge. In the first condition, students were asked to learn information with the intention of recalling it. In the second condition, students were asked to process new information critically and evaluatively. In the third condition, students were asked to process the new information creatively. Only in the third condition did students see implications of the knowledge and apply what they had learned.

Instructing students to be able to recall and/or critically evaluate material only taps the left-brain abilities of logical, analytical, and sequential thinking. In a world where it is vital that students see both present and future implications and applications of relevant knowledge, it is important that the creative thinking capacity of the whole brain be activated.

INCUBATION

Another vital factor in the facilitation of whole-brain creative thinking is the management of incubation. Incubation is the second stage in the Wallas (1926) model of creative thinking (preparation, incubation, illumination, verification).

Teacher-training programs generally stress preparation and verification and omit incubation and illumination. There are some practical reasons for this. The skills involved in the preparation and verification of knowledge can be logically and sequentially organized. They involve the normal, waking state of consciousness. The lessons can be designed to fit prescribed blocks of time. Student responses can be objectively evaluated.

The process of incubation differs in all of the above respects. Incubation involves skills common to the intuitive domain. These may include (but are not necessarily limited to) relaxation, meditation, creative imaging, dream exploration, and precognition (Rockenstein, 1988).

Incubation involves different states of consciousness. Wallas (1926) defines incubation as a time when the thinker is not consciously thinking about the problem. Gowan (1979) interprets Wallas' definition of incubation as:

> any state of relaxation of the conscious cognition (left cerebral hemisphere function), such as, but not confined to, dreams, daydreams, fantasy, hypnosis, meditation, diversion, play, etc., which allows subliminal processes (right hemisphere functions) to operate. He saw preparation (academic discipline), as the necessary, and incubation (relaxation), as the sufficient condition for creative insights to emerge. (p. 39)

The time required for incubation on a problem or project may vary from situation to situation and from one student to another. Khatena comments:

> Incubation is an important activity of the brain in the creative process; it is that stage in creative thinking and problem solving when mental events, earlier set in motion by deliberate and intensive preparation, are energized to become autonomous for the occurrence of fruitful insights that lead to good solutions to problems. The time taken may vary from a moment to days and months and is beyond the awareness of the creator. (1982, pp. 107–108.

Incubation is a difficult activity to evaluate objectively. Khatena lists the following characteristics of incubation:

1. It depends much on intensive and careful preparation.
2. It requires no conscious or voluntary thinking of the problem in hand.
3. It functions (under optimum conditions) either through relaxation or rest with no interference from conscious thought about the problem or, when attention is given to solving other problems, through a series of incubations.
4. It facilitates right-hemisphere or creative imagination imagery for creative solutions. (1982, p. 108)

As difficult as incubation is to manage and evaluate, the inclusion of incubation time may be essential to the facilitation of whole-brain creative thinking. Torrance contends, "the process of incubation is the key element involved in putting together the specialized functions of the left and right cerebral hemispheres" (1981, p. 104)

Torrance supplies the following guidelines for an instructional model that will succeed in enhancing the chances that incubation and creative thinking of a high quality will occur:

1. States of consciousness other than the logical, wakeful state must be activated at least for brief intermittent periods.
2. Intellectual, volitional, and emotional functions must all be brought into play together.
3. There must be realistic encounters with a problem, intense absorption, involvement, and commitment, and heightened consciousness or awareness.
4. Opposite, contradictory, or antithetical concepts, images or ideas must be confronted simultaneously.
5. Visual, kinesthetic, auditory, and other sensory modes of thought must be brought into play. (Perhaps at least two of these are necessary for successful incubation of creative solutions). (1979b, pp. 25–26)

MEASURING CREATIVITY

A variety of instruments are available for studying creativity. Almost all of them reflect a rational (logical, analytical) view of creativity. The following instruments measure creative style or personality:

1. *What Kind of Person Are You?* (Khatena & Torrance, 1976). This instrument provides a measure of the creative personality style and consists of 50 objectively scored, forced choice items. Factor scores include: acceptance of authority, self confidence, awareness of others, and disciplined imagination.
2. *Something about Myself* (Khatena & Torrance, 1976). This is a 50-item checklist of creative achievements, behaviors, and motivations. Derived factors include: environmental sensitivity, intuitiveness, intellectuality, and individuality.
3. *Adaptation–Innovation Inventory* (Kirton, 1977). This inventory places individuals on a continuum ranging from adaptation to innovation. It identifies 32 personality characteristics, including: conformity, originality, and risk-taking behavior.
4. *Torrance Tests of Creative Thinking, Figural and Verbal Forms*

(Torrance, 1974). Each of the three figural and seven verbal activities contained in this instrument was designed to measure a different type of creative thinking. All of the activities are open-ended. Both forms yield scores for fluency, flexibility, and originality. The figural form yields an elaboration score and scores for a variety of creativity indicators such as: unusual visual perspective, resistance to premature closure, abstractness of titles, humor, expression of emotion, colorfulness of imagery, and fantasy. Over 1,000 studies using these tests have been reported, and a large number of them supply a great deal of validity and reliability data.

5. *Sounds and Images* (Khatena & Torrance, 1973). This instrument measures originality. Subjects are asked to describe the images suggested by each of a series of four sounds. The sequence is presented three times with instructions that encourage increased imaginativeness and mind stretching.

Research which correlates scores on creativity measures with Your Style of Learning and Thinking (Torrance et al., 1977) yields some interesting results. Scores on creativity instruments correlate significantly and positively with right-hemispheric learning styles and negatively and significantly with left-hemispheric learning styles. The results for the integrative style are inconsistent and generally rather low. This research would seem to support the view of creativity as a right-brain function rather than as a whole-brain function, as the authors have maintained throughout this chapter. If creativity is a whole-brain function, it would seem that we should find a high, positive correlation between creativity measures and the integrative style on Your Style of Learning and Thinking.

We offer two plausible explanations for this apparent inconsistency: (a) Since creativity has traditionally been viewed as a right-hemispheric ability, tests of creativity may measure only those creative factors associated with right-brain thinking; (b) because the concept of whole-brain learning and teaching is new, the integrative style, as it appears today, may not be a true whole-brain style. If, for example, a subject taking the SOLAT marks that he or she has no preference for either algebra or geometry, this could mean that he or she is good at neither rather than master of both.

NEW DIRECTIONS IN TEACHING AND RESEARCH

The authors would like to see three developments in education relevant to learning styles and learning strategies: (a) emphasis on the learning style that uses the fully functioning brain, (b) development of teaching–learning strategies that develop the fully functioning brain, and (c) the design of measurement tools that verify the operation and/or evaluate the products of the fully functioning brain.

As a first step in these new directions, teachers and teacher educators must work together to develop whole-brain units of learning that combine objectives from the cognitive, affective, and intuitive domains. The process of whole-brain curriculum development must be learned and then widely shared. Once whole-brain thinking is a process that can be observed, new instruments for assessing creativity and brain style can be developed which will measure whole-brain usage and creative thinking.

REFERENCES

Aaron, I. E., & Fortson, L. R. (1968, May). Sing a song of readiness. *Early Years*, pp. 41–43.

Bloom, B. S., Englehart, M. B., Furst, E. G., Hill, W. H., & Krathwohl, D. R. (1964). *Taxonomy of educational objectives, handbook I: Cognitive domain*. New York: McKay.

Fischer, B. B., & Fischer, L. F. (1979). Learning styles in teaching and learning. *Educational Leadership, 36*, 245–254.

Fortson, L. R. (1970). A creative-aesthetic approach to readiness and beginning reading and mathematics in the kindergarten. (Doctoral dissertation, University of Georgia, 1969). *Dissertation Abstracts International, 30*, 5339 A.

Gregorc, A. F. (1982). *An adult's guide to style*. Maynard, MA: Gabriel Systems.

Gowan, J. C. (1979). The production of creativity through right hemisphere imagery. *Journal of Creative Behavior, 13* (1), 39–51.

Jung, C. G. (1921). Psychological types. In H. Read, M. Fordham, & G. Adler (Eds.), *Collected works of C. G. Jung* (Vol. 6). Princeton, NJ: Princeton University.

Khatena, J. (1982). *Educational psychology for the gifted*. New York: Wiley.

Khatena, J., & Torrance, E. P. (1973). *Norms technical manual: Thinking creatively with sounds and words*. Bensenville, IL: Scholastic Testing Service.

Khatena, J., & Torrance, E. P. (1976). *Manual for Khatena–Torrance creative perception inventory*. Chicago: Stoelting.

Kirton, M. J. (1977). *Research edition: Kirton adaption-innovation inventory*. Windsor, Berkshire, England: NFER Publishing Co.

Kolb, D. A., Rubin, I. M., & McIntyre, J. M. (1979). *Organizational psychology: An experiential approach* (3rd ed.). Englewood Cliffs, NJ: Prentice-Hall.

Krathwohl, D. R., Bloom, B. S., Masia, R. (1964). *Taxonomy of educational objectives, handbook II: Affective domain*. New York: McKay.

Lotas, A. (1979). *The Lotas teaching preference questionnaire (LTPO)*. Unpublished manuscript.

McCarthy, B. (1980). *The 4 mat system*. Arlington Heights, IL: EXCELL.

Ornstein, R. E. (1972). *The psychology of consciousness*. New York: Viking.

Reynolds, C. R., & Torrance, E. P. (1978). Perceived changes in styles of learning and thinking (hemisphericity) through direct and indirect training. *Journal of Creative Behavior, 12*, 247–252.

Rockenstein, Z. L. (1988). *Training the creative/intuitive mind*. Buffalo, NY: Bearly Ltd.

Taggart, W., & Torrance, E. P. (1984). *Human information processing survey: Administrator's manual*. Bensenville, IL: Scholastic Testing Service.

Torrance, E. P. (1974). *Norms-technical manual: Torrance tests of creative thinking*. Bensenville, IL: Scholastic Testing Service.

Torrance, E. P. (1975). Sociodrama as a creative problem-solving approach to studying the future. *Journal of Creative Behavior, 9* (3), 183–187.

Torrance, E. P. (1978). Healing qualities of creative behavior. *Creative Child and Adult Quarterly, 3*, 146–158.

Torrance, E. P. (1979a). *The search for satori and creativity*. Buffalo, NY: Creative Education Foundation.

Torrance, E. P. (1979b). An instructional model for enhancing incubation. *Journal of Creative Behavior, 13* (1), 23–35.

Torrance, E. P. (1979c). Developing creativity instructional models according to the sociodrama model. *Creative Child and Adult Quarterly, 4*, 9–19.

Torrance, E. P. (1981). Implications of whole-brained theories of learning and thinking for computer-based instruction. *Journal of Computer-Based Instruction, 7* (4), 99–105.

Torrance, E. P. (1982). Hemisphericity and creative functioning. *Journal of Research and Development in Education, 15* (3), 29–37.

Torrance, E. P., & Forston, L. R. (1968, Sept–Oct). Creativity among children and the creative-aesthetic approach. *Education*, pp. 1–3.

Torrance, E. P., & Frasier, M. M. (1983). Styles of learning and thinking and biographical inventory measures. *Creative Child and Adult Quarterly, 8*, 206–210.

Torrance, E. P., & Harmon, J. A. (1961). Effects of memory, evaluative, and creative reading sets on test performance. *Journal of Educational Psychology, 52*, 207–214.

Torrance, E. P., Reynolds, C. R., & Ball, O. E. (1977). Your style of learning and thinking, forms A and B: Preliminary norms, abbreviated technical notes, scoring keys, and selected references. *Gifted Child Quarterly, 21*, 563–573.

Wallas, G. (1926). *The art of thought*. London: Jonathan Cape.

Williams, L. V. (1983). *Teaching for the two-sided mind*. Englewood Cliffs, NJ: Prentice Hall.

CHAPTER 11

Assessment and Training of Student Learning Strategies

CLAIRE E. WEINSTEIN

Learning-to-learn phenomena have been examined from a wide variety of perspectives (Anderson, 1985; Brown, Bransford, Ferrara & Campione, 1983; Dillon & Schmeck, 1983; Kirby, 1984; Pressley & Levin, 1983a, 1983b; Weinstein & Mayer, 1985). While, in general, this development has served to enrich the field of study, it has also created enormous definitional problems. For the purposes of this chapter, attention is focused on a subarea called learning strategies. Learning strategies are considered to be any behaviors or thoughts that facilitate encoding in such a way that knowledge integration and retrieval are enhanced. More specifically, these thoughts and behaviors constitute organized plans of action designed to achieve a goal (Anderson, 1985; Paris, in press; Weinstein & Mayer, 1985). Examples of learning strategies include actively rehearsing, summarizing, paraphrasing, imaging, elaborating, and outlining.

This chapter is organized around several themes. First, a categorical scheme for conceptualizing learning strategies is presented. Next, some issues related to assessment and research methodologies are presented. Finally, approaches to teaching learning strategies are discussed.

CLAIRE E. WEINSTEIN • Department of Educational Psychology, University of Texas at Austin, Austin, Texas 78712.

INTRODUCTION

For many years studies of human learning were dominated by the behaviorist school of thought in psychology. This resulted in a total dependence on the effects of external events as determinants of what was acquired. With the rise in interest in the role of organizational processes and information transformations that take place within the learner, the interest of many researchers was refocused on what had come to be regarded as the black box of the human mind (Melton & Martin, 1972). Many of these earlier studies represented attempts to demonstrate the roles that learners could or did play in facilitating their own learning and recall. Much of the emphasis in these studies was on the extent to which the use of mnemonic devices could enhance recognition or recall memory. Based on the success of these early studies, some researchers went on to examine the processes that underlie the use of mnemonic strategies (e.g.. Bower, 1970; Paivio, 1971). This work contributed to an evolving interest in the remediation of learning deficits in academically disadvantaged and academically underprepared students. If the processes and procedures that underlie effective learning could be taught, or enhanced, then an additional and possibly very potent form of remediation could be developed. It was this idea that underlies the motivation for much of the work that has been done in the area of learning strategies, particularly when the focus is on the adult learner.

In the late 1960s and into the middle of the next decade, the majority of investigators in this area concentrated on demonstrating the effectiveness of training designed to teach the use of one or more mnemonic strategies or techniques (e.g., Borkowski & Kamfonik, 1972; Rohwer, 1966, 1970; Wood, 1967; Yuille & Catchpole, 1973). The tasks used most frequently in this work included paired-associate learning, serial list learning, and free recall learning. Notice that these tasks tend to be associated more with laboratory research tasks than with real-world natural language processing activities. A major change in the more current literature is to focus attention on ecologically valid tasks, particularly those needed to succeed in a postsecondary educational setting (e.g., Dansereau, in press; McCombs, in press; Nickerson, Salter, Shepard, & Herrnstein, 1984; Wittrock, 1985). This change in focus to more applied aspects of cognition has affected the ways learning strategies are now conceptualized, the methods used to measure their acquisition and use, and the procedures and materials used to teach them.

TYPES OF LEARNING STRATEGIES

Given the relatively young and somewhat disorganized nature of the field, there is not yet one organizational scheme that is generally accepted as a way of classifying learning strategies. However, Weinstein and Mayer (1985) attemped to create a set of categories that reflected both the current state of research and practice. Each separate category is composed of methods that can be used by learners to influence one or more aspects of the encoding process. The ultimate goal for any of these activities is to enhance learning outcomes and performance.

Rehearsal Strategies for Basic Learning Tasks. An example of a strategies in this category would be repeating, in correct serial order, the names of the colors in the spectrum. There are a number of different educational tasks that require simple recall. This is particularly true at the lower educational levels and in introductory courses at the postsecondary level. A major difference between experts and novices in many content areas appears to be related to the knowledge base that they possess (Chi, Feltovich, & Glaser, 1981; Gagne, 1985; Larkin, 1981). While the structure, organization, and integration of this knowledge base is most important for expert decision making and problem solving, the acquisition of the basic knowledge needed to create a more unified data base is often the first step. As Schmeck (1983) notes, it may not be possible for even the highly intelligent students to engage in deeper forms of information processing until they acquire this knowledge base.

Rehearsal Strategies for Complex Learning Tasks. The learning tasks in this category are more complex and tend to involve knowledge that extends beyond the superficial learning of lists or unrelated bits of information. Strategies in this category would include copying and underlining material presented in a lecture. Generally, they involve repetition aimed at literal reproduction. Like the methods discussed above, these activities seem particularly effective when they provide further opportunities for more meaningful processing to take place, such as the use of elaboration, organization, or comprehension monitoring.

Elaboration Strategies for Basic Learning Tasks. Elaboration involves adding some sort of symbolic construction to what one is trying to learn as a way to make it more meaningful. This can be accomplished using either verbal or imaginal constructions. For example, the use of mental imagery to help remember the action sequence described in a play and the use of a sentence to relate a country and its major industrial product are both elaborations. The creation of effective elaborations requires that the learner be actively involved in processing the to-be-learned information. Numerous studies have shown this to be an important prerequisite for meaningful learning, versus superficial encoding for recall (Cermak & Craik, 1979; Rigney, 1976; Weinstein, 1982; see also chapters by Entwistle, Marton, and Schmeck, this volume).

Elaboration Strategies for Complex Learning Tasks. Activities in this category include creating analogies, paraphrasing, and using prior knowledge, experiences, attitudes, and beliefs to help make the new information more meaningful. Again, the major goal of each of these activities is to get the learner actively involved in building bridges between what the learner already knows (in the broadest sense of this term) and what he or she is trying to understand. Trying to apply a principle to everyday experience, relating the content of one course to the content of another, relating what was presented earlier in a lecture to the current discussion, trying to use a problem-solving strategy in a new situation, summarizing an argument, all of these are different ways to elaborate.

Organizational Strategies for Basic Learning Tasks. The strategy in this category focus on methods used to translate information into another form that will make it easier to understand. The facilitating effect is usually attributed to the processing involved in accomplishing the transformation as well as the structure imposed. Examples of methods in this category include grouping the battles of World War II by geographic location, organizing animals by their taxonomic category, and listing foreign vocabulary words by their parts of speech. In each of these examples an existing or created scheme is used to impose organization on an otherwise unordered set of items. Notice that organizational strategies, like elaboration strategies, require a more active role on the part of the learner than simply rote or rehearsal strategies.

Organizational Strategies for Complex Learning Tasks. Organizational strategies can also be very useful for more-complex tasks. Common examples of the use of this method with complex tasks include outlining a chapter of a textbook, creating a conceptual diagram of cause–effect interrelationships, and creating a hierarchy of sources to use in writing a term paper. Here, too, it is both the process and the product which seem to contribute to the effectiveness of the method.

Comprehension Monitoring Strategies. Metacognition is used to refer to individuals' knowledge about their own cognitive processes as well as their abilities to control these processes by organizing, monitoring, and modifying them as a function of learning outcomes and feedback (Brown, 1975, 1978; Brown *et al.,* 1983; Cavanaugh & Perlmutter, 1982; Flavell, 1970, 1981). A subarea within metacognition that is particularly relevant to the present discussion is called *comprehension monitoring.* Operationally, comprehension monitoring involves establishing learning goals, assessing the degree to which these goals are being met, and, if necessary, modifying the strategies being used to facilitate goal attainment. Comprehension monitoring requires several types of knowledge on the part of learners. First, they need to know something about themselves as learners. For example, what are their preferred learning styles? What subjects are easier or harder for them to understand? What are their best and worst times of day? This type of knowledge helps individuals to know how to schedule their study activities and the kinds of resources or assistance they will need to perform efficiently and effectively.

Learners also need to have some knowledge about the nature of the task or tasks they are about to perform as well as the anticipated or desired outcomes. It is difficult to reach a goal if you do not know what the goal is (see Entwistle, Chapter 2, Marton, Chapter 3). For example, many students experience great difficulty reading a textbook in spite of the large amount of time and effort they devote to the task. In our own research with a learning-to-learn course we have developed at the University of Texas, the problem often turns out to be that the student does not know how to read a textbook. Many of these individuals do not know how to select main ideas and important details for further study. They treat every sentence as if it were just as important as every other sentence. Not knowing about different text structures or how to identify important information can make reading a textbook an almost impossible task. Thus, it is important that students have an understanding of what is required by different school tasks.

It is also important to access relevant prior knowledge. This can serve two functions. First, it helps with understanding the new material. However, it also helps with preparing for the new learning by instantiating relevant schemata and providing some guidelines for checking the accuracy of new knowledge.

Finally, it is necessary to have some knowledge of strategies that can be used to guide learning or that can be called upon to help when a comprehension problem is encountered. This type of knowledge includes knowing about methods in each of the categories already described. It also includes being able to actually use these methods and knowing when they are appropriate to use. Thus, comprehension monitoring is very intimately related to the selection and use of other strategies in any given learning activity.

Assessing the degree to which goals are met is one of the central tasks in comprehension monitoring. This task is usually accomplished through some form of self-questioning, broadly defined. There are a wide variety of specific methods that could be used to assess one's level of understanding. For instance, attempting to apply a new principle, using a chapter summary to create questions to answer while reading, self-testing while reviewing lecture notes, or attempting to teach the information to someone else (or even pretending that you are teaching it to someone else) are all examples of ways in which we could assess our level of understanding. It is important to note that many of these activities overlap with strategies presented in earlier categories. This categorical scheme is not meant to imply orthogonality among the classes of methods. In fact, there is a great deal of overlap between categories. For example, trying to apply a principle to a new situation can be a form of elaboration, thereby enhancing encoding, but it can also be a way to help monitor one's understanding of the principle to see if further study is needed. This interdependence among strategies makes them very difficult to study, particularly when the researcher attempts to isolate the effects of just one type of strategy. The problem is similar to teaching students about a car. Although we discuss separately the ignition system, the braking system, the steering system, and so forth, we know that driving a car is an integrated activity composed of many subskills and requiring varied knowledge. The emergent properties of the integrated system that represents driving a car, however, are too complex to present. It is the same with the strategies that underlie a systematic approach to studying and learning. The whole is too complex to teach or use for conceptual guidance in research, so we reduce it for utility and lose several degrees of precision.

Affective Strategies. Affective strategies help to create and maintain suitable internal and external climates for learning (Dansereau *et al.*, 1979; McCombs, in press; Palmer & Goetz, in press; Weinstein & Underwood, 1985). Although these strategies may not be directly responsible for knowledge or skill acquisition, they help to create a context in which effective learning can take place. Examples of affective strategies include using relaxation and positive self-talk to reduce performance anxiety, finding a quiet place to study to reduce external distractions, and establishing priorities and setting a time schedule as a way to reduce procrastination. Each of these methods is designed to help focus the limited processing capacity of the human information processing system on the learning goal. Eliminating both external and internal distractions contributes to enhanced attention and concentration.

LEARNING STRATEGIES ASSESSMENT

The rapidly expanding interest in learning strategies assessment is the result of several causes. Among them is the increasingly large number of academically underprepared or disadvantaged students entering postsecondary institutions. In response to this influx of students with special needs, many institutions have created special programs to address academic deficits (Noel & Levitz, 1982; Weinstein & Underwood, 1985). However, the successful implementation and evaluation of training programs and courses designed to teach learning strategies requires reliable and valid means for measuring students' entry-level deficits and their progress. Having the means to diagnose student deficits could contribute significantly to the design of instruction, and having the means to monitor progress and course outcomes could contribute significantly to evaluating and improving the effectiveness of the training.

Another reason for the increasing interest in the area of assessment relates to both basic and applied research interests in information processing. The measurement issue in cognitive research is a major stumbling block to progress (see Garner, in press, for a discussion of this issue). Since cognitive researchers focus on topics that reflect processes that are usually not available to direct measurement, indirect forms of assessment must be developed for more precise research hypotheses to be amenable to study. In response to this need there has been a renewed focus on variations of self-report methodologies that could be used to help gather data about covert strategies.

APPROACHES TO ASSESSMENT

One result of the pressures for the creation of useful assessment methods has been the development of a number of instruments designed to measure varying aspects of learning strategy use. Many of these instruments build on the measures that were created to assess students' study practices. Several of these measures are available commercially. A review of a subset of both commercially published as well as developmental or research instruments indicated that many of them concentrate on quite traditional areas of study skills such as note taking, study attitudes towards school and learning, text marking, and test taking (Schulte & Weinstein, 1981; Weinstein, Zimmermann, & Palmer, in press). The specific topics included in these measures are highly variable. This is, in part, a reflection of the definition problem discussed earlier and, in part, a reflection of the relative importance attached to different skills by different authors. Generally, the format used for these instruments requires some type of self-report response. While the data reported for many of these instruments are quite limited, reliabilities are usually found to be in the acceptable (Anastasi, 1976) range of .80 and above. However, many of the subscales, particularly those that are relatively short, are often found to have somewhat lower reliabilities (.46 to .93).

Since the purpose of many of these measures is to either predict academic performance, counsel students about their study skills, or screen students for entry into or exit from remedial courses, they often used what Svensson (1977) called a "correlational approach." This method of item selection and instrument design emphasizes behaviors, thoughts, and activities that correlate with successful studying but that may not be the direct causes of successful learning and achievement. (For example, many successful students may keep their desk tops clean but that does not necessarily mean that students can raise their grades by cleaning their desks!) Thus, many of the items on these inventories have little use for someone interested in using them as a basis for re-mediation or for forming the basis for experimental interventions. Many of the authors of these measures selected or created items on the basis of how well they distinguished between students with high and low grade point averages who had similar IQ and achievement test scores (Brown, 1964; Brown & Holtzman, 1967; Carter, 1985; Christensen, 1968).

Given the way many of the items on study skills instruments are selected, they tend to yield limited information about how students study or learn. Rather, the emphasis tends to be on either historical or preference information or correlational factors that stress the conditions under which students study. This approach is quite different from what Svensson (1977) called a "functional approach" that stresses identifying differences in how students learn that directly seem to affect learning outcomes and academic achievement. It was this approach that guided the development of the Learning and Study Strategies Inventory (Weinstein, Schulte, & Cascallar, 1983; Weinstein *et al.*, in press).

THE LASSI

The Learning and Study Strategies Inventory (LASSI) was developed as part of the Cognitive Learning Strategies Project at the University of Texas at Austin. Given the problems identified with previous instruments, an attempt was made to create a measure that could be used for diagnosis and that could facilitate the design of remedial learning strategies instruction. Thus, the focus was on either covert or overt thoughts and behaviors that relate to successful learning *and that could be altered* through educational interventions. In addition, an attempt was made to emphasize items that reflected the functional approach of Svensson.

The earliest step in the development of the LASSI involved analyzing the instruments reviewed by Weinstein and Schulte (1981). This work was supplemented by a review of 47 study skills books, manuals, and program or curriculum guides (see Weinstein *et al.*, 1983 for a description of this developmental work). The topics and subtopics identified in this process were subjected to repeated reviews and analyses using expert judges to create a categorical scheme that could be used to guide item creation or selection. These initial categorical schemes were used to create the item pools from which the final items were eventually selected.

Sources for the initial item pool included published, unpublished, and experimental instruments, researchers and practitioners in the area of learning strategies, staff members on the project, and psychometric consultants. This first pool of 645 items was trimmed down as a result of several analyses and a variety of pilot and field studies. A wide variety of item elimination criteria were used, including correlations with grade point average, correlations with the Marlowe–Crowne Social-Desirability Scale, and item content that stressed specialized skills such as creating a bibliography or vocabulary building. Redundant items and those which elicited a very narrow range of responses were also eliminated.

As a result of these steps, a version of the LASSI containing 90 items was constructed. One of the first studies conducted with this instrument examined its test–retest reliability. Ninety undergraduates from an introductory educational psychology course completed the LASSI on two different occasions, separated by a 3- to 4-week interval. The students were given 45 minutes in which to complete their task. A test–retest correlation of .88 for the total instrument was obtained.

Using this version of the LASSI, a set of 10 scales measuring different clusters of learning strategies and study attitudes was developed. This process was accomplished by a team of expert judges using several iterations of a modified Delphi technique and by analyses of the scale structures. (See Table 1 for a sample of the items from each of the scales.) The topics covered by the 10 scales are anxiety, attitude, concentration, information processing, motivation, scheduling, selecting the main idea, self-testing, study aids, and test strategies.

The Anxiety scale focuses on the degree to which students worry about school and their performance (see Entwistle's discussion of fear of failure, Chapter 2, and Chapter 6 by McCarthy & Schmeck, this volume). Do students worry so much that it is hard to concentrate? Are they easily discouraged about grades? Are they nervous even if they are well prepared for a test? The Attitude scale contains items addressing attitude and interest in college. Is school important and worthwhile to the students? How clear are they about their own educational goals? (Once again, see Chapter 2 by Entwistle and Chapter 6 by McCarthy and Schmeck for related discussions.) Concentration items focus on students' ability to pay close attention to academic tasks. Are they easily distracted? Can they focus their attention (see McCarthy & Schmeck,

Table 1. Sample Items from the LASSI Scales

Scale (# of items)	Sample item
Anxiety (10)	1. Worrying about doing poorly interferes with my concentration on tests. 2. When I begin an examination, I feel pretty confident that I will do well. 3. Even when I'm well prepared for a test, I feel very anxious.
Attitude (4)	1. Success in school is very important to me. 2. I feel confused and undecided as to what my educational goals should be. 3. In my opinion, what is taught in my courses is not worth learning.
Concentration (8)	1. I often find that I have been reading but don't know what it was all about. 2. I concentrate fully when studying. 3. I find that during lectures I think of other things and don't really listen to what is being said.
Information Processing (17)	1. I try to find relationships between what I am learning and what I already know. 2. When I study I try to somehow organize the material in my mind. 3. When having difficulty recalling something, I make an effort to recall something else that might be related to it.
Motivation (14)	1. I read the textbooks assigned for my classes. 2. I hurry my assignments trying to get them out of the way rather than doing a good job. 3. I seem to be able to find all kinds of excuses for not studying.
Scheduling (5)	1. I only study when there is the pressure of a test. 2. I make good use of daytime study hours between classes. 3. At the beginning of a study period I organize my work so that I will use the time most effectively.
Selecting Main Idea (4)	1. My underlining is helpful when I review text material. 2. I have difficulty identifying the important points in my reading. 3. Often when studying I seem to get lost in details and "can't see the forest for the trees."
Self-Testing (5)	1. I stop periodically while reading and mentally go over or review what was said. 2. I go over homework assignments when reviewing class materials. 3. I seldom review except just before tests.
Study Aids (8)	1. I do not work through practice exercises and sample problems. 2. When they are available, I attend group review sessions. 3. I make simple charts, diagrams, or tables to summarize material in my courses.
Test Strategies (13)	1. I think through the meaning of test questions before I begin to answer them. 2. I have difficulty adapting my studying to different types of courses. 3. When I take a test, I realize I have studied the wrong material.

Chapter 6)? The Information Processing scale contains items addressing a number of different areas. In fact, studies are currently under way to examine how this scale might be subdivided to provide more useful diagnostic information so that more specific remediation might result. Currently, the areas addressed include the use of imaginal and verbal elaboration, comprehension monitoring, and reasoning.

The next scale is called Motivation (cf. Entwistle, Chapter 2). The items on this scale address willingness to work hard, diligence, and self-discipline. Do the students stay up-to-date in class assignments? Do they easily lose interest in their classes? Items on the Scheduling scale examine students' use of time-management principles for academic tasks. Are they well organized? Do they anticipate scheduling problems? Selecting the Main Idea items address students' ability to pick out important information for further study. Can they focus on the key points in a lecture? Can they decide what to underline in a textbook? The next scale, Self-Testing, focuses on reviewing and preparing for classes and tests. Most of the items deal with some aspect of comprehension monitoring. Do the students review before a test? Do they stop periodically while reading to review the content? Items on the Study Aids scale examine the degree to which students use support techniques or materials to help them learn and remember new information. Do they complete practice exercises and sample problems? Do they use or create organizational aids? The last scale, Test Strategies, focuses on students' approach toward taking tests and examinations. Do they prepare appropriately? Do they try to tie the material together?

As can be seen in Table 1, the number of items in the various scales ranges from a low of 4 to a high of 17. Part of our current work involves adding new items to the scales that currently have less than 8 (Attitude, Scheduling, Select Main Idea, and Self-Testing). In addition, the subdivision of the Information Processing Scale and the addition of new scales is also being examined.

A number of studies have been conducted to examine the psychometric properties of the LASSI. The data from a total of 783 incoming freshmen at a small private college in the eastern United States were used to calculate coefficient alphas for each of the scales (see Table 2). The resulting coefficients ranged from a low of .60 to a high of .88, with the low coefficients associated with the scales having the fewest number of items. (This is one of the reasons that additional items are being developed for these scales.) These data were also used to develop a preliminary set of norms of the various scales. In a study presently underway, data from approximately 800 students from the entering class in a large public university located in the southwestern United States are being used to validate these results. Only preliminary data are available, but the results are very encouraging. Thus far, only minor

Table 2. Test–Retest and Alpha Reliabilities for the
LASSI Scales

Scale (# of items)	Test–retest reliability	Alpha reliability
Anxiety (10)	.81	.82
Attitude (4)	.64	.60
Concentration (8)	.80	.82
Information Pro- cessing (17)	.79	.88
Motivation (14)	.79	.87
Scheduling (5)	.77	.69
Selecting Main Idea (4)	.64	.61
Self-Testing (5)	.66	.65
Study Aids (8)	.70	.69
Test Strategies (13)	.79	.83

differences have been found for the alpha reliabilities and norms of the
scales. This high degree of agreement indicates a high degree of stability
in these data.

Test–retest reliabilities for the scales have also been obtained. Using
the sample of 96 students previously described, and a 3- to 4-week
interval, the data set was created. The reliability values ranged from a
low of .64 to a high of .81 (see Table 2). Again, the scales with the lowest
reliability coefficients were the ones that also contain the fewest number
of items.

The validity of the LASSI has been examined using a variety of
approaches. When possible, the scale scores have been compared to
other measures, or scales, assessing similar factors or constructs. For
example, scores on the Information Processing Scale of the LASSI were
correlated with scores on the Elaborative Processing Scale of Schmeck's
Inventory of Learning Processes (Schmeck, in press; Schmeck, Ribich, &
Ramanaiah, 1977). The correlation was .60. Another approach has compared the scores on some of the LASSI scales to appropriate performance
measures. For example, scores on the Select Main Idea scale were compared to scores on classroom tasks involving identifying the main ideas in
a series of textbook and reading selections. Correlation coefficients of .40
and above have been obtained.

The final approach used to obtain validity data relates to the purposes for which the LASSI was originally designed. This approach has
concentrated on how successfully the LASSI can be used by practitioners
and teachers in postsecondary settings. Professors, counselors, ad-

visors, and developmental specialists at more than 15 different locations in the United States and Mexico have used the LASSI on a trial basis. Thus far, the results have been very encouraging. Users report few, if any, administration problems and a high degree of usefulness.

Part of the motivation for developing the LASSI was the need for a valid and reliable assessment method for use in both the research and the development activities that are conducted as part of the Cognitive Learning Strategies Project. In particular, there was a need for an instrument that could be used to diagnose the strengths and weaknesses of students who participate in the learning-to-learn course developed to test out the research in a real-world setting. This course, which is described in more detail in the next section, has also been used to help establish user data for the LASSI.

LEARNING STRATEGIES TRAINING (POSTSECONDARY)

Learning strategies training programs have been developed for a variety of reasons. Often, they are used by researchers to investigate the effectiveness of strategy components or interactions among components. These programs are also used to examine instructional procedures, transfer, and generalization of strategy use. Finally, they are often developed as part of a larger remedial or enrichment program for educationally disadvantaged or underprepared students.

APPROACHES TO LEARNING STRATEGIES TRAINING

A number of different methods have been used to implement learning strategies training at the postsecondary level. The first method, *embedded instruction*, concentrates on incorporating learning strategies training into existing educational materials, particularly print materials and workbooks (e.g., Jones, in press; Jones, Amiran, & Katims, 1985; Sticht, 1979). Jones' work, in particular, has involved teaching, reinforcing, and cueing the use of strategies from all eight categories in the materials developed as part of the Chicago Mastery Learning Reading Program and as part of the Basic Skills Program of the United States Army. These creative materials have been repeatedly field tested and found to contribute significantly to the reading comprehension of the students involved. Embedded curricular materials are most effective when there are very large numbers of students to teach, problems with frequent teacher turnover or reassignments, or too few qualified instructors for the number of students requiring instruction. When these conditions do not apply, the heuristic nature of learning strategies indicates that they could be taught best in a more direct fashion using a teacher, aide, or developmental education specialist. The following method uses this latter approach.

Another approach uses existing instructional interventions to teach learning strategies. Unlike the embedded approach, the use of a meta-curriculum to teach learning strategies involves teaching them along with the regular content material in existing classes or training programs (Weinstein, 1982). The instructor uses methods that demonstrate, cue, and reinforce the acquisition and use of strategies from all of the different categories. It is a metacurriculum in the sense that it requires an analysis of the regular course curriculum and the learning demands that it places on the students.

Implementing the metacurriculum requires the instructor to integrate learning strategies instruction into the planned and unplanned activities that go on during class. For example, when assigning a textbook for a course, a teacher could pause and discuss the strategies one could use to preview and use a textbook. The assignment of a term paper or project is an excellent time to discuss time management. When using an analogy to help explain a difficult concept is a good time to also discuss elaboration, the role it plays in learning, and how students can use this method on their own. Notice that in each of these examples what is required is that the teacher use a planned or an unplanned activity to focus on the types of learning strategies that might be particularly effective to accomplish the relevant learning goal. By making this information explicit, explaining to students how to use the strategy, providing opportunities for practice and feedback, and periodically reviewing how various strategies can be combined to create an effective study system, instructors are implementing the metacurriculum.

Most researchers and practitioners have tended to use some form of *adjunct approach* to learning strategies training. Using an adjunct approach involves creating some form of supplementary instruction. This can take the form of anything from a 2-hour workshop on a particular strategy to a semester-long course teaching strategies from each of the eight categories. Dansereau (1985, in press), McCombs (1981, 1982a, 1982b, in press), and Weinstein (Weinstein, Butterfield, Schmidt, & Poythress, 1983; Weinstein & Underwood, 1985) have all focused on creating adjunct programs for postsecondary students in job or college settings.

Many of the ideas and methods discussed so far in this chapter have been implemented in a three-credit lower-division learning strategies course created as part of the Cognitive Learning Strategies Project at the University of Texas at Austin. A description of the course, relevant evaluation data, and future directions for both research and development in this area is now presented.

A Course in Individual Learning Skills

The learning strategies course offered at the University of Texas is part of the undergraduate program in educational psychology. Originally, the course was developed solely as a real-world laboratory to test out research findings described in the literature and from our own laboratory (Underwood, 1982). Over time, the service aspect of the course became at least equally important. Currently, 35 sections of approximately 25 students each are offered each year. This does not meet the demand, but it does exhaust our capacity to staff and support the sections. The type of student registering for this course is quite variable. However, the majority are lower-division students with either a history of academic difficulty or students who have encountered problems in their studies at the University of Texas at Austin. Among the remaining students, many are advised to take this course in preparation for advanced studies or training.

The overall goal of the course is to help students take more responsibility for their own learning. Strategies and skills from each of the categories identified by Weinstein and Mayer (1985) are presented (see the Appendix for a detailed overview of the course topics). A variety of instructional methods are used, but the emphasis, given the procedural nature of much of the content, is on guided practice and feedback (Anderson, 1985; Gagne, 1985). To facilitate a transfer, these exercises are taken from a wide variety of content areas and task types. To facilitate integration, the strategies are discussed in a cyclic manner. First, the instructor briefly introduces the strategy and identifies how it can be used to address a student-identification problem. This discussion is always related back to the model of the successful student presented at the beginning of the semester. Next, the key elements of the strategy are presented along with a few examples. Given the heuristic nature of most learning strategies, this is immediately followed by practice and feedback sessions so students can begin to incorporate the method into their repertoire. Over time, the use of the strategy is reviewed, and its relationship to other strategies identified. This is designed to help the student form a more systematic approach to studying and learning rather than just providing a bag of tricks (see Schmeck's, in press, discussion of the need to encourage a "unified learning outcome").

The course is evaluated extensively. Part of the data for evaluation is obtained from the entry and exit measures administered to students. This data includes scores on the LASSI, the Survey of Study Habits and

Attitudes (Brown & Holtzman, 1967), the Trait Anxiety Inventory Portion of the State–Trait Anxiety Inventory (Spielberger, Gorsuch, & Luschene, 1970), the Test Attitude Inventory (Spielberger. Gonzalez, Taylor, Algaze, & Anton, 1978), and the Nelson–Denny Reading Test (Brown, Nelson, & Denny, 1973). In addition, information is also obtained from class examination scores, homework assignments, in-class activities, student journals, and practice exercises. We have also been able to run several studies that allowed us to obtain follow-up data on some of our students. Finally, the university has helped us to obtain copies of the students' course evaluation surveys.

The patterns we find in these data sets are very exciting. The course has consistently led to significant pre-to-post changes on all of the measures with the exception of the Trait Anxiety Inventory. This result was expected and predicted, however, due to the nature of the underlying construct. The encouraging fact is that all of our anxiety measures show a very significant improvement in student attitudes and reported decreases in anxiety-related performance problems.

These changes on the self-report measures are backed up by significant improvements on the performance measures. The quality of student work on the in-class and homework assignments shows definite improvement over the course of the semester (as judged by a team of outside experts). Scores on the Nelson–Denny Reading Test show improvements ranging from 14 to 34 percentile points. Finally, there are significant increases in academic grade point averages compiled from the students' regular coursework (after controlling for the normal increases one would expect as a function of time). Indirect evidence for the effectiveness of the course is also provided by the current increase in student enrollment (the course originally had 4 sections per year instead of 36) and the reports of academic advisors from a variety of departments at the university.

In addition to being used to help with prescriptions for individual students, these data are also used to guide the continuing development of the course. For example, data from the LASSI indicated that more instructional emphasis was needed on information processing strategies, and early data from the Test Attitude Inventory indicated that a component focusing on coping with performance anxiety needed to be expanded.

CONCLUDING COMMENTS

The work described in this chapter is still in a relatively early stage of development. Cognitive and educational psychologists have much to learn about the processes and knowledge needed for effective learning.

The categorical scheme derived by Weinstein and Mayer (1985) was meant more to stimulate thought about this area than as a definitive classification. While it summarizes our current state of knowledge, there are many weaknesses. For example, how can strategies be tied to content domains? Many researchers and theoreticians now believe that both generic and content–domain-dependent strategies must be identified and taught (e.g., Gagne, 1985; Glaser, 1984).

There are also many unsolved problems in the area of assessment. It will be hard for cognitive psychologists to continue to contribute significantly to educational needs unless we can improve our ability to measure, no matter how indirectly, the underlying mediational mechanisms that affect final performance. Continuing research into the development of diagnostic instruments such as the LASSI is a step in that direction.

Finally, the need for courses or educational experiences that focus on the development of student learning strategies will remain for years to come. The changing demographics of higher education lead to widespread predictions that more and more students will enter postsecondary settings with an inadequate academic background. Since many academically disadvantaged and underprepared students evidence serious learning strategies deficits, it will be crucial that remediation and enrichment be provided.

APPENDIX

COURSE TOPICS

UNIT: Successful Learning
      Part One: Becoming a Successful Student
      Part Two: Training Your Mind

1. There are certain skills, behaviors and attitudes that distinguish successful learners from those who are not so successful. Part One of this unit describes the characteristics of a successful learner and focuses on a model that can aid students in dealing effectively with academic dissatisfactions. This model of a successful learner incorporates the following variables: motivation, attention, understanding, recall ability, and reduced stress (see "Handout" below).

2. The ability to encode and recall information is a skill which can be developed and improved. In part two of this unit the student is introduced to elementary principles of learning and cognition that lead to a discussion of the differences between rote learning and meaningful learning. These include ways to generate (for oneself) interest in a topic area, the importance of distributed practice and review, how to decide upon goals for learning, connecting new information with existing knowledge, relating new information to everyday life

experiences as much as possible, and applying new information. These suggestions provide the student with an appropriate framework for becoming an active learner and for using cognitive learning strategies drawn from information processing models.

HANDOUT: Becoming a successful student

Motivation

Stress-Free   **Attention**

Recall   **Understanding**

There are certain skills . . .
There are certain behaviors . . .
There are certain attitudes . . .
that distinguish successful learners from those who are not so successful.

If you learn these skills and behaviors and attitudes—and practice them—then you too can be successful in school.

What exactly *are* the characteristics of a successful learner?

1. Motivation—The successful student has an inner drive that makes him or her want to do well. S/He accepts responsibility for doing his/her own learning, and when s/he does succeed s/he knows it was because of his/her own efforts. S/He succeeded because s/he wanted to, because s/he tried his/her best, and *luck* had *nothing* to do with it.

2. Attention—A successful learner also is able to pay attention to what is going on at the moment. Instead of daydreaming about yesterday or thinking about what s/he's going to do tomorrow, s/he can concentrate all his or her attention on school-related tasks. S/He will ignore or reduce outside distractions. If his/her roommate insists on playing the stereo at 120 decibels, then someone who is determined to learn his/her homework or do his/her reading will go to the library or someplace where s/he isn't interfered with.

3. Understanding—The successful student also makes an effort to understand the ideas presented in school. When s/he realizes s/he doesn't know enough about a topic to understand it, then s/he gets help, either from the teacher or by talking to other students or by doing some more reading.

4. Recall—A successful learner also is able to recall, and remember, the knowledge, main ideas and principles that s/he needs to know. S/He does this by *using* the learning strategies that s/he has either learned on his/her own—or has been taught to use in a class similar to this one.

5. Relatively Stress-free—In addition, the successful learner can do all this in a relatively relaxed way—hopefully without too much worry, too much frustration, or too much anxiety.

UNIT: Time Management
    Part One: Scheduling
    Part Two: Procrastination

1. There are many demands made on a student's time. The emphasis of this unit is to help students structure time so that activities necessary for academic success are accomplished, and there is still time for personal and leisure activities. The value of scheduling and its effect on stress reduction are discussed in this context. Suggestions are given for setting goals, getting organized, establishing study routines, and studying "on the run." Several different types of scheduling are then demonstrated. These include (1) a personal activities diary, (2) weekly and monthly academic scheduling forms, (3) "to do" lists, and (4) the "COPE" system (Margaret R. Barr, Center for Teaching Effectiveness, University of Texas, Austin, Texas, undated xerox copy).

2. Procrastination is a major obstacle to good time management. Factors that aid and abet procrastination (e.g., inappropriate commitments, perfectionism, and self-deception) are dealt with, but the emphasis is on ways and means to overcome the habit of procrastination. Procedures for reducing this habit range from the behavioral (e.g., a reward and punishment system) to the cognitive (e.g., establishing positive self-talk).[1] Additional procedures include written reminders, the five-minute plan, and setting realistic goals. Students are encouraged to deal simultaneously with the behaviors, emotions, and cognitions attached to procrastination.

UNIT: Problem Solving

Dealing with academically related problems is often confusing and overwhelming for the target student population. In this unit students are presented with a problem solving model that will help them deal more effectively with their school-related problems. The seven-step process includes: (1) accepting responsibility for taking care of the problem and being accountable for actions taken; (2) collecting and examining information about the problem; (3) defining what the actual problem is; (4) generating ideas for solving the problem; (5) choosing a plan of action; (6) taking the action; and (7) evaluating whether or not the action taken was effective in solving the problem. Students implement this model over a period of seven weeks and turn in a progress report for each step.

UNIT: Cognitive Learning Strategies

Most current models of information processing suggest that it is necessary to process information at a "deep" or "semantic" level if there is to be adequate understanding, retention, and recall of information. In accordance with this notion, students are presented with a rationale for using the following cognitive learning strategies: imaginal elaboration, verbal elaboration, and organizational strategies, such as grouping. The characteristics of each strategy are discussed, and students are provided with practice exercises. This material is also related to current conceptions of knowledge acquisition, such as schema theory.

In addition, contrasts are drawn between primary and support strategies. Primary strategies are operations performed on the materials to be remembered.

---

[1]Materials adapted from A. Ellis & W. J. Knaus, *Overcoming Procrastination*. New York: New American Library, 1979.

These may range from purely cognitive strategies such as imagery and verbal elaboration to more mechanical strategies such as note taking and highlighting of textual materials. Support strategies are methods that help the learner maintain a suitable psychological climate for learning or help establish an appropriate learning attitude. These strategies may range from techniques for coping with loss of concentration to the use of physical relaxation routines. Students are also asked to think of ways that the two types of strategies may be used in combination to build a strong study system.

UNIT: Concentration

Concentration is a difficult skill to present because it is a by-product and only happens when we do not think about it. However, the habit of concentration can be developed through self-discipline and practice in becoming actively involved in studying and learning. Discussion revolves around strategies for focusing attention such as highlighting, note taking, and outlining, and many cognitive strategies for increasing level of involvement, such as relating the material to-be-learned to already-learned information, organizing it, and generating interest through questioning strategies.

Attention is also given to the relationships between concentration and metacognitive awareness as well as between concentration and the learner as an active processor of information.

UNIT: Listening

The focus of this unit is listening for important information and understanding in an academic setting. It is necessary for students to become active listeners by improving their listening habits, by learning what to listen for, and by becoming involved with the speaker. Differences between hearing and listening are noted, and students are asked to think of good listening as an active process. Several listening problems such as close-mindedness, paying false attention, and daydreaming are discussed, and relevant "cures" for such maladies are presented. These cures include learning how to prepare to listen, becoming aware of the speaker as an individual with information to share, noting and asking relevant questions, thinking ahead, and looking beyond the speakers' mannerisms and idiosyncracies to the content of the message.

UNIT: Selecting Important Ideas

This unit deals with differentiating important from supporting information. A discussion of organizational schemes used in written materials provides a framework for information on using context, using the author's signs and signals, and recognizing key ideas in reading passages. Also emphasized are the ability to recognize different styles of writing, the different places topic sentences may be found, and the importance of flexibility when trying to determine main ideas. These skills are also related to listening activities.

UNIT: Note Taking

Nearly all students take notes. This unit integrates what the student has learned about good listening skills and finding important ideas with techniques for efficient note taking (see examples below).

Effective utilization of notes is also discussed in some depth with an emphasis on thinking about and summarizing key ideas, as well as immediate and periodic reviews.

Note Taking

1. Get a written record of each class.
2. Read your textbook in ADVANCE.
3. Use a note-taking system (e.g., modified Cornell model).
4. Use a modified outline form.
5. Watch for signals of importance (e.g., gestures, key words).
6. Write down examples.
7. Write down connections between ideas.
8. Leave blank spaces for what you miss.
9. Don't stop taking notes toward the end of class.
10. Review as soon as possible after class.

UNIT: Text-Marking and Outlining

Concentration, attention, and recall are improved only when *thinking* precedes marking, highlighting or outlining of the textbook. In Part One of this unit, methods for selecting important ideas are reviewed, and a procedure for active text marking is presented. This procedure emphasizes the value of thinking before marking, the summarization of graphic data, and the identification of relationships among major ideas.

Part Two of the unit is a brief overview of an outlining system. Discussion centers on the major ways that an author may develop a topic, connecting details to major points, and the proper notation for formal outlines.

UNIT: Pre-, During-, and Post-Reading Strategies

Good reading comprehension is a crucial skill at the college level. This unit describes processes for developing good reading comprehension as well as techniques for improving speed and flexibility.

A comprehensive study-reading system involves three stages: (1) a preview, which provides a framework for understanding what the author is writing about; (2) active reading, in which the learner engages in conscious, purposeful, elaborative reading; and (3) a post-reading stage (review), in which the learner evaluates the knowledge gained from the reading and ascertains whether or not there are still gaps in her knowledge.

Reading speed and flexibility are other important skills for students, since many have never learned to vary the way they read to suit the material. A review of organizational schemes used by writers, skimming and scanning exercises, and opportunities to practice are provided to help students increase reading flexibility.

Note: Much of the material already presented in the course is actively and directly integrated into this section.

UNIT: Reading Comprehension/Comprehension Monitoring

Poor learners often do not recognize that they have failed to comprehend material being studied. In addition, even if they do recognize their lack of understanding they may not know how to correct the situation. In this unit students are taught to deliberately analyze their understanding of materials being studied, and whenever comprehension is incomplete, to switch to a more effective processing strategy.

Several strategies useful for monitoring comprehension and active processing are presented. Examples include (1) paraphrasing or interpreting difficult passages into the learner's own terms; (2) formulating questions and answers about the material; (3) rehearsing an explanation of the material that the learner might give to a fellow student; and (4) using strategies to aid comprehension, such as using visual imagery to picture how all the information ties together. Note: Much of the previous material is integrated into this section.

UNIT: Stress, Sanity, and Survival in Academia

Many times students' grades do not reflect their actual abilities, and a major factor is often stress. They get anxious at test time, feel overwhelmed by the amount of work expected of them, or panic because they feel inadequate to accomplish many tasks. The focus of this unit is on how to manage stress in an academic setting. An overview of a model for handling stress is introduced. The model presents stress as a condition that results from our perceptions and/or beliefs about certain events. This allows us to gain and maintain some control over how we choose to react to situations, thus reducing the amount of stress experienced.

Ways that stress may be reduced include changing the situation at an environmental level, weakening the connection between the event and physiological/emotional arousal; and changing irrational beliefs, assumptions, and ineffective ways of thinking to be more reality oriented. Techniques for staying task oriented and exchanging negative self-talk for positive self-talk are also presented.

UNIT: Test-Taking Skills

Exams are an integral part of academic life. Many students face them with a do-or-die attitude and not much else to help them through. In this unit successful preparation and test-taking techniques for both objective and essay tests are presented.

First, a general explanation of how to review for exams is given. The discussion that follows centers on how to study for and take objective tests and how to study for and take essay exams. In the second part of the unit the focus is on a discussion of several related topics. These include "reasoning through to an answer," "test-wiseness principles," "factors influencing failure," "cramming," and "how to make a study-plan guide."

UNIT: Reducing Test Anxiety

This unit is introduced with an unannounced pop quiz. This generates an extremely active discussion in which feelings of hostility and negative thoughts about testing are discussed by the students. The instructor uses feedback from the students to provide examples of how negative self-talk and self-orientation can keep students from doing their best work on exams.

The rest of the lesson is devoted to a discussion of the components of test anxiety and several cognitive and behavioral techniques that can be used before and during an evaluative situation to reduce anxiety to an endurable or less-interfering level. These techniques include actively challenging irrational and negative types of thinking, the practice of thought stopping, how to overcome blocking, using physical relaxation and mind-quieting exercises, and the practicalities of being well-prepared for any exam.

Acknowledgments

The research reported in this chapter was supported in part by Contracts No. MDA903-79-C-0391 and MDA903-82-C-0122 with the Army Research Institute for the Behavioral and Social Sciences. Views and conclusions contained in this chapter are those of the author and should not be interpreted as necessarily representing the official policies, either expressed or implied, of the Army Research Institute, or of the United States government.

REFERENCES

Anastasi, A. (1976). *Psychological testing.* New York: Macmillan.

Anderson, J. R. (1985). *Cognitive psychology and its implications* (2nd ed.). New York: Freeman.

Borkowski, J. G., & Kamfonik, A. (1972). Verbal mediation in moderately retarded children: Effects of successive mediational experiences. *American Journal of Mental Deficiency, 77,* 157–162.

Bower, G. H. (1970). Analysis of a mnemonic device. *American Psychologist, 58,* 496–510.

Brown, A. L. (1975). The development of memory: Knowing, knowing about knowing, and knowing how to know. In H. W. Reese (Ed.), *Advances in child development and behavior* (Vol. 10, pp. 103–152). New York: Academic Press.

Brown, A. L. (1978). Knowing when, where, and how to remember: A problem of metacognition. In R. V. Glaser (Ed.), *Advances in instructional psychology* (pp. 77–163). Hillsdale, NJ: Lawrence Erlbaum.

Brown, A. L., Bransford, W. F., Ferrara, R., & Campione, J. (1983). Learning, remembering, and understanding. In J. Flavell & E. Markman (Eds.), *Handbook of child psychology* (Vol. 3, pp. 77–166). New York: Wiley.

Brown, J. I., Nelson, M. J., & Denny, E. C. (1973). *Nelson–Denny reading test* Boston: Houghton Mifflin.

Brown, W. F. (1964). *Effective Study Test.* San Marcos, TX: Effective Study Materials.

Brown, W. F., & Holtzman. W. H. (1967). *Survey of study habits and attitudes.* New York: The Psychological Corporation.

Carter, H. D. (1958). *California study methods survey.* Monterey, CA: California Test Bureau.

Cavanaugh, J. C., & Perlmutter, M. (1982). Metamemory: A critical examination. *Child Development, 53*(1), 11–28.

Cermak, L. S., & Craik, F. I. M. (1979). *Levels of processing in human memory.* Hillsdale, NJ: Lawrence Erlbaum.

Chi, M. T. H., Feltovich, P. J., & Glaser, R. (1981). Categorization and representation of physics problems by experts and novices. *Cognitive Science, 5,* 121–152.

Christensen, F. A. (1968). *College adjustment and study skills inventory.* Berea, OH: Personal Growth Press.

Dansereau, D. F. (1985). Learning strategy research. In J. Segal, S. Chipman, & R. Glaser (Eds.), *Relating instruction to basic research.* Hillsdale, NJ: Lawrence Erlbaum.

Dansereau, D. F. (in press). Cooperative learning strategies. In C. E. Weinstein, E. T. Goetz, & P. A. Alexander (Eds.), *Learning and study strategies: Issues in assessment, instruction, and evaluation.* New York: Academic Press.

Dansereau, D. F., Collins, K. W., McDonald, B. A., Holley, C. C. P., Garland, J., Diekhoff, G., & Evans, S. H. (1979). Development and evaluation of a learning strategy training program. *Journal of Educational Psychology, 71,* 64–73.

Dillon, R. F., & Schmeck, R. R. (1983). *Individual differences in cognition.* New York: Academic Press.

Flavell, J. H. (1970). Developmental studies of mediated memory. In H. W. Reese & L. P. Lipsitt (Eds.), *Advances in child development and behavior* (Vol. 5). New York: Academic Press.

Flavell, J. H. (1981). Cognitive monitoring. In P. Dickson (Ed.), *Children's oral communication skills.* New York: Academic Press.

Gagne, E. D. (1985). *The cognitive psychology of school learning.* Boston: Little, Brown.

Garner, R. (in press). Verbal-report data on cognitive and metacognitive strategies. In C. E. Weinstein, E. T. Goetz, & P. A. Alexander (Eds.), *Learning and study strategies: Issues in assessment, instruction, and evaluation.* New York: Academic Press.

Glaser, R. (1984). Education and thinking: The role of knowledge. *American Psychologist, 39*(2), 93–104.

Jones, B. F. (in press). Test learning strategy instruction: Guidelines from theory and practice. In C. E. Weinstein, E. T. Goetz, & P. A. Alexander (Eds.), *Learning and study strategies: Issues in assessment, instruction, and evaluation.* New York: Academic Press.

Jones, B. F., Amiran, M. R., & Katims, M. (1985). Embedding structural information and strategy instructions in reading and writing instructional texts: Two models of development. In J. Segal, S. Chipman, & R. Glaser (Eds.), *Relating instruction to basic research.* Hillsdale, NJ: Lawrence Erlbaum.

Kirby, J. R. (Ed.). (1984). *Cognitive strategies and educational performance.* New York: Academic Press.

Larkin, J. H. (1981). Cognition of learning physics. *American Journal of Physics, 49,* 534–541.

McCombs, B. L. (1981, April). *Transitional learning strategies research into practice: Focus on the technical training student.* Paper presented at the annual meeting of the American Educational Research Association, Los Angeles, CA.

McCombs, B. L. (1982a). Transitioning learning strategies research into practice: Focus on the student in technical training. *Journal of Instructional Development, 5*(2), 10–17.

McCombs, B. L. (1982b). Learner satisfaction and motivation: Capitalizing on strategies for positive self control. *Performance and Instruction, 21*(4), 3–6.

McCombs, B. L. (in press). Motivational skills training: Combining metacognitive, cognitive, and affective learning strategies. In C. E. Weinstein, E. T. Goetz, & P. A. Alexander (Eds.), *Learning and study strategies: Issues in assessment, instruction, and evaluation.* New York: Academic Press.

Melton, A. W., & Martin, E. (Eds.). (1972). *Coding processes in human memory.* Washington, D.C.: Winston.

Nickerson, R. S., Salter, W., Shepard, S., & Herrnstein, J. (1984). *The teaching of learning strategies* (Report No. 5578). Cambridge, MA: Bolt, Beranek, and Newman.

Noel, L., & Levitz, R. (Eds.). (1982). *How to succeed with academically underprepared students.* Iowa City: American College Testing Service, National Center for Advancing Educational Practice.

Paivio, A. (1971). *Imagery and verbal processes.* New York: Holt.

Palmer, D. J., & Goetz, E. T. (in press). Selection and use of study strategies: The role of the studier's beliefs about self and strategies. In C. E. Weinstein, E. T. Goetz, & P. A. Alexander (Eds.), *Learning and study strategies: Issues in assessment, instruction, and evaluation.* New York: Academic Press.

Paris, S. C. (in press). Theories and metaphors about learning strategies. In C. E. Weinstein, E. T. Goetz, & P. A. Alexander (Eds.), *Learning and study strategies: Issues in assessment, instruction, and evaluation.* New York: Academic Press.

Pressley, M., & Levin, J. R. (Eds.). (1983a). *Cognitive strategy research: Educational applications.* New York: Springer-Verlag.

Pressley, M., & Levin, J. R. (Eds.). (1983b). *Cognitive strategy research: Psychological foundations.* New York: Springer-Verlag.

Rigney, J. W. (1976). *On cognitive strategies for facilitating acquisition, retention, and retrieval in teaching and education* (Tech. Rep. No. 78). Los Angeles: University of Southern California, Department of Psychology.

Rohwer, W. D., Jr. (1966). Constraints, syntax, and meaning in paired-associate learning. *Journal of Verbal Learning and Verbal Behavior, 5,* 541–547.

Rohwer, W. D., Jr. (1970). Images and pictures in children's learning. *Psychological Bulletin, 73,* 393–403.

Schmeck, R. R. (1983). Learning styles of college students. In R. Dillon & R. Schmeck (Eds.), *Individual differences in cognition.* New York: Academic Press.

Schmeck, R. R. (in press). Individual differences and learning strategies training. Should we accommodate to personal attributes, or change them? In C. E. Weinstein, E. T. Goetz, & P. A. Alexander (Eds.), *Learning and study strategies: Issues in assessment, instruction, and evaluation.* New York: Academic Press.

Schmeck, R. R., Ribich, F., & Ramanaiah, N. (1977). Development of a self-report inventory for assessing individual differences in learning processes. *Applied Psychological Measurement, 1,* 413–431.

Schulte, A. C., & Weinstein, C. E. (1981, April). *Inventories to assess cognitive learning strategies.* Paper presented at the annual meeting of the American Educational Research Association.

Spielberger, C. D., Gonzalez, H. P., Taylor, C. J., Algaze, B., & Anton, W. D. (1978). Examination stress and test anxiety. In C. D. Spielberger & I. G. Sarason (Eds.), *Anxiety and stress* (Vol. 5). New York: Hemisphere/Wiley.

Spielberger, C. D., Gorsuch, R. L., & Luschene, R. E. (1970). *Manual for the state–trait anxiety inventory.* Palo Alto, CA: Consulting Psychologists Press.

Sticht, T. G. (1979). Developing literacy and learning strategies in organization ` ·ettings. In H. F. O'Neil, Jr., & C. D. Spielberger (Eds.), *Cognitive and affective learning* s.`· ·gies. New York: Academic Press.

Svensson, L. (1977). On qualitative differences in learning: III—study skill and learning. *British Journal of Educational Psychology, 47,* 233–243.

Underwood, V. L. (1982). *Self-management skills for college students: A program in how to learn.* Unpublished doctoral dissertation, University of Texas at Austin.

Weinstein, C. E. (1982). Training students to use elaboration learning strategies. *Contemporary Educational Psychology, 7,* 301–311.

Weinstein, C. E., Butterfield, P. J., Schmidt, C. A., & Poythress, M. (1983). *An experimental program for remediating learning strategies deficits in academically underprepared students*

(Final Report). Alexandria, VA: Army Research Institute for the Behavioral and Social Sciences.

Weinstein, C. E., & Mayer, R. E. (1985). The teaching of learning strategies. In M. C. Wittrock (Ed.), *Handbook of research on teaching* (3rd ed.). New York: Macmillan.

Weinstein, C. E., Schulte, A. C., & Cascallar, E. C. (1983). *The Learning and Study Strategies Inventory (LASSI): Initial design and development* (Final Report). Alexandria, VA: Army Research Institute for the Behavioral and Social Sciences.

Weinstein, C. E., & Underwood, V. L. (1985). Learning strategies: The *how* of learning. In J. Segal, S. Chipman, & R. Glaser (Eds.), *Relating instruction to basic research*. Hillsdale, NJ: Lawrence Erlbaum.

Weinstein, C. E., Zimmerman, S. A., & Palmer, D. R. (in press). Assessing learning strategies: The design and development of the LASSI. In C. E. Weinstein, E. T. Goetz, & P. A. Alexander (Eds.), *Learning and study strategies: Issues in assessment, instruction, and evaluation*. New York: Academic Press.

Wittrock, M. C. (1985). Students' thought processes. In M. C. Wittrock (Ed.), *Handbook of research on teaching* (3rd ed.). New York: Macmillan.

Wood, G. C. (1967). Mnemonic systems in recall. *Journal of Educational Psychology, 58,* 1–27.

Yuille, J. C., & Catchpole, M. J. (1973). Associative learning and imagery training in children. *Journal of Experimental Child Psychology, 16,* 403–412.

CHAPTER 12

Strategies and Styles of Learning

An Integration of Varied Perspectives

RONALD RAY SCHMECK

The way we go about accomplishing learning will of course depend upon what we conceive of learning to be. I begin this concluding chapter by discussing definitions of learning. Then, I deal with the approaches students take to the task of learning in school. Approaches are the observable attempts of students to adapt to school, and they reflect both the school environment and the students themselves—individuals made up of unique past experiences and unique styles of perceiving and thinking. I consider some of the variables that contribute to the individuality of the student, including motives, self-concepts, and cognitive styles. I end by considering ways of improving learning, but since we can do little to change personality and cognitive style directly, suggestions generally involve modifications to the school environment.

WHAT IS LEARNING?

Traditional psychologists define learning as relatively permanent changes in behavior. Rightly or wrongly, changes in *verbal* behavior seem to be the focus of most school learning. Furthermore, most of the

---

RONALD RAY SCHMECK • Department of Psychology, Southern Illinois University, Carbondale, Ilinois 62901.

changes measured in the school setting reflect *recall* as demonstrated through reproduction or recognition of the verbal material. Marton, Pask, and Ramsden have all emphasized that changes in verbal behavior indicating recall do not necessarily mean that a student has achieved an understanding, and they argue that understanding should also be an official part of the definition of school learning.

Marton emphasizes that we should strive to measure not only whether the students understand a particular topic but also *how* they understand it. In his own research, he has used a measure that he refers to as "retelling the text," a measure similar in some ways to one Pask calls "teachback." Pask says that people understand a concept when they can derive it from their own mental structures. Pask states, "An 'understood topic' is one for which teachback has been obtained. Teachback involves not only saying what other topics a topic may be derived from, but also how the other topics relate to reproduce the one that is to be understood. It is not enough merely to parrot back a definition; the topic must be used in a novel way that shows the learner's ability to manipulate topics and their entailments and produce a novel interaction" (Chapter 4). Pask goes on to note that, in addition to recall, teachback involves prediction "in Bruner's sense of going beyond the information given," and he adds that "understood topics are resilient" (Chapter 4).

Entwistle, Marton, and Ramsden all discuss research (e.g., Säljö, 1982; Van Rossum & Schenck, 1984) concerned with the conception that students hold of the learning process. If you ask students what learning means to them, different students will describe different conceptions of the process. At one end of a continuum you will find a quantitative conception in which learning is described as the accumulation of facts or bits and pieces of information, or knowledge. At the other end of the continuum, you will find students who have a more qualitative view in which learning is seen to involve the interpretation and reinterpretation of experience to produce self-actualization or personal growth and development. Similarly, with regard to conception of writing, Biggs describes a study by Hounsell (1984) in which students on the quantitative end of the continuum who saw writing as "a loose collection of thoughts and ideas" were contrasted with those on the qualitative end who felt that "data and organization were subordinate to the overall interpretative stance adopted by the writer" (Biggs, Chapter 8).

Marton has pointed out on several occasions that teachers hold conceptions of the learning process similar to those Säljö found in students and that may explain where students get their conceptions. Entwistle, Marton, and Ramsden all point out that students sense the relation between learning process and learning outcome, and they study so as to produce the outcome that they expect the teacher to assess. Ramsden says, "The evaluation process provides a signal to students about the kind of learning they are expected to carry out; they adapt by choosing strategies that will apparently maximize success" (Chapter 7). If students see teachers rewarding the parroting of words from textbooks and lectures, they will memorize those words literally through repetition and recitation, and they will acquire not only facts but also shallow, quantitative conceptions of the learning process.

As Marton points out, the student with a quantitative view of learning does not include arriving at a new, personal conceptualization of something in his or her definition of the process. If the author of a textbook has tried to encourage the development of some new conceptualization or way of interpreting reality, a student with a quantitative conception of learning will simply memorize the original words of the author as though they were "facts." As noted above, Pask felt that topics were understood only when students could *derive them from their own mental structures.* Yet, Säljö (1982) says students with a quantitative conception of learning "do not see it as the purpose of the overall situation they are in [i.e., school] to confront their preconceived assumptions with ideas presented by the author" (p. 186). Obviously, the latter students are not likely to achieve what Pask is calling an understanding.

Das agrees with Luria (e.g., 1981) that it is the nature of a fully functioning brain to continue to integrate information after it has been coded, associating neural codes of related experiences to continue to form higher-level codes. Indeed, most of the human cortex is not projection area, in which simple and initial codings of sensory experience and motor programming occur, but rather it is association area where a sort of *re*coding can occur through interrelating and integrating coded information. This integration (or higher-level coding of lower-level codes) should be included in our definition of learning. and our tests should assess it as one of the expected outcomes of learning.

Our authors are not denying that recall is part of learning. Students sometimes have to "memorize" in order to add new words, ideas, and algorithms to their cognitive tool kits. Also, perhaps minimal amounts of experience have to be coded before more integrative functions can operate. Das (1980) says of one high-level, integrative function (planning): "results demonstrated . . . that planning evolves from coding . . . at an earlier state of competence, planning and coding are not independent" (p. 149). Thus, perhaps memorization may be especially necessary in early phases of learning in new and unfamiliar content areas. However, learning also includes recoding—Das' "information integration" and Marton's "interpretation of coded experiences from new and different perspectives."

In summary, from a behavioral point of view, learning is a relatively permanent change in behavior and, in the school setting, a relatively permanent change in verbal behavior. Furthermore, the measures of learning used in most schools and in most research labs, for that matter, assess recall but rarely understanding of verbal information. Yet, seeing a phenomenon from a new point of view, interpreting reality in a new and different way, or integrating initially separate bits of information may be more important in the long run than being able to recall a list of facts or rules or memorizing someone else's conclusion without understanding its derivation. We saw above that qualitative researchers who allowed learners to tell them what learning "meant" reported that the most mature students include "self-actualization and seeing reality from new points of view" in their definitions of the process. Furthermore, Luria's research (cf. Das, Chapter 5) suggests that it is the nature of a fully functioning brain to continually integrate experience, in addition to coding it (cf. Marton, Chapter 3).

The remainder of the chapter examines school learning from the perspective of a classic "person by situation interaction"—students perceiving, reacting to, and adapting to school settings. Past experiences and interpretations, as they are influenced by cognitive style, determine students' perceptions of the demands made by the school setting. Reactions to these demands produce feedback (further experience) which further determines future perceptions and behaviors. I begin with the approaches students take, reflecting both the environment and the students themselves. Then, I review factors determining the individuality of the student (the "person"), and finally, review ways of improving learning by altering the situation.

APPROACHES TO LEARNING

Biggs defined an *approach* to learning as "the learning processes that emerge from students' perceptions of the academic task, as influenced by their personal characteristics" (Chapter 8). Later he said, "approaches to learning stem from the interaction, mediated by metalearning, between the general orientations that an individual displays across particular learning situations and over time, on the one hand, and the current task and situational demands, on the other" (Chapter 8).

In Biggs' view, an approach to learning represents the deployment of a learning strategy based upon metacognitive knowledge (similar to Das' "planning"). Biggs notes, "a self-conscious and planful approach to learning thus requires, first, that students are aware of their motives and intentions, of their own cognitive resources, and of the demands of academic tasks; and second, that they are able to control those resources and monitor their consequent performance" (Chapter 8). Most of the authors of the present text would agree that two basic approaches to learning are "surface and deep." I discuss them one at a time.

Marton notes that a *surface approach* to learning leads to a learning outcome that is essentially a literal reproduction of the words of text-book authors or instructors. Furthermore, the surface approach does not include perception of the holistic structure of information but instead *atomizes* it into disconnected bits and pieces that are memorized through repetition. Thus, individuals taking a surface approach are likely to have a quantitative conception of the process. If the outcome is organized at all, it is merely a stringing together of the memorized bits and pieces of information.

Marton suggests that individuals taking a surface approach fail to derive full meaning, including implications and connections, from information because they fail to perceive the structure of the information in the first place. The learner taking a surface approach often doesn't perceive that two things are related, much less that they are hierarchically related. I suggest below that this perceptual failure can occur when learners have not developed or do not apply the brain's more "global" skills during studying. Also, in Das' terms, such a learner would not fully integrate information that has been coded.

In the context of writing, Biggs referred to a *knowledge-telling* approach; he also uses the terms *linear* and *bed-to-bed* writing (in which writers simply list what happened from the time they got out of bed in the morning until they went to bed at night without any attempt to interpret or make sense of their experiences). With regard to one such student, Biggs commented upon "the inadequacy of her own inner resources" and her "need to latch on to any cues to define the boundaries of the knowledge she is to retell" (Chapter 8). McCarthy and Schmeck argue that such an "inadequacy of inner resources" results from insufficient development of a self-concept, or integrated identity.

On the other end of the continuum of approaches to learning, we have what Marton calls a *deep approach*, which produces an outcome that represents the "communicative intent" of the author or instructor rather than a literal reproduction of his or her strings of words. A deep approach, according to Marton, includes perception of the holistic organization of material studied, and the components of the learning outcome are hierarchically nested rather than simply being strung together sequentially. The person who takes a deep approach to learning has a qualitative conception of the process, including the interpretation and reinterpretation of experience leading ultimately to self-actualization.

Kirby and Marton note that students who take such an approach to reading a text will have the intention of *extracting meaning* from words, not focusing on words as an end in themselves but rather going from words to suppositions regarding meaning and back to the actual words again. Kirby says, "there must be a rather careful balancing and cross-checking of evidence and interpretations, with the details constituting evidence for the more abstract propositions or interpretations" (Chapter 9).

Similarly, with regard to writing, Biggs reports that students who take a deep approach describe the writing of an essay as the preparation of an integrated argument supported by evidence, whereas those taking a surface approach say merely that it involves the presentation of facts in an ordered form. Biggs also notes that writers taking a deep approach use a "reflective strategy" involving interpretation and integration of components, producing higher-order knowledge from lower-order inputs. In reflective writing, one "treats one's own thought as the object of further thought" (Biggs, Chapter 8).

Elsewhere Biggs says, "A deep approach involves metacognition, in that the search for meaning involves one in monitoring and reshaping one's own thought, whereas a surface approach is simply reactive" (p. 48). Biggs emphasizes that writers who take a deep approach focus their attention more at the discourse level and less at the word or even the sentence level, postponing low-level editing until after initial composition. This is reminiscent of Marton's original description of the distinguishing characteristic of a deep approach to reading—focusing attention on intended meanings more than on letters and words.

As suggested above, Marton emphasizes that a deep approach requires that students be sensitive to relations among topics—to structure. He says, "changes in meaning originate from acts of structuring; but on the other hand, acts of structuring presuppose changes in meaning; the two aspects of the learner's activity thus being intertwined in a dialectical interplay" (Chapter 3). This latter quote reminds me of Biggs' description of "reflective writing" mentioned above—one's thoughts treated as the object of further thought.

Marton notes that, "in order to establish a structure, that is, relations between components, these components have to be seen in relation to each other, they have to be seen as parts of the same whole" (Chapter 3). Ironically, both Biggs and Marton note that a surface strategy seems to include an element of perceptual style that actually interferes with perceptions of relations: "the reproductive nature of a surface strategy . . . omits *or avoids* the interrelations that may exist between components of the task" (Biggs, Chapter 8, italics added). I argue below that one of the reasons that students may take a surface approach to a reading or writing task is that they lack the holistic or global perceptual and cognitive skills that permit them to see interrelations and structure. In this sense, cognitive style sets limits to the approaches to learning that one can take.

Ramsden describes experiments by Säljö (1975), who structured situations to prompt students to take either a surface or deep approach. He found that most students were adaptable, versatile, and fully sensitive to the situation, but there were some who took a surface approach even when a deep approach was called for. Furthermore, Ramsden says that in general, "surface approaches could be induced in students relatively easily, while changes in the types of questions asked did not necessarily lead to the use of deep approaches" (Chapter 7). Since the situation was varied as part of the experiment, such style-like persistence (i.e., use of a surface approach in a situation which called for a deep approach) would seem to be due to personal characteristics of students, something they bring with them to the situation. Ramsden says, "It is perhaps the case that some students perceive the environment as one demanding shallow memorization even when the instructor intends for the reverse to be true."

A student learning in a classroom context is involved in a "person by situation interaction" in which styles and motives of individuals influence perception of situational cues and moderate reactions to the situation. Personal style affects approach, but we can only see the person's approach, not his or her style. Because of their desire to emphasize this complex person-by-situation chemistry, Entwistle and Ramsden label cross-situational consistency or regularity in approach to school learning an "orientation to studying" and reserve the word *style* for the information processing routines that are more traitlike and are traditionally called *cognitive* styles.

MOTIVES, SELF-CONCEPT, AND ORIENTATION

Since an orientation to studying indicates cross-situational consistency in approach to learning, it is worth repeating Biggs' definition of approach: "the learning processes that emerge from students' perceptions of the academic task, as influenced by their personal characteristics" (Chapter 8). Thus, personal characteristics influence perception of the situation, and the stability of those characteristics account for cross-situational consistency in behavior. The most stable personal characteristic of all is probably cognitive style, but motives also tend to be relatively stable. Perception involves an act of classification (e.g., "this is a *test*"), and if a particular motive is very strong (e.g., fear of evaluation), then it may excessively influence the perceptual categorization or prototyping process perhaps by narrowing cue utilization (e.g., to some people "everything looks like a test"). This is where Entwistle's "motives" and McCarthy and Schmeck's discussion of "self-esteem" become important. Entwistle notes that qualitative analysis of interviews with students have always revealed that one of the most crucial components of approach to learning is the student's *intentions*. Motives describe the broad personal concerns that affect perception and generate intentions. These motives are related to the mechanisms that students have developed for maintaining their self-esteem, as discussed by McCarthy and Schmeck.

Entwistle and Wilson (1977) used factor analysis to reveal three basic motives of students successful in school. Factor analyses separated three groups of successful students: one motivated by "hope for success" (Atkinson & Feather, 1966), one by "fear of failure" (Birney, Burdick & Teevan, 1969), and one by "academic interest." Thus, we have need for achievement, fear of failure, and sincere interest in the subject matter. Similarly, Fransson (1977) demonstrated the importance of threat, or anxiety, and intrinsic motivation as determiners of approach. Perceptions seemed to result as much from the motives of students as from the actual learning situation, and these perceptions ultimately affected the approach students took. For example, Fransson (1977) found students' routine level of text anxiety (fear-of-failure motive) had a bigger effect on their approach to learning than did the level of threat that he actually tried to create within the situation.

Let's review the three motives and the three related orientations to studying discussed by Entwistle (Chapter 2). The three orientations are meaning, reproducing, and achieving. If a student has the habit of using a deep approach across varying situations, this is an indicator of what Entwistle calls a *meaning orientation*. A bias in favor of taking a surface approach across a variety of situations would be an indicator of a *reproducing orientation*. And cross-situational consistency in using what Entwistle calls a strategic approach suggests the presence of an *achieving orientation*. The three orientations described by Biggs in Chapter 8 are very similar to these.

The three motives associated with the three orientations are need for achievement, fear of failure, and personal interest. Entwistle says of the achieving orientation: "The strategic approach, linked to competitive achievement motivation, describes the tactics used by students mainly concerned with reinforcing their academic self-concept through repeated demonstrations of intellectual mastery" (Chapter 2). We also have Biggs definition: "The affective orientation of [such] students . . . is based on manifesting one's excellence relative to other students, specifically in obtaining grades that are as high as possible" (Chapter 8). Similarly, Eison and his colleagues (1981, 1982; Eison & Pollio, 1985; Eison, Pollio, &

Milton, 1986) suggest that the critical motivational indicator is the extent to which grades dominate the students perceptions. Eison distinguishes between "grade-oriented" and "learning-oriented" students. The difference between students with an achieving orientation motivated by the achievement motive and students with a reproducing orientation, motivated by fear of failure, concerns expectations. While achieving students are drawn by expectations of success, seeking to increase their "score," students with fear of failure, although similarly needful, are nagged by self-doubts and strive to "get by" while securing as little damage as possible.

I and my colleagues found that students who perform poorly at writing essays report strong self-doubts (low self-efficacy) with regard to such tasks (Meier, McCarthy, & Schmeck, 1984). Also, those who notice most the surface (e.g., rhyme) features of texts tend to be higher on neuroticism (Schmeck & Spofford, in press). This same type of individual is high on both chronic and evaluation-related anxieties (Schmeck & Ribich, 1978; see Schmeck, 1983, for a lengthy discussion). Entwistle (Chapter 2) and Fransson (1977) emphasize the relationships between fear of failure and surface approaches that they have found in their own research.

Entwistle states that for the student with a reproducing orientation, there is a "perception of learning as something imposed by an external authority . . . learning is seen narrowly in terms of the prescribed syllabus and the specific task requirements. What is to be learned is limited to the knowledge presented, and so the processes of learning become altogether more mechanical, concentrating on overlearning and verbatim recall. Although considerable effort may still be put into this type of learning, there is less chance of even the details being remembered. . . . Even facts have to be embedded within a semantic framework if they are to be readily recalled out of the immediate context in which they were initially learned" (Chapter 2).

Biggs notes that one particular student with a reproducing orientation commented that when writing an essay she felt you had to "give back what you've been given" (Chapter 8), and as noted above, Biggs argued that this attitude "reflects . . . the inadequacy of her own inner resources and the need therefore to latch on to any cues to define the boundaries of the knowledge she is to retell." In one case, he points out that it was the student with a reproducing orientation who got the lower grade on an essay in spite of the fact that it was her thinking "that was dominated by the function of summative evaluation that the essay is to serve." Also with regard to creativity, Biggs suggested that students with a reproducing orientation actively *avoid* originality, writing for the instructor "under pressure to conform to his *presumed* biases" (Chapter 8).

Although the motives of achievement and fear of failure differ with regard to the expectations that students have, that is, success versus failure, the two are quite similar in another respect. McCarthy and Schmeck note that in both cases individuals look outward, *look to others,* for evidence of self-worth. This can be contrasted with the more "intrinsic" motivation of students who take a truly deep approach to learning. Fransson (1977) reported that students who were reading out of personal interest took a deep approach. Entwistle describes the students who habitually take a deep approach as having a meaning orientation—"an inclination to learn out of interest, as a form of personal development, it may also be seen to indicate how the intention to understand is empirically and logically linked to subsequent learning processes necessitated by that intention . . . these learning processes are found to include selection of salient material, organization of that material, reasoning, questioning, relating, and personalizing" (Chapter 2). As indicated above, Eison (1982) describes such a student as "learning-oriented" rather than "grade-oriented" (Eison & Pollio, 1985; Eison, Pollio, & Milton, 1986). Eison has published a scale for assessing differences between students on this dimension. It is called the LOGO Scale (i.e., Learning-Oriented–Grade-Oriented; Eison, 1981).

Everyone has personal interests of one sort or another. However, when interests or motives involve defending against self-doubts, McCarthy and Schmeck point out that other motives tend to assume a secondary position on the individual's personal agenda. It is as though the person has a compulsion to above all else "look good" (or avoid "looking bad") to others—anchoring virtually all self-esteem in the external environment (see McCarthy & Schmeck, Chapter 6). This agenda can prevent achieving or failure-avoidant students from having true self-interest, that is, it can keep them from perceiving their more "subtle passions." As Entwistle says, the distinction is "between learning for personal understanding and development and learning necessitated by fulfilling the requirements of others" (Chapter 2).

McCarthy and Schmeck argue that self-esteem of achieving and failure-avoidant students is not self-sustaining. Such students are nagged by doubts regarding self-worth and personal adequacy. Somehow, through accidents of development, they seem to never have been sufficiently convinced that they had a full complement of "basic physical and cognitive equipment." They seem to have a constant need to prove something, and those with an achievement motive are convinced that they *can* do it, while those with a fear of failure are convinced they *can't* (at least not alone). McCarthy and Schmeck argue that students with a meaning orientation have a greater reserve of unconditional self-respect, allowing them to shift their attention to subtle personal interests regardless of interests and needs of other people. This freedom allows them, from time to time, to pursue their inner voices—that is, to self-actualize.

Biggs reports evidence that the achieving orientation is often married in different individuals to either deep or surface approaches to learning, yielding two subtypes of achieving students: "deep-achievers" and "surface-achievers." Similarly, Entwistle reported evidence that the achievement motive can be "allied with deep, surface, or strategic approaches, depending on the student's individual conceptions of learning and purposes in studying" (Chapter 2). It is interesting to speculate that students with intense fears of failure might on occasion progress from *surface* to *surface-achieving* to *deep-achieving* and ultimately to *deep* in their habitual approach to learning. Periodic success experienced by students habitually taking a surface approach might slowly shift expectations from fear of failure to hope for success, thereby making them "surface-achievers." They may then eventually experience enough success to put aside self-esteem issues on occasion and become aware of personal interests and opinions, leading the students to become "deep-achievers" and ultimately fully "deep" in their approach to learning.

I noted above that personal characteristics influence *perception* of situations, and stability of personal characteristics can account for cross-situational consistency in a person's behavior. I also suggested that the most stable characteristic of all was cognitive style. I turn now to a discussion of that characteristic.

COGNITIVE STYLES

I feel that all cognitive styles can be encompassed by one broad, inclusive dimension of individual difference, labeled "global versus analytic" by Kirby (Chapter 9), "holist versus serialist" by Pask (Chapter 4), and "right versus left-brained" by Torrance and Rockenstein (Chapter 10). "Field-dependent versus field-independent" is a related dimension studied at length by Witkin and his colleagues (e.g., Witkin, Moore, Goodenough, & Cox, 1977). The term "global versus articulated (or differentiated)" has also been applied to this dimension of perceptual or attentional style. "Impulsive versus reflective" (Kogan, 1976), and "category breadth" (Wallach & Kogan, 1965) are likewise relevant. I am arguing that all of these, at some level of abstraction. are reflections of a single dimension that I label "global versus analytic," similar to Kirby's terminology (Chapter 9). I would like to describe these two dimensions, and then at the end of this section relate them to approaches to learning and the more style-like orientations to studying.

THE TWO STYLES

In general, it is important to note that what I am calling two "styles" are actually two extreme ends on a continuum that in the extreme are not softened by the influence of the opposing end. Kirby (Chapter 9) says it is like describing two "partial styles," with the ultimate developmental position being a synthesis of the two. I discuss this further below.

People with an extreme *analytic* style are field independent and have focused attention, noticing and remembering details. They have an interest in operations and procedures, or the "proper" ways of doing things and prefer step-by-step, sequential organizational schemes. Their thinking, like their attention, is more controlled and consciously directed than that of individuals with a global style. This control and focus of attention allows them to divorce feelings from objective "facts." They are gifted at critical and logical thinking. They are also gifted at seeing differences between apparently similar experiences, in contrast to the global thinker, who is gifted at seeing similarities between apparently different experiences.

Individuals with a *global* style are field dependent with attention tending toward scanning, leading to the formation of global impressions rather than more precisely articulated codes. Rather than linear and sequential, their organizational schemes involve more random or multiple accessibility of components, allowing numerous and varied associations between coded experiences. Their thinking is more intuitive than that of an analytic person, including entry of feelings into decisions. The emphasis on conscious control and directing of thoughts is less evident, and global individuals are likely to be more impulsive than analytic thinkers. Also, as noted above, they are more gifted at seeing similarities than differences.

Both Das and Kirby make distinctions between simultaneous and successive coding processes. Kirby says, "simultaneous processing involves the coding of a set of information into a unitary representation which is gestaltic or quasi-spatial in nature, whereas successive processing involves the coding of information into a sequence or temporally dependent series" (Chapter 9). Das notes (Chapter 5) that people have "preferred modes of processing," and Kirby adds, "I would suggest that the global style and its strategies employ simultaneous processing, while the analytic style and its strategies employ successive processing. . . . The synthetic style consists of the integration and orchestration of these clusters of styles, strategies, and skills."

Pask studied individuals who were in the process of trying to understand a body of information. By having them request information and externalize their thinking, he could observe stylistic differences. He found that "serialists" (presumably individuals with an analytic style) "showed intention to search for specific data," while "holists" (presumably with a global style) "test a large predicate or relational hypothesis" (see p. 12 in Pask's Chapter 4). Interestingly, Pask found that serialist learners actually examine less data overall than holists, searching step by step to confirm or disconfirm one specific hypothesis at a time. In general, holists scan large amounts of data searching for patterns and relations. Pask also reported that holists had a greater tolerance for uncertainty than did serialists with regard to the "correctness" of their hypotheses. Like Kirby, Pask argues that the best cognitive style for "understanding" isn't really a style at all in the traditional sense but is more like the *absence* of rigid, style-like consistency. He labels this latter state a "versatile style" (similar to Kirby's "synthetic style").

Before looking at the development of cognitive style, let's examine the relationship between cognitive style and approach to learning or, more appropriately, orientation to studying.

STYLE VERSUS ORIENTATION

As noted earlier, the orientation a person takes to studying reflects a habitual, cross-situational preference for one of the approaches to learning, and such a preference is determined by the person's motives and cognitive style. Earlier, I discussed motives as determiners of orientation to studying, and now I turn to cognitive style. Marton believes atomistic and sequential structuring of information (the type typical of Kirby's analytic style) are most prevalent in surface approaches to learning, while holistic and hierarchical structuring (Kirby's global style) are more common in deep approaches. This should not be taken to suggest that analytic style and surface approach or global style and deep approach are the same, but they are certainly related.

Several of our authors argue that extreme reliance on an analytic style of cognition (what Pask calls an "improvidence" pathology) virtually forces students to take a surface approach to learning. Indeed, Pask (Chapter 4) specifically describes one type of serialist who relies solely on rote memory. Likewise, I noted earlier that after emphasizing the importance of structuring information, Marton states, "in order to establish a structure, that is, relations between components, these components have to be seen in relation to each other, they have to be seen as parts of the same whole" (Chapter 3). I likewise noted earlier that Biggs maintains, "the reproductive nature of a surface strategy . . . omits or avoids the interrelations that may exist between components of the task. . ." (Chapter 8). What I am suggesting is that the deeper structures of information are not noticed by many students taking a surface approach to learning because they have an extremely analytic (focused) cognitive style. As Pask notes, "sensitivity to the relations of topics" is part of a global style of cognition (not an analytic style).

Yet, students showing only an extreme global style of cognition— the pathology Pask labels "globetrotting"—are not necessarily able to take a deep approach either. In addition to perception of relations and patterns, a truly deep approach requires critical evaluation, a hallmark of the analytic cognitive style and what Torrance and Rockenstein call "creating-by-improving." The approach to learning taken by Pask's globetrotting (extremely global) individual is probably what Kirby calls "primitive deep," Entwistle describes as "disorganized," and Biggs (1984) describes as "idealist"—oriented toward meaningful learning but lacking appropriate organization and generally performing very poorly in the school setting. If such globetrotters survive the school experience at all, they probably do it by pragmatically memorizing, just like the extremely analytic individual, otherwise they are no longer in the school system.

True *understanding* resulting from a meaning orientation and deep approach requires Pask's "versatile style," or Kirby's "synthetic style." According to Pask, a versatile style permits "the integration of both local and global rules . . . both serial strategies and holistic strategies . . . needed to achieve an understanding." Entwistle (1981, and Chapter 2, this volume) has emphasized that a deep approach (or meaning orientation) to any task, whether problem solving, reading, writing, decision making, or learning, requires proficiency in, and integration of, both modes of functioning: globally seeing connections (relation) in the data to form conclusions or generalizations and critically evaluating and revising those conclusions in light of further analysis of the evidence.

Torrance and Rockenstein (Chapter 10) argue that thinking focused predominantly in the right hemisphere of the brain (presumably global thinking) is necessary for "creating-by-inventing," while thinking involving the left hemisphere (analytic thinking) is conducive to "creating-by-improving." Torrance and Rockenstein emphasize that a truly creative contribution to culture and technology requires both modes of functioning, something that they call "whole-brain thinking."

Marton speaks of cycling from experience to interpretation of experience and back to experience again, hopefully seeing it from a new perspective. Also, Marton emphasizes periodic "structuring" as a vital component of a deep approach to learning. He says, "changes in meaning originate from acts of structuring; but on the other hand, acts of structuring presuppose changes in meaning; the two aspects of the learner's activity thus being intertwined in a dialectical interplay" (Chapter 3). Entwistle found such versatility to be rare, with few students "able to carry through all the component processes demanded by a fully deep approach which would have resulted in a fully deep level of understanding (Chapter 2).

Turning now to suggestions regarding the developmental process from which this versatility in functioning arises, keep in mind that cognitive style and approach to learning interact dynamically. Cognitive style influences approach to learning and approach to learning determines the nature of the learning outcome (neural traces, programs. etc.) which, in time, may change the person, including his or her cognitive style. Shapiro (1965) suggested a sort of crystallization process in which the style we practiced most in the past leaves traces, making it more and more likely we'll use the same style in the future. Shapiro has said that what we perceive is a result of what we attend to, and what we attend to is a result of the actual stimulus situation plus what we remember about that type of situation from our last experience of it. If we form global impressions, we will remember global impressions and notice global features in the future. If we notice specific details, we will remember details and be attuned to them next time.

Style becomes more and more "crystallized" as we approach subsequent tasks with perceptual category systems and interpretations developed in the past. Schmeck (1983) provides a detailed description of an experiment regarding retrieval cues ("hints") and cognitive style used in a memory task. He and his colleague Mark Spofford found that "deep, meaningful learners" profited most from deep (semantic) retrieval cues ("hints"), while "surface learners" profited most from being given very shallow, *rhyme* cues. Perhaps, as Shapiro (1965) says, that which was meaningful to the subjects in the past, that which caught their attention, will tend to catch their attention in the future and will perhaps lead more and more to crystallization of a "style" of cognition.

DEVELOPMENT OF COGNITIVE STYLE

Kirby's explanation for the development of reading comprehension has implications with regard to the development of cognitive style in general. In his own words, "The three phases of reading skill development are analogous to three different reading styles. . . . The global phase represents a style . . . relying far more on expectations and predicted meanings than is wise . . . characterized by a disinclination to analyze the printed word carefully . . . often termed impulsive. . . . The analytic phase is . . . too much data driven . . . corresponds to Pask's 'improvidence' pathology, discussed in his chapter . . . focuses on the identification (naming) of words rather than the extraction of meaning. . . . The synthetic style, on the other hand, requires . . . both sorts of skills . . . similar to the 'versatile' style discussed by Pask in his chapter" (Kirby, Chapter 9). Kirby also suggests that reading skill develops in spiral fashion. Students may have achieved an advanced synthetic style for performing lower-level tasks such as simple "word identification" but still be using a less-advanced global style to perform higher-level, more-difficult tasks such as "meaning generation."

Furthermore, in the performance of any type of task people can get stuck, or developmentally fixated, in either the global or analytic stage of functioning. Students begin reading with a global and not very successful style, and then they achieve some success through focused analysis of written symbols—as Kirby says, they "crack the code." This is the point at which global skills must be reintegrated to achieve higher-level comprehension. Das and Kirby note that when children first start achieving success at reading, analytic skill definitely predicts performance. However, at higher levels of reading comprehension measures of *global* skill correlate most with performance. Das says, "simultaneous processing may be necessary for the development of a more-advanced level of comprehension" (Chapter 5), and Kirby notes that the highest levels of reading comprehension require a synthetic style: "in contrasting good and poor readers, we are not contrasting one style with another but rather contrasting two partial styles with an integrated one" (Kirby, Chapter 9).

Theoretically then, at the highest level of cognitive development everyone would have a synthetic cognitive style. However, the student with an analytic style is temporarily on "safe ground" since he or she just achieved some success. Integration at this point temporarily disrupts a working solution, that is, disrupts the smooth flow of success. McCarthy and Schmeck argue that the integration of global and analytical skills necessary for higher-level comprehension may require a reserve of unconditional self-esteem that individuals can fall back upon when success rates are reduced temporarily during new integrative learning. This may explain the origin of cognitive style. Some children with doubts regarding self-worth learn to overcome basic fears of inadequacy by "proving" themselves, that is, by establishing conditional worth in a context of achievement and competition. This required, as Kirby says, that they "crack the code" using analytic skills. McCarthy and Schmeck suggest that this new feeling of worth acquired with controlled, analytic forms of thinking is difficult to give up, even temporarily. The student who clings to this way of feeling "OK" might continue to demonstrate an analytic cognitive style.

On the other hand, if early doubts resulting from insufficient unconditional regard cannot even be overcome through personal achievements (e.g., if the person has difficulty "cracking the code" or doesn't get enough approval–attention from others for achievements), then the student may be left with neither positive regard nor hope of earning it, leaving vague, unconscious fears that he or she cannot make it alone—an uneasiness manifested whenever independent thought and action or competition are called for. In general, such individuals are happier, even in adulthood, if they have someone else (a teacher) or something else (e.g., a set of rules) "to depend upon," that is, they are happier if someone else takes responsibility. This may result in fixation on global, field-dependent styles of thinking—childlike and undirected.

The reader interested in empirical relationships between parenting style and cognitive style of children should read an excellent review by Rothbart and Posner (1985). The latter authors report that mothers who are sensitive to subtle gestures and other behavioral indicators of infant impulses (intentions?) seem to help the infants implement those impulses and thereby promote development of a sense of self, an internal source of direction. Dyk (1969) reported that these infants became more field independent than is the case in those infants with mothers who tend to "twist" infants expressions to somehow satisfy their own needs or fears. This latter parenting style hinders the development of a sense of self in the infant and results in a child who is more field dependent. The reader is urged also to refer to a discussion by Winnicott (1965) that links these same parenting styles to development of what he calls the "false-self," an identity dependent solely upon the influences of other people.

With regard to *writing*, Biggs presented interviews with two students who took a surface approach. He notes, "Both these last two students show, in various degrees of desperation, the need to turn to external resources to structure their work—to, as it were, tell them what to say" (Chapter 8). With regard to Anne (a surface learner) and Emma (a deep learner) he says, "It is interesting and important to note that Anne and Emma had the same marker, yet only Anne felt under pressure to conform to his *presumed* biases. Her need to 'give back what you've been given' thus reflects rather the inadequacy of her own inner resources and the need therefore to latch on to any cues to define the boundaries of the knowledge she is to *retell*. Not surprisingly, Emma obtained a higher grade for the essay than did Anne, despite the fact that it is Anne's thinking that is dominated by the function of . . . evaluation that the essay is to serve."

Biggs stated that students who took a surface approach to writing often reviewed and revised too frequently and too soon, especially at the word and sentence level. Such students would experience writer's block more frequently. This suggests too much emphasis on analytic skill, or Torrance and Rockenstein's creating-by-improving, and too little willingness to think globally, or as Torrance and Rockenstein put it, to create-by-inventing. Such students seem compelled to improve before inventing is complete, and that may be why the writer's block occurs. Biggs also suggests that students with a surface approach to learning actively avoid originality in their writing, believing that you should only "give back what you've been given" (Chapter 8). The emphasis on revising and criticizing coupled with avoidance of originality again suggests that surface writers have excess analytic (left-brained) thinking and insufficient global (right-brained) thinking. Once again, I'm reminded of Entwistle's (Chapter 2) finding that many students attempting to take a deep approach to learning either spend a disproportionate amount of time relating ideas without examining evidence sufficiently or spend too much time on factual details without having a clear overview. In either case, the outcome falls short of a deep level of understanding.

I turn now to an attempt to apply to education the ideas discussed in this text and summarized in the present chapter. We will see that varied approaches to research and to theory building have in fact led to plenty of agreement with regard to what is needed to improve education.

IMPROVING EDUCATION

It is conceivable (cf. Craik & Lockhart, 1972; Schmeck, 1981, 1983; Schmeck, Ribich, & Ramanaiah, 1977) that one could structure learning situations so that some subjects would perform better if they were *not* *trying* to learn. These subjects would learn more if they were instructed to perform a task that forced them to process information deeply and elaborately while remaining unaware that their memory was to be tested. This suggests that the cognitive processes engaged when people *try* to learn are less effective for learning than the processes that occur when they are instructed to perform tasks that draw attention to meanings. For example, they would do better if asked to make judgments concerning, for example, the category membership of a piece of information, or a comparison between it and some other information, or to perform some sort of elaboration using their personal experiences. The subjects in question apparently see the instructions to "learn" as demanding something other than the latter activities, for example, they may see it as a demand for repetition in preparation for some sort of recitation (cf. Schmeck, 1981).

Ramsden says, "Context differences impose on or suggest to students different strategies of learning; individuals try to adapt to the demands and opportunities presented by the content of what is to be learned and its institutional setting." Furthermore, he states that, "students never receive teachers' instructions completely passively . . . they adapt to the context by trying 'to deliver what the teacher is predicted to reward'" (Chapter 7). The point of this and the previous paragraph is that when students confront a situation that demands learning (e.g., school), they employ the cognitive processes that they believe to be appropriate for the task, and their decisions are based on past experience with such tasks. They do not necessarily employ the deep approach that is necessary for an understanding to develop.

Approach to learning begins with one's definition of learning, but it involves other things as well. For example, even if students want to understand material, their fears (cf. Entwistle. Chapter 2, and McCarthy and Schmeck, Chapter 6) or the level to which they've developed their cognitive skills (cf. Kirby, Chapter 9) may make it difficult for them to engage in the activities that lead to understanding. Since it all begins with one's definition (or conception) of learning, I begin the next section, concerning ways to improve education, with that topic.

REDEFINING LEARNING

I noted at the beginning of this chapter that teachers who hold shallow, quantitative conceptions of the learning process, defining it as some sort of accumulation of bits and pieces of information, are likely to make demands on students which teach them to define learning, to define their responsibilities as students, in a similar quantitative fashion. For example, Ramsden said that, "There is evidence that the learning tasks set in the early elementary school are influential in developing a quantitative and unreflective conception of learning" (Chapter 7).

Thus, we have the students Marton (Chapter 3) described, who leave university physics or economics classes with passing or even high grades and yet have no understanding of the most basic concepts that lie at the root of the various facts and rules that they so successfully memorized. Marton says, "How is it possible that educational experiences so often fail to bring about conceptual changes in the most fundamental respects? The fact is that students may acquire huge bodies of knowledge (clusters of facts) without appropriating the conceptualizations on which those bodies of knowledge are based." Similarly, we have adults who do not see it as their function to reflect, form opinions, evaluate, disagree, oppose, challenge, conceptualize and reconceptualize, or integrate information in meaningful ways. We have adults who plod along without thought until, at roughly 10-year intervals, they have what has come to be popularly known as the "midlife crisis"—permitting themselves for one brief period to ask "What does it all mean?"

I agree with Marton that those of us who want to influence the direction of education should begin by urging current and future educators to reevaluate their definitions of learning. On a very general level, teachers can ask themselves to what extent quantitative indices (e.g., number, frequency, speed, size) dominate their assignment of school grades. Do qualitative judgments enter the process (e.g.. novelty or degree of differentiation and integration in an essay)? Do quantitative scores ever reflect the presence of a justification or argument on the part of the student rather than simple rote memory? Generally, the more that judgments of quality and cognitive processes (not just products) enter into grade assignments, the more likely it is that teachers are including information integration and self-actualization in their definitions of learning.

The most concrete (most "operational") definition of learning offered by the teacher is the classroom test used to determine the student's grade. Ramsden says, "Several investigations have identified methods of student assessment as the most critical situational influence on learning strategies." And further, "The evaluation process provides a signal to students about the kind of learning they are expected to carry out; they adapt by choosing strategies that will apparently maximize success" (Chapter 7).

I noted earlier that Das (and Luria, e.g., 1981) emphasizes that, while the brain does code experience, it also continues to integrate it. The classroom tests of many teachers convey to students the importance of coding but not necessarily the importance of integrating—of seeing connections and implications, deriving meaning. Marton describes it as arriving at a new conceptualization of something, a new way of interpreting reality, and confronting preconceived assumptions with ideas presented by authors and teachers to arrive at something new, something that students can truly call their own—an *understanding* rather than a memorization.

Ramsden says, "If the evaluation of student learning does not go beyond what can be unreflectively retained in the memory, then misunderstandings may never be revealed, despite the fact that students have successfully negotiated examinations." Entwistle emphasizes that deep test questions focus on the nature of the relations between conclusions and evidence, a process Kirby describes as "balancing and cross-checking of evidence and interpretations, with the details constituting evidence for the more abstract propositions or interpretations" (Chapter 9).

With regard to evaluation aimed at assigning grades, Ramsden cites evidence that holistic approaches are more common with written assignments (essays) and atomistic approaches are more common with multiple-choice and short-answer tests. Pask believes that understanding is best assessed by demanding some form of "teachback," which involves the student in "saying what other topics a topic may be derived from, but also how the other topics relate to reproduce the one that is to be understood. It is not enough merely to parrot back a definition; the topic must be used in a novel way that shows the learner's ability to manipulate topics and their entailments and produce a novel interaction" (Chapter 4). Pask also feels that understanding is indicated by extrapolation and prediction in Bruner's sense of "going beyond the information given."

A deep approach to learning is the only way to accomplish understanding, and tests that signal students that understanding will be assessed also encourage them to take deep approaches to learning. However, Marton emphasized that if we succeed in our attempts to get teachers to include self-actualization and seeing things from new and uniquely individual perspectives in their definitions of learning (and their tests), then we will have to be prepared to offer assistance to those students who have never thought of learning this way. If we can get teachers to redesign their tests—the operational definitions of their goals—then students will look for something different in the instruction. When we alter the demands we make on students, they will alter the demands they make on us. Those teachers who ask for understanding but do not teach the students how to achieve an understanding will be pressured to do so. I turn now to a discussion of ways to encourage the deep approach to learning that is so necessary if an understanding is to be accomplished.

SKILL AND STRATEGY TRAINING PROGRAMS

One way to encourage a meaning orientation to studying is to design a special training program to teach the necessary skills and strategies. Weinstein (Chapter 11) uses the label "adjunct approach" to describe special (often extracurricular) programs designed to train students to use certain learning strategies. She describes such a program which she has developed. Her description of the extensive research, development, and evaluation that has gone into it and her review of similar programs should prove invaluable to anyone planning to teach study skills.

Weinstein also discusses two ways to provide training in learning strategies as part of regular university courses. Regarding one of these techniques, she says, "*embedded instruction* concentrates on incorporating learning strategies training into existing educational materials, particularly printed materials and workbooks." The other approach, referred to as a "metacurriculum," "requires the instructor to integrate learning strategies instruction into the planned and unplanned activities that go on during class . . . to focus on the types of learning strategies that might be particularly effective to accomplish the relevant learning goal" (Chapter 11). Thus, when the teacher assigns a term paper. he or she may use that occasion to insert a half-hour presentation on the nature of a deep approach to writing. The interested reader is referred to Weinstein's chapter for an excellent review of these programs.

We can also try to encourage deep approaches to learning by encouraging the general development of cognitive skills, especially the versatility in cognitive style that is so necessary if the student is to take a deep approach to any learning task. If the student is predominantly global, we can encourage analytic skills; if he or she is predominantly analytic, we can encourage global skills. Both Das and Kirby mention programs for training students to code information in unfamiliar or underdeveloped processing modes. Das adds that, "The actual type of information processing which is selected depends upon (a) the individual's preferred mode of processing (which is influenced by an individual's experience, sociocultural and genetic factors); (b) the task demands, and (c) the interaction between preferred mode and task demands" (Chapter 5).

Kirby (Chapter 9) says, "it is important to recognize the basis of errors that readers make . . . the trick seems to be to get children to recognize that they are using an inappropriate strategy, and to design a task in which they spontaneously use a strategy comparable to the appropriate one" (cf. Marton, Chapter 3). Also, Kirby emphasizes that there is a difference between *strategy reorientation* as an intervention goal and *skill development* as a goal. Strategy reorientation involves awareness and intentions, encouraging the student to include a skill in his or her plans.

Das emphasizes the importance of developing planning skills. He discusses a study that divided subjects into the best and worst planners and says that in a follow-up 3 years later the top planners were easier to locate, seemed to have more successfully adjusted to adult life, more easily got the "gist" of a written passage and remembered it better, were less impulsive, made more inferences, and more flexibly modified incorrect hypotheses (see the subsection "Encouraging Development" below).

The reader interested in skills training should be certain to consult Ramsden (Chapter 7), who cautions that "interventions are themselves a part of the context of learning. Interventions do not exist separately from the remainder of the students' experience; they are interpreted just as learning is interpreted, in their educational context." In a training program, the students with a reproducing orientation may pay close attention to mnemonic strategies while ignoring or misunderstanding coverage of more meaningful strategies. Likewise, the designer of a training program may intend to teach a deep approach to learning, but students with a strong achievement orientation may only intend to learn to *act* as though they process information deeply. The reader is reminded of the our earlier mention of Winnicott's (1965) "false-self." Achievment-oriented students may intend to use what they learn in a training program to produce test answers and essays that "look" deep to an instructor (e.g., by rote memorizing certain arguments). "Teaching students to become more strategic cannot ensure that faculty goals are met. Teachers need to be aware that the student's interpretation of the advantages of a learning skills intervention may well be different from their own" (Ramsden, Chapter 7).

IMPROVING TEACHING

Good teaching helps the student to improve his or her approach to learning; it doesn't just involve delivering content. Good teaching helps students learn to focus on meanings, not just symbols, to perceive the underlying structure of content, to relate conclusions and evidence, and to include self-reference and self-expression in their list of available learning strategies. Even the student's orientation to studying is somewhat changeable. As Ramsden says, "stability of orientation does not imply fixity. Orientations to studying are changeable and responsive to the context of teaching, evaluation, and curriculum" (Chapter 7). As instructors, we can often use the control which we have over the context to influence the student's choice of strategy and tactics. Ramsden argues that, "so far as contextual variables are in the control of instructors, it is possible to structure the environment of learning in such a way that adaptive responses are congruent with the instructors' aims. . . . A nontrivial educational question is how to present tasks so as to engage the student at a deep level." For example, "A combination of high perceived workload and limited choice over study methods was strongly associated with high scores on surface approaches" (Ramsden, Chapter 7).

If we repeatedly encourage students to process the subject matter at a surface level, we are also nurturing a reproducing orientation to studying, and if we repeatedly encourage a deep engagement, we nurture a meaning orientation to studying, and perhaps to life in general. Ramsden believes that contextual effects operate directly as well as indirectly with direct effects, related to the fact that some material by its very nature can only be memorized, while indirect effects relate to the students *perceptions* which bring past experiences to bear. "It is assumed that students strive to *adapt* to the context" (Ramsden, Chapter 7, italics added).

Marton says that the teacher who wants to encourage a deep approach to learning should emphasize *interpretation*. In this regard, Luria (1981) notes that the two main aspects of language are pointing (reference to concrete objects and events) and deriving meaning (relating objects and events into a system of categories). Marton suggests that too often our teaching fails to include the second aspect, *deriving meaning*. Too often we fail to produce conceptual changes in students and merely teach facts without considering the conceptions that make those facts interesting or meaningful. As I noted above, Marton describes studies that show that students often come out of university courses as conceptually undeveloped as they were when they went in, even if they do know more facts. Too often students and teachers alike fail to see changes in one's conceptions (or interpretations) of reality as what learning is really about. One way for teachers to monitor this aspect of their teaching is to ask themselves, "why am I teaching these facts; what do they *imply*; what do they *mean*?"

Marton emphasizes that teachers must concentrate on changing students' perceptions of the educational context and the phenomena being taught. He suggests that teachers can sometimes get students to alter their perception of the subject matter or the educational context by encouraging a new perspective much as a Gestalt psychologist might seek to alter perceptual figure–ground relations to produce insight or shifts in category systems. For example, we can sometimes get students to focus attention on that which at first glance appears as the background of a problem (the "space around the problem"). If for even one instant background is perceived as figure and figure as background, we may produce a "perceptual shift," revealing heretofore unperceived structures or relations among parts, or produce a "category shift," revealing heretofore unnoticed systems of categories that might apply or changes in those categories that are already being applied.

For example, to alter students' approaches to reading and writing, we might try to get them to focus on meanings as figure, allowing the symbols on the page to become ground—"there is no one 'magic way' to express a particular meaning." Likewise, we might influence orientation to studying or to education in general by getting students to focus on reality and it's interpretations, allowing an upcoming test to become ground—"education is about *understanding reality*; if I understand reality, I don't need to worry about the test."

The authors of the present text have proposed various ways of incorporating the development of new, personal interpretations into our instructional objectives. Ramsdan proposes altering tests and giving more writing assignments. Biggs agrees with regard to writing but emphasizes that we must teach a *reflective* approach to writing—one's own thoughts about content viewed as a legitimate subject for further thought. Torrance and Rockenstein want us to teach both inventing and improving as forms of creativity. McCarthy and Schmeck want teachers to encourage creative self-expression in a supportive environment— realizing that self-expression has to precede self-improvement (you can't change who you are if you don't "know" who you are). In a similar manner, Schmeck and Meier (1984) emphasized the importance of using previously coded personal experience and integrations thereof to code new information within the school and university settings. Entwistle and Kirby emphasize the development of versatile cognitive functioning—relating evidence and conclusions in cyclical fashion, generalizing from details then referring back to details to justify or revise the generalizations in a never ending cycle of cognitive growth.

Teacher as a Social Object

In addition to noting the cognitive uses of languages (e.g., derivation of meaning), Luria (1981) also noted that it serves invaluable social functions (e.g., pointing). Furthermore, he suggests that the social roots and funcfions of language affect its development as a tool for thinking. Thus, the teacher's role as a social object cannot be ignored if we are to improve teaching and ultimately improve students' thinking. Rogers (1969) was very emphatic on this point, as are McCarthy and Schmeck in the present volume (Chapter 6). Good teaching includes a concern for students as human beings, not just the delivering of lectures and making of assignments. Ramsden notes that good teaching includes empathy, not making unreasonable demands, respect for student individuality, some freedom of choice regarding how to learn and what to learn, and relevance (either as perceived by the student directly or as apparently perceived by teachers and reflected in their enthusiasm).

McCarthy and Schmeck emphasize the need to control the "critical eye" that so many of us have developed in our role as teacher. They refer to Torrance and Rockenstein's distinction between creating by inventing and creating by improving. The first requires a safe, noncritical environment for self-expression. The second requires a critical environment where errors are noted and corrected. They state, "Our fear is that too many schools and too many teachers place most of their emphasis upon improving, upon 'catching' students in the act of making errors. We feel that school systems and teachers need to permit and reward some of the self-expression that is implicit in creating by inventing, the kind of self-expression that leads to self-discovery, self-awareness, and ultimately to integration and adult cognitive functioning" (McCarthy and Schmeck, Chapter 6).

McCarthy and Schmeck also argued that there are certain student's who will suffer severely from the use of competition as a motivator. There is nothing wrong with competition if the students have a reserve of unconditional positive regard for themselves. However, the conception of self held by some students leads them to experience extreme anxiety, inhibit self-expression, and pursue a surface approach whenever social comparison (and potential failure) are emphasized. As opposed to these students with fear of failure, the achieving students in our classes may be greatly energized by competition, but there are some drawbacks here as well. Specifically, the need to compete (to win) will often dominate intentions to the point that students fail to perceive their own inner needs, values, and opinions, failing to ever express their true selves. Since self-awareness is a key to encouraging overall cognitive development, we may in fact be doing "achievers" a long-term and subtle disservice by continually using their need to succeed as a way of accomplishing our own short-term course objectives.

Encouraging Development

The author of the present text all emphasize the importance of developing versatility in cognitive functioning, learning to use both global and analytic cognitive skills in a synthesis that can be called neither a "global style" nor an "analytic style" but is an amalgam of the two. McCarthy and Schmeck feel that awareness and acceptance of one's own feelings, thoughts, and memories are essential for such versatility to develop. They argue that personal meaning, or identify, derives from a reflective self turned toward its own past experiences, and they emphasize the following quotation: "Progress in knowledge . . . involves more than the accumulation of objectively valid cognitions; it means the growth of a subject progressively better equipped to know and to be the validating source of the knowledge it has or acquires" (Rogers, 1983, p. 44). McCarthy and Schmeck argue that the developing identity (or self-concept) is the ultimate "organizer" of all experience. Learning, when viewed as broadly as possible, is the creative development of an identity—a self.

Das (1980; and Chapter 5) suggests that development proceeds from coding, through integration, to planning. Das says, "intelligent behavior cannot be limited to merely coding, to analysis and synthesis of sensory input, but also involves using the coded information consciously to attain a desired goal" (1980, p. 150). He further states that "results demonstrated . . . that planning evolves from coding and that at an earlier state of competence, planning and coding are not independent" (Das, 1980, p. 149). Earlier in this same paper, Das notes that

Eccles felt self-consciousness or reflection of the mind upon itself was at the root of synthesis or integration (cf. Popper & Eccles, 1977). Das (1980) agrees with Luria that the catalysts and milieu for the development of consciousness are social. Likewise, McCarthy and Schmeck (Chapter 6) argue that delayed development results from insufficient unconditional positive regard, leading either to a dependent style ("I am OK if someone else takes responsibility") or a counterdependent style ("I never need anyone"). In any case, the demands made by others and admiration coming from others wields excessive influence upon behavior. Individuals with too little unconditional regard feel they have to constantly "prove something," and they imagine themselves either ill-prepared or exceptionally prepared for this fantasied task. Either way they distort reality. If students are "trying to prove something" for the purpose of maintaining self-esteem, they may find it difficult to accept or admit certain things about themselves and the world. Yet, self-awareness requires acceptance of that which is discovered. If students can't "accept" what they see, they tend to "distort" what they see, and you can't be aware of reality if you are distorting reality.

Of course, if students enter our classrooms with so little self-respect that they are unable to freely accept reality, it's unlikely we will reverse that process. However, McCarthy and Schmeck argue that distortion of (or awareness of) reality are on a continuum. People vary in awareness because of variation in personal motives. Teachers can at least avoid making matters worse by focusing on competition, threat of failure, criticism, and the like. Two conditions are necessary to encourage development in the classroom. First, students have to feel that their circumstances, including their core, or "the cards they've been dealt," are acceptable or will ultimately become acceptable with adaptation. Somehow teachers have to communicate trust in the processes that unfold naturally from within. Second, students have to believe that this human essence in which the teacher believes is dynamic and constantly growing, and they should feel that one of the aims of education is to nurture it. I am reminded of the title of one of Carl Rogers' books, *On Becoming a Person* (1961). Rogers felt the purpose of education was human development, development of individuals who would be able to express their true selves in independent action guided ultimately by personal values.

Several of the authors of the present text have emphasized the importance of self-awareness for encouraging integration and versatility in cognitive functioning. Earlier, we had this quotation from Biggs: "a self-conscious and planful approach to learning thus requires, first, that students are aware of their motives and intentions, of their own cognitive resources, and of the demands of academic tasks; and second, that they are able to control those resources and monitor their consequent performance" (Chapter 8). Ramsden says, "teachers will need to be involved, as part of their professional development, in systematic analyses of their students' perspectives on learning tasks, and in studying how subject matter is conceptualized and understood by students. . . . Teaching students to become more aware of their own motives and resources and to select and use them appropriately is a component of such activity by faculty" (Chapter 7).

Marton suggests that, "We can try to make the students aware of their own way of approaching a learning task and understanding its content, against a background of an awareness of the alternative ways. . . . Realizing that there are different ways of thinking and different ways of going about a learning task can be a very efficient way not only of enhancing one's understanding of the specific learning task, but also of transcending it, that is, of learning to learn in a very genuine sense of the word" (Chapter 3). And Pask states, "Among other methods of promoting these general learning-to-learn decision skills, we have the possibility of administering stylistic tests to a group and then giving them feedback regarding their scores . . . and encourage free discussion of the relative advantages of each approach" (Chapter 4).

We can also gently encourage students to take personal responsibility for their learning and, thus, ultimately for their development. Biggs (1986; Chapter 8, this volume) discusses the importance of metacognition and the sense of personal responsibility (internal locus of control) that seems to be required for metacognition to develop. He says that, "a deep approach involves metacognition, in that the search for meaning involves one in monitoring and reshaping one's own thought, whereas a surface approach is simply reactive." With regard to personal responsibility, he refers to the "sense of internal locus of control, which is an important component of metalearning." He notes that, "the control aspect of metalearning typically did not develop until the end of senior high school; earlier in the case of highly motivated and internally controlled students, later, if at all, in unmotivated or externally controlled students." And in yet another context, he presents evidence that deep writers try to add a personal touch in order to make an essay "their own"—"this sense of proprieotiality likewise stems from an internal locus of control, in 'integrating the task with oneself' . . . and is characteristic of a deep approach" (Chapter 8).

I agree with Entwistle (1981, and in this volume) that it is important to continue to distinguish between orientation and style. Orientation to studying involves more than cognitive style, it also involves motives and intentions. The teacher has little control over the student's style but has a lot of control over the situation, and by structuring the situation, the teacher can influence the student's perceptions and thus their motives and approaches to learning. By influencing approach to learning, we influence the learning outcome—and the outcome ultimately becomes part of the person. Thus, over time, the teacher may also influence cognitive style. As Kirby emphasized, cognitive style is not fixed, it is dynammic and growing.

Both Biggs and Marton note that, since students taking a surface approach don't attend to the structure of information to begin with, it is not surprising that they don't perceive the structure. I would argue that this is related to attentional or perceptual style, in particular to excess emphasis on what Kirby calls an analytic style of processing. I feel that the global style is needed to perceive the structure of information. However, Pask noted it is the analytic style that is most consistently related to grades in school, especially in certain specializations such as the technologies. Ramsden made a similar observation. This suggests that schools give analytic skills more emphasis than global cognitive skills, and Pask noted that many students with excess emphasis on analytic functions rote memorize (take a surface approach) in order to pass examinations. I would agree with Torrance and Rockenstein that schools need to encourage students to exercise all of their brain's potential, not just their analytic or critical functions.

In conclusion, I should add that none of these suggestions is easy to implement in an educational system which is part of a larger cultural entity and which serves many functions not necessarily altruistically aimed to help the individual student. Ramsden (Chapter 7) says, "Changes to teaching to maximize the probability of faculty aims being met may not be practicable without substantial revision of the management of academic units and without major alterations to traditional disciplinary boundaries and reward systems in some undergraduate courses, especially professional programs." McCarthy and Schmeck state, "Some of the more radical solutions proposed for this problem (e.g., Rogers, 1969) have not been implemented because societies (e.g., the corporations that hire graduates) place great emphasis upon rank-ordering people. However, we would argue for compromises, even little ones" (Chapter 6). It is my hope that this text has suggested a few workable compromises.

REFERENCES

Atkinson, J. W., & Feather, N. T. (1966). *A theory of achievement motivation*. New York: Wiley.

Biggs, J. B. (1984). Learning strategies, student motivation patterns, and subjectively perceived success. J. R. Kirby (Ed.), *Cognitive strategies and educational performance*. Orlando, FL: Academic Press.

Birney, R. C., Burdick, H., & Teevan, R. C. (1969). *Fear of failure.* New York: Van Nostrand.

Craik, F. . M., & Lockhart, R. S. (1972). Levels of processing: A framework for memory research. *Journal of Verbal Learning and Verbal Beahvior, 11,* 671–684.

Das, J. P. (1980). Planning: Theoretical considerations and empirical evidence. *Psychological Research* (W. Germany), *41,* 141–151.

Dyk, R. B. (1969). An exploratory study of mother–child interaction in infancy as related to the development of differentiation. *Journal of the American Academy of Child Psychiatry, 8,* 657–691.

Eison, J. A. (1981). A new instrument of assessing students' orientations toward grades and learning. *Psychological Reports, 48,* 919–924.

Eison, J. A. (1982). Educational and personal dimensions of learning- and grade-oriented students. *Psychological Reports, 51,* 867–870.

Eison, J. A., & Pollio, H. R. (1985, September). A multidimensional approach to the definition of college students' learning styles. *Journal of College Student Personnel.*

Eison, J. A., Pollio, H. R., & Milton, 0. (1986). Educational and personal characteristics of four different types of learning- and grade-oriented students. *Contemporary Educational Psychology, 11,* 54–67.

Entwistle, N. J. (1981). *Styles of learning and teaching.* Chichester: Wiley.

Entwistle, N. J., & Wilson, J. D. (1977). *Degrees of excellence: The academic achievement game.* London: Hodder and Stoughton.

Fransson, A. (1977). On qualitative differences in learning: IV. Effects of motivation and text anxiety on process and outcome. *British Journal of Educational Psychology, 47,* 244–257.

Hounsell, D. A. (1984). *Students' conceptions of essay writing.* Unpublsihed Ph.D. Thesis, University of Lancaster.

Kogan, N. (1976). *Cognitive styles in infancy and early childhood.* Hillsdale, NJ: Lawrence Erlbaum.

Luria, A. R. (1981). *Language and cognition.* New York: Wiley.

Meier, S., McCarthy, P., & Schmeck, R. R. (1984). Validity of self-efficacy as a predictor of writing performance. *Cognitive therapy and research, 8,* 107–120.

Popper, K. R., & Eccles, J. C. (1977). *The self and its brain.* Berlin: Springer.

Rogers, C. R. (1961). *On becoming a person: A therapists view of psychotherapy.* Boston: Houghton Mifflin.

Rogers, C. R. (1969). *Freedom to learn.* Columbus, OH: Merrill.

Rothbart, M. K., & Posner, M. I. (1985) Temperament and the development of self regulation. In L. C. Hartlage & L. F. Telzrow (Eds.), *The neuropsychology of individual differences.* New York: Plenum Press.

Säljö, R. (1975). *Qualitative differences in learning as a function of the learner's conception of the task.* Gothenberg: Acta Universitatis Gothoburgensis.

Säljö, R. (1982). *Learning and understanding: A study of differences in constructing meaning from a text.* Gothenburg: Acta Universitatis Gothoburgensis.

Schmeck, R. R. (1981). Improving learning by improving thinking. *Educational Leadership, 38,* 384–385.

Schmeck, R. R. (1983). Learning styles of college students. In Dillon, R. F., & Schmeck, R. R. (Eds.). *Individual differences in cognition, Volume 1.* New York: Academic Press.

Schmeck, R. R., & Meier, S. (1984). Self-reference as a learning strategy and a learning style. *Human Learning, 3,* 9–17.

Schmeck, R. R., & Ribich, F. D. (1978). Construct validation of the inventory of learning processes. *Applied Psycological Measurement, 2,* 551–562.

Schmeck, R. R., & Spofford, M. (in press). Attention to semantic verbal attributes as a function of individual differences in arousal and learning strategy. *Contemporary Educational Psychology.*

Schmeck, R. R., Ribich, F. D., & Ramanaiah, N. (1977). Development of a self-report inventory for assessing individual differences in learning processes. *Applied Psychological Measurement, 1,* 413–431.

Shapiro, D. (1965). *Neurotic styles.* New York: Basic Books.

Van Rossum, E. J., & Schenk, S. M. (1984). The relationship between learning conception, study strategy, and learning outcome. *British Journal of Educational Psychology, 54,* 73–83.

Wallach, M. A., & Kogan, N. (1965). *Modes of thinking in young children.* New York: Holt, Rinehart & Winston.

Winnicott, D. W. (1965) *The maturational processes and the facilitating environment.* New York: International Universities Press.

Witkin, H. A., Moore, C. A., Goodenough, D. R., & Cox, P. W. (1977). Field-dependent and field-independent cognitive styles and their educational implications. *Review of Educational Research,* 1–64.

Index

ISBN 0-306-42860-1

90000